MICHAEL CAINE

MICHAEL CAINE
A Class Act

CHRISTOPHER BRAY

faber and faber

First published in 2005
by Faber and Faber Limited
3 Queen Square London WC1N 3AU

Typeset by RefineCatch Limited, Bungay, Suffolk
Printed in England by Mackays of Chatham, plc

The right of Christopher Bray to be identified as author
of this work has been asserted in accordance with Section 77
of the Copyright, Designs and Patents Act 1988

A CIP record for this book is available from the British Library

ISBN 0–571–21682–X

10 9 8 7 6 5 4 3 2

Contents

Introduction

*I was about to say that . . . you were the British film industry's
biggest asset in the second half of the twentieth century . . . [but]
I would offer one possible rival, and that is Michael Caine.*
  David Sylvester talking to Ken Adam[1]

Psychoanalyst, cat burglar, playwright, architect, reporter, gangland
villain, secret agent . . . was ever a movie star cast in as varied a set of
roles as Michael Caine? There are bit-part players whose filmic CVs
range far and wide over the different professions, but in the major
league, perhaps only Peter Sellers's retinue can stand shoulder to shoulder with that of Caine. And even here, the comparison is unfair. Sellers's
portrait gallery was hung largely with grotesques; Caine's characters
have all been limned with a stylized naturalism that requires rather
more in terms of both craft and observation.

Indeed, so 'natural' have many of Caine's performances been that
they have often been taken for non-performances. Discussing this
book at a dinner party a couple of years ago, a friend of a friend
expressed puzzlement at my choice of subject: 'Michael Caine? But
he's always just Michael Caine.' Well, up to a point . . . For one thing,
being even momentarily oneself, as most of us know, is no small
achievement. For another, Caine's characters have all been singular
creations. But as Caine himself once put it: 'I have played everything
from an upper-crust officer to a Nazi to a transvestite psychopathic
killer, and the audience says there's Michael Caine playing himself
again.'[2] And again: 'I've never played myself. I've never played a rich
man. I've rarely played a father, a family man. And I've never played
anyone famous . . . There's no sense that I've ever learnt to do anything, or that I do it with skill. No matter who I play, everyone here is
convinced I'm playing myself.'[3]

Caine's problem is that, almost unique amongst movie stars, he is
also a character actor. Had he been content to play the part of the
superstar – to play, that is, minor variations on one role throughout
his career – nobody would have carped. The idea that 'he's always just
Michael Caine' wouldn't have been a criticism. Nobody knocks Clint
Eastwood for doing a Clint Eastwood, although even now, further
into his seventies than Caine, he trades largely in roles similar to those
he has been playing all his working life. Caine is different. He is

always on the lookout for parts that will stretch him. Like the repertory actor he once was, he is willing to have a go at anything. 'If you don't make many films,' he said recently, 'you won't make many bad ones . . . [but] when you're my age you must look back and regret the things you did and not the things you didn't do.'4

Regrets, Caine has a few. With more than a hundred films to his name, how could he not? So sure of his talent is he that it is almost as though he believes his presence will redeem any script. Like the post-war Britain that made his name, Caine is convinced against all the evidence that whatever he is involved in will come good in the end. And indeed, for all those regrets, Caine has done surprisingly little that is reprehensible. He has always given of his best. 'Decades of duff directors,' wrote Brian Case, 'have made him self-sufficient.'5 Like the hero of Patrick McGilligan's fine book *Cagney: The Actor as Auteur*,6 Caine has many times been his own director; not in the sense of standing behind the camera barking orders, but in the sense that his presence bulks so large in post-war British culture that he brings to any new movie accretions of meaning that even the most determinedly authorial director would find it hard to subvert.

The 'new critical' idea of the work of art as something magically untouched by the strains and stresses of the day was perhaps always a pious fiction. Books, paintings, poetry – all artworks are linked, by whatever tenuous threads, to the spirit of their age, the movement of their times. And this is more than doubly so with the movies, the art form that is also always and everywhere an industry. The Hollywood producer Samuel Goldwyn said that if you wanted to send a message you should do so via Western Union, but the fact is that movies are messengers whether their makers intend it or not. John Ford said that all he did was make westerns, but if you want to know how twentieth-century America went on dreaming about the manifest destiny bodied forth in its promised land even as capitalism was busy laying it waste, then Ford's westerns are the place to go. Alfred Hitchcock said that his movies weren't 'slices of life . . . [but] slices of cake', but you would have to be blind and deaf to miss out on what Hitchcock's work tells us about, for example, the battle of the sexes. In *Duck Soup* (1933) even the Marx Brothers have things to say about the nature of power.

Certainly, if you want to understand something of the change Britain has gone through in its post-war years, then Michael Caine is as good a lens as any to look through. Nor is this merely because Caine has, right from the first, been willing to hold pungently forth on the state of the nation. It is more the fact that Caine's life trajectory mirrors so precisely larger movements in the nation around him. A similar claim could be made for just about any working-class movie star born contemporaneously – Sean Connery, say,[7] or Albert Finney.[8] But while Connery's first forty years or so can be read as microcosmic of Britain's, Caine is unique in having gone on echoing his country's mindset and mood swings throughout his life. Nations tell stories about themselves, and one of the stories Britain has been telling itself for the past four or five decades is Michael Caine.

Which is a way of saying that this is a book not about Michael Caine but about 'Michael Caine'. Writing, thirty-odd years ago, about the auteur theory, Peter Wollen suggested that in talking of movie directors we need to distinguish between, say, Howard Hawks – the man who, among other things, directed a bunch of Hollywood movies – and 'Howard Hawks' – the man discernible in however ghostly a form across and between that bunch of movies.[9] As for directors, so for actors. I am not largely concerned in these pages with what might be called the 'real' Michael Caine. What interests me is the figurative Caine served up in the cinema and on TV.

'There have been', wrote Caine in the Foreword to his own life story, 'at least seven biographies of me.'[10] By my count there had been at that time (1992) precisely one book on Caine's life, William Hall's *Raising Caine*.[11] All future writers on Caine will be indebted to him for that book – indeed, given the number of similar chronological cock-ups in *What's It All About*, Caine himself seems to have relied on it rather heavily – but that is not to say that Hall, a one-time tabloid newspaper reporter, had closed his subject off. For all his showbiz gossip and tittle-tattle, Hall had little to say about what it is that matters about Caine, namely, his work. Much less did Michael Freedland in his 1999 book, *Michael Caine*.[12] Anne Billson's *My Name Is Michael Caine*[13] and David Bishop's *Starring Michael Caine*,[14] on the other hand, are both movie-buff books, though the buffery rather gets in the way of any critical insight. I hope that the present book – still only the *sixth* about Caine – will go some way towards filling that gap.

Christopher Bray
London, September 2004

Part One
SEI

Coercion created slavery, the cowardice of the slaves perpetuated it.
Rousseau, *The Social Contract*

I 1933–37

In the little world in which children have their existence, whosoever brings them up, there is nothing so finely perceived and so finely felt, as injustice.

Charles Dickens[1]

In September 2003, Sir Michael Caine was quoted as saying that he refused to open mail that failed to address him by his correct title. The next month, Sir Michael's old pal Sir Roger Moore said this was nonsense. Sir Michael would never not open an envelope – because there was always the chance that it might contain a cheque.[2] It was a joke, but like many jokes it made a serious point. Money and class have been the twin obsessions of Caine's life.

Certainly, he has never been ashamed of the fact that international stardom has made him a lot of money. 'I've been rich and I've been poor,' he once said. 'Rich is better any day.'[3] Not that he became an actor with the sole aim of earning himself a fortune. 'I would have carried on in this business even for just a few quid a week in repertory,' he told a television interviewer a few years ago.[4] And perhaps he would. Certainly, it cannot have been the hope of untold riches that sustained him through more than a decade of low-grade repertory work in the theatre and walk-on parts in more than a hundred television plays. On the other hand, since becoming a star, Caine has never turned down work that might have been thought beneath him. Even today, at seventy-two, it seems he is willing to appear in any movie, good or bad.

Many actors like to keep working, of course. The motivation is partly existential – actors don't really feel fully alive unless they are pretending to be somebody else. But it is partly egotistical, too – like all self-employed freelancers of whatever trade (and since the demise of the studio system all actors have essentially been freelancers), they have to keep proving to other people that they can do what they say they can do. The cliché is that you are only as good as your last per-formance, though it often feels more like you are only as good as your *next* performance. Whatever the stresses and strains of the actor's life, they are as nothing when compared with the stresses and strains on the actor who isn't acting. 'I think, therefore I am,' wrote Descartes in proof of his existence. The actor sees things from the other end of the telescope: 'I am, therefore I am not someone else, therefore I am not.'

None of which gets us anywhere near an explanation for Michael

Caine's appearances in, say, *On Deadly Ground* (1994). How could one of the finest movie actors there has ever been want to, need to, star in such a film? Is it possible that he is so convinced of his talents that he believes an appearance by him can redeem any movie, no matter how bad the script? And even if we could prove that theory, how would we account for Caine's acceptance of an offer, in the early nineties, to reprise the role of Harry Palmer, the character who made him a star, in a pair of low-budget updates? Caine famously said of his appearance in *Jaws: The Revenge* (1987), 'I have never seen the film but by all accounts it was terrible. However, I HAVE seen the house that it built, and it is terrific. What is more, the film has now gone but the house is still with me and continues to be one of the greatest sources of pleasure and happiness in my life.'5 It's an excuse, of course, but there is an excuse for the excuse in that Caine made his foray into the *Jaws* series at a time when he needed to move house and was short of cash. Moreover, *Jaws: The Revenge*, while no masterpiece, is far from being the least interesting of the entries in the Steven Spielberg-inaugurated mini-genre. Ham-fisted it may be, but the movie has a psychoanalytic undertow that spins it into an arena of rather more interest than its star's quip quite allows. No amount of what the late Orson Welles once called 'dollar book Freud', on the other hand, could convincingly explain a mess like *Bullet to Beijing* (1996).

And so, in the end, you have to come down on the side of common sense and agree that Michael Caine likes to work so much because he remembers when times were hard and there was no work to be had. At some very deep level he still inhabits the unstable, insecure world of his early days. The novelist John Updike, who was born a year earlier than Michael Caine into an America as dumbstruck by the Depression as Great Britain was, has remarked of his own prodigious rate of production that people of his generation 'acquired in hard times a habit of work and came to adulthood in times when work paid off'.6 Caine would nod an Amen to that sentiment. As he has more than once quipped, 'In order to fund a high-class lifestyle, it is sometimes necessary to make a lot of low-class films.' Granted, but how does he come to choose the duds? 'First of all I choose the great ones, and if none of them come, I choose the mediocre ones, and if they don't come – I choose the ones that are going to pay the rent.'7 And there is no denying the fact, as we shall see, that Michael Caine knows what it is to worry about paying the rent.

He was born Maurice Joseph Micklewhite on 14 March 1933 in St Olave's Hospital, Rotherhithe, south-east London. It was a cold,

grim day in what is anyway one of the colder, grimmer months of the
London calendar. But things were colder and grimmer than usual that
year. Historians and economists generally consider 1933 to be the
nadir of the thirties, those ten years that W. H. Auden famously characterized as a 'low, dishonest decade'.[8] Six weeks before the young
Micklewhite came into the world, Adolf Hitler had been appointed
Chancellor of Germany. Five days before he was born, the SS opened
its first concentration camp.[9] Nor were things any rosier on the home
front. The Great Depression had sunk the countries of the developed
world to their lowest depths. Four years earlier, the Wall Street Crash
had sent shock waves through the world economy; when the future
Michael Caine came into the world, their reverberations could still be
felt from Brooklyn to Berlin to Bermondsey.

Maurice Micklewhite senior had married Ellen Frances Maria
Burchell fifteen months earlier at St Stephen's Church, Southwark,
on 12 December 1931. Three months before the wedding, Ramsay
MacDonald's National Government (a coalition of left, right and centre parties which dominated British politics throughout the thirties)
had finally decided to take the pound off the Gold Standard. The result
was a devaluation of the pound from $4.86 to a new parity of $3.40.
Export prospects improved, of course, but job prospects merely kept
on worsening. All the same, MacDonald forced through a measure that
cut unemployment benefits by 10 per cent. As one observer remarked
at the time, the end of parity between gold and sterling was 'For most
Britons born before 1910 . . . the biggest shock that we had known or
were to know.'[10] Times were tough and getting tougher.

Certainly, life at 283 Weston Street – a snaky thoroughfare in that
grimy warren between London Bridge station and the Old Kent Road
wherein the Micklewhites rented a single room – was no picnic. The big
problem was that Maurice senior wasn't bringing any money home. In
1933, thirty-four-year-old[11] Maurice senior was, like another three
million or so men in the United Kingdom (at the time, around one in
five of the country's working population), out of work. Until recently,
like generations of Micklewhites before him, he had been a porter at
Billingsgate fish market, a short walk away across the river Thames.
After the slump, when the world economy stumbled back into action,
he would return to carting those clammy, sloppy crates around that
vast, icy warehouse.

Maurice senior, of course, left no record of his labours at Billingsgate,
so we must be grateful to George Orwell who, fresh from his exploits
hop-picking in Kent, helped out at the market in September 1931.
Though the work was arduous – 'it knocks it out of your thighs

and elbows' – you never got enough of it to tire you out. For helping a porter push his barrow 'up the 'ill', Orwell was paid twopence a time. Competition was fierce and Orwell reckoned he never made more than 1s 6d (7.5p in today's decimalized money) out of the 5 a.m.-to-midday shift.[12] Fish porters themselves, though, Orwell reckoned to be earning between £4 and £5 a week – a reasonable wage in the thirties, giving them plenty of money for drink. Though a Billingsgate porter's work was finished by noon, many of them never made it home before the evening, or even later.

But £100 a week would not have been enough to tempt Orwell to work there regularly. As far as he was concerned, the stench that hung around him during and after his labours at Billingsgate was unbearable. Moreover, the kitchen at his lodging house 'smelt permanently of fish, and the sinks were blocked with rotting fish guts which stank horribly'.[13] If Caine has any such olfactory memories he has chosen not to share them, though he has said that he would never eat any of the fish his father brought home each day.[14] And seventy years after Orwell's sufferings he was still remembering the spectral glow given off by the phosphorescent smoked haddock that were stored in his bedroom as a child.[15]

As a teenager, Maurice junior would use his weekends to help out at Billingsgate, but he was adamant that he would never work there full-time.[16] Moreover, he has made it plain that he believes fish-portering was beneath his father: 'My father was a typical example of ability thrown away . . . He was a man of much greater intelligence than his background and education allowed him to use. He had a good mind, but was never given a chance to do anything with it.'[17] This is as it may be, though the fact remains that until comparatively recently the British economy could survive, if not by brawn alone, then at least with comparatively little brain. However bright Maurice senior was (and given his eldest son's native wit and intelligence it is a fair guess that he was indeed bright), the Britain of the thirties had little need of such men. Not that the son saw the father as a paragon of virtue. At times, indeed, the boy's impatience with what he regards as his father's shortcomings has bubbled to the surface. 'I was disappointed in him,' Caine has admitted. 'A young lad wants his father to be the epitome of things, and I saw the gambling particularly as a terrible weakness. I don't like weakness in people and I try to avoid it myself. And while I've drunk alcohol, nobody has ever seen me drunk or out of control. No one. Ever.'[18] No indeed, though few people who have seen more than one Michael Caine film will have missed him *acting* drunk. Whether or not because of what he witnessed at his childhood home,

Caine is one of the best stage drunks the movies have ever had and he has put the skill to use in numerous pictures.

Drink, of course, has long been seen as the curse of the working classes, and there is no need to doubt that life was far from easy for Maurice senior. There are several photographs of him in his son's auto-biography, one of them taken, one surmises from Caine's back-combed bouffant and wide-lapelled jacket, sometime in 1954 or '55. Born on 20 February 1899, Maurice senior's features are going by the time of this photo. No more the pin-eyed, knife-chinned bombardier of the 1925 photograph also reproduced. No more the stick-thin Michael Caine lookalike who can be spied in another picture at his Billingsgate labours. In the fifties picture, Maurice senior's jaw has thickened even as his hair has thinned, but his shoulders are still thrust back and a cigarette hangs casually loose in his fingers as he gives the camera a look at once relaxed and questioning. He isn't frightened, like so many people were (and still are) of whoever it is with the Box Brownie. Here, one finds oneself thinking, is where Maurice junior must have got at least some of the confidence needed to keep working through his own lean years of the fifties and early sixties. Here too, perhaps, is where Maurice junior got his famous, much-prized, relaxation in front of a camera.

From the pictures we have of her, it is fair to say that Maurice's mother, Ellen, was too pudgy and pasty, too short and stout, to ever have been considered a looker. But there is a photograph of her holding the young Maurice in Caine's autobiography that gives the impression of someone who knows her worth. Standing so as to look at the camera straight on, she has about her a kind of sweetened pride. She holds her head slightly back, a posture that gives her an almost imperious air – and certainly the air of someone who will not suffer fools gladly. Sharp-eyed and certain of herself, she may not have had much of an education, but nor, one guesses, was she someone who would easily be bamboozled.

She was born on 10 May 1900, making her thirty-two when she gave birth to the Micklewhites' first son. Maurice junior was not, however, Ellen's first child. Just shy of eight years earlier, on 11 July 1925, she had given destitute birth to another boy, christened David William, in a Salvation Army hospital across the river in Hackney. Who the father was the records have not vouchsafed. Caine has wondered whether David may have been, in fact, not his half-brother but his brother proper.[19] But though Maurice senior and Ellen had known each other since their schooldays together, there is no evidence to prove the matter one way or the other. It may have been that Maurice senior had no knowledge at all of David's existence. Caine himself, however, is certain that he knew nothing of his having an older brother until 1991, the year after his mother died, and he was rung up in Los Angeles by a reporter from a Sunday newspaper keen to break the news to him.

The bigger mystery is that although Ellen had kept David's existence a secret, she had somehow contrived to visit him pretty much every Monday of her life. Shortly after David was born, he was diagnosed with epilepsy (a disease not as easily treated in the twenties as it is today). After a brief but troubled adoption, he was at first kept in a school for mental defectives, then in a home for disturbed children. Subsequently, he spent the bulk of his life in a Surrey hospital. A brooding slab of Victorian gothic, the hospital sits half hidden by trees atop a hill in south Croydon, and its name must give us pause. It was called Cane Hill.[20]

Michael Caine has always insisted that he took his stage name (actually his second stage name: he called himself Michael Scott during the early to mid-fifties) from *The Caine Mutiny* (1954), a hit movie starring his favourite actor, Humphrey Bogart. There is no need to doubt this story, of course, but nor should we ignore the fact that Ellen Micklewhite often told the teenage Maurice of her visits to a mentally ill 'cousin' in Cane Hill.[21] Whether she told him any more than that we do not know, although surely if she had wanted to keep the fact of David's existence a complete secret from her family it would have been more logical for her not to mention these visits at all. Whatever the truth, one does not have to be a psycho-analyst to see that the word Cane (or Caine) had been resonating in Maurice Micklewhite's mind for years before he chose his stage name.

Shortly after Maurice junior's birth, his parents moved a little more than a mile further south, to a *two*-room flat in Urlwin Street off the Camberwell Road – then, as now, one of the shabbiest, most squalid areas of the capital. As George Orwell points out in *Down and Out in Paris and London* (published the year Maurice junior was born): 'It is a curious but well-known fact that bugs are much commoner in south than north London.'[22] Prejudice? Probably, though the prejudice was (and is) far from being confined to Orwell. The philosopher Bryan Magee, who was born in Hoxton three years before Maurice junior, in 1930, has said that like most north Londoners he thinks of south London as 'a foreign country'.[23] Moreover, 'I have London in the marrow of my bones, and an inexpressible, almost immoderate love of it, but I have never felt south London to be a part of it. South London is for the most part a recently created dormitory, brought into being in

only the last two centuries by the railways. Real London is nearly all
north of the river.'²⁴ South London, then, was second-class London,
though this being England there were some areas of it even further
down the scale. As the novelist and critic V. S. Pritchett, who was born
the year after Maurice senior, in 1900, and brought up in Camberwell,
wrote of the area: 'The south of London has always been unfashion-
able and its people have stuck to a village life of their own; they were
often poorish, but poverty or rather not having much money yet
managing on it has its divisions and subdivisions of status.'²⁵

Squalid: Urlwin St, where Maurice grew up. © Christopher Bray

And despite their new two-roomed flat, the Micklewhites were
decidely poorish. The year Maurice junior was born, the housing stock
in the borough of Stepney, just across the river from the Micklewhite
household, was described thus: 'damp, dilapidation of every kind,
obsolete design and construction, vermin . . . abound throughout the
whole borough, and impart to much of it a character of unrelieved
defectiveness . . . the only real remedy would seem to be the reconstruction of the whole borough.'²⁶ The only reason to think life in the
borough of Bermondsey was any different is that, given the anti-south
London prejudice, it is probable things had been allowed to descend
much further into wrack and ruin.

Room at the top: The Micklewhites's two-room flat. © Christopher Bray

The thirties was, of course, the decade of Metroland, of Londoners' great escape to Betjemanian suburbia. But not everybody had the money to escape. And if your job, when you had a job, was just a couple of miles away at Billingsgate market, a job, moreover, that had been in your family for generations, then perhaps you wouldn't want to escape. Escape into the suburban middle class was to be one of the major themes of the books and plays that stormed the English literary citadel around the time Maurice junior became Michael Caine. But a quarter of a century earlier escape meant little more than running away – disappearing into the same life somewhere else. Those who didn't fancy disappearing stayed put.

Alas, the damp and dilapidation stayed too. Mass reconstruction was to come to run-down parts of London like Stepney and Bermondsey, though not for more than another decade, after Hitler's planes and bombs had done their worst. Admittedly, the Micklewhites Weston Street home was demolished when Maurice junior was just six months old 'as part of a slum clearance project',[27] but that didn't mean that things looked up much for the family. The flat in Urlwin Street – really just the top floor of a tiny Victorian terrace – was marginally less cramped than its predecessor, but the arrival of Maurice's younger brother Stanley a couple of years later soon put paid to such luxury.

They shared the house, which rattled as the trains clattered across the railway bridge adjoining the terrace, with another four, similarly cramped, families. They shared the toilet too – a cold, clammy lean-to at the bottom of the garden, a full five flights down from the Micklewhite residence. To make matters worse, young Maurice grew up suffering from the bone-weakening disease rickets, which meant that he had to wear surgically modified shoes. Getting up and down those flights of stairs was no small feat for him.

Rickets is caused by a deficiency in vitamin D (Maurice's sufferings might, perhaps, have been eased if he had eaten a little more of that phosphorescent fish his father brought home from Billingsgate) and is therefore treatable. But blepharitis, which the boy was born with, is incurable. An inflammation of the eyelids, blepharitis is what gave Michael Caine those thick, hooded, nacre-lined eyelids that have come in so handy when he plays the villain or camps things up slightly – or, as has often happened, does both at the same time.

And the villain was, in fact, the very first role he found himself playing. From the age of three, around the time that his brother Stanley was born, Maurice junior would be sent by Ellen Micklewhite to answer the front doorbell and inform the man who had just rung it that his mummy wasn't in. Thus was the rent payment postponed for another week. Plainly, we have no idea as to the quality of the performances on offer, but whatever their strengths and weaknesses the connection they must have forged in their interpreter's mind between the pecuniary and the histrionic could not be but significant.

For all the licensed dishonesty at home, when, aged just four, Maurice Micklewhite fetched up at the John Ruskin infant school just around the corner from Urlwin Street, he quickly got himself a reputation for being too good for his own good. His blond curls and baby blue eyes gave him something of the look of Shirley Temple and led one of the teachers to gift him the unenviable nickname of 'Bubbles'.[28] Teacher's-pet types never have an easy time of it, and young Maurice was soon returning home bruised and dirtied, his shirts and shorts torn. But things can't have been made any easier by the fact that his mother took to coming round to the school herself and belting all the lads who had been picking on her son. The teacher's pet was a mummy's boy, too.

Nice little learner: Maurice's infant school, John Ruskin. © Christopher Bray

He was also becoming something of a movie buff. The Mia Farrow character in Woody Allen's *The Purple Rose of Cairo* (1985) wasn't the only person to find solace in the silver screen during the Great Depression of the thirties – the golden era for British cinema-going. Fred Astaire and Ginger Rogers, Barbara Stanwyck, Betty Grable, Humphrey Bogart, Jimmy Cagney, Shirley Temple herself, of course – such were just a few of the names and faces to be worshipped at the pictures in the decade of Maurice Micklewhite's birth. The Lone Ranger is the first hero he remembers having seen as a child, though it is a fair bet that Johnny Weissmuller's *Tarzan* series and *Snow White and the Seven Dwarfs* (released in 1937, the year Maurice was introduced to the pictures) featured in his daydreams. The next year, when Maurice was five, Errol Flynn starred in that miracle of Hollywood hokum, Michael Curtiz's *The Adventures of Robin Hood*, and it is tempting to wonder whether he saw that movie, too. Certainly, several of the roles that were to make him a star in the sixties were updates of Flynn's most famous role. In pictures like *The Ipcress File* (1965) and *Gambit* (1966) Caine made a name for himself playing the poor but savvy nobody out to take whatever he could from the needlessly rich. One way or another, the movies would have him for life.

2 1938–46

War educates the senses.
   Ralph Waldo Emerson[1]

Away from the glamour of the cinema, though, the already less-than-pretty slums of south London were beginning to look even more unattractive. War with Germany was looming, and Hitler's bombers were likely to be soon flying overhead. The country's fears were made concrete at the end of September 1938, when 38 million gas masks were issued – one for every man, woman and (not-too-small) child.[2] In the event of a catastrophe, they were intended to aid breathing, though the first one Maurice junior was issued with came with its own built-in catastrophe. After a few minutes of accustoming himself to its operation in the school playground, he keeled over. The mask had been letting him breathe out properly but had not been allowing fresh air back in. Even today, Caine says, he can't abide the smell of rubber.

Not so the smell of the English countryside, which the young Micklewhite loved from his first taste of it. Peter Ackroyd wrote of Dickens, he 'places all the poverty and horror in the world in London, all of its peace and seclusion in the neighbouring countryside'.[3] He might have been talking about Caine, who writes of his evacuation from London, a year or so after that ill-starred début with a gas mask, with the liberated glee of David Copperfield.[4] More than half a century on, in Caine's telling of it, the countryside comes as a literal breath of fresh air to a boy hitherto trapped in the sour stifle of the city.

The countryside in question, at least at first, was part of the Royal County of Berkshire. Together with his three-year-old brother and his classmates from John Ruskin School, Maurice junior was put on a train at Waterloo station. Many hours but only forty-odd miles or so later, they decanted in the village of Wargrave, a couple of miles upstream from Henley-on-Thames. The children were assembled in the village hall, fed a little and then made to stand on parade. That way, the local families could come and get a good look at their new guests and pick the ones they wouldn't mind having at home with them.

After the best part of an unsupervised day on a train, few of this pack of south London urchins can have been anything but grubby, though the Micklewhite brothers evidently won the prize in the filth stakes. Certainly, as Caine's Dickensian memory filters it, Stanley and he were the only two children left in the hall at the end of the day. Nobody wanted them. At last, though, an attractive and kindly elderly lady, to whom the vicar and his minions seemed most deferential, took a fancy to the two brothers. It was a fancy they returned when she took them outside and instructed them to get in her Rolls-Royce. Once in it, they were taken to a house that looked 'like a castle'.5 It turned out to have servants, as well as sufficient rooms to give the boys their first taste of sleeping alone. It was like something out of a dream or one of those Hollywood movies Maurice had seen.

Once again, though, there was a Dickensian twist to the tale. After just one night's solitary sleep, a local official came to advise the boys' host that, lovely though her house was, it was further than regulations allowed from the local school. The boys would have to be moved. And not even moved together. They ended up in separate houses. Maurice, in fact, ended up in the broom cupboard, locked in there for a full day, the victim of a dictatorial martinet given to beating the boys in her care. Thankfully, a teacher at the local school spotted the bruises on Maurice's legs and got in touch with the local NSPCC. They in turn contacted the boy's mother, and she got herself to Wargrave as fast as she could. They were back in London the same night.

They weren't there long. The bombs that had been feared were now dropping all over the town. Hitler had dreams of razing St Paul's cathedral, and though there is a world of difference between the area around Wren's masterpiece and that around Urlwin Street, there isn't much more between them than two miles as a crow – or a bomber – flies. Not surprisingly, many of the bombs aimed at the City ended up falling on Camberwell. After Maurice senior was called for service in the Royal Artillery and London was all but set ablaze under the German Blitz of autumn 1940, his wife decided it was time to get her boys out to the country again. This time, though, she would be going with them.

Norfolk was their destination, a tiny village called North Runcton Green, a couple of miles west of King's Lynn. Along with ten other London families, the Micklewhites were put up at Church Farm, a disused farmhouse with a wood stove and a tin bath. 'The village children did their best to make it welcoming,' remembers local historian Rod Humby, 'collecting furniture and utensils from around the village. Even so, it must have been crowded and basic. It must also have been a tremendous culture shock for the city dweller and villagers alike.'6

Culture-shocked or not, the Micklewhites spent three and a half years in Church Farm, and Michael Caine has long numbered his days there as among the happiest in his life. The clean air and open spaces did wonders for his health, and he took to the farming life with relish. Sheep-shearing, pheasant-beating, haymaking, threshing, herding cattle – young Maurice loved them all. 'He enjoyed being in the country,' remembered John Fuller, a local lad whose father owned Church Farm. 'He used to ride out everywhere in the lorries with my father – sitting in-between the front seats. My father often said that if he ever went away without him, Maurice would let the pigs or cattle out because he went without him!'7 Though Caine has always declared himself proud of his London roots, he has been more ambivalent about the locale he grew up in. Twenty years after his evacuation to Norfolk, Caine would applaud the wholesale destruction of much of the south-east London he had known as a child: 'It's a good feeling to see that little lot coming down,' he said. 'I don't dig this Keep Britain Historical rubbish. The Elephant was picturesque – if you didn't live there.'8 Church Farm, though, has retained its charms for him. Returning to North Runcton over the years, Caine has implored his childhood friend to never pull the farm down. 'I said, "I'll promise I won't pull it down . . . the bugger might fall down!" '9

Early in 1944, though, the Micklewhites left Church Farm, moving to a big house at the edge of the village. The Grange sounds like the address of a house in one of those British films young Maurice had so taken against at the pictures – the kind of place where girls with names like Bunty would have lemonade parties thrown for them. Nonetheless, in one of those quaint Dickensian ironies with which his life is replete, Maurice found himself resident there – and loving every minute of it. Indeed, to hear Caine talk about it, he mapped out a whole new future for himself while living at The Grange.

The Micklewhites went there because its owners – a timber merchant called Irwine English and his wife Constance – needed a cook, and Ellen was given the job. Used to making the best out of the cheaper cuts of meat, the food she had to work on at The Grange must have come as a revelation to her. Certainly, her eldest son, who had tasted something of the good life at that Berkshire 'castle', was about to have his eyes opened to *la vie deluxe* proper. Pheasant, caviare, ports and wines – such were the foods Ellen was serving up to the residents of The Grange, and she made sure any leftovers found their way on to her sons' plates. Michael Caine the gourmet dates his fondness for the good things in life to his stay at The Grange, though he would have to have been a prodigally epicurean child to have really developed a taste for fish roe and well-hung game so young in life. Nonetheless, there is no need to disbelieve his bigger point: here was a world he had hitherto only dreamed of made flesh.

Things were looking up for him at the village school, too. His teacher there, a Miss Linton, saw great potential in this eleven-year-old

Londoner and took to pointing out books in the school library she thought he ought to read. She even entered him for the scholarship exam that, if passed, would allow him entrance to the grammar-school system and the right to an education beyond the statutory leaving age of fourteen. On 3 March 1944, Maurice duly sat the exam – the first time any pupil at North Runcton school had done so. Hopes were high, though there was a problem: even if the lad did pass the exam, his family could hardly afford to keep him in school. Which is when Irwine English, who had been much taken with his cook's eldest son, came to the rescue: he would pay for the boy's education, scholarship pass or not.

In the event, there was no need to worry. On 28 July Miss Linton recorded in her school logbook: 'We have today been notified that Maurice Micklewhite, an evacuee billeted here since he was seven years old, from London, has passed the LCC [London County Council] scholarship exam which he took from this school last March.'[10] An LCC exam meant an LCC scholarship, and until the Micklewhites returned home after the war Maurice was subsequently a pupil of the Hackney Downs Grammar School. This was not, of course, the nearest grammar school to their home in Urlwin Street, but it was the nearest London grammar to North Runcton. Hackney Downs had moved to King's Lynn for the duration of the war, and it was to King's Lynn that Maurice now travelled each day.

Hackney Downs, infamous recently as one of the worst schools in the country, was closed down in 1995.[11] Half a century before, though, it had been an institution to be reckoned with. Its pupils back then were mainly the children of ambitious and industrious Jewish families; over the years, Hackney Downs has given the country two life peers and two university vice-chancellors. More importantly in this context, perhaps, the school has also given us, besides Michael Caine, two other masters of dramatic menace: Harold Pinter and Steven Berkoff.

The school brought out the best in young Maurice. Indeed, had he remained a pupil there, one wonders whether there would have ever been a Michael Caine. He worked hard at Hackney Downs, and as a naturally bright boy he might have gone on to do very well on the academic front. But in 1945 the war ended, and the next year the Micklewhites returned to south London. Maurice's schooling was as good as over.

Hitler's bombs having all but destroyed Urlwin Street, the council gave the Micklewhites a new home: a prefabricated house in Marshall Gardens, a mile or so up the Walworth Road at the Elephant and

Castle. It was made of asbestos, but at least it had electricity and running water – both improvements on the gas lighting and outside lavatory of the family's previous home. Indeed, Ellen Micklewhite was to live there for the best part of twenty years, until the mid-sixties, when the star of *The Ipcress File* (1965) could afford to buy her something a little more plush.

The new stability at home wasn't reflected, though, in Maurice's performance at school. The Elephant and Castle falling far outside the Hackney Downs catchment area, Maurice became a pupil at Wilson's Grammar School down the road in Camberwell. Wilson's modelled itself after the great British public schools,[12] and if it wasn't quite Dotheboys Hall, nonetheless it was a regime of rules and regulations. All the pupils had to wear a uniform, for instance. This was not cheap, but the future Michael Caine was one of the first generation to benefit from free education in a welfare state. Should a pupil's family be sufficiently poor, then his uniform would be paid for by means of a government grant. The school's appointed tailor was not far from Urlwin Street in the Camberwell New Road. There, a pupil would be measured for his thick woollen jacket and trousers – itchy attire that, while merely uncomfortable during the autumn and spring terms, attained heights of tortuous prickliness in the summer term. Certainly, it made the young Micklewhite prickle: he seems to have hated Wilson's from day one.

He was thirteen now, a bad age for clever boys with an independent streak, and all the promise he had shown while at Hackney Downs' King's Lynn billet was quickly dissipated. Wilson's was only a short bus ride away from the Elephant, but Maurice seems to have found the mile or so that separated him from his parents during the day rather liberating. The biographer Brian Masters, who became a pupil at Wilson's the year after Maurice left the school, remembers him 'as a rather dull chap',[13] although evidently he was not so dull as to avoid getting into trouble. William Mattingly, one of Maurice's classmates, remembers him having 'a pretty coarse tongue. "Arsehole" he used quite frequently. And various other words. They were being thrown into the conversation deliberately to shock us. He did not want to be accepted. There was something within him that deliberately was telling him to stand out from the crowd, and the best way for him to be unique was to be a loner with a chip on his shoulder. I think he developed it himself as a form of self-defence.'[14]

Unsurprisingly, perhaps, Maurice spent little time at the school, bunking off as frequently as he could get away with it. The school's sports fields were a further bus ride away from home, in leafy Dulwich,

Rebel daze: Wilson's grammar school, at which Maurice turned into a trouble-maker.
© Christopher Bray

but before it got halfway there, the bus passed the Tower in Peckham, a cinema at which they changed the programme twice a week. That childhood passion for the movies had only grown stronger as Maurice moved into adolescence, and rather than play cricket or soccer with the other lads from Wilson's, he preferred to while away his afternoons in the company of Jimmy Cagney and Humphrey Bogart.

Bogart talked back and got away with it. Schoolboys who tried the same trick invariably found themselves being punished. Wilson's policy for dealing with misbehaviour was to send unruly pupils to the Prefects' Room. Punishments escalated dependent on the scale of the misdemeanour: a pupil could be detained in school after hours, given errands to do, write lines, or be beaten with a plimsoll. If, however, he had been irredeemably wicked, the pupil would be caned by the Head Prefect or School Captain. Few weeks went by without Maurice suffering a lashing.

There is nothing very unusual about any of this, of course, except for the fact that Maurice's rebellious nature had been nowhere in evidence at the Hackney Downs' billet in King's Lynn. One cannot help wondering whether what the boy was kicking against was not Wilson's Grammar School itself but the fact that it was sited in south-east London, that run-down area he had believed himself to have escaped from. His return to Camberwell seemed to him perhaps like one of those nightmares in which the dreamer runs and runs and runs only to find himself running straight into whatever it is he is running away from. Whatever, when he left Wilson's, aged sixteen, the academic promise of just a few years earlier had evaporated. He had scraped through the School Certificate exams for English Literature and Language, French, Geography, History and Art, but the passes were testimony to native wit, not to any hard work on his part.

Despite his rebellion in the face of educational authority, however, Maurice had something of an autodidactic streak. The English teacher at Wilson's, Eric Watson, had managed to instil in his otherwise troublesome pupil a passion for reading and encouraged him to join the local public library. 'I used to read like mad,' he said of his adolescence a few years later. 'Fourteen books a week. I think that's what ruined my eyes. Because my father would call out in a voice brooking no contradiction, "I want that light out in that bedroom, Maurice." I'd turn out the light, of course, and go on reading under the blanket. With an electric torch.'[15]

Among the books Caine remembers having read by torchlight are Norman Mailer's début novel *The Naked and the Dead* and James Jones's *From Here to Eternity*.[16] In point of fact, the Jones novel was

not published until 1951, a couple of years after Maurice had left
school, but one gets Caine's drift. American literature served up a
picture of a country and a culture far less hidebound, far less crippled
by the stagnating effects of the class system than the one he was
growing up in.

So too the American cinema. Maurice's childhood love of the pictures had become by the time of his adolescence an ardent passion,
but it was always Hollywood movies he favoured. For all the British
cinema's emphasis on low-key realism, he found American films far
less fantastical. He wasn't alone in doing so, of course. Long before
today's global marketplace, Hollywood movies were pitched at as
wide an audience as possible. Not so the British cinema, especially the
pre-sixties British cinema, a large percentage of whose output was
all but incomprehensible to most of its compatriots. 'For years and
years,' wrote the *Spectator*'s film critic Isabel Quigly in 1959, 'we have
known that the British film picture of ourselves was phoney. Everyone
in the country knew it, it was one of the big national lies that everyone
concurred in.'[17]

Certainly, Maurice junior, his own voice a cacophony of swallowed
vowels and glottal stops, realized very early on that homegrown
films – with their cut-glass accented élite and their obligatorily chirpy,
lord-love-a-duck cockneys – merely perpetuated the class stereotypes
that the ruling élite wanted perpetuated. Interviewed by the BBC
shortly after his seventieth birthday he could still warm to the theme:
'[The cinema gave us] very few British role models . . . war films [were]
about [the] upper classes . . . English actors seemed a bit prissy . . . I
identified with Americans, but the one person I did identify with was
Johnny Mills in *This Happy Breed* [1944].'[18]

The fantasy status of British cinema bred in Maurice his own fantasy.
Unlike the average movie fan, he didn't just want a life like the one being
projected up on that screen; he wanted to be up there on the screen
projecting life. But he wanted the life he projected to be more real than
what he had had to sit through as a boy. Being of working-class stock he
took it for granted that if he did ever get a chance to act it would be in
working-class roles. But he was determined that, if and when such roles
were offered him, he would play them as *people* and not just types.

Once, outside the Elephant and Castle's Trocadero cinema, young
Maurice met Anthony Wager, the boy star of David Lean's *Great
Expectations* (1946). Michael Caine remembers his young self as having been bowled over at meeting a real movie actor, but something
inside him must have wondered how this young man had come to be
cast in the Dickens film.[19] Wager was never convincing as the young

Pip. Not for a moment could anyone believe that this prim, scrubbed cherub had been born and bred in a Kentish blacksmithery. Wager, like all Lean's young stars, was a public schoolboy through and through, and he was far more suited to the snobbishly genteel Pip of the story's second movement than he was to its rough-house early days. Maurice Micklewhite, though – he might have been born to play the part.

3 1947-52

Players, Sir! I look on them as no better than creatures set upon tables and joint stools to make faces and produce laughter, like dancing dogs.
Samuel Johnson[1]

Maurice had made his acting début at Christmas 1943, while still an evacuee in North Runcton. History does not record how the future movie star coped with his role as Baron Fitznoodle, the father of the two ugly sisters, in the school production of *Cinderella*. But whatever the audience made of it, Maurice enjoyed himself. Certainly, when, back in London after the war, the opportunity to get on stage again presented itself, he seized it.

Clubland, as its name at least half suggests, was a youth club in the Walworth Road. Run by a local man of the cloth, the Rev. Charles Butterworth, the club doubled as a sports hall for the local boys and a drama group for the girls. A PR guru before the job had been heard of, Butterworth talked Richard Attenborough and Maurice's British cinema favourite, John Mills, into becoming patrons, and its premises were visited more than once by Queen Mary. What Her Royal Highness made of the club and its members and environs has gone unrecorded, though we do know that during a walkabout tour of the East End of London in the thirties she was heard to bewilderedly ask the local residents, 'Why, why do you live here?'[2]

In his autobiography, Caine claims to have joined the drama group because of a combination of clumsiness and lust. In love from afar with one of the drama group's leading lights, one Amy Hood, the fourteen-year-old Maurice took to playing basketball in the Clubland gym. One day, though, he stumbled into a rehearsal session by mistake and was welcomed with open arms by the teacher: 'We haven't got any boys . . . you are the first one to join this year.'[3]

And indeed he may have been. Even today, acting – indeed, any kind of stage work – is regarded as a rather effeminate hobby for boys. Sixty years ago, a quarter of a century before the legalization of homosexual acts between consenting adults, acting was still regarded as a kind of surrogate buggery. And no more so than in strongly working-class areas such as the one Maurice grew up in. As late as 1983, when Peter Tatchell stood for the Labour party in the parliamentary seat of Southwark and Bermondsey (the constituency in which the Micklewhites had lived),

Playtime: Clubland, site of Maurice's first stage show. © Christopher Bray

Tatchell was vilified by the locals for being openly gay. For the first time in decades, the constituency failed to return its Labour candidate to Parliament. The homophobic graffiti daubed round the borough during that gruesome by-election was a fearful spectacle. (And remained so for many years afterwards: anti-Tatchell graffiti could still be spotted, flaking and peeling and weathered by the years, well into the nineties.) What, one has to wonder, did Maurice Micklewhite senior's mates at the pub and the bookies' make of Maurice junior's acting ambitions? Not much, one guesses. Certainly, he did not pay the boy's subscription fees to Clubland. 'When I was fourteen, I asked my father for £2 to pay a quarter's fees at drama school but he didn't have it,' remembered Michael Caine many years later.[4] Didn't have it or wouldn't give it? More than once over the years, Maurice senior asked his thespian son whether he was a 'nancy boy'.

'Micklewhite looked bent,' remembers Maurice junior's childhood friend, the sometime boxer cum actor Nosher Powell. 'He looked a poof. He was good-looking, [had] long wavy hair, and he was quiet . . . I thought he had as much chance of being an actor as me being heavyweight champion of the world . . . I said, "Get your father to get you a job at Billingsgate." '5 The description, if not the logic, is impeccable, but what is most striking about this image of the teenage Maurice is how little it chimes with the contemporaneous one we have of him from a mile down the road at Wilson's Grammar. What has happened to the hot-blooded tearaway of Kelly House? Was the rebel without a cause act just that – a pose devised to distract attention from his puta- tively effete existence elsewhere? Was he getting into hot water at school in order to reassure his father that, far from being a homosexu- al, he was really just another averagely troublesome boy? Whatever the truth, the stark differences in opinion about the teenage Maurice point to someone already well able to compartmentalize the different spheres of his existence. More than one of his co-stars has marvelled over the years at Michael Caine's ability to switch off his performance once the day's shoot is over.

One of his earliest appearances in a Clubland production was as one of the titular characters in Karel Capek's 1920 play *Rossums' Universal Robots*, which tells the story of a group of robots whose creator has managed to endow them with souls; alas, the near-human robots make their mission in life the destruction of humanity proper. Caine has said he didn't understand much of what was going on in the play. Nonetheless, one cannot help but wonder how he approached the role. What, after all, could be more difficult than playing a robot with feel- ings? How does a robot with feelings differ from a robot without them? How, more to the point, does a robot with feelings differ from a human being? Whatever his answers, he was rewarded for his efforts with his first review, in the Clubland magazine: 'Maurice Micklewhite played the robot who spoke in a dull mechanical monotonous voice to perfection.'6

Dull, mechanical, monotonous – the words sound (and were pre- sumably intended to sound) pejorative. But while one does not want to make any great claims for Maurice's performance, it is possible to see in that report of his acting something of Michael Caine the natu- ralistic star. Right from the start, it seems, he put the lessons he had learned from all those Hollywood movies into practice – to play things down rather than up, to breathe in rather than breathe out. Like the robot he played, in other words, he was ahead of his time.

Maurice left school at the age of sixteen, in the summer of 1949. The bright young lad of a few years earlier had done no more than all right in his final exams, and in the eighteen or so months before he was obliged to commence his National Service he trod water with a series of dead-end jobs. He fetched up first at Peak Films, a small company that specialized in weddings and 8mm tourist shorts of the sights of

London. There he learned something of the technicalities of movie-making – the functions of the different lights and lenses and such like – the kind of technicalities, in fact, that Michael Caine has always been adamant that aspirant actors ought to know about. Acting, he has long been at pains to point out, is a practical as well as a creative art. Those actors who know what effect a given light or lens is going to have on what they are doing are not only advantaging themselves: they are true professionals because they understand that no matter how famous they are, they are still only one of the cogs in an enormous machine.

Such was the basic lesson he learned from a first reading of the Russian film-maker V. I. Pudovkin's *Film Acting* (translated into English by Ivor Montagu in 1949), which Maurice borrowed from the Southwark Public Library. A director rather than an actor, Pudovkin was convinced that montage – the editing together of separate images – was the crux of movie art. Meaning, he argued, never inhered in a single image but was, rather, constructed by the movement from one image to the next. Movie acting, it followed, was as much a construct of the director as of any individual performer.

To prove what seemed at the time a somewhat outlandish claim, Pudovkin adduced the editing experiment carried out by another Russian film-maker, Lev Kuleshov. Kuleshov constructed a short film that consisted of a series of images of objects – a child at play, a woman's corpse, a bowl of soup – intercut with another series of images of an actor's face reacting to the preceding object. Having shown the film to an audience, Kuleshov asked them to describe the performance of the actor. Their response was enthusiastic: the actor, they said, looked happy watching the child, sad looking at the dead woman, and hungry looking at the soup. At which point Kuleshov told them that the shots of the actor were all the same – they had read the successive emotions into his face *because* of the preceding images.

Pudovkin, in other words, confirmed Maurice's essential belief about movie acting – that less is more and that, therefore, the high-flown histrionics of the British *theatrical* tradition have no place in the *cinema*. A believer above all in the primacy of entertainment, Michael Caine has never been remotely interested in modernist drama or film. Nonetheless, as a young would-be actor there was an undeniably avant-garde streak about him. His naturalistic instincts cut right across the grain of the British film industry. For the best part of a decade they would cost him dear.

Before those troubles, though, there was military life to endure. In 1951, Maurice received his call-up papers for the two years of National

Service every eighteen-year-old boy then had to go through. On 17 May that year he became a soldier. 'Every man thinks the worse of himself for not having been a soldier,' said Dr Johnson, and as usual he had a point. But it is probably equally true that every man who has been a soldier without volunteering thinks the worse of the people who volunteered him. Maurice had grown up with a diffuse detestation of the class system based largely on a mix of personal experience and Hollywood movies; during his two years in the Royal Fusiliers those feelings would gain in focus and force. And within a year or two of his being back in civvy street, several writers were to start embodying this class-consciousness in some of the canonical English plays and novels of the second half of the twentieth century.

For now, though, life was simply dull and repetitive. National Service,

> empty for the most part of any useful occupation, did not inspire
> one with a sense of urgent readiness for patriotic duty. This was
> why most National Servicemen resented, with varying degrees of
> bitterness, the confiscation of their freedom for two of the best
> years of their lives. The Services, and successive governments, failed
> abysmally to give any kind of positive or constructive meaning to
> National Service. Those of us who did it felt, not that we were being
> trained to be useful in a national emergency . . . but that we were
> being maintained as a cheap standing army, occupied with futile
> and demeaning tasks.[7]

That is the novelist David Lodge, another south London boy, born a couple of years after Maurice, in 1935. Moreover, thanks to his having taken a degree, Lodge did not actually begin his National Service until 1955, four years later than Maurice. Why does this matter? Because the key difference between the two men's National Service is that, while both of them wasted a lot of time on such tasks as painting coal and shaking leaves off trees,[8] Lodge saw no active service. Maurice, on the other hand, emphatically did.

The Korean War[9] had been raging for a couple of years when Maurice and several of his conscript friends were made an offer they could refuse. Sign on for another year of drudge in the army, they were told, or be sent to Korea and complete only their two years' statutory service. It was quite possible that being sent to Korea would mean death (up to 4 million people, 750 of them British troops,[10] were killed during the three-year war), but as far as Maurice was concerned an early death was better than a late departure from the army. He signed up for the war and became Fusilier 22486547 of the Royal Fusiliers' 1st Battalion.

They set sail from Liverpool on 26 June 1952, bound for Pusan, Korea, by way of Port Said, Aden, Colombo, Singapore and Hong Kong on the *Empire Halladale*. The journey was to take forty days, during which time Maurice and his shipmates were told that, as well as their sundry mundane duties, they must spend the mornings sun-bathing on deck to toughen up their skins in readiness for action in the fierce heat of Korea. By the time they got there even the most pallid blond – such as Maurice himself – was well-prepared for the scorching sun. What they weren't ready for was the filth and degradation – rats, flies, mosquitoes, clap-ridden whores – and all around the smell of the human shit that the locals used as compost. 'When I first saw that place,' Caine has remembered, 'I felt I'd been living in luxury all my life.'[11]

Not that there wasn't fun to be had. 'Why is it all you blokes want to go to the Far East? Bet you think it's all beer and brothels, don't you. Well it is – for about two weeks of the year, on your annual leave. The rest of the time it's flies and heat and patrols and dysentery.'[12] Thus the sergeant to his dreamy squad in *Ginger, You're Barmy*. David Lodge knew of what he wrote. There were indeed a lot of beer and brothels in Korea, though Maurice steered well clear of the latter. Instead, he became the camp's self-appointed VD expert, a position which led him into near Ortonesque pseudo-medical escapades in the latrines. It was not, apparently, enough for some of the chaps that he took a look at their equipment and pronounced them in the clear; they wanted Maurice to get his own equipment out so that they could carry out a compare and contrast exercise.

Given his later reputation as a ladykiller, one wonders how the teenage Maurice could remain so abstemious. In his memoir, he claims that, as well as an instinctive loathing for commercial sex, he had a dread of the clap: 'I was petrified of catching anything since I'd seen the VD film they had shown us on the ship. I've seen some horror films in my time but that one scared the life out of me. There was a terrify-ing rumour going around, about a disease called Black Syphilis which, the story went, was incurable and you went insane and were locked away until you died and the army informed your parents you had been killed in action.'[13] Which is fine as far as it goes, but why did this horror film not affect everyone who saw it in the same way? How hard must it have been for an inexperienced teenager to resist the blandish-ments of easy sex? Was it the fear of insanity and being locked away that really terrified Ellen Micklewhite's second son?

Life in the army was bad enough without the clap anyway. Night-time guard duties were the worst, especially for a small band of men with out-of-date equipment. As Richard Hoggart has pointed out, the arms the average British soldier was using in Korea were the same as he would have been using ten years previously: 'No magnificent and sophisticated new electronics from the arms industry in the intervening years.'[14] Or as Maurice Micklewhite put it, with rather less diplomacy: 'Why are we expected to fight a Chinese army which numbers in the millions with a bolt-loading, single-shot rifle? The Americans have at least a semi-automatic carbine for the same job.'[15] The reward for having such a questioning mind was the task of cleaning a US machine gun – an enormous Browning still covered in the pounds of packing grease it had travelled to Korea in.

On one night-guard, during which they had to patrol no-man's-land, Maurice and a couple of other conscripts found themselves being tracked by Koreans through the pitch-black. After a few moments' soul-searching, the men decided to charge back at the Koreans, screaming. Alas, they had miscalculated: the Koreans were, in fact, ahead of them, nearer to the British camp. By some miracle of circuitousness, however, Maurice and the other men managed to find their way back behind the British lines. Michael Caine says in his autobiography that the experience taught him to believe that 'if anyone takes me, they're going to have to pay'.[16] It sounds like a line from *Get Carter* – as well it might: because what Korea also taught Maurice, of course, is how to play the hard man.

Moreover, Korea showed everyone in Britain with eyes to see that the so-called 'special relationship' the country had with the USA was highly one-sided. Ever since the end of the 1939–45 war, British politicians of both left and right had claimed that one of their post-imperial missions in life was to guide America through the troubled waters of a world it didn't really understand. In reality, the Americans were making all the decisions, and the British were no more than willing lapdogs. Both Clement Attlee, prime minister from 1945–51, and his successor Winston Churchill demanded of America 'a place on the bridge within reach of the wheel'[17] in foreign affairs. Both were rebuffed. Three years after the end of the Korean War, the Suez crisis would put paid to any lingering fantasies of Britain's being a world power, but the angry young men who came along in tandem with Suez had learned their basic lessons from Korea.

Certainly, what Korea most taught that proto-angry young man Maurice Micklewhite was something he had long suspected: that too often those in authority do not merit their position; indeed, will probably be the opposite of authoritative when the moment for authority arrives. He was by no means the only squaddie to learn these lessons in this (or any other) war, of course. But he was one of the few squaddies who put their knowledge to some practical use. Michael Caine's breakthrough performance as the arrogantly incompetent fop Gonville Bromhead in *Zulu* (1964) might well have been just as technically as perfect as it is had its creator not spent a year in Korea. It could not, though, have spoken to audiences quite so powerfully had it not so plainly come from the actor's heart.

4 1953–56

Most marriages don't add two people together. They subtract one from the other.

Ian Fleming, *Diamonds Are Forever*[1]

Michael Scott was born in Leicester Square at the age of twenty. Maurice Micklewhite gave birth to him while pondering a job application in the spring of 1953. After being demobbed from the army, Maurice had returned to the family's Camberwell prefab: home is the hero. And indeed, home was the only place where he got a hero's welcome. After the Second World War the people of Britain had been promised a land fit for heroes. After the Korean War they were still waiting for it. Money was still tight. Food was still rationed. The age of affluence was just around the corner, but for now it was still very much the age of austerity.

Doubtless Maurice senior suggested once more to his eldest son that he join him in working at Billingsgate; instead, he fetched up down the road at Smithfield meat market. There, he was employed by a company called Lovell and Christmas, mixing different qualities of butter into a one-size-fits-all homogeneous mulch. The class system returned, however, at the wrapping stage, when the blocks of butter were wrapped and labelled differently depending on where they were going to end up being sold. Gold paper for Knightsbridge, greaseproof for the Elephant and Castle.

It would have been a dead-end job for a would-be star were it not for the old-timer Maurice palled up with who, according to one version of the story, had known the theatre critic James Agate.[2] Another version has it that the workmate in question had a daughter who was trying to make it as a singer and thus knew some of the ins and outs of show business.[3] Hearing of the young man's ambitions, he suggested he start buying the *Stage*, the theatrical newspaper that carries the job-vacancy advertisements for the acting profession. The following weekend Maurice took himself off to the West End to pick up a copy.

There is something touching about the idea of a would-be actor not knowing of the existence of the *Stage*, but we should remember that Maurice was going about things the old-fashioned way, trying to break into show business without having studied at drama school. Not that he thought this a disadvantage. Even if he could have afforded to go to RADA or one of the other theatrical colleges, Maurice wouldn't have

wanted to. As he saw it, stage schools churned out stilted clones by the
dozen – high-blown athletic types with a spring in their step and a plum
in their throat. Such places were no training ground for actors who
wanted to portray something approximating to the empirical world
they witnessed and dealt with every day. RADA and its like were not
the places to learn about realism. Indeed, weren't the American movie
stars he so admired even now absorbing the hyper-realist tenets of the
Stanislavsky Method? In the England of the early fifties, of course,
there was nowhere to go to learn about the Method, but it is still somewhat ironic that Maurice was to learn his stagecraft from an old-school
repertory manager whose love of posturing declamation wouldn't have
looked out of place in the Georgian theatre.

His name was Alwyn D. Fox and, as well having written a handful of radio plays and trodden the occasional West End board, he
ran a troupe called the Westminster Repertory Company. Alas, the
Westminster Repertory Company was located not where its name
might suggest but in Horsham, thirty miles or so from the centre of
London, in West Sussex.

'Assistant Stage Manager, occasional walk-on parts' ran the ad in the
Stage that caught Maurice's eye that morning in Leicester Square. Appli-
cants for the job had to provide a picture of themselves, so he duly took
himself off to Jerome's studio in Oxford Street to be photographed.4
The result, all high-lit cheekbones and eyelashes suffused in a sepia
glow, wasn't, perhaps, what Maurice junior would have had in mind,
but Michael Scott could see its virtues. And it was Michael Scott who
signed the accompanying letter and posted it off to Horsham.

Alwyn D. Fox liked the cut of Michael Scott's key-lit jib. Like the
majority of men in the theatre, he was a homosexual, although even
the most rampant heterosexual would have found it hard to gainsay
the beauty of this would-be assistant stage manager. He stood tall at
six foot two, was lean and tanned from his time in Korea, and hauling
that butter around at Smithfield hadn't done his musculature any
harm. Throw in those high cheekbones, those near effeminately long
eyelashes and a mouth with a propensity to pout and you have yourself 95 per cent of a stage presence; the rest can be learned. Fox offered
him £2.10s a week (£2.50 – around a third of the average weekly wage
at the time5 and just about enough to pay for his board and lodgings).
Michael Scott's apprenticeship had begun.

Despite Fox's own histrionics, he seems to have had a keen eye for
ham on the part of his underlings. Certainly Caine, one of the best
screen drunks there has ever been, has credited Fox with helping him
create a believable picture of drunkenness. 'What the hell do you think

you're doing?' asked Fox as his new charge, playing Hindley Earnshaw in the Horsham production of *Wuthering Heights*, stumbled and stuttered across the stage. 'I'm playing a drunk, sir,' replied Scott. 'No you're not,' rasped Fox. 'You're an actor who's trying to walk crooked and trying to speak in a slurred voice. Don't you realise that a drunk is a man who's trying to walk straight and speak properly?'[6]

Such dressings down notwithstanding, there wasn't all that much realism to be found in the productions put on by the Westminster Rep. In his first show with them, *The Case of Lady Camber*, Michael Scott played a doctor, although 'never convincingly', according to the *West Sussex County Times*.[7] He got better reviews for his drunken fumblings in *Wuthering Heights* the next week, and better again for a comedy turn as a cockney butler in *The Sport of Kings*: 'The best thing he has done locally . . . his transformation on learning of his master's misdemeanours is a grand piece of comic contrast.'[8] As is Caine's own recollection of the review: 'It was a real stinker! But it did me the world of good. Tell a Cockney he's no good, and he'll dedicate his life to proving otherwise.'[9] Perhaps his memory deceived him, although there is no denying that Michael Caine has spent the bulk of his career being affronted by complimentary reviews.

It was at Horsham, too, that he began the highly practical training that was to stand him in good stead in the movies. Michael Caine has played down his off-stage responsibilities with the Westminster Rep, but an assistant stage manager is as important as anyone out there in front of the footlights. And just as he had used his lowly job in the film industry to learn something of cinematic techniques, so at Horsham did he school himself in the technicalities of the theatre. Set design and construction, lighting, curtain-pulling – he learned them all. Above all, he learned about timing. One of the stage manager's big jobs, after all, is making sure people are on stage where and when they should be, accompanied by the right props. Caine's performance as the effete but irascible theatre producer in the movie of the Michael Frayn farce *Noises Off* (1992) makes the fullest visible use of this experience that we have.

But Terence Stamp benefited from it years before *Noises Off*, when he was up for the title role in Peter Ustinov's movie of *Billy Budd* (1962). To get the part would be an enormous break, and Stamp was understandably nervous. Caine, then Stamp's flatmate, helped him learn his lines and then took him through the process of standing in the right place at the right time by having him walk across their living-room floor until his toes were touching the blade of a bread knife. 'It is critical for the actor to hit the mark laid down,' he told Stamp. 'These marks . . . are the cameraman's only way of keeping an actor in perfect focus. If you can't master it, you might as well give up right away.'[10] Since Stamp got the part, the lesson clearly paid off, though what is interesting is that nobody on the movie had mentioned anything about marks: it had been Caine who decreed that such matters were what would count most at the audition. There was no ethereal talk about motivation or character. Practicalities were what counted. Caine the technician knew that you had to get the basics right before you could build on them. He could all but hit his mark running. As Stamp says of him: 'He could feel a chalk mark through the crepe soles of his desert boots.'[11]

Back in the early days at Horsham, though, the great technician had been known to muff things. During a performance of the now long-forgotten *The Case of Mrs Barry*, the extremely tall hat he was wearing got caught up in what must have been some extremely flimsy scenery and took the top off a doorway. In another production, the victim of a practical joke, he came on wearing half a pound of lipstick and eye-shadow. But we learn as much from our mistakes as from our masterstrokes, and given the speed of turnround in a post-war provincial repertory theatre – a new play to be learned and performed each week – Michael Scott was getting a crash course in the acting trade. Thirty years later, Woody Allen talked about Michael Caine as so much more versatile than the bulk of Hollywood leading men: 'Michael can play a CIA agent or a comic role and he gets a great kick out of playing either. England has a tradition of men of all ages because of its vital theater, [sic.] (?) and the films are not always about gangsters or gunfighters riding into town. They're normal human beings.'[12]

All that was long in the future, but as that summer of 1953 turned to autumn and the Korean War ended, the former Maurice Micklewhite could have been forgiven for allowing himself the thought that things were beginning to happen for him. Korea, however, wasn't quite done with him. Back in July, during the run of *Wuthering Heights*, one of Hindley Earnshaw's drunken falls had seemed a little too real: Michael Scott had struggled through a performance while running a high fever, and after the show an ambulance was called for and he was stretchered off to hospital. He was back at work a few days later, but by October he was hospitalized, the fever raging once more. All through the war he had done everything he could to avoid catching a sexually transmitted disease. Not all diseases, though, are transmitted sexually and Korea had left him suffering from a particularly vicious type of malaria. He would not live, a doctor in the hospital told him, much beyond his early forties.

He spent seven weeks in hospital, and then a few weeks convalescing at home. After that the man who had been told he had little more than a decade to live went back to Horsham ('We'll do some horror plays,'

quipped Alwyn D. Fox after catching sight of his rising star[13]), though
not for long. The army wrote to offer him the chance of a cure for the
malaria – or an even earlier death: the treatment was to be by way of
an experiment, and he was to be one of the guinea pigs. Being a guinea
pig involved no more than being strapped to a bed for ten days in the
army hospital at Roehampton and taking a course of pills. The pills
thickened the blood so much that the straps were a necessity in order
that the patients not fall over and knock themselves out. It was
a long and unpleasant ten days, then, but at the end of them he was
pronounced cured. Michael Scott returned to Maurice Micklewhite's
home once more, to be fattened up on his mother's bread pudding[14] in
preparation for a prodigal's return to Westminster Rep.

Home is the hero: Caine with his mother at her house in Camberwell. His brother
Stanley is in the background. © Getty Images

When he got back to Horsham this time, though, Fox was nowhere
to be seen. The theatre was empty. The Westminster Repertory company had gone bust, and Michael Scott was looking for work again. In
all probability this wasn't the bad news it might at first have seemed.
He had learned a good deal at Horsham, but it is highly likely that it
is all he would ever have learned there. Fox had given him his first big

break, but if there were going to be more breaks he would have to hunt them out.

The place to hunt, of course, was the ads pages of the *Stage*, which, one week early in 1954, carried an ad for 'experienced juveniles' at the Lowestoft Theatre on the Suffolk coast. Prospective candidates had to write to the company producer, one Jackson Stanley, who, the ad informed them, was currently preparing a production of a show called *George and Margaret*. Coincidentally, this was one of the plays that Michael Scott was to have appeared in at Horsham before he had fallen ill. And though he had never read the play, he reasoned he had heard enough about it to claim to have appeared in it for Alwyn D. Fox, playing, he wrote in his application for the job, the titular male character. He might as well have claimed to have played Godot, for the character of George, while much mentioned in this repertory warhorse, never actually appears on stage. The play is built around the imminent arrival of George and Margaret, but ends before they ever get there.

So it was perhaps only for purposes of his own merriment that Stanley summoned Michael Scott for an interview – an interview which began ominously: 'What have we here, then,' rasped the producer, 'apart from a bloody liar?'[15] What he had here was, in fact, a reasonable stage actor, as the applicant managed to prove after he had talked Stanley into giving him the audition he had putatively invited him down for. After he had run through a few scenes from *Wuthering Heights* and *The Sport of Kings*, Michael Scott was taken on by the Lowestoft Theatre. His salary was to be virtually double what he had been earning at Horsham – £4.10s (£4.50) a week.

The company was, Caine remembers, a notch up from that in Horsham. He has described Jackson Stanley as a good producer, if only because he encouraged his actors to do less but think more. During one rehearsal the new boy was bawled out and asked why he was doing nothing. 'I'm doing nothing because I haven't got any lines for a long while.' 'No,' boomed Stanley, 'but you are thinking of wonderful lines to say, and then deciding not to say them. Remember always to listen – that is half of acting.'[16] And a big half, too, one thinks watching Michael Caine at work in *Alfie* (1966), say, or *Educating Rita* (1983). One is apt to picture those movies as talky, but they are full of silences too – the silences of a man totally in control of his effects.

Meanwhile, Michael Scott was falling in love. The leading lady at the Lowestoft Theatre was one Patricia Haines. Almost two years older than him, a tall, green-eyed RADA graduate from the north country, she ought to have been way out of his class. As in every other working arena, there is an unspoken sexual hierarchy in the theatre which decrees that, while the boss can sleep with anyone, everyone else must stick to their own level. Leading ladies, accordingly, put out for leading men and producers. They do not get involved with juvenile leads.

Except that this one did. And just as it would be for a whole generation of women a decade later, it was his eyelashes that entranced her. 'It was as if they were dusted with pollen,'[17] she said years later in what was a perhaps unconsciously apt metaphor. Because though the couple were married within weeks of their meeting, within months of their marriage they discovered that they were pretty much allergic to each other.

The wedding was held at Lowestoft registry office on 3 April 1954, the just-twenty-one-year-old groom's address being given as 17 Cleveland Road, Lowestoft, and the twenty-two-year-old bride's as that of her parents – 139 Springfield Road, Sheffield 7. Patricia's parents – Claire and Reginald Arthur Haines (the Chief Clerk with the Sheffield Education Authority) – acted as the couple's witnesses. There is no record of anyone from Maurice's family being present.

Things began as they meant to go on – disastrously – with Caine, drunk under the table by his father-in-law at the reception, unable to do what bridegrooms are meant to do on their wedding night. So much one learns from Caine's memoir, but otherwise he is here very short on detail – not a failing observable at every point of his book. This first marriage is written up almost as a drive-by shooting incident: no dates, no motivation, no attempt at understanding what was going on. What was it, though, that prompted this shy young virgin from the back streets of south London to marry so suddenly? To be sure, pre-marital sex was not quite as easily come by in the early fifties as it would be a decade or so later. Indeed, the statistics show that three quarters of all girls were married by the time they reached the age of twenty-five.[18] As Peter Lewis has pointed out, 'The Fifties were not a permissive era. The pressure to marry young went along with a renewed convention of pre-marital chastity.'[19] Even granted what Lewis describes as the 'favourite theme of Fifties writers . . . upward sexual mobility',[20] a theme Michael Scott was making flesh in his relationship with Patricia, there is still about the speed of this affair as if Michael wanted to prove something, to himself as much as to anyone else. Something wasteful too, for it was not to last overlong.

By the end of 1954, Michael and Patricia had had enough of Suffolk rep. They moved to London to try their luck in the major acting league.

They rented a small house in Stockwell Park Walk[21] that was the property of Michael's eighty-year-old aunt. With its easy tube access to the
centre of London, Brixton – just a mile or so south of the Elephant and
Castle – had for many years been popular with actors, though by the
mid-fifties the area was in decline. Certainly, to a middle-class Yorkshire
girl like Patricia it must have been something of a come-down.

Perhaps that is why the couple agreed that it should be Patricia who
carried on trying her luck at acting while Michael went out to work on
rather more mundane jobs – at an industrial laundry, washing up in
restaurant kitchens, helping out as a plumber's mate – so as to pay the
bills. 'I was merely keeping alive while waiting for my next chance at
acting,' he remembered a decade or so later. 'I had dozens of jobs.'[22]
Times might have been tough for Michael Scott the would-be star, but
they were relatively easy on Michael Scott the seeker of casual employ-
ment. A year later, in 1955, there were a mere 200,000 people on the
dole – still the lowest unemployment figure of Britain's post-war
years.[23] Even if Patricia had no luck finding any stage or TV work,[24]
the chances of she and her husband going hungry were slim.

There was still Michael's ambition to feed, of course, although – as
noted already – if he were to do so he would have to change his name
again. There was, his new West End agent – Jimmy Fraser of the high-
powered West End agency Fraser and Dunlop – told him, another actor
called Michael Scott already doing the rounds. So it was that Michael
Caine made his professional début towards the end of 1954 in an
adaptation of Dickens's second Christmas ghost story, The Chimes. A
production of Joan Littlewood's Theatre Workshop in Stratford, east
London, the show's three-month run commenced on 30 November –
and was roundly trashed by the critics.

A keen theorist of theatrical technique, Littlewood (who once made
her troupe rehearse a prison drama in a well on the roof of the theatre
workshop so that they could 'experience the architectural bleakness of
a prison yard'[25]) was one of the first people in England to make use of
the Method school of acting on which we have already touched. First
made famous by Marlon Brando's performance as Stanley Kowalski in
Elia Kazan's movie of the Tennessee Williams play A Streetcar Named
Desire (1951), the Method called for an improvisatory approach to
acting, relying less on the actor's imagination than on his recollection
of emotional experiences. In time, Michael Caine would learn a lot
from the example of Method stars like Brando, James Dean and Paul
Newman, but in late 1954 their techniques were still a mystery to him.

Although her new charge had already forsworn the doublet-and-hose
school of histrionics, Littlewood (whose theatre has been characterized

as being run like a 'benevolent dictatorship'[26]) still found Caine an irritant. 'This is a group theatre,' she barked at him as he made his first entrance in a rehearsal of *The Chimes*. 'I'm not having . . . any of this star nonsense. You bury your individuality in the character for the good of the group and the play as a whole.'[27] The fish porter's son from the Elephant and Castle, meanwhile, had little patience with what would come to be known as trendy lefties, and Littlewood – a Brechtian communist who believed the goal of theatre to be the emancipation of the working class – was as leftie as they came. Sparks were bound to fly. When *The Chimes* came to the end of its run, so did Caine's relationship with the Theatre Workshop.

Things weren't going well at home, either. The sight of two fiercely competitive, struggling actors living in close proximity is never a pretty one, and it gets less pretty when it is agreed that one of them must put his ambitions on hold to see that the bills are paid. And uglier still when the one whose ambitions are not on hold isn't blazing a trail. The newlywed Scotts' flat in Brixton was a time bomb waiting to go off.

Matters weren't helped when Maurice Micklewhite senior fell ill with what he had been told was rheumatism of the spine. In fact, the doctor said to Caine, the fifty-six-year-old Maurice was suffering from cancer of the liver. He had no more than a few months to live. Early in 1956 he was moved to the St Giles Hospital, a spit from Wilson's Grammar in Camberwell. There, on 8 March 1956, a few days before his eldest son's twenty-third birthday, he died. 'Good luck to you, son,' were his dying words. 'The only time he ever encouraged me,'[28] Caine was to remember many years later. Maybe so, but the encouragement came at the right time. Michael Caine's luck was about to change for the better. He got his first part in a movie.

Part Two
WI

The toughest thing about success is that you've got to keep on being a success.
  Irving Berlin

5 1956–63

There is no more sombre enemy of good art than the pram in the hall.
  Cyril Connolly[1]

As the fifties wore on it became more and more apparent that Britain was changing. The old order might not have quite been crumbling; nonetheless, there was a feeling that it had been given its notice. The Korean War had sounded a discreet warning about post-WWII Britain's hopes of maintaining her imperial status. By the end of 1956 the blaring siren that was the Suez crisis had woken even the bluffest armchair colonel from Tunbridge Wells to the fact that the imperial game was up. Suez put paid once and for all to the idea that Britain could still influence events by force. Having marched British troops into Egypt in protest at Colonel Nasser's nationalization of the Suez Canal, Prime Minister Anthony Eden then had to march them back out again when the USA refused to support him. Eden's failed campaign resulted in a curiously contradictory double-shock effect. On the one hand, the British people were ashamed of their country for having indulged in the kind of imperialist bully-boy tactics it had just fought a war against. On the other, they found it hard to believe that Britain could no longer fight and win wherever and whenever it chose. Its people unable wholeheartedly either to endorse or condemn her, Britain turned entropically in on herself. The age of mass irony was born.

In fact, the first major public attack on post-imperial Britain had scorched across the London stage a few months before the Suez crisis. John Osborne's *Look Back in Anger*, a play that took no hostages, had an eerily prophetic air about it. Its hero was Jimmy Porter, a ranting nihilist whose tirades against his wife, friends, in-laws, parents – even himself – were saved from tedium only by the potency of their poetry. No stage character since Shakespeare's had had such reserves of rhetorical overdrive. In one of his most famous diatribes, Porter bemoans his impotent lot thus:

I suppose people of our generation aren't able to die for good
causes any longer. We all had that done for us, in the thirties
when we were still kids. There aren't any good, brave causes left.
If the big bang does come, and we all get killed off, it won't be
in aid of the old-fashioned, grand design. It'll just be for the

Brave New-nothing-very-much-thank-you. About as pointless and inglorious as standing in front of a bus.[2]

Post-Suez Britain six months before the fact.

Diffuse and unfocused, Porter's ire struck a chord with anyone remotely ambitious in fifties Britain. Certainly, he spoke to Michael Caine, who once called *Look Back in Anger* 'the play that changed everything for the working-class actor in the British theatre'.[3] As Peter Vansittart has suggested, Porter's magnificent invective articulated 'the contempt and resentment of those who, despite the Century of the Common Man, could see privileges still earned by lack of talent . . . Old Boy controls rampant in an England of meaningless work.'[4] Caine, though, responded to Jimmy Porter's accent as much as he did to what he said. Kenneth Haigh, who played Porter for the show's opening run, might have trained at the Central School for Speech and Drama, but he had made no attempt to lose the accent his upbringing in Mexborough, a mining village near Doncaster, had bequeathed him.

For all its subsequent mould-breaking status, however, Osborne's play was hardly formally adventurous. While in later works he would borrow distantiation effects from the likes of Brecht, Osborne's first hit is as cosily anti-modernist as anything by, say, Terence Rattigan. Had it been any otherwise it is doubtful whether *Look Back in Anger* could have spoken to the likes of Michael Caine, who has always been adamant that before anything else plays and films must entertain people.

Similarly, despite the revolutionary hopes that have since been pinned to it, Osborne's play was hardly a work of class antagonism. As the historian Maurice Cranston remarked in 1957, detectable behind Osborne's attacks on the upper classes was a desire to have been born into them.[5] It would be stretching things to tar Michael Caine with the same brush.[6] Equally, to think of Caine as some kind of class warrior storming the citadels of privilege is mere romantic inflation.[7] Yes, Caine has said that one of the goals of his working life is the honest representation of the working classes on the silver screen. On the other hand, he has always maintained that he simply does not comprehend why those same working classes don't want to rise above their station. As he told one interviewer, 'When somebody says to me: "I'm proud to be a Cockney," I say "What else are you proud of? What do you DO?" '[8]

Meanwhile, the cockney actor *manqué* was doing very little. 'And introducing Michael Caine,' it says on the sleeve to the 2002 video release of *A Hill in Korea* (1956). It is all rather more grand than the treatment he gets in the movie itself. There he is, listed right at the bottom of the end credits, having failed to make the opening credits at all. As for Caine himself, given that his character Lockyer is one of the few low-ranking soldiers that survives the movie's running time of just over an hour, he is off screen an awful lot of time. And when he *is* on, he has little to do. Ten minutes in he gets to say, 'Morning . . . get us the light programme,' but he has to wait another three quarters of an hour before being allowed to run on to the set shouting: 'Sir, sir, Sgt Payne spotted Kim.' The line delivered, he is allowed a brief pause and a glance to camera, behind which the main action of the scene – the death of Stanley Baker's Corporal Ryker – is taking place. Caine's Lockyer gulps and moves towards Baker, a move that results in his first medium-close shot for the camera, while saying, 'Pity, he was the toughest bloke we'd got.' The close shot is as brief as the director can make it though. Even as he arrives at his glottal-stopped peroration, Caine is turning on his heels and running out of shot. A couple of minutes later he gets his third and final snatch of dialogue: 'I wonder what time it is.'

A *Hill in Korea* is a typical British picture of its time, right down to the chirrups and trills of its Malcolm Arnold Festival of Britain-style score. It's the kind of movie that would become unthinkable within half a decade. The heroes of the novels of John Braine and Alan Sillitoe (and the movies which grew out of them) had no time for the deeply striated class system that holds the small troupe of chaps from Blighty tightly in place in Julian Amyes's film. Indeed, *A Hill in Korea* can be seen as a kind of prototype *Zulu* (1964): a movie in which a small troupe of isolated but plucky Brits take on a mighty army of foreigners and some-how manage to win the day. What the earlier film lacks, though, is *Zulu*'s powerful undertow of class conflict.

George Baker, his speech at once clipped and casual as the almost wilfully relaxed troupe commander Lieutenant Butler, serves up one of his best stiff-upper-lipped turns, while Stanley Baker (emphatically no relation) is all sweat and stutter and panic. All the other stock types of the day are there, too. Stephen Boyd, in his third movie, is the pretty boy destined for an early death, while Robert Shaw is the muscle.

Given the paucity of his dialogue, Private Lockyer was hardly a part that was going to break Caine into the big time, either. Yes, there were early signs of the sixties icon to come – when he has little to do Caine is already hollowing his cheeks and pouting his lips – but he hasn't yet worked out how to give his clench-jawed blankness the diffident sexiness that would so mark him out a decade later.

Nonetheless, it could be argued that Caine pulled his screen début off rather too well. Even here, fresh from the blather and bombast of

provincial rep, he underplays his every scene with spectacular abandon. Few actors respond to other actors as well as Caine , and even in
1956 he had the skill mastered. Clearly, being bawled out for doing
nothing on the stage at Horsham Rep had paid off. Halfway through
the movie, Caine's Lockyer has to watch while the straw-hutted village
he and the rest of his troupe are hiding in is burned to the ground by
the local militia. While the other actors in the shot mop their brows
and exchange worried glances, Caine just lets his jaw go slack and his
eyes gape in a marvellous image of panic held in check by the routines
of military training. With the hindsight of half a century it is clear that
this is Caine's scene (his biggest in the movie); back in 1956, though,
when the British cinema was dominated by piping, posturing poseurs,
he must have seemed like a dumb automaton. 'I'm not keeping *him* on
my books,' you can almost hear Caine's agent saying.

And indeed he didn't. Shortly after the shoot, Jimmy Fraser summarily dismissed Caine from Fraser and Dunlop's client list. Fraser
had seen an early cut of the movie and thought little of his erstwhile
client's achievement in it, though when pressed for concrete criticism
all he could do was mumble something about how Caine ought to get
his eyelashes dyed.

In fact, he had got the part as much on the strength of his war
record as his acting abilities. The producers wanted a technical advi-
sor on the movie, and thanks to his time in Korea, Caine fitted the bill
perfectly. Not that he had any more to do in his off-screen capacity
than he had on screen. Given that *A Hill in Korea* was a piece of bog-
standard British B-movie melodrama, little technical advice was actually called for. Indeed, though Caine told Julian Amyes that British
troops in Korea had tended to spread themselves rather widely during
an advance, for the purposes of the camera they ended up being photographed as closely together as Arthur Lowe and John Le Mesurier in
the end credits of *Dad's Army*. The reason was simple: the crew didn't
have a lens with a wide enough focal length to let the chaps separate
for the shot. And even if they had had such a lens, the resulting image
would have been full of empty space.

Not that Caine cared overmuch. He was being paid £100 a week
whether or not his advice was heeded, and the shoot was scheduled to
last eight weeks. Moreover, Amyes's Korean 'locations' turned out to
be in Portugal. Caine believed that the landscape most similar to that
of Korea was to be found in Wales, but he was sage enough to keep his
counsel on the matter. He wanted some time in the sun.

He wanted some time away from his problems at home, too. Two
years after their wedding, he and Patricia were getting on less and less

well. Rows and jealousies over work were common, yet mutual poverty kept them together. The £800 Caine earned for *A Hill in Korea* was the first serious money either of them had ever seen. But instead of making things easier for them, it seems to have made them worse. When, shortly after Caine's movie début opened in British cinemas in September 1956, Patricia announced that she was pregnant, she lit the fuse on the time bomb that was their marriage.

A note of caution is due here. There is some confusion as to when the couple actually separated. The rough-hewn chronology to be found in William Hall's biography, in Caine's autobiography and in various interviews he has given over the years would lead you to believe that Caine abandoned his wife and child some time in the late summer or early autumn of 1955. Hall, for instance, says that the child was six months old when Caine walked out on her and her mother.[9] Caine merely calls the girl he abandoned his 'new baby'.[10] Both books agree that, having left his new family, Caine moved back into his parents' house and helped nurse his father in the months before his death. But the fact is that the Micklewhites' daughter had not even been conceived, let alone born, at the time of her grandfather's death.

Dominique Ann Micklewhite was born in Sheffield on 14 August 1957. She was named after Dominique Françon, Caine's favourite fictional heroine, from Ayn Rand's 1943 novel *The Fountainhead*. Unreadable now, Rand's sub-Nietzschean, crypto-totalitarian rant had a cult following in Britain and America during the forties and fifties. Her core themes were simple enough: it is only hard-working individuals who achieve anything; therefore, *laissez-faire* capitalism (out of fashion in Britain since around the time of Maurice Micklewhite junior's birth) is the most congenial system for the exercise of talent; and altruism is a vice while selfishness is a virtue. Pity poor Dominique, born twenty-five years ahead of her time.

Nonetheless, it was doubtless such a belief system that helped Caine steer himself through the next few rocky years. Since Dominique was born in Sheffield, while Patricia was back staying with *her* parents, it is possible that Caine had abandoned his wife while she was pregnant. Or it may have been that the couple did not break up until after the birth of their child. Whatever, within months of Dominique's arrival, Caine and Patricia had separated and the baby was resident with her grandparents in Yorkshire, where she was to spend the rest of her childhood. Caine, to borrow the title John Barry was to give the theme he wrote for *The Ipcress File* (1965), was 'a man alone'.

But even solitaries must pay their way. Certainly Patricia was adamant that Caine pay his share of the costs of bringing up their baby. Too much of the time, though, he was all but broke. At one point, Ellen Micklewhite had to contribute to her granddaughter's maintenance on her son's behalf.

The problem was that, even after *A Hill in Korea*, work was hardly pouring his way. After the Jimmy Fraser fiasco, Caine had quickly enough found himself a new agent in Josephine Burton. Unfortunately, Burton lacked the clout of Fraser and Dunlop, and try as she might to make good the shortfall with the kind of quiet industriousness her new client approved of, Caine was more often out of work than in it. So began Caine's long – very long – apprenticeship.

Julian Amyes had liked Caine's performance in *A Hill in Korea* well enough to cast him as Boudousse in a TV production of Anouilh's *The Lark*, which went out live on 11 November 1956, but other offers were still few and far between. For the next six or seven years Caine was to stumble around from one tin-pot TV play to another. He had bit parts in *The Adventures of* both *Sir Lancelot* and *William Tell*, various *Plays of the Week* and in more than one episode of *Dixon of Dock Green*.

On the big screen, he was visible for a moment in Gordon Parry's movie of that old repertory warhorse *Sailor Beware* (1956), and had uncredited walk-ons in the Norman Wisdom comedy *The Bulldog Breed* (1960) and Peter Sellers' early masterpiece *The Wrong Arm of the Law* (1962). He is said to have a part in André de Toth's Nazi espionage yarn *The Two-Headed Spy* (1958), although the present writer has had no luck spotting him. Nor, one presumes, did de Toth, who didn't work with Caine again until ten years later, when he acted as executive producer on the third Harry Palmer movie, *Billion Dollar Brain* (1967).

Occasionally, he would be cast in a movie that held the promise of bigger things. In Carol Reed's *The Key* (1958), for instance, he was playing opposite the likes of William Holden, Trevor Howard and Sophia Loren. In the event, though, not one of Caine's scenes made the final cut.

And so he kept on not being noticed. He was an uncredited prisoner of war in *Carve Her Name with Pride* (1958), a picture directed by Lewis Gilbert. Eight years later, Gilbert was to seal Caine's international star status when he directed him in *Alfie* (1966). He has, though, no memory of Caine's presence in the earlier film.

Similarly, the producer Cubby Broccoli (who was later to make his fortune with the Bond movies) has no recollection of Caine's having worked on his movie *How to Murder a Rich Uncle* (1957).

'We made a string of pictures in those days,' said Broccoli. 'Long after . . . I ran into Michael Caine, who said to me, "Cubby, you probably wouldn't remember it, but did you know I once worked in a picture for you?"

'He was right: I didn't remember it.

' "When was that?" I asked.

' "It was back in 1956, on *How to Murder a Rich Uncle*. You short-listed two of us for a small part on the picture, though you needed only one. You looked at us both, but finally chose me. It wasn't much of a part. I had a scene where I was punting up the Thames with a pretty girl, in a sort of background shot. Do you remember the other actor with me, the one you rejected?"

' "No I don't remember . . . who was it?"

' "It was Sean Connery." '[11]

Though Caine had beaten Connery to that movie, when the two men next met professionally (they bumped into one another often enough on the rounds of London theatrical parties and were already, in fact, firm friends) it was Connery who had the upper hand. He had the lead role in the BBC production of Rod Serling's boxing drama *Requiem for a Heavyweight*, which went out on Sunday, 31 March 1957. Connery played a punch-drunk prizefighter by the name of Mountain McClintock; Caine, meanwhile, had another of his uncredited parts as a boxer who gets summarily taken to pieces by McClintock. The day after the show's transmission, the phone at Connery's agency never stopped ringing and he received offers from both Rank and Twentieth Century Fox. And while nothing much came of this interest until five years later, when he got the part of James Bond, Connery would at least be getting roles with more than a line or two of dialogue to them for the remainder of the fifties. When, Caine could have been forgiven for wondering, was *his* agent's phone going to start ringing?

Things went from bad to worse when Josephine Burton died during an appendectomy. Having worked so little, Caine found it a struggle to get another agent, and when he was signed up it was by Pat Larthe, who dealt primarily in modelling work. Nonetheless, as the fifties approached their end, Larthe did manage to fix her newest signing up for an interview with Robert Lennard, the Casting Director of the Associated British Picture Corporation, who numbered among his discoveries Audrey Hepburn and Richard Todd. The ABPC was run along the lines of the pre-war Hollywood studios, with actors on contract, drawing a regular salary and taking whatever job the company deemed them fit for. Alas, what Lennard deemed Michael Caine fit for was a change of career. 'I know this business well,' he counselled the struggling hopeful, 'and I can assure you that you have no future in it.'[12]

Caine was angered by this advice, as well he might have been, but who was he to demur? As the months and years went by and he stumbled from one miserable TV show to another, was consigned to the cutting-room floor on picture after picture, he cannot but have occasionally wondered whether Lennard had a point. Even when things did happen for him, they did so only half-heartedly.

Early in 1959, for instance, Caine was cast as the understudy to one of the leads in Willis Hall's anti-war play, *The Long and the Short and the Tall*, to be directed by Lindsay Anderson at the New Theatre (now the Albery). Hall had written the part of Private Bamforth with the then hot and happening Albert Finney in mind, but in the event the man Caine was to understudy turned out to be Peter O'Toole. Even at that early stage of his career, O'Toole had something of a reputation as a drinker, but despite turning up late occasionally a little the worse for wear, he never actually missed a performance of the show. Which meant that his understudy never got to go on stage as Bamforth in its West End run.

Caine did, however, get to go on as Bamforth in the show's nationwide post-London tour. While everyone else from the original cast – O'Toole, Edward Judd, Robert Shaw, Richard Harris – had moved on to other things, Caine finally got to play the part he had been hearing every night for three months and more. As the old hand of the cast, he found himself travelling in a position of some importance. Not only was his £16 a week salary more than 33 per cent higher than the other members of the cast,[13] his inside-out knowledge of the play licensed his pointing newcomers in the right direction. One of the actors who benefited most from such tips was Terence Stamp.

Stamp, who had been born and bred in Plaistow in London's East End, was playing Private Whittaker, what Caine referred to as the drama's token 'gormless northerner'.[14] The problem with Stamp's Whittaker, thought Caine, was that it was almost too good. In his notes to the cast, Hall had mentioned that Whittaker is from the Newcastle area, and Stamp had dutifully gone out and worked hard on perfecting a Geordie accent. Caine, though, suggested losing such specificity and turning Whittaker into an all-purpose northern type. This was an idea Caine would put into practice himself a few years hence, when he played *Zulu*'s Lieutenant Gonville Bromhead not as an Etonian or Harrovian (and certainly not as an impersonation of anyone famous who had actually attended either of those places) but as a composite public-school fop. The suggestion worked for Stamp, too. From the moment he started following Caine's advice, he got bigger laughs in every performance.

For all his knowledge of the show, though, when *The Long and the Short and the Tall* came to be filmed, in 1960, Caine wasn't considered for the movie. Instead, the part of Bamforth was filled by Laurence Harvey (cast on the back of his performance as Joe – angry young man – Lampton in *Room at the Top* filmed the previous year). A shame this, because Bamforth – a cut-price Jimmy Porter cum prototype Harry Palmer – was a part made for Caine. Certainly, Hall's screenplay, though no masterpiece, deserved better than Harvey's squawking cockney caricature. A Lithuanian educated in South Africa, Harvey's mispronounced vowels and diphthongs result in a cacophonous Bamforth no less insulting to the Caine's class origins than any of the Richard Todd-style stiff-upper-lipped movies he had grown up loathing.

But it was the presence of two other actors that made the movie of *The Long and the Short and the Tall* look like a kind of proleptic take on the Caine CV. Ronald Fraser's Macleish, for instance, is a dress rehearsal for his role as Campbell opposite Caine's Tosh Hearne in Robert Aldrich's *Too Late the Hero* (1970). More important, though, is the presence of Richard Harris as Bamforth's hectoring nemesis Johnstone, for the relationship between Johnstone and Bamforth was to be echoed off screen as Caine's and Harris's respective careers developed. A few years later, Harris refused to 'play second fiddle to Caine' in André de Toth's *Play Dirty*.[15] By the mid-nineties, as we shall see, the Caine/Harris spats had become a full-blown feud.

The Long and the Short and the Tall tour came to an end in February 1960, by which time Caine and Terence Stamp had cemented a serious friendship. So much so that Stamp suggested to Caine that he move into the flat he and several other friends had on a cheap let in Harley Street, W1. It was to be the first of several surprisingly salubrious addresses the two struggling actors shared over the next few years, during which time they collaborated on a screenplay called *Over the River*. This last was a highly autobiographical story about a young south London boy making it good and moving north of the Thames. It was never filmed.

Things weren't improving for Caine on the personal front either. Sleeping late in his Harley Street bed one morning, he was roused by a violent knocking on the front door. Upon answering it, he was confronted by two men who asked whether he was Maurice Joseph Micklewhite and would he like to accompany them to the Magistrates'

Court in Marlborough Street? He spent several hours in a cell before being arraigned on a charge of having failed to pay child maintenance to his estranged wife. Defenceless, Caine was forced to empty his pockets in front of the court, producing the princely sum of £3.10s (£3.50). This sum was duly confiscated and Caine was told he would have to pay the same amount to his estranged wife every week or go to jail.

Fortunately, a paying job was just around the corner. Caine won a part in a new play by a new writer: Harold Pinter. *The Room* had opened at the Hampstead Theatre three weeks into the new decade. Now, a couple of months on, it was transferring to the West End, to the Royal Court no less, and Caine was replacing John Rees in the part of Mr Sands.

The homecoming: Caine with Harold Pinter (centre) and Pinter's then wife, *Alfie* co-star Vivien Merchant. © British Film Institute

The Room, it is now clear, was archetypal Pinter – a shabby, claustrophobic set; a put-upon woman and a taciturn husband; several mysterious visitors – but at the time it must have seemed almost wilfully obscure.Certainly, Caine, who played one of the play's mysterious visitors, has always maintained that he was baffled by it. But his lack of understanding did the show little harm, since an air of numinous doubt is essential to Pinter. And the benefits were mutual, because no playwright has encouraged his actors to understand that less can be more as much as Pinter. Indeed, Pinter's work can be read as a critique of the grandiloquent/histrionic school of acting that had so dominated the London stage and the British film industry until well into the fifties. Caine's Mr Sands had, quite literally, no more than a couple of walk-ons in Pinter's play. Nonetheless, its lessons in theatrical quietism were to stay with him for the rest of his working life.

With a couple of movie appearances that year (the Norman Wisdom comedy *The Bulldog Breed* and *A Foxhole in Cairo*, a true story about espionage in WWII) and half a dozen small roles on television, things were finally beginning to look up for Michael Caine. Although Terence Stamp's recollection of their leaving the Harley Street flat is that they were forced to downsize for lack of work, Caine remembers the move being prompted by an increase in his earnings. And given that the downsizing exercise took them to a one-bedroomed flat just south of Hyde Park, at 12 Ennismore Gardens, Knightsbridge, it is probable that Caine's memory is the more accurate. Knightsbridge has long been one of the most expensive areas of London.

Not that Caine and Stamp can be thought of as having been doing well. Even allowing for inflation, the cost of renting a property in London was considerably cheaper forty years ago than it is today. Moreover, the pictures we have of Caine from the early sixties are of a painfully thin man. Stamp says that Caine introduced him to the idea of walking everywhere so as to save money, but on the evidence of Caine's brief appearance in *The Day the Earth Caught Fire* (1961), he wasn't eating much either.

Nor was he likely to be after the dressing down he received from Val Guest, the director of the movie. Caine played a traffic policeman in the film, and while saying the one line of dialogue the script had allotted him, he let his helmet slip down over the top of his face.[16] Guest flew into a rage, telling Caine that he'd never work in the cinema again. Even for as old a hand in the British film industry as Guest, such curses rang slightly hollow. Guest had been around a long time, but he didn't have that kind of clout. Nonetheless, the outburst worried Caine sufficiently for him to come up with a contingency plan should he really not find any more movie work. He and Stamp (whose own career, it should be remembered, was not even going as well as Caine's) agreed that whichever one of them was earning would forthwith pay the rent.

On 22 August 1961, just a month after Caine's disastrous day's filming on *The Day the Earth Caught Fire*, the BBC aired a one-off play by Johnny Speight called *The Compartment*. Speight was later to write that long-running BBC sitcom *Till Death Us Do Part*, and *The Compartment* was an early run-through of his obsession with the British class system. It starred Frank Finlay (who had played opposite Caine in the touring version of *The Long and the Short and the Tall*) as a middle-class gentleman who, at least for the duration of the play, wants nothing more than a quiet journey in the train he is on. Opposite him in the compartment is Caine as a working-class bloke insistent that the two of them have a conversation. Finlay's character will have none of it, though, and he spends the best part of TV play's forty-five-minutes ignoring Caine – until the latter snaps and pulls a gun.

Class conflict, slow-burning silences, barely suppressed violence: Speight was clearly trying to occupy the Pinter territory Caine understood so well. And although the critics weren't bowled over by his performance – lamenting, for instance, his gun-toting lout's monotone lack of control – one of London's most important agents was. Dennis Selinger – then Peter Sellers' agent, later to represent Roger Moore and Sean Connery – wrote to Caine saying he had liked his performance in *The Compartment* and that if he wanted an agent he should give him a call. Ironically, Caine had himself only recently written to Selinger asking for representation, though at that time he had been given short shrift. Nonetheless, Caine accepted the invitation, remaining on Selinger's books until the latter's death in 1998. His ship might not have quite come in, but it could at least be sighted on the horizon.

And he was in desperate need of such good news, because his flatmate's career was now sailing ahead at full steam. Stamp had won himself the title role in Peter Ustinov's movie of the Herman Melville story *Billy Budd* (1962). It was a big opportunity, though one that had the unfortunate effect of setting Stamp in stone as the doomed innocent. Like Caine a couple of years later, Stamp found that his star image stuck. The problem was that Stamp's star image was far less malleable than Caine's. After a handful of movies there was little he could do with his doomed innocence other than live up to it. While great claims were made for Stamp's work with Pier Paolo Pasolini in the late sixties, their blank numbness boded ill for his future career. Stamp, in other words, got the earlier break but ended up having the shorter run. Nevertheless, as 1961 became 1962 it was he who paid the bulk of the rent for that flat in Knightsbridge. At times Caine was even reduced to having money thrust into his hand by the fledgling he had taken under his wing only a couple of years earlier.

And so, while Stamp went off to make a big movie, Caine found himself stuck in the rut of more routine TV plays and more one-shot

Bosom buddy: Caine's flatmate Terence Stamp hit the big-time first in *Billy Budd*.
© The Kobal Collection

movie walk-ons. After a year and more with Selinger, he was put up
for the part of the cockney narrator Meff in the New Arts Theatre's
production of *Next Time I'll Sing to You*, alongside Barry Foster, Liz
Fraser and Peter McEnery. When, towards the end of February 1963,
the show transferred to the Criterion, Caine could have been forgiven
for congratulating himself: even though he was earning only £7 a
week[17] he had made it to the West End – just a couple of weeks before

his thirtieth birthday. And when the *Sunday Telegraph*'s Alan Brien found space to say that 'Michael Caine's jaunty cockiness [was] a joy to watch,'[18] Caine's own joy can hardly have been much confined.

After ten years of treading the boards, Caine had learned a lot, not only about stagecraft but also about the requirements of different kinds of writer. He had served time in the repertory regulars of the post-war years but had an instinctive understanding, too, of the newer school of 'angry young men' plays of Osborne and Arnold Wesker. On top of that, he had actually acted in a play by the newest of the new kids on the block, Harold Pinter, whose numb, neurasthenic narratives were perfectly suited to an actor whose desire was to play down the conventions of movie acting.

For all that wealth of training and experience, though, Caine had, it should be remembered, little of substance to show for it. As the curtain went up on another performance of *Next Time I'll Sing to You* he must have wondered whether he was destined for a career playing nothing more than chirpy, chippy Londoners. Certainly, it must have seemed so the day that Dennis Selinger called with the news that the film director Cy Endfield and the actor Stanley Baker were on the lookout for someone to fill the cockney cameo in a historical epic they were putting together.

Poshed up: The Cockney Caine was cast as an old-Etonian in his break-through movie, *Zulu*. © British Film Institute

You can be in the Horseguards and still be common, dear.
Terence Rattigan[1]

With his roles in *A Hill in Korea* and *The Long and the Short and the Tall* under his belt, Caine had every chance of winning the part of Private Hook, *Zulu*'s indolent, insubordinate, immiserated cockney of cliché. Hook wasn't a big part, not really much bigger than Caine's role as Lockyer in *A Hill in Korea*, but Endfield and Baker's project was unquestionably going to be a bigger film. Caine would have had reason to be excited by the director's track record, too. A few years earlier Endfield had given Caine's old friend Sean Connery a similarly small role in a low-budget picture called *Hell Drivers* (1957). Now, Connery was an international star.

So the omens were good for Caine as he walked into the bar below the Prince of Wales Theatre for his audition at 10 o'clock one morning in early March 1963. What he didn't know is that Endfield had already found his Private Hook in an East End actor called James Booth. Apprised of this information, Caine turned on his heel and started to walk. Then, just before he got through the door, Endfield called him back. He had another idea for this tall, fair-haired, high-cheekboned young man. Providing Caine could put on an upper-class accent, Endfield was willing to give him a screen test opposite the movie's star, Stanley Baker. Caine, having demonstrated the poshest vowels he could muster, was told he would be reading for the part of an officer in the picture, one Lieutenant Gonville Bromhead.

Shell-shocked and nervous, Caine did not make a good job of the screen test a couple of days later. Or so he thought. It may have been, in fact, that his angsty read-through convinced Endfield he had his Gonville Bromhead. As conceived in Endfield and John Prebble's original script, Gonville Bromhead was an effete public-school fop, a donkey to the fierce Welsh lions in his charge. Caine's dithering, doubt-ridden screen test might just have looked like a masterly spot of character acting. Nonetheless, Caine left the Fleet Street basement where the read-through had taken place in a state of some distress.

The next day, Stamp has remembered, was 13 March – the eve of Caine's thirtieth birthday.[2] On the strength of Stamp's earnings from *Billy Budd*, the two men were by now sharing a two-bedroomed flat in Ebury Street, SW1, and that night they had been invited to a cocktail party in their ritzy new neighbourhood. In a bid to take Caine out of himself, Stamp insisted they go along. Alas, the first person Caine set eyes on at the party was Cy Endfield, who spent the rest of the evening avoiding Caine's gaze. Only towards the end of the night did the by now cocktail-fuelled Caine muster the courage to approach his prospective director. The news, said Endfield, was both good and bad. The screen test had been as lousy as Caine had feared. On the other hand, Endfield was still convinced Caine was right for the part and was doing all he could to convince the Paramount Pictures' executives to go along with him. Meanwhile, Caine would just have to sit tight.

A fraught few weeks passed, but Endfield turned out to be as good as his word. Caine was summoned to see Joe Levine, the President of Embassy Pictures, the company that was making *Zulu*, and told that if he wanted the part he would have to sign up with them for a seven-year contract. Unsurprisingly, Caine grabbed Levine's pen. A few days later he gave his last performance in *Next Time I'll Sing to You*, packed his bags and took a plane to Africa.

Zulu (1963) took up sixteen weeks of location work in the Drakensburg mountains in northern South Africa. During those four months Caine got a belated crash course in life on a big movie – its long hours, its repetitions, its tedium, its air of barely suppressed panic. He learned, too, that at least one half of W. C. Fields' celebrated diktat about working with children and animals was true. On day one of filming, Caine had to walk with a horse that didn't want to walk with him. On day two, he had to ride his steed across a shallow stretch of water. Instead, the horse bucked and threw its mount into the pond. But then Maurice Micklewhite, his childhood friend Nosher Powell has remembered, 'hated horses. He couldn't ride a donkey at Ramsgate.'[3]

And his problems didn't end there. His line readings were no good. Caine has only fifty-two lines of dialogue in *Zulu*'s 135 minutes' running time, but something was badly wrong whenever he spoke one of them. Together with Endfield, Caine had decided to give Gonville Bromhead a piping old-boy trill. In front of the camera, though, Caine was coming on like a frightened castrato, and Endfield was forever having to shout 'Cut!' As soon as his operatic swoops had been pointed out to him, of course, Caine the master technician knew what was going wrong. His first-big-part nerves were causing him to constrict his throat, and this was in turn leading him to lift his shoulders – two actions guaranteed to raise the voice by an octave or more.

Dressing down: Caine relaxes on the *Zulu* shoot. © British Film Institute

Things didn't get any better when Caine went, for the first and last time in his career, to view the daily rushes. Having thought carefully while still in London about how he would play Gonville Bromhead, Caine had decided to pull his pith helmet well down on his forehead and shield his eyes in shadow. That way, he figured, when Gonville Bromhead needed to really hammer a point home to his men he could tilt his head back slightly and let the sun hit his eyes, inflaming them with a kind of manic power. Within seconds of the first rushes being projected on to the screen, though, Caine heard someone behind him ask why on earth this fool was wearing his hat in front of his face. Caine fled to the latrine and threw up.

To be fair, it probably wasn't just nervous shock that had made him queasy. Like a lot of the cast and crew, Caine spent an awful lot of the location shoot on *Zulu* in the latrine. Still, there was nothing psychosomatic about the distress he felt when a secretary surreptitiously passed him a telegram addressed to Stanley Baker from the Paramount moneymen back in London. They had seen the rushes, too, and wanted Caine off the movie. This guy, they said, didn't know what to do with his hands.

Now usually, to be sure, analyzing what an actor does with his hands is a pretty reliable way of separating the novice from the expert. Inexperienced actors fumble and fidget; old hands' hands tend to be well-nigh invisible until required for action. But the fact was that, relative newcomer or not, Caine knew exactly what he was doing with his hands. He was keeping them behind his back. While getting into character, Caine had noticed that Prince Philip the Duke of Edinburgh often walked with his arms held behind his back (he still does, as, of course, does Prince Charles; Mike Yarwood's famous impersonation of Charles was based almost entirely on the habit). By means of a little psychological extrapolation, Caine decided that the habit had come about because the Prince was so protected from the world around him by his bodyguards that he felt no need to keep his arms at the side ready for action against any potential danger. Gonville Bromhead, Caine thought, should show the same sense of effortless, relaxed power when he was on walkabout. And fortunately for him, while the Paramount executives couldn't see the virtues in his performance, Stanley Baker could and he stood by his decision to have him in the movie.

Indeed Baker, perhaps the British cinema's first genuine working-class star, took Caine very seriously as an actor. Five years after *Zulu*, his production company would put up the money for *The Italian Job* (1969), and Baker more than once came up with movie ideas for Caine and himself to star in. Moreover, he had listened long and hard on the flight from London when Caine had suggested that Baker's Lieutenant Chard might look stronger if Caine's Gonville Bromhead were made to look stronger too. As we have seen, the movie as written envisaged Gonville Bromhead as a limp-wristed public-school dandy. Baker, a firebrand Welshman with as many chips on his shoulder as Caine, saw *Zulu* at least in part as a political parable on the parasitic decadence of the upper classes and the concomitant potency and vitality of the lower classes. Effectively, what Caine was suggesting was that they beef up this structural opposition by letting him play Gonville Bromhead not as a snivelling incompetent wet but as a strong officer, albeit one misguided by his class allegiances.

Baker was won over by the argument and won Endfield over in turn – a victory which probably did more to seal Michael Caine's fate as a movie star than anything else he has ever done. Had Caine been made to play Gonville Bromhead as a stuttering fop, it is likely the character would have been forgotten after the second reel and his creator relegated to the third league. As it is, when one reporter arrived on the set for a chat with its most reliably big name, Jack Hawkins (who all but disappears from the narrative himself after the first reel),

Hawkins said the journalist could do himself a favour by talking to Caine. 'He,' Hawkins assured him, 'is going to steal this picture.'[4]

Not that there was much to steal. The basic problem with *Zulu*, which tells an extraordinary, even incredible, true story of a British victory against all the odds, is that it is almost entirely lacking in drama. The action takes place over the course of a single day – 22 January 1879, when 105 fit men of the South Wales Borderers, fighting under the orders of two young lieutenants, Chard and Gonville Bromhead, beat back a horde of 4,000 Zulu warriors at Rorke's Drift mission station. From the middle of the afternoon until nightfall on that terrible day, wave after wave of Zulus attacked the soldiers, burning out the station hospital as they did so. But the discipline of the soldiers won the day, so much so that when the Zulus finally retired they sang a song of salute to their gallant victors. Subsequently, eleven of the men stationed at Rorke's Drift were awarded Victoria Crosses.

A true story, then, and a relatively well-known one. But *Zulu* doesn't lack excitement merely because we all know how it is going to end. Indeed, it has its spectacular moments. No matter how many times you have sat through the movie, nothing can prepare you for the awesome sight of Rorke's Drift's tiny mission station as it is surrounded by those 4,000 Zulu warriors. Then again, given enough money it is all but impossible to fluff the power of such a pageant – the paraphernalia of tribal warfare invariably looks a treat in saturated big-screen colour. But only musicals can get by on spectacle alone. The average movie needs a strong narrative drive and interesting characters if it is to have a chance of succeeding.

Even were it not well-known already, *Zulu*'s storyline – a few plucky Brits take on an army of marauding primitives – could never be described as the strongest of plots. But its characters, too, aren't much more than perfunctory sketches. That otherwise eternally reliable actor Jack Hawkins is reduced by the exigencies of his part as a cowardly cleric to mussing his hair while going ape, and James Booth's Hook, the cockney layabout who comes good in the end, is little more than a sub-Dickensian caricature. Booth – who was appearing opposite Paul Scofield in *King Lear* while he was filming his scenes for *Zulu* – serves up a series of sweaty, grimacing rants, but he plays them as if projecting to the back row of the National Theatre. He gives Hook his all, but the part is so little worked out that his all is far too much.

Worse, the movie's anachronistic subplot of class antagonism – Baker as a prototype Jimmy Porter and Caine as his Flashman-style nemesis – is treated with such cursory abandon that it never really sparks into life.[5] Baker's Chard was meant to be the heart of the picture and his ongoing battle for control of the station with Caine's Gonville Bromhead the narrative motor. But though Baker is rarely off screen, one's sense of the movie is that he is hardly there at all. The pressures of producing while at the same time acting, said Baker's wife Ellen, had got to him:

> It rained for the first eleven days so they started twelve days behind schedule . . . Stanley's face showed the strain, he was so preoccupied and worried . . . The film was shot in sequence. And in the first sequences there was supposed to be no strain, when everything was going calmly and tranquilly – in the story I mean . . . [That is why] there are one or two very strange shots of Stanley standing around at the beginning of the film. Cy Endfield . . . did two days of close-ups of Stanley at the end of the film to insert in the picture because the responsibilities and strains showed up so much on Stanley's face during the first days of shooting.[6]

On top of that, Baker's Chard suffers from being badly underwritten. Most of all, though, he suffers from having his every scene arrogated by the power of Caine's Gonville Bromhead. So much so that it is impossible not to wonder whether Baker ever subsequently regretted giving Caine his head and allowing him to play the part as rather more than an upper-class buffoon, because there is no doubt that Caine not only did what Jack Hawkins said he would and stole the movie; he also threw its allegoric subtext way out of kilter.

What *Zulu* needed was Howard Hawks in the director's chair. Hawks would have stripped out the battle scenes (which take up rather more than half the movie) and turned it into a tight little drama about the privileged but empty-headed Gonville Bromhead coming to respect the quiet professionalism of the lowly Chard. Indeed, Caine's Gonville Bromhead is introduced in classic Hawksian fashion, haughtily shooting at (and missing) a panther. The scene is meant to give us a sneaky laugh at this swaggering poltroon, but Caine's Gonville Bromhead brushes the incident aside with such dignified aplomb that you can't help but respect him. Gonville Bromhead is so relaxed about his authority that Baker's Chard can't really pick a fight with him. Near the start of the movie the two men have a set-to about who has superiority (it turns out to be Chard), but Caine's effortlessly dandified Gonville Bromhead is so little perturbed by being usurped that Chard's assumption of power seems merely that: an assumption.

By turning a two-dimensional fall guy into a full-blooded character, Caine had raised the level of *Zulu*'s game considerably. The problem was that Baker, for whatever reasons, was unable to breathe life into his own role. Other than loosening his collar when the heat is on, he doesn't change one jot throughout the action. As the movie opens, Chard is all foam and fire; as it ends, he's all fire and foam. Caine's Gonville Bromhead, on the other hand, moves from naive self-belief through to doubt and then dread. When we first meet him, riding into frame on horseback, his back is ramrod straight and there is a delicious effeteness about his delicate sweeps of wrist and riding crop. By the end of the movie, though, he has wearied. The top half of his body seems to have folded in on itself, while his shoulders have risen in a kind of hysterical parody of machismo. Gonville Bromhead might not be bloody, but he is bowed nonetheless.

Not that Caine's first major movie performance was perfect. As Alexander Walker has pointed out, Gonville Bromhead's cut-glass vowels veer dangerously near the East End at times.[7] Moreover, even in the bloodiest of battles no genuine public schoolboy would bare his teeth (especially teeth with what are patently NHS fillings). For the most part though, Caine cuts a convincing figure as the movie's gentleman officer. The irony is, of course, that he had spent more than ten years preparing to play the kind of character who would have been bent on taking the wind out of Gonville Bromhead's sails. As we have seen, had circumstances not prevented his getting it, Caine would have been a shoo-in for the role of the 'Socialistic malingerer'[8] Hooke. On the other hand, had Baker not grabbed the role himself, Caine could easily have filled Lieutenant Chard's boots, too.

But Caine's expectations in 1963 were not ours today. Nobody save a few other struggling actors had heard of him before *Zulu*, and nobody had any expectations as to what he could and couldn't do. Though Caine had spent the post-*Look Back in Anger* years conceiving of himself as an angry young man, Cy Endfield was adamant that he didn't look the part. 'My idea of a Cockney,' Endfield told him at their first meeting, 'is [of] a little, down-trodden, working-class man.'[9] He had a point, though one that even as he spoke was being ground down by history. As Terence Stamp had recently remarked: 'There's a new kind of Englishman that I think the general public will be interested in. He's very masculine, very swinging, very aware, well-dressed and all that but with great physical and mental strength. He's the working-class boy with a few bob as opposed to the chinless wonder. French girls and American girls used to look on Englishmen as idiots because they only saw the ones that could afford to travel. Now they're seeing the new type and they think they're great.'[10] Doubtless the wish was father to the thought; nonetheless, Stamp's point was well made. It wasn't so much that the class barriers were coming down as that they were being made visible. Endfield's belief that Caine didn't look like a cockney went halfway towards the sixties realization that class or status was as much a performance as it was an inheritance. Caine's achievement in his first major role was to make concrete this rather abstract historical concept; if for no other reason, he had earned the £4,000 he was paid for *Zulu*.

It was far and away the most money he had ever earned and far better than the £17-a-week average man's wage in 1963 Britain.[11] In movie terms, though, it was modest pay for more than four months work. The previous year, as Caine knew only too well, his flatmate had been paid £4,000 for a mere ten days' work on his second film, *Term of Trial* (1962).[12] Still, at least he had that seven-year contract with Joe Levine, which guaranteed him a salary of $1,500 a week. Or did he? The contract was written in such a way that while Caine couldn't get out of it, Embassy Pictures could drop him whenever they wanted to. And after seeing *Zulu* they wanted to.

The reason was simple: Levine thought Caine's Gonville Bromhead looked gay. In vain did Caine point out that the script had called for a certain effeteness. Levine said that was fair enough, but Caine's looks were such that he seemed gay anyway. Those bright, powder-blue eyes with their daringly long eyelashes, those luxuriant blond tresses, the lazy swish and sway he had given Bromhead's gait – all had contributed to a fine character study; now, though, it looked as if they were conspiring to sabotage his future.

And so, with *Zulu* not set to open until the new year, Caine went back to the drudge of looking for work. Without his knowing it, he was being considered for the title role in a play that was transferring to the West End from Bernard Miles's Mermaid Theatre. John Neville had played the part at the Mermaid, but he was unavailable for the run at the Duchess Theatre and Miles's then artistic director, Joss Ackland, put up Caine's name. Glenda Jackson, the show's leading lady, lent Ackland her enthusiastic support, but the plan was scuppered by the financial backer, Peter Saunders, who refused to countenance the idea of someone 'I had never heard of' appearing in one of his shows.[13] The show in question was Bill Naughton's *Alfie*. Three years later, the movie version of Naughton's story would seal Caine's reputation as an international star. On the stage, though, it was not to be. Caine's valedictory performance in *Next Time I'll Sing to You* turned out to be his farewell to live theatre. He has never acted on stage again.

Zulu was no more than politely reviewed, but Caine's performance was the one most singled out for positive comment. The movie had its première at the Plaza cinema in Piccadilly on 22 January 1964 – the eighty-fifth anniversary of the battle of Rorke's Drift. As well as the usual roster of stars and hangers-on, the show was attended by Welsh VCs of the First and Second World Wars. Ellen Micklewhite, though invited to the première by her son, declined for fear of feeling 'awkward'.[14] She did turn up to see her son make his big entrance into the cinema, though. She took a bus up to the West End from Brixton, stood outside in the crowds to cheer him on, and then went home the way she had come.

Caine himself no longer had need of that bus, but he would occasionally make the same journey back to his mother's home for Sunday lunch. On his way, he said, he liked to stop off at the Elephant and Castle to have a look at the clearance of the slums where he had grown up three decades earlier. The Elephant was a dungeon, he said and not all the kids got out.'[15] As 1964 got into its stride, and Caine was reduced to accepting the part of Horatio in a TV production of *Hamlet*, he could have been forgiven for wondering whether he had really escaped himself.

Right angle: Caine overcomes another gimmicky camera set-up in
The Ipcress File. © British Film Institute

Most secret agents of the mind, I should think, take advantage of the chief characteristic of real secret agents. Not only have the latter no need to be outwardly different from other men; they must not be different.
  Kingsley Amis[1]

In 1957, the theatre and movie director Lindsay Anderson delivered himself of the opinion that 'a young actor with a regional or cockney accent had better lose it quick . . . for where are his chances of stardom?'[2] Within five years of that statement, a former truck driver and coffin polisher from Edinburgh was Britain's biggest star and well on the way to being one of the world's biggest stars, too. The character of James Bond had, to be sure, smoothed down the rougher edges of Sean Connery's Edinburgh brogue, but, as the evidence of countless mimics attests, there were still more than a few Scottish vowel sounds in the average Connery line reading.

Caine has described himself as 'amazed' at the casting of Connery as Bond. 'I was sure they'd give it to Rex [Harrison] because he was your living image of upper-crust good living.'[3] Certainly, Bond's original creator, Ian Fleming, was taken aback by the man chosen to bring his character to life on the big screen. Connery, said Fleming, hadn't been quite what he had had in mind when he was writing the 007 novels, although he would be if he were to do them over again.

Michael Caine was still an unknown when Len Deighton was working on his début spy novel, *The Ipcress File*, but Deighton can have had no Fleming-like qualms about the casting of Caine in the lead role when the book was turned into a movie three years later. Indeed, Deighton has claimed that he had long thought of Caine as a potential screen Palmer, 'but to my eternal disgrace I never mentioned the part to him. He later told me it was the first book he'd ever bought. I think he meant hardback book. He shared a place with Terence Stamp, who says that Caine used to wake him up saying: "This man in this book, he's just like me. If they ever make a film of it they should have me in it." Stamp says he told him they wouldn't make a film of the lousy book and even if they did he wouldn't get a part.'[4]

Nor was Caine producer Harry Saltzman's first choice for the part. Saltzman, who had made his fortune co-producing the Bond movies, had originally wanted[5] Harry H. Corbett of the BBC sitcom Steptoe & Son for the role. His next idea was for Christopher Plummer to play the movie's then still-anonymous lead, though it is not just hindsight that renders this casting notion astonishing. Plummer, who had recently been seen in Anthony Mann's costume picture *The Fall of the Roman Empire* (1964), was a pleasant enough light lead with a nice line in hidden depths, but not by any stretch of the imagination could he have been right for Deighton's wounded class antagonist. For one thing, he looked too healthy, too rosy-cheeked, to represent the undernourished lot of the post-war British working man. For another, his bright-eyed slyness carried with it more than a hint of self-regard. A Plummer Palmer could never have imagined himself put upon by the forces of the old school tie. Plummer's shoulders were always back and his back was always straight, and the thought of this beaming, overebullient matinee idol preening himself while pounding the streets of the seedier sides of Soho (as Deighton's hero does for the first quarter of the novel) is a ludicrous one. Fortunately for Saltzman, Plummer had other plans – chief among them taking himself off to the alps to carol 'Edelweiss' at Julie Andrews in *The Sound of Music* (1965).

Richard Harris was Saltzman's next choice, but he turned the part down, too, a decision he later rued. 'I've been guilty of a lack of judgement in my roles,' he told Sean Connery on the set of Martin Ritt's *The Molly Maguires* (1969). 'I turned down *The Ipcress File* which went to Michael Caine, but I did *Caprice* [1967] with Doris Day.'[6] Little wonder, perhaps, that the thought of supporting Caine in *Play Dirty* (1968) a few years later rankled Harris so.

Stories differ about how Saltzman came to cast the virtually unknown Caine in *The Ipcress File*. One version has him dining out at that sixties theatrical hang-out the Pickwick Club in Great Newport Street, spotting Caine across the room, calling him over and offering him the part – no line readings, no costume try-outs, no more than a couple of minutes of chat. A somewhat more credible version holds that Dennis Selinger, having heard that Saltzman was on the lookout for a new leading man, arranged for him to see a pre-release screening of *Zulu*. Selinger then had Caine shadow Saltzman until he got noticed.

It is likely that there is some truth to each of these stories, both of which have been related by Caine at different stages of his career.[7] As a producer on the Bond series, Saltzman knew Caine's old friend Connery. Moreover, during post-production on *Zulu*, Caine had befriended the movie's composer, John Barry, and subsequently the two men had a regular Friday lunch date at the Pickwick. Barry, of course, was most famous for his Bond-movie soundtracks and was thus another link with Saltzman.[8]

Nor is there any need to doubt that casting was for Saltzman the relaxed affair Caine has described. Three years earlier, when he had first been in the frame for the part of the smoothly urbane Bond, Sean

Connery had turned up for his audition/interview wearing a lumber jacket and jeans and had ended up all but picking a fight with Saltzman, his co-producer Cubby Broccoli and their director, Terence Young. But after he had left the interview, and the three men watched him from on high as Connery padded gracefully across the street below, Saltzman said he knew he was their Bond. Something similar seems to have happened in the Pickwick that night. Saltzman (like Joe Levine before him) said he wanted more from Caine than just one movie. The two men signed a seven-year contract, guaranteeing Caine earnings of £50,000 a year – twice the money Connery had been paid for *Dr No* (1962) three years earlier9 – and Saltzman half the money Caine made working for anyone else.

Saltzman might have made his fortune out of Bond, but he had made his name with a very different animal: the so-called kitchen-sink dramas of the late fifties and early sixties. Movies like *Room at the Top* (1959), *The Loneliness of the Long Distance Runner* (1962) and *A Kind of Loving* (1962) – all of them intimate, gritty, black-and-white dramas – had replaced the big, Technicolor, stiff-upper-lipped wartime movies of the mid-fifties. Along with the change in these movies' sense of scale, setting and lifestyle, came a difference in their interests in class. Whereas war films like *The Dam Busters* (1954) – or, on a rather less renowned scale, *A Hill in Korea* – can be seen as parables of the stratified joys of the English class system, the kitchen-sink movies were all about people struggling to break free from such demarcated niceties. The kitchen-sink heroes were inheritors of the angry young man tradition, and while none of them could be called political activists, neither could they be thought happy with the status quo.

For all their subversive tug, though, only one of the kitchen-sink movies is in any way distinguished: the Saltzman-produced *Saturday Night and Sunday Morning* (1960). Only in this film did the hero's lowering resentment of Britain's pigeonholing class system seem more than a function of plotting. Saltzman had wanted Peter O'Toole to play the film's lead, but his co-producer Tony Richardson and the director Karel Reisz both wanted Albert Finney for the part of the regally insubordinate Arthur Seaton. Reisz and Richardson won, Finney was cast and Saltzman learned that the star of a movie need not look like a conventional leading man.

Four years on and, like any canny financier, Saltzman wanted to hedge his bets, the bulk of which were by now placed on James Bond. What if the glittery consumerist bubble the Bond movies so gloriously incarnated was to burst? What if the post-imperialist fantasy of Bond was to wither as the lessons of the Suez crisis permeated every layer of British society? What if Harold Wilson's first Labour government (which was elected on 15 October 1964, just as work on filming *The Ipcress File* began[10]) really did pursue its stated aim of 'sweeping away ... outmoded ideas ... the old boy network ... [of Government by] a closed and privileged circle'?[11] In an attempt to cover all the bases, Saltzman was determined that the hero of his new spy movie would, in fact, be an anti-hero – a lower-class anti-hero with a *Saturday Night and Sunday Morning*-like kicking-against-the-pricks attitude:

> PALMER: Er [*pause*], is that my B107, sir?

> COLONEL ROSS: As if you didn't know. And it makes awful reading, Palmer. You just love the army don't you?

> PALMER [*with deadpan irony*]: Yes, sir, I just love the army [*pause*], sir.

Admittedly, Saltzman's Bond had little enough respect for his superiors.[12] Sean Connery's 007 was forever making sly digs at his boss, M, and laughing in the face of his armourer, Q, and his more fanciful gadgetry. But in the end the Bond of the movies believed in his job because he instinctively believed that his country was in the right. Not so Caine's Palmer, who makes no bones about the fact that all he is out for is himself. At the end of *The Ipcress File*, he doesn't gun down Guy Green's traitorous Dalby because he has been betraying his country but because, as Palmer puts it, 'you used me'.

Shambling around London in his macintosh overcoat, Caine's Palmer reminds you less of Sean Connery's dinner-jacketed 007 than one of Robert Mitchum's stumblebum fall guys – one of those characters who has ambled into the plot of his movie by accident. Caine's Palmer is a post-Suez cynic who believes heroism is for fools. He is not, though, a radical and has no interest in seizing control from the powers that be. Like Arthur Seaton or Kingsley Amis's Lucky Jim, Caine's Palmer has no grandiloquent ideas about changing the system. What annoys him is merely the fact that the system so often works against his own needs and desires. Caine's first achievement in developing the role was to find a way of suggesting that Palmer's quiet subversions were personal and not political. Hence Harry's habit of opening and closing his mouth for a split second the moment before he delivers each gobbet of ironic insubordination:

> PALMER [*momentarily dropping his jaw*]: Er [*pause*], is this a promotion, sir?

COLONEL ROSS: Sort of.

PALMER: Any more money?

ROSS: Let's see, you're on £1,300 pay and allowances.

PALMER: Yes, sir.

ROSS: I'll try and get you £1,400.

PALMER: Oh, thank you, sir. Now I can get that new infra-red grill.

ROSS: Well, save your money. Where you're going you won't have time for cooking. Dalby works his men. And he doesn't have my sense of humour.

PALMER: Yes, sir. [*Momentary drop of jaw*] I will miss that, sir.

Ever since *The Ipcress File*, headline writers have loved to describe its star's chip-on-the-shoulder wit as 'The Caine Mutiny', but it is a moot point which came first. Was Caine cast in *Ipcress* because of his mocking deadpan take on the status quo, or did playing Harry Palmer encourage an air of insubordination in his creator? Certainly, Palmer is a role Caine has been happy to play off screen for the past four decades. When, in the early nineties, he became a reborn hero for Chris Evans and the *Loaded* generation's lad culture, it was for such moments of sly cheek that Caine was most loved.

Howard Hawks once said that what he most liked about Humphrey Bogart was his capacity for projecting insolence. Caine, as we have seen, worshipped Bogart, and there is little doubt that he saw Harry Palmer as his chance of playing a Bogart-type role – the compromised hero forever being given the runaround by the powers that be that Bogart had made his own, most famously in Hawks's *The Big Sleep* (1946).[13] Harry Palmer, though, was no Philip Marlowe and the result was that Caine ended up commenting on, rather than updating, Bogart's most canonic image. Crucially, Caine's Palmer had no sense of moral rectitude. Bogart's Marlowe, a man who wouldn't cheat on anyone, was an update of the chivalric knights of old. Caine's Palmer was a cashiered NCO with a shady past that allowed his superiors to strongarm him into work he would otherwise have avoided. Like Marlowe, Caine's Palmer was forever being bamboozled by the vicissitudes of the plots he found himself involved in.[14] In the Bond movies there was never any doubt as to the identity of the villain (or what villainy he was up to). The Palmer trilogy began to open up the spy figure to existential doubt and dread – to question the wherewithal of his assignments. Caine's Palmer might not have been as morally culpable as the villains he was up against (as

Richard Burton's hero would be in *The Spy Who Came in from the Cold* [1965] or Laurence Harvey's in *A Dandy in Aspic* [1968]), but nor was he at all convinced that Queen and country came first. There was, in other words, no moral high ground in the Deighton version of the spying game. One of Caine's big achievements in *The Ipcress File* was to sweeten Palmer's corruptibility, to turn him into a Lucky Jim-style figure and suggest that, in a society where everyone is on the make, only the gullible aren't themselves out for a spot of gulling.

Effectively, Caine's presence in the Palmer trilogy democratized the espionage game. Sean Connery had brought a plebeian whiff to Bond, but Connery Bond's pleasures were still those of Fleming's high-living original: fine wines and languorous lunches. Palmer's tastes were considerably down the scale: home-cooked omelettes and tinned mushrooms. Stuck on an ice floe in a Helsinki sauna in *Billion Dollar Brain* (1967), Harry asks – in one of Caine's finest throwaway moments – for a cup of tea. While Connery's Bond motored on the consumerist fantasies of the sixties – effortless sex with sun and sand thrown in for good measure, Caine's Palmer chugged along on the down-at-heel reality of post-imperial Britain. Like many a hero of sixties British movies – Ray Brooks in *The Knack and How to Get It* (1965), Oliver Reed in *The Jokers* (1966), Lynn Redgrave and Rita Tushingham in *Smashing Time* (1967) – Harry gets around on London's red buses.

Unlike so many of those swinging London pictures, though – unlike, too, the bulk of the entries in the espionage genre (1966 saw the release of more than fifty spy movies) – *The Ipcress File*, despite the complexities of its plotting, still makes a kind of sense. Why has the movie lasted? In the main, because of Caine's resolutely untheatrical performance, his steely devotion to downplaying every scene. In Deighton's novel, the hero says of an early meeting with his boss that he 'twitched face muscles to look like a man paying attention'.[15] In the movie, Caine has the disadvantage of not being able to tell us what he is doing; nonetheless, he proved himself for the first of many times one of the best 'twitchers' in the business. Time and again in *The Ipcress File*, Caine shows he can communicate more with his face in a long or medium shot than many an actor can with a close-up.

What is the more remarkable is that he did this in his début starring role, while surrounded by director Sidney J. Furie's gimmicky framing and ponderous wide-angle shots. Without Caine's (admittedly highly stylized) naturalism, *The Ipcress File* would look and feel very badly dated. Perhaps because he was the director of the film that gave him his first big part, Furie's praises have long been sung by Caine, but less partial viewers have rarely been won over by the pyrotechnics of his style. Fortunately, Caine never let Furie's more absurd camera set-ups put him off his stride. In one shot, a corpse is gazed down on from ceiling height through the innards of a lampshade. In another, a fight is filmed through the tiny window frames of a red telephone booth. Against such self-conscious compositions, though, Caine refuses to strain for effect. Already, he knew just how little he had to do to communicate meaning. When Palmer plays the Ipcress cassette on the office tape deck, the camera observes his and his boss Dalby's reactions to its radiophonic cacophony. As Dalby, Nigel Green reverts to his theatrical roots, arching one eyebrow and then the other, pursing and unpursing his lips. Caine, though, just stands his ground, allowing no more than a look of surly bafflement to ghost across his face. As the critic Geoffrey Nowell-Smith noted at the time, Caine's Palmer 'stands out as a human being, while his superiors are puppets'.[16]

At last, the lessons absorbed from that reading of Pudovkin's *Film Acting* fifteen years earlier were paying off. At one point in the movie, the camera watches Caine's Palmer for a few seconds as he gazes at something outside his office window. Caine's expression is good-humoured, slightly amused with itself, but beyond that the moment is impossible to read. Then the camera cuts to a shot of a couple of pretty girls walking across the road, and Caine's expression becomes full of meaning. How confident this nascent star was! How certain of his effects! Only an actor who knows how much the camera and the editing room can do for him would dare to do so little.[17]

There were theatrical influences at work on Caine, too, of course, chief among them those of Harold Pinter. Shortly after *The Ipcress File* was released, Pinter was contracted to write the screenplay for an adaptation of Adam Hall's spy thriller *The Quiller Memorandum* (1966), and in doing so he found a mainstream voice for the claustrophobic, class-conscious dialogues he had been writing for the stage. Nobody could pretend that Bill Canaway and James Doran's screenplay for *The Ipcress File* is up there with Pinter; nonetheless, its air of chippiness and ambiguity has something of Pinter's quiet menace. Caine's appearance in Pinter's *The Room* a couple of years earlier had shown him how even the most innocuous line of dialogue could be freighted with threat, while his ability to wrongfoot the rhythm of a sentence can make any line sound a little gnomic.

And all this, of course, while he was wearing spectacles. Caine has often pointed out that he was the first leading man since Harold Lloyd to act with glasses on. What he has not remarked on is the iconic status those thick, dark frames helped to give both performers. Lloyd's lily-white ingenue face is unimaginable without that ironically heavy figure eight etched at ninety degrees across it – unimaginable and unforgettable. So too for Caine: Harry Palmer's hang-jawed, four-eyed, *faux* confusion became quite as defining an image as Connery's quizzical deadpan. Moreover, while not quite in the Sean Connery league, Michael Caine was a beautiful young man, and the decision to let him keep his spectacles on while playing Palmer was a subtle way of pointing up his beauty, of letting it catch the light. Certainly, those specs gave Caine's Palmer an effortlessly flirtatious air. In *The Big Sleep*, Bogart knows he is about to score with Dorothy Malone's seductive bookstore owner when she removes her glasses. In *The Ipcress File* the foreplay is reversed: Sue Lloyd, playing a potential femme fatale, asks Harry if he always wears his glasses, to which he replies that he takes them off to go to bed. Lloyd ponders for a moment and then removes his spectacles, and the audience is treated to its first shot of Caine's naked face – a picture of baffled expectation.

For Caine's Palmer was a new kind of British sexual hero – a man unafraid of women, yet one who is perfectly willing to let them make the first move. Hollywood movies had hitherto habitually associated English leading men with a kind of fastidious asexuality. Sean Connery's permanently predatory Bond had begun to change things, but there was a touch of the neanderthal about his sexual politicking. *Diamonds Are Forever* (1971) opens with Connery removing a girl's bikini top only to then threaten to strangle her with it. The scene, which comes complete with a bad pun, is written for laughs, but Connery's beefy lasciviousness always lent such moments a whiff of sadistic pleasure.

Caine's Palmer turned this on its head. Without seeming at all effeminate, he let the girl take the lead. That he managed this after having first gone shopping for food and then cooking it for the girl is a measure of the subtlety of his performance. For the seduction in *The Ipcress File* has none of the obligatory feel of similar scenes in so many movies: it isn't just there to vouchsafe Harry's heterosexuality. When he tells Lloyd's Jean that he's 'going to cook her the best meal you've ever had', Caine's Palmer dulls his eyes a little as if to prove that he is neither showing off nor merely trying to get her into bed. He is trying, in fact, to do that most un-Bond-like thing: establish the basis for a relationship. Accordingly, Caine's Palmer always looked like he could get hurt. In all of the three original Palmer movies, Harry gets properly hung up on one or other girl. Invariably, the girl he is hung up on hangs him out to dry, but the point is that Caine at least gets to do some proper acting with and around women. Connery's Bond, let alone Dean Martin's Matt Helm, would have run a mile.

Not that the films in the Palmer trilogy were any more realistic than the other entries in the spy genre. 'Grey, gritty . . . that's the effect we are seeking,' Sydney J. Furie told a reporter on set one rainy day. 'The film is being shot in colour, but so monochrome you'd hardly notice. This is meant to be spying for real, whereas the Bond films are for glamour-pusses and jokes.'[18] 'I should say this will be a thoroughly uncommercial film,' Furie told another interviewer during filming.[19] 'You wouldn't think you could make an uncommercial film about spies these days, but I think I'm going to do it!' He didn't, of course. The movie did highly respectable business at the box office, for despite its ad-libbed supermarket shopping scene, despite the resolutely naturalistic playing of Caine, and despite its attentiveness to the surface of mundane existence – the credits, for instance, play out over a close-up of Palmer's hands as they grind and filter a cup of coffee – The Ipcress File is not a slice of English neo-realism but as stylized a thriller as Goldfinger (1964).

Like Bond, Harry seems to be the only person around who can put two and two together and solve whatever mysteries life has this week served up for him. Like Bond, he has a habit of falling into the villain's clutches around the time the projectionist is loading up the penultimate reel. And Like Bond, Harry has what everyone else who has hitherto met the villain hasn't – the strength of mind and body to resist his tortures. Indeed, the movie climaxes with a rather anti-climactic brainwashing sequence – all psychedelic lights and droning synthesised noises – that Harry somehow magically finds it within himself the capacity to resist.

And yet, as Geoffrey Nowell-Smith argued at the time, Palmer's eventual heroism is less than conventional: 'For the first time in a British film heroism is no longer the prerogative of a tight-lipped aristocracy imbued with the public school ethos. Nor is it seen as a patriotic abnegation, the sacrifice of the individual to the nation. This cockney joker, a classic anti-hero if ever there was one, becomes a true hero through his will to survive. And his power of survival resides not in class conditioning . . . but in the assertion of his own individuality.'[20] This is well said, but what is most striking about Nowell-Smith's comments is that they are as applicable to Caine as to Harry Palmer. Ever since the release of The Ipcress File Caine has been keen to play up to Palmer's image of cockney rebel.

Even today, almost four decades on, he still gleefully relates the story of how the manager of the Rolls-Royce showroom off Bond Street laughed at the cockney upstart who wanted to buy one of his motors. Undaunted, Caine went to another Rolls-Royce garage, bought the car he wanted and promptly went back to the first showroom, raising two fingers at the manager as he passed.[21] Whether or not things happened with quite such dramatic pungency, the episode irresistibly calls to mind an incident early on in Deighton's original novel, *The Ipcress File*. The nameless hero is having the first of many spats with his new boss Dalby over a claim for lunch expenses at a very upmarket restaurant: 'Ross said you were an impertinent,' rasps Dalby. 'You'll impertinent your way out of here before long.' At which point the Palmer figure's first-person narration resumes: 'His [Dalby's] rage had gone suddenly, but it seemed a shame to leave it like that.' A shame because the narrator is convinced that what Dalby is so hot under the collar about is not the cost of the meal being claimed for but 'the thought of a sergeant brushing waiters with him at the Mirabelle'.[22] What is at stake, in other words, is class, not money.

This slippage between performer and performance would happen again the year after *The Ipcress File* when Caine went out of his way to live up to the poster line of his next movie: 'Michael Caine IS Alfie'. A month before the film's British release, Caine told a journalist about the women he was mixing with in Hollywood: 'They're dollier here than anywhere I've ever been. They come strictly under the Strong Men Sobbed category. They're like unbroken horses – very independent. They've never been controlled by anybody, you see. If you do break them, they're grateful, as all women are. After that, all they need is to be fed three times a day and shown who's master. Just like horses.'[23] This is less Caine talking than it is Alfie Elkins – early evidence of his creator's instinctive genius for the mechanics of PR. Unlike Sean Connery, who quickly came to loathe his fans' belief that he really was James Bond, Caine had realized that the best way to deal with stardom was to remain in character whenever you were in public. How better to hold on to your privacy than by going along with the widespread fantasy of what your life consists of? How better to obscure the obvious but boring fact that Michael Caine was such a hard worker he had little time for relaxation and relationships than by being seen out with an endless stream of beautiful women?

In terms of creating a star image for himself, Caine's strategy of conflating performer and performance paid off. In terms of establishing himself as a serious actor, though, its results were rather less successful. While Geoffrey Nowell-Smith had thought Caine's performance in *The Ipcress File* 'superb',[24] critical reaction was elsewhere mixed. Patrick Gibbs applauded Caine's decision to adopt 'the correct but by no means simple course of under-playing',[25] but while Philip Oakes found Caine's Palmer 'skilfully, even wittily assembled' he also thought him a 'triumph ... of engineering, not invention. The parts are documented, but never examined.'[26] *The Times*'s anonymous critic praised Caine's 'real interpretation of a particular man in a particular situation', but the *Sunday Express*'s reviewer thought it 'the most dreary and colourless performance I have seen in years'.[27]

Whatever the critics' differences, audiences loved *The Ipcress File*. Caine's cockney spy even went over big in America, where he characterized the reviews as 'extremely good'.[28] Within a few months of the movie's opening, Caine was one of the iconic figures in Harold Wilson's white-hot world of technology. And in May 1965 he was one of those photographed for David Bailey's *Box of Pin-Ups*, a collection of thirty-six black-and-white high-contrast portraits of the new great and good that came complete with a short essay by the film critic Francis Wyndham.

The Caine photograph is probably the most famous picture ever taken of him. Side-lit and shot through a wide-angle lens, a cigarette dangling from his mouth, he looks more of a villain than the Kray twins (whose company, along with that of Cecil Beaton, John Lennon and Paul McCartney, Rudolf Nureyev and Jean Shrimpton, Caine was keeping within the confines of Bailey's box). Four decades on, this picture remains one of the canonic images of the sixties. Why so? Because it crystallizes so many of the era's contradictory strains. Bailey shot the picture on high-speed film, the grainy result evoking memories of the naturalistic kitchen-sink school that had been such a help to Caine. But the lighting for the image was far from naturalistic: harsh, angular and selective, it reminds us of German expressionism rather than low-key British realism. The cigarette hanging from Caine's lips evokes the tough-guy cool of the Bogart he had grown up hymning; on the other hand, the elegant sweep of his eyelashes, crisply captured by Bailey's key light, presage the androgynous impulse London was to be tugged by for the next 10 years. In short, Bailey's portrait of Caine emblematized the big changes that were happening in Britain at the time. At once stylized and streetwise, tough and tender, noir-ish and nerdy, Caine's face seemed laden with the tensions of the decade – a decade torn between loyalty to the old world that had given birth to this excitingly meritocratic new one and the wish to rush headlong into whatever was novel, now and never the same again.

Outside Bailey's box, the company Caine was keeping was no less celebrated. In August 1965, he joined a syndicate that was putting £70,000 into a West End night club. Fellow investors included Stamp, the singer Anthony Newley, the dress designer Mary Quant, Sydney J. Furie and Bailey himself. The syndicate had been formed by the theatrical agent Felice Gordon, who said the idea behind the club was to give its starry investors an informal place in which they could relax.[29] As such, it was the first of many such ventures for Caine. Over the years he has shown himself to have a keen business sense, putting his money into many a club and restaurant.

And so, financially secure at last, Caine found himself a new flat, this time near Marble Arch in Albion Close. Though the location couldn't be faulted, the flat was hardly the lap of luxury, boasting only a master bedroom and a small spare room. But Stamp had gone to Hollywood to film *The Collector* (1965) with William Wyler, and Caine was now living on his own. Or so he maintains. Stamp had other ideas. On his return from the States, he assumed that Caine's spare room was his and his new girlfriend Jean Shrimpton's for the taking.

At which point accounts diverge. Caine told the couple they could stay with him only until they'd found somewhere of their own. Stamp, though, was adamant that he and Caine had been committed to flat-sharing for the long term. Who was telling the truth? Probably they both were. Caine, the hard-headed materialist bent on career, career, career had doubtless seen sharing a flat as a very useful way of making ends meet. Stamp, the more relaxed proto-hippie, had doubtless thought their loose-living deal could go on for ever. 'I'd still be sharing a flat with him now if it had been up to me,' he said, decades later.[30]

Whatever, Stamp knew it was time to move on when Caine cancelled the delivery of his daily paper. 'Looking back,' he wrote, 'there was an aspect of Mike that he played very close to the chest. He had a very tough time in the business and I think that during that time he must have been honing a dream about how it would be when he made it.'[30] Over the next couple of years that dream was to become reality.

Top of the world, ma!
  White Heat[1]

Fooling around: Caine with Shelley Winters in *Alfie*. © British Film Institute

The years 1965–67 were Michael Caine's best ever on a professional level. After more than a decade of slow, grinding ascent, he had finally reached the summit. He was a star the world over. During those three years, he made the movies that both moulded and commented upon his image. During those three years, he got the best run of consecutive reviews of his career. There have been high spots since then, of course – some of them sufficiently high to surpass Caine's achievements of the mid-sixties. But *Get Carter* (1971) aside, there has been nothing so self-defining, no movie that distilled the essence of Michael Caine at quite the same proof as *Alfie* (1966) and the Harry Palmer trilogy did. As the years wore on, Caine would get richer and richer, but the sweetest moments of success for him were still these first – not merely because they had been so hard-won, but because they allowed him the fullest expression of his essential being. It would not be true to say that it was downhill all the way after, say, *Billion Dollar Brain* (1967), but for long stretches of the decades that followed Caine could certainly be said to have been coasting.

The mid-sixties helped to define Caine, but he in his turn helped to define them. His heavy-rimmed spectacles are as essential a component of the period's iconography as John Lennon's wire rims or Mick Jagger's suggestive pout. Like the Beatles and the Rolling Stones, like David Bailey and Terence Donovan, like Mary Quant and Vidal Sassoon, Caine was a harbinger of the new meritocracy that was to be brought in on the wave of Harold Wilson's Labour governments of 1964–70. 'For about 10 years,' Caine has said, 'I was always in the wrong place at the wrong time. When it all changed, I was in the right place at the right time.'[2] Indeed he was. Before Caine, the typical British movie hero was either a nob or a wannabe nob. After Caine, local accents became more and more acceptable – so much so that even public-school-educated journalists and television presenters would take to speaking the ersatz London dialect of mockney. Where would the likes of, say, Johnny Vaughan or Jamie Oliver be without Caine's example – perhaps most crucially his example in *Alfie*?

If *The Ipcress File* had been a spy thriller refracted through the lens of the kitchen-sink drama, then *Alfie* was a kitchen-sink drama refracted through the multicoloured, kaleidoscopic gaze of the swinging London movie. In spite of its kitchen-sink status (and a kitchen sink really does figure in the narrative), *Alfie* was one of the first pictures to breathe the fresh air of the new Britain – the Britain that came into being as the drab constrictions of the post-war austerity mindset were finally snapped apart by the exuberant, moneyed amorality of the sixties. Joe Lampton in John Braine's *Room at the Top* had spent the bulk of the book dreaming about all the beautiful expensive objects that lay beyond his grasp. The Alfie of Bill Naughton's play-turned-book-turned-movie, on the other hand, was a satisfied consumer fetishist right from the off:

> I've took out my big white handkerchief and folded it carefully over my left lapel. I was wearing a navy-blue lightweight suit, in a material called Tonik, made by Dormeuil, and I didn't want it

spoiling. I don't care whether a bird uses Max Factor Mattfilm or Outdoor Girl from Woolworth's, if she starts purring up against your lapel, it won't look the better for it.[3]

A cold-hearted cynic out for what he could get, Alfie was far closer to the spirited deadpan decadence of Connery's Bond than Harry Palmer ever had been. Caine's first achievement in creating the character was to play Alfie with the brash self-confidence of the assured star.

The part might have been made for him, though it had not always seemed so. A couple of years earlier, as we have seen, Caine had failed to get the part when Naughton's original stage version of the story transferred to the West End. Moreover, when the show had been taken to Broadway in December 1964, Terry Stamp was given the role. Stamp's wide-eyed beauty and air of holy innocence could never have served the part well (the New York production closed within days), but Stamp's appropriation of another coveted role must have left Caine smarting again. Insult was added to injury when, despite Stamp's having made a mess of the part on Broadway, he was considered for the movie while he was staying with Caine at Albion Close. Fortunately for Caine, the disastrous New York run had put Stamp off the role. He 'decided he couldn't carry on with it', the movie's director, Lewis Gilbert, has remembered,[4] though even then Caine was not considered for the role. James Booth, the man who had been cast for the part of Hook in *Zulu* before Caine had ever had a chance to read for it, was in the frame, as was another Caine acquaintance, showbiz renaissance man Anthony Newley. Meanwhile, James Woolf, who was at one point to have produced the movie, wanted to give the part of Alfie to his friend Laurence Harvey. It was only Harvey's being cast in the West End production of *Camelot* that forced him to demur.

Lewis Gilbert's son, John, however, had an idea. 'We were desperate for a cockney to play the part,' said the director, 'and my son – who was associate producer and a friend of Caine's – said: "What about Michael?" Michael hadn't done a lot at that point. But when I saw *The Ipcress File*, I was impressed. So I rang Paramount and said: "There's only one person who can play this part, and that's Michael Caine." "Michael who?" they said. "We've never heard of him." "You will," I said. "Trust me." They said: "OK, it's just a cheap little British film, you go ahead and make it." '[5]

Those Paramount big boys were, of course, speaking before Caine's name was finally made when *The Ipcress File* was released (Gilbert had seen only a rough cut of the movie[6]). *Alfie* was shot during the autumn and winter of 1965–6, but by the time the movie arrived in British cinemas, on 24 March 1966 – a year and a week after the release of *Ipcress*, the longest career interregnum that Caine would have for quite some time – the posters were screaming James Bond-style that 'Michael Caine IS Alfie'.[7]

And indeed, from its opening moments the movie invites you to confuse actor and role. Like Tony Richardson's then recent movie of *Tom Jones* (1963) with Albert Finney and like Olivier's *Richard III* (1955), Caine's Alfie kick-starts his film with a soliloquy to the audience. A few years earlier, Caine had bridled when Joan Littlewood attempted to instil in him a little theatrical modernism. Here, though, in only his second big role, he proves himself a master of Brechtian alienation technique. 'I suppose you all think you're gonna see the titles now,' he says to the audience in the movie's opening moments. 'Well, you're not, so relax.' The film is studded with such jokey asides, the best of them occurring when Caine's Alfie goes to hospital to have his ailing lungs checked out. While Eleanor Bron's doctor requests him to 'breathe in', 'say ninety-nine' and the like, Caine's Alfie punctuates the medical examination with his own straight-to-camera analysis of what is wrong with him.

Stephen Farber, in an interesting but finally unconvincing analysis of the movie, suggests that Alfie's asides are as much heartbroken as they are Brechtian. Alfie, writes Farber, 'cannot bear to be alone, even in his thoughts and he is constantly making us his confidantes and conspirers by punctuating his remarks with a "Know what I mean?" '[8] For Farber, Alfie is not a charming cynic but a victim of alienated ennui: 'There are no real people to share his confidences, as there were in the theater [*sic*], but I think this gives his asides an additional pathos; in the very effort to make a friend of the camera we see Alfie's desperate fight against impersonality and loneliness more clearly than stage asides could ever have suggested. Alfie sweeps absolutely everything aside in his insatiable search for a sympathetic audience.'[9]

Exponentially desperate for attention, Farber's Alfie sounds like a refugee from the *nouvelle vague*. Yet though he tosses into the mix some half-hearted homages to the cinema of the sixties new wave – a jump-cut here, some black-and-white slo-mo scenes there – Lewis Gilbert is far from being another François Truffaut. Nor is Caine's Alfie really a modernist hero. Alfie's asides to the audience may well destabilize narrative conventions, but they also offer the audience a way of cosying up to what would otherwise be a thoroughly unpleasant character. Without his shallow, side-of-the-mouth charm, Caine's Alfie would be as insufferable a monster as Olivier's Richard III. And like Olivier's Richard, Caine's Alfie is a highly theatrical declaimer. Throughout the movie

Caine's voice is raised an octave or more to the high pitch he has reserved in subsequent pictures for moments of incipient hysteria. Unlike Olivier, though, Caine doesn't back up the vocal histrionics with any physical outlandishness. By contrast with Larry's lip-smacking Richard, Caine's Alfie is an altogether more pursed performance.

The problem is that the movie as a whole lacks Caine's subtlety and stealth. The plot is simplicity itself. Alfie Elkins is a heartless man about town, moving from one girl to another without a care . . . until one of them, a married woman, finds herself pregnant. At which point the narrative falls back on that stock scene of the kitchen-sink drama, the back-street abortion, though here, it should be said, the scene ends up as anything but stock. After Denholm Elliott's seedy doctor has done his work, Vivien Merchant – Harold Pinter's then wife, with whom Caine had appeared on stage in *The Room* – raises the movie's temperature, yelping and yowling in the madness of her loss and pain. Merchant was never better on the movie screen, and her power seems to spur Caine on for the rest of the scene. After the abortion, when Alfie steps through the curtain into the tiny kitchen where the dead child lies, Caine treats the camera to the best close-ups of his career to date. Gilbert, overemphatic as usual, moves his camera in even more tightly for a couple of shots, but Caine resists the temptation to do anything more than let his eyes water and his face crumple. Given the bragadoccio extravaganza that is the rest of his performance, the scene is a quiet miracle of control.

And it needed to be, because Alfie's emotional about-turn is merely the movie's most flagrant have-its-cake-and-eat-it moment. It wants us to joke along with Alfie's loud-mouthed troublemaking, but it also wants to warn us that such insurrection invariably hurts the rebel more than it does the rebelled against. Just as the movie appropriates the elements of modernist drama to tell an essentially backward-looking story, so it uses the era of sexual liberation to warn its audience that too much freedom is a bad thing.

Shelley Winters and the aforementioned Vivien Merchant aside, for instance, none of the girls in the movie exists any more concretely in narrative terms than they do in Alfie's squalid fantasy world. Jane Asher's Annie is particularly guilty here; though her part is as badly underwritten as those of Shirley Anne Field, Millicent Martin and all the other women in Alfie's life, Asher's decision to underplay the role cripples the character. As Caine's Alfie caws snidely to the audience about what he sees as Annie's overattentive stupidity, Asher merely stands there, blank as a start-of-term blackboard, incapable of summoning any response to his litany of insults.

But if the girls are stereotypes, get a load of the guys. The movie sees its male characters not as human beings but as variants on the old sexist opposition of womanhood: angels or whores. Alfie, of course, is the whore, while Graham Stark's friendly bus conductor Humphrey is an angel – a man who refuses to see wrong and can only do right. The baldness of the opposition confirms, if confirmation were needed, that we are not dealing here with a movie interested in the real world. For all its attention to squalor, for all its documentary feel for the streets and squares of London, the world of Alfie is as hollow as Blofeld's volcano in Gilbert's next movie, *You Only Live Twice* (1967).

Certainly, Alfie's realization at the end of the picture that there must be more to life than the casual flings he has hitherto treated himself to is utterly unconvincing. Earlier kitchen-sink Lotharios – Harvey in *Room at the Top*, Finney in *Saturday Night and Sunday Morning* – had got their marital comeuppance by the time their story came to an end. Essentially, those movies were sour little morality tales, their morality a legacy of the strictures of post-war austerity. Connery's Bond, who loved and left his women with an abandon licensed by the consumer age, changed all that, though not overnight. Caine's achievement – at the end of an otherwise depressingly regressive movie – is to make Alfie's change of heart feel tacked on for the sake of convention:

> When I look back on my little life and the birds I've known, and think of all the things they've done for me and the little I've done for them, you'd think I'd had the best of it all along the line. But what have I got out of it? I got a bob or two, some decent clothes, a car. I've got me health back and I ain't attached. But I ain't got my peace of mind, and if you ain't got that you ain't got nothing. I don't know, it seems to me if they ain't got you one way then they've got you another. So what's it all about, that's what I keep asking myself, what's it all about? Know what I mean?

On the narrative level the answer is no, but Caine's sly undercutting of the lines, twisting his body awkwardly as if to suggest that the words are being forced out of him by some unseen hand, nicely maintains the (admittedly nasty) integrity of the character. Naughton's Alfie bemoans the fact that he hasn't found a girl to settle down with. Caine's Alfie, though, is up to his old tricks, charming his audience with whatever it wants to hear. As Michael Bracewell has argued, Alfie is 'filled with the contradictions that run throughout Caine's career. Because here he is in the Sixties, era of permissiveness, era of sexual liberation, making an incredibly reactionary film about sex.'[10] The point is well-made, though it doesn't go quite far enough. By refusing to give in to the conventional change of heart he is assigned by the narrative, Caine's *Alfie* is rather more daringly Brechtian than his writer or director quite understood. Caine's refusal to endorse the sugar-coated *Alfie* the movie wants to end with showed that the angry young man could see deeper within himself than some of his more vainglorious predecessors.

Caine was nominated for the Best Actor Oscar for his performance in *Alfie*. He didn't win it, but he did win the right to consider himself a star. In the course of the next three years alone, he would take the leading role in as many films as he had had walk-ons in during the decade leading up to *Zulu*.

Away from the screen he became a regular in newspaper gossip columns, his starry status being attested to there by the readiness with which *Alfie's* restless spirit was treated as that of the actor who had created him. Just as Harry Palmer had crystallized the tensions of a quietly rebellious age, so Alfie was an emblem of the rapidly shifting sexual politics of the mid-sixties. Even the *Spectator's* high-minded film critic, Isabel Quigly, seemed guilty of conflating character and actor when she talked about Alfie thus: 'Vain, easy-going, autocratic, physically fastidious, cowardly, undomestic, irresistible, he is the sort of man once thought totally unEnglish but now being fished out of the proletarian pond where Englishness of the traditional sort never flourished. Like the new bright clothes on the new bright boys, he suggests a subterranean national character rising to surprise even the locals.'[11] Not since Somerset Maugham had pronounced the titular character of Kingsley Amis's *Lucky Jim* 'scum' had a fictional character been upbraided so.

Not that Caine was worried overmuch by the confusion. He seized the opportunity to hide behind the Alfie image with both hands. For years afterwards, Caine sat back while reporter after reporter turned interviews with him into mini-dramas about the recurring life of Alfie Elkins. Later on, when he was more firmly established, Caine would take issue with what he rightly saw as lazy journalism, but in those early days he was happy to ride the publicity wave. 'It's not difficult getting girls,' he told an interviewer shortly after he had been cast in *Alfie*. 'After all, girls will go out with a short, fat man with money, so why wouldn't they go out with a tall, thin one? And it helps being well known . . . Course you don't know whether a bird's just out with you because of who you are – but who cares? It's not too unpleasant, sorting the wheat from the chaff.'[12] Moments later, Caine is quoting S. J. Perelman, but there is no getting away from the fact that it could be Alfie doing the talking. Like Marlon Brando, whom Caine also mentions in the interview, he was getting into character. But the character was getting into him, too.

'Many of the people here,' Francis Wyndham had written in the text accompanying Bailey's *Box of Pin-Ups*, 'have gone all out for the immediate rewards of success: quick money, quick fame, quick sex – a brave thing to do'. Caine had spent too long at the coalface of the acting trade to really be characterized as being after quick money or fame. But quick sex was what the papers required of him after his image-defining turn in *Alfie*. From the spring of 1966 on, Caine was rarely seen out without a beautiful woman on his arm.

Even more rarely, though, was he seen out with the same woman more than a couple of times. The roll-call of talent Caine was linked with during the second half of the sixties was long and impressive. There was Camilla Sparv (later to marry Robert Evans) and Edina Ronay (daughter of the food connoisseur Egon, whom he started dating when she was only seventeen – fifteen years his junior – ditching her shortly after the première of *Alfie*). There was Bianca de Macias (later to be Bianca Jagger) and Alexandra Bastedo (later the eye-candy in the TV series *The Champions* [1968–9], who said he dropped her after one date because she was still a virgin.[13]

The women in his life were ditched as quickly as they were dated, usually because they were proving a tie that an aggressive go-getting actor could do without. Fame, money and beautiful women: such, argued Freud, was the artist's tripartite structure of desire. He might have been talking about Caine, although in Caine's case money was always the most important. 'Glamour,' as Wyndham noted in the notes to those Bailey pictures, 'dates fast . . . and his pin-ups have a heroic look: isolated, invulnerable, lost.'[14] Caine might have looked invulnerable, but he didn't feel it. Certainly, he had no faith in the idea that he had any long-term future in the movie world. Broke for too long, he would take anything that came his way. For the first decade and more of his working life he had earned next to nothing. 'That's why I'm working like I am now . . . I want . . . an average of £25 a week through the whole of my life . . . I want to earn a million dollars in the next five years so it'll even out.'[15] And so, just two months after *Alfie* had opened at British cinemas, Caine was back with his second film of the year.

The Wrong Box (1966), though, was not what was required. Caine has subsequently claimed that he had signed up for the movie before *The Ipcress File* had made him a star;[16] be this as it may, his decision to appear in Bryan Forbes's picture offers the first evidence of his seemingly wilful inability to sort wheat from chaff. Dennis Selinger had said that the surest way to become an international star was to be in four or five movies a year, but *The Wrong Box* was never going to boost anyone's career. Film historian Robert Murphy may have gone over the top when he suggested that the film 'ought to be shipped to a desert island and screened continuously to those responsible'.[17] All the same, one knows what he means.

Caine and Forbes had met back in the late fifties at the Under Thirties Club, a cheap West End eatery popular with actors. Like Caine a not-quite cockney, Forbes had been born in Leytonstone – the same area of East London where Alfred Hitchcock had grown up a generation or so before him. He had started out as an actor, but lacking the height and looks for anything but character parts he had worked himself up to become, in impressively short order, a writer and then a director. His first movies behind the camera – *Whistle Down the Wind* (1961), *The L-Shaped Room* (1962) and *Séance on a Wet Afternoon* (1964) – were small-scale black-and-white dramas that showed both a good ear for naturalistic dialogue and a tin ear for expositional cliché. While there was no denying that Forbes could tell a story, nor could it be gainsaid that he strained for seriousness.[18] Seemingly unsure of the intrinsic import of any of his stories, Forbes would weigh them down with all manner of sententious freight. For its first hour or so, for instance, *Séance on a Wet Afternoon* functions beautifully as a slow-moving psychological thriller, and could have been one of the British cinema's bleakest studies of a failed marriage were it not for Forbes's insistence on gimmicky camera angles.

All of which might suggest that he was not the ideal man to direct a farcical black comedy like *The Wrong Box*. And indeed, the movie is a disaster from its opening moments.[19] Adapted from a viciously funny Robert Louis Stevenson short story by Larry Gelbart and Burt Shevelove (who had just had a massive hit with *A Funny Thing Happened on the Way to the Forum* [1966]; Gelbart would later co-create the TV series of *M*A*S*H* and write the Dustin Hoffman sex-change comedy *Tootsie* [1982]), *The Wrong Box* tells the story of several people all bent on killing one another in order to inherit a vast sum. One would-be comical death follows another, the idea being, one imagines, to come up with something reminiscent of Robert Hamer's dark masterpiece, *Kind Hearts and Coronets* (1949). Forbes, though, failed to grasp that if you want your humour bin-liner black then you must play your comedy as if it were a drama. Instead, everything is played for laughs. And so we get John Mills, that most regimentedly unphysical of actors, falling over a lot; Peter Sellers in a fright wig and *Goon Show* voice; and Peter Cook wandering around in tattered trousers. Throw in Cook's long-time comedy partner Dudley Moore, Tony Hancock, a scene-stealing Ralph Richardson and, of course, Caine himself, and you have yourself an entry in that sixties movie sub-genre, the multi-star vehicle.

There is no doubt, though, whom the movie considered its biggest star: Michael Caine. The story revolves around him and he appears in far more of its many busy scenes than any of its other big names. In fact, *The Wrong Box* makes sense only when read as a joshing deconstruction of its leading man's new-found stardom. Less than a year after being a virtual unknown, Caine was being given licence to monkey around with his screen image. Unsurprisingly, then, his character in the movie is also called Michael – Michael Finsbury. Lest we fail to get it, however, the script has an undertaker ask him if that is 'Finsbury as in the London area'. No doubt, then, that the movie wants to remind us that under that cherub-cheeked blond beauty with his clipped public-school tones beats the heart of a cockney lad.

The problem is that though Caine is clearly having fun sending his image up, the effect is to make him less than convincing as the dumb-struck lover. In his first big scene, opposite what the intertitle calls 'The girl he worships from afar' (played by Forbes's wife Nanette Newman), Caine's bashful diffidence and gap-speeched fawning seems not so much a study from life as from TV. He is playing the scene exactly as Harry H. Corbett was playing similar scenes in BBC television's then biggest sitcom, *Steptoe and Son*. Moreover, such grovelling sits uneasy on Caine's aesthetically stooped shoulders and lolling head. Partly, of course, this is down to the *Alfie* effect, but mostly it is due to the fact that swapping Harry Palmer's horn rims for a daintily elegant pair of gold-framed spectacles and his dirty mac for a tweedy Norfolk coat cannot disguise Caine's beauty.

Despite the changes in costume and appearance, Caine abjures the big effects most of the rest of the cast spend their time stumbling through. Ironically, the resultant relaxed naturalism is far more in tune with the sly, throwaway gags Gelbart and Shevelove waste on everyone else. Unfortunately, as the shy boy who wouldn't hurt a fly, Caine gets not one funny line to say. Perhaps that is why Dilys Powell, reviewing the film in the *Sunday Times*, thought Caine not quite up to the mark (though she was fair enough to point out that had she not seen *Alfie* and known how good Caine could be, she would have thought nothing amiss with his performance).[20]

The movie was reasonably well received, however, everywhere but Britain, where the social revolution inaugurated by the angry young men was proceeding apace. Crucially, in March 1966 (the month of *Alfie*'s release), the Wilson government went to the country for the second time in two years. This time it won a solid majority – up from just four in the election of October 1964 to ninety-seven. The country was hungry for change, and the twee Victoriana of *The Wrong Box*[21] ill-fitted that mood. Even as Forbes was releasing the film, the Beatles were unloading *Revolver* – that vinyl call to arms that marched the early sixties into the late sixties – on the world. Even had it been of any more intrinsic worth, *The Wrong Box* would have been the wrong film for Britain in 1966.

Not that Caine was worried overmuch by the critical reaction to the movie. As far as he was concerned, 1966 was the first year he had no downtime between jobs since his days with Westminster Rep twelve years earlier. Like a snooker player whose opponent has kept him away from the balls too long, Caine wasn't going to turn the chance of a big break down when it came along. He wanted to keep busy. He wanted to prove to himself that everything that had happened to him over the past couple of years really had happened – and the best way of doing that was to keep on doing it. And so in 1966 Caine managed, not for the last time, to star in three movies on the trot. The third of these would finally take him to work in Hollywood.

The movie was called *Gambit* (1966) and, interestingly enough, Bryan Forbes was involved again – or, rather, had been involved. Forbes had written an early version of the movie's script (so early a version that it ended up bearing little relation to the finished product[22]), when the leading man was to have been Cary Grant. It was not, of course, to be. Grant had given up acting by the mid-sixties, though it is unlikely that he would have taken the part anyway. Not only was he rather too old for the role, but he had effectively played it before, a decade earlier, when he had starred in one of the classiest light thrillers there has ever been: Alfred Hitchcock's *To Catch a Thief* (1955).

While a highly watchable entry in sixties cinema's second most populous genre, the caper movie, *Gambit* isn't in the Hitchcock league. Nonetheless, Caine must have jumped at the opportunity to play a role originally conceived for Grant. Though he had grown up adoring Bogart's impudent cool, Caine had long been fond of Grant, too. Grant (whom Caine had befriended while filming *The Wrong Box* on location in Bath – Grant's mother still lived in his home town of Bristol and he visited her as often as he could) was Hollywood's prime emblem of classlessness. His sexless physical elegance (he had trained as a circus gymnast) and curiously hybrid accent – mid-Atlantic meets west-country burr meets South Kensington posh – rendered him unplaceable in any conventional social hierarchy, British or American. Grant brought to his every role a kind of democratic élan, the smoothed-down sheen of a fantasy world in which all class conflict has been resolved.[23]

As rewritten for Caine, however, the part of cockney con man Harry Dean foregrounds the restrictive stratifications of the British class system, revealing them in the process to be as much about performance as protocol. The plot is simple enough: Caine's Harry hires dancing girl Nicole Chang (Shirley MacLaine) to be his vital accomplice in a daring burglary. Nicole is the spitting image of the late wife of a middle-eastern millionaire, Ahmad Shahbandar (Herbert Lom), and Harry's plan is that she and her 'husband' Sir Harold Dean infiltrate Shahbandar's empire so that she can work her charms on him while Harry robs him of a priceless ancient Egyptian statue. For long stretches of the movie, then, Caine's cockney chancer is pretending to be a titled gent, the joke being that in the consumerist meritocracy of the sixties such status no longer cuts any ice. When Caine's Sir Harold checks into the Hotel Dammuz he is surprised that he receives no red-carpet treatment, and even more shocked to discover that nobody else in the movie gives a fig for this Old Etonian stuffed shirt. *Gambit*'s only real distinction lies in this hall-of-mirrors quality: it is a movie in which that successful but class-conscious young actor Michael Caine plays an on-the-make cockney who still believes you have to pretend to be upper class if you want to get on in the world.

A couple of years earlier, while filming *The Ipcress File*, Caine had claimed that 'Coming from south London . . . I have a fine ear for class structure in the voice. I'm playing Harry [Palmer] in a dead-neutral meritocrat's accent.'[24] *Gambit* was Caine's first big chance since *Zulu* to show off his finely tuned class antennae. Ronald Neame, who directed the picture, was a bit over the top when he described Caine as 'a "chameleon" like Alec Guinness . . . he can slip from cockney to upper crust without missing a beat'.[25] Nonetheless, Caine's quick-fire changes from yob to nob are the highlight of the picture. As the movie's co-writer Alvin Sargent has said: 'Michael Caine is the best kind of person to write dialogue for. There's something musical about his delivery.'[26]

To be sure, just as with *Zulu*'s Gonville Bromhead, a jarring note from the gutter occasionally punctuates Sir Harold's otherwise rarefied upper-class tones. But the physical changes Caine puts himself through as he moves from being Harry to Sir Harold and back again are flawless. As Sir Harold, Caine thrusts his shoulders up and back, projecting the upper classes' slight but permanent air of discomfort with matters bodily. Sir Harold's walk is rigid and reined in, especially when set against Harry's rather more mobile, hip-swaying amble. While Sir Harold (like

Gonville Bromhead) apes Prince Philip's habit of keeping his hands behind his back, Harry's arms flash and flail around him, especially when he is attempting to make a point. And while Harry is forever shouting and barking orders, Sir Harold never raises his voice much above a stage whisper. As Nicole says of him at one point: 'My husband never shows his emotions – he's English, you know.'

That scene points up a nice creative friction between Caine's laid-back naturalism and MacLaine's almost calculated vivacity. *Gambit*'s narrative logic, however – Nicole out wining and dining with Shahbandar while Harry robs his penthouse apartment – dictates that the two of them aren't actually together on screen that much. Ronald Neame has said that the picture suffered at the box office because 'There were several similar films being released at the same time – *Topkapi* (1964), *Ocean's Eleven* (1960), *The Jokers* (1967).'[27] It's a fair point, though there is no denying that what really crippled Neame's movie was the fact that its central relationship never really comes to life. Caine gets some fine comedy out of Harry's flustered rages with MacLaine's wilful Nicole – to see him in full rhetorical flight against what he sees as her air-headed disobedience is to be put in mind of Grant's impotent fluster with Katharine Hepburn in Hawks's *Bringing Up Baby* (1939) – but he never quite convinces you that Harry is attracted to Nicole despite himself. When, three quarters of the way through the movie, Harry blurts out that he loves her, Nicole looks shocked – as well she might. Caine has never held her glance for a moment too long, never pondered anything she has said for any potential double meaning. Indeed when, just before he goes into action, Nicole looks longingly at Harry and tells him she hopes he isn't 'one of those spies who gets blown up', you half expect Caine to turn round and say no he isn't: he is one of those spies who files his own paperwork and scrambles his own eggs, and she ought to know because she had seen *The Ipcress File* like everyone else.

And she had. 'I just loved his acting and what he did . . . in *The Ipcress File*,' MacLaine has remembered.[28] Fortunately for Caine, MacLaine's contract stipulated that she had the right to choose her leading man, and he was cast in *Gambit* accordingly. Shooting began in December 1965, and though Caine had visited New York earlier in the year (on a brief pre-release publicity tour for *Alfie* and *The Ipcress File*), this was to be his first stay of any duration in the United States. 'When he came to my luxurious office,' Ronald Neame has remembered, 'his first comment was, "This is the life, Ron." . . . He asked if he could use the phone to call England . . . he settled behind the desk, and had a long chat with his girlfriend. "Ron," he said as he hung up.

"This is a bit of all right over 'ere." '[29]

Characteristically, what most caught Caine's eye was the efficiency of Hollywood's industrial relations. 'In England, you're usually in a factory with a lot of extremely kind technicians who are going to help you do something which you want to do . . . and they're very nice and helpful, but it's to help *you* to make *your* picture, not theirs. There's no question of "our" picture, and this is . . . like all British industry, partly the fault of the unions and partly the fault of the management inasmuch as the unions treat the whole thing obviously without any artistic merit whatsoever, and British producers . . . treat the technicians . . . the way [they] treat British working class people in restaurants.' In Hollywood, on the other hand, '*Everybody* is *making* pictures . . . everybody is making *our* picture.'[30] Caine loved Hollywood's collectivist ethos, its Britain-in-the-blitz sense of one-for-all-and-all-for-one. A decade later he would come in for a lot of criticism for quitting England for Los Angeles, but only a cynic could say he made the move solely for money.

Life in Hollywood was not all work, of course. At a party at Danny Kaye's house he bumped into Prince Philip, who apparently referred to him as 'old Ipcress',[30] and he was seen around town with several of Tinseltown's then hottest dates, Natalie Wood, Nancy Sinatra and Carol Lynley among them. Nonetheless, one takes with a pinch of salt Caine's claim that while in Hollywood he gained a reputation for being a party animal. 'Most stars here go to bed early because they're afraid of looking horrible in the morning,' he said. 'I look horrible all the time, so I have the advantage. In any event, I sleep between takes during the day. So I can stay up late with impunity, whoever she is . . . They seem convinced that we English are just a bunch of Limey fags and I'm determined to change the image.'[31] What one is listening to here is the *Alfie* publicity machine churning at full speed. Even those who dislike his movies could not deny that Caine works hard. The parties that he attended while in Hollywood were as much work as they were play. At one of them he met Otto Preminger, who said he had a part for him. *Hurry Sundown* was to be one of five films Caine released the following year.

Loon of Love: Caine with Francoise D'orleac in *Billion Dollar Brain*. © British Film Institute

Progress in art consists not in extending one's limits, but in knowing them better.

Georges Braque[1]

Before the Preminger shoot, though, Caine was booked to film *Funeral in Berlin* (1966), the second Harry Palmer movie, although with his new mood of self-conscious sex appeal it would have been closer to the mark to rechristen him Harry Charmer.

Given the success of *The Ipcress File*, Harry Saltzman had doubled the budget for the new picture. Len Deighton's original *Ipcress* novel had been as globe-trotting as anything by Ian Fleming. The movie, however, had been severely reined in by budgetary constraints. Even Ken Adam, the set designer responsible for blowing millions of pounds on the Bond movies, got to build only one set for *Ipcress*. Shooting abroad had been out of the question, the original novel's jaunts to the Middle East being replaced by a torture scene in a derelict London warehouse masquerading as being somewhere behind the Iron Curtain. For *Funeral in Berlin*, though, location shooting was insisted on. And while Berlin might not be the Bahamas, nonetheless Palmer's travels in his second movie could not help but take him away from his kitchen-sink origins.

The Michael Caine who flew to Berlin in the spring of 1966 was a reasonably well-travelled man. He had fought a war in Korea and made a movie about that war in Portugal. He had shot a movie in the United States and had, a year earlier, appeared at the Cannes film festival to puff *The Ipcress File*. (Indeed, before the *Funeral in Berlin* shoot was over, he would return to Cannes, this time to puff *Alfie*.) Nonetheless, on his arrival in Berlin he found himself as disoriented as Christopher Isherwood had claimed to be three decades earlier in his autobiographical novels *Mr Norris Changes Trains* and *Goodbye to Berlin*. During *Funeral in Berlin*, Palmer visits a transvestite club, and though he affects the air of relaxed insubordination he does around everyone ('See you later, love,' he says with casually flirtatious irony to one make-up-caked temptress), Caine himself found the club somewhat unsettling. When one of the acts got up to do 'her' bit – a rendition of the Shirley Temple number 'On the Good Ship Lollipop' – Caine told the hat-check girl how weird he found all this. She replied by telling him that Shirley Temple was her father.[2]

Palmer's rather warmer humour in the new movie was due largely to the presence of a new director. In place of Sydney J. Furie (who was trying his hand in Hollywood), Saltzman had hired Guy Hamilton. Hamilton had just finished making *Goldfinger* (1964), the sprightliest Bond movie in the series thus far, and he was determined that *Funeral in Berlin* should breathe something of 007's air of camp high jinks. One result of this approach is that Caine delivers pretty much his every line of dialogue as if it were a throwaway gag.

Another result of Hamilton's emphasis on laughs is that the movie is all but incomprehensible. Even after repeated viewings, Deighton's plot – as sifted through Evan Jones's script – is unfathomable. As Tom Milne wrote at the time, 'it becomes difficult to remember who is watching who and why, or indeed whether anybody *was* watching anybody at any given moment'.³ Milne's point is well made, though he misses its corollary: that despite the impossibility of knowing who's watching whom, nobody in the audience can take their eyes off Caine. Indeed, it's almost as if the deadpan obscurantism of *Funeral in Berlin* was designed to be so wilfully uninvolving that the star quality of its leading man would be thrown into relief. While *The Ipcress File* had been filled with all manner of self-regarding camera angles and compositions, *Funeral in Berlin* turns out to be the more modernist movie in that it is constantly playing around with the notion of an undercover agent who is also a world-famous sex symbol. Early on in the movie, when Palmer is given his identity papers for the trip to Berlin, he affects disappointment at the false name he has been allotted. 'I don't feel like Edmund Dorf,' he says. 'Can't I be Rock Hunter? I want to be Rock Hunter.' Hallam (Hugh Burden), the officer in charge of passport issues, looks long-sufferingly at Palmer before telling him, 'You aren't the type' – which is exactly the kind of remark Michael Caine might have expected from a casting agent until only a year or two earlier.

Later on, after Palmer has checked into his Berlin hotel, there is a delicious moment when a girl catches his eye in the lobby. Caine's Palmer shambles and shuffles past her, glancing at her from the corner of his eye, twisting his head round to keep her in view as he moves. Caine contrives to make Palmer's sequence of manoeuvres here at once gawky and graceful; Palmer moves with a sensuous diffidence that both mocks and celebrates Caine's new-found status as international sex symbol. He might be the star of the movie, but it is he who seems star-struck by this Eastern European beauty (Eva Renzi). So much so that *she* ends up picking *him* up, the joke being hammered home in the next scene, when Palmer tells his contacts he is suspicious of the girl precisely because she treated him like a matinee idol.

Given Caine's new starry status, the movie is careful to play down the original novel's continued insistence on Harry's class-conscious angry young man stuff. 'Really work at the insubordinate bit, don't you?' a girlfriend says to Caine's Palmer at the start of the movie, and work at it he does. Palmer's shoulders still slope and his mouth still hangs agape, but only when he is in the company of those he wishes to offend. When Caine's Palmer tells his boss Ross (Guy Doleman – practically the movie's only hanger-on from *Ipcress*) that 'I want to get on in life,' he does so with the inert irony of Eric Morecambe – another man in thick spectacles who was making a name for himself at the time. By the time Palmer is at work in Berlin, though, the angry young man stuff is forgotten, as Caine and Hamilton work to turn this convoluted spy thriller into something akin to bedroom comedy.

Funeral in Berlin is no masterpiece. The movie is clumsily edited, has a lacklustre score (especially when set beside John Barry's music for *The Ipcress File* and Richard Rodney Bennett's for *Billion Dollar Brain*) and is awkwardly paced. For all that, Caine somehow manages both to play self-deprecatingly Pirandello-esque games with Palmer and make him recognizably human. By the end of the film, when Harry has to leave Eva Renzi's Samantha Steel in Berlin, there is an exchange of looks between them that hints at a depth of feeling hitherto not thought of in Palmer (and never thought of in Bond). Developing Harry's humanity would be one of Caine's central projects in the third Palmer movie, *Billion Dollar Brain*.

In 1953, Billy Wilder cast Otto Preminger as the Nazi concentration camp commandant in his film *Stalag 17*. Egged on by Wilder, Preminger played the part with the brutal theatricality he was famous for on his own movie sets. While shooting *Margin for Error* (1943), Preminger had so loudly ordered an actor who was struggling with his lines to 'Relax!' that the man in question fainted.[4] Not surprisingly, Preminger had ever since had a reputation for being one of Hollywood's more tyrannical directors. As Caine told the *New York Times* during the filming of *Hurry Sundown* in the late summer of 1966: 'He loves to embarrass actors in front of other people to tear down their egos. He's only happy if everybody else is miserable. Still, if you can keep his paranoia from beating you down, you can learn a lot from this guy.'[5] And so, on day one of the shoot, Caine set about ribbing Preminger, telling him he was dealing with 'a very shy little flower, and if anybody ever shouted at me I would burst into tears and go into my dressing room and not come out for the rest of the day'. Preminger laughed and told Caine that 'he would never shout at Alfie'.[6] And nor, it would seem, did he, although pretty much everyone else on the movie felt Preminger's lash.

Why did he leave Caine alone? Professionalism, one surmises. Unlike so many of the most-loved Hollywood directors – Welles, Ophüls, Kubrick – Preminger had no reputation for profligacy. Instead, he was regarded as a director with far too much of the producer about him. Shooting *Exodus* (1960) – his adaptation of Leon Uris's novel about the founding of the modern state of Israel – Preminger was told that a shadow from a boom had found its way into one of the movie's key shots. Unfortunately, the sun had gone down and they would have to retake the scene tomorrow. Preminger, though, refused, saying that he had a schedule to stick to. Easy to damn such sloppiness, but, like Caine, Preminger knew the movies were an industry before they were an art form. While his reputation as an artist might suffer because of that errant boom, his reputation as a reliable craftsman who brought his projects in on time and on budget would remain unsullied. Like Caine, Preminger believed there was a corollary to the old adage that you were only as good as your last picture: you could always do better in your next one.

Not that Caine, who was paid $20,000 a week for *Hurry Sundown*, was doing badly. Preminger had been daring in casting Caine as a wealthy deep-southern bigot in this tale of racism, greed and lust, but during quiet moments of the *Funeral in Berlin* shoot Caine had taken time to listen to recordings of the local accent. As with *Zulu* and *Gambit*, the resultant voice wasn't perfect but it was still very good. Caine's southern vowels are almost impeccable throughout the movie, though he failed to capture the right pitch and pace. He speaks too many of his lines too high and too fast and with altogether too much energy when they are heard against the lazy, lugubrious drawls of the rest of the cast. Nonetheless, film reviewers on America's southern newspapers lauded Caine's imitation of their vowel sounds. Critics back home in the UK, though, were having none of it and lambasted him for his efforts. In doing so they were more than a little unfair, although four decades on, it is easy to see why Caine's fellow country-men were so wrongfooted by his southern accent. The problem lies not in Caine's voice but in his visage. By the time of *Hurry Sundown*, Caine was a national icon. He had one of the country's most recognizable faces, and a highly recognizable voice to go with it. The sight of this very familiar face uttering mightily unfamiliar sounds could hardly have been anything but disconcerting to those critics who knew the Caine of old. Not for the last time, Caine's problems were caused by his aesthetic schizophrenia. Was he a movie star or a character actor?

For Preminger, he was doubtless the former. Indeed, when he joshed Caine that he couldn't bring himself to shout at Alfie, he half gave the game away. In a sense, the character Caine plays in *Hurry Sundown* is an American Alfie – cynical, amoral, hard-bitten and with both eyes fixed firmly on the main chance. Caine's Henry Warren even has Alfie-style sex with his best friend's bride-to-be – on the front seat of his car. But where Alfie's villainies extended only as far as the bedroom, Warren is a full-blooded bad guy – a grab-the-block-screw-the-neighbours land developer, a prototype J. R. Ewing from the later television series *Dallas*.

Given the melodramatic plotting and dialogue – nobody throughout the entire film says anything other than what is on his or her mind – Caine would have done well to play Warren as a bombastic impotent. Instead, while everyone around him sets off fireworks, Caine sticks with the low-key naturalism that had made his name. 'Villainy doesn't exist outside of books or movies,' Caine said at the time. 'In real life men are not heroes or villains – but both at the same time. What I do is show the sadness of the man – whether he is Alfie or Warren . . . The sadness of a man who destroys others and destroys himself.'[7] It was a good point, though it would have required an altogether more subtle picture to do it justice. Caine's Warren ought to have been a fruity patriarch with a lascivious glint in his eye and a winning way with one-liners. As Caine plays him, though, he is a priggish dullard every bit as out of place in the steamy South as Marlon Brando was in Lewis Milestone's *Mutiny on the Bounty* (1962). To watch Caine try to play scenes of domestic crisis naturalistically opposite Jane Fonda's mocking, flutter-eyed, southern Gothic belle is to wish he would make the effort to catch the daily rushes.

Yet though Caine had misread the movie disastrously, *Hurry Sundown* was not a complete waste of time for him. Preminger's slow, objective camera style taught Caine that his Pudovkinian belief in editing as the essential tool in film-making was mistaken. Sometimes it was not enough to rely on meaning being put into a performance at the cutting bench. 'What I did learn from Otto,' Caine said several years after making the movie, 'was how to do long takes . . . up to seven minutes. I like those shots when I see them.'[8] At the end of the movie, when Caine's Warren has accidentally killed his young friend Charles (Steve Sanders), Preminger's camera moves in tight on his face the better to observe the devastation. In truth, Caine crumples his features a little *too* slowly, but the scene makes its point nonetheless. Caine, meanwhile, would put such lessons to very good use a few years later when he acted opposite Laurence Olivier in *Sleuth*.

Profitable or not, the *Hurry Sundown* shoot was a far from happy one. Though the best-selling novel by K. B. Gilden, on which the film was based, was set in Georgia, Preminger decided to shoot the movie in Louisiana. The town scenes were filmed in St Francisville – then the centre of the Ku Klux Klan's Louisiana operation. The movie's many black actors were given restricted use of the town's services, and it was only when Preminger threatened to call the movie off that the hotel he and the rest of the crew were staying in allowed one of its swimming pools to become 'integrated' so that blacks and whites could swim together. When slashed car tyres and threatening phone calls were reported, the hotel was put under armed protection from state troopers. 'You soon learn how to survive here,' Caine said. 'You don't go into any bar, for instance, which has a pick-up truck outside it. Pick-up trucks mean trouble and their owners are more likely to be members of the Ku Klux Klan.'[9] Characteristically, though, he saw the conflict in more homegrown terms. 'To be a cockney is . . . like what the negroes complain about in America,' he explained shortly before *Hurry Sundown* opened. 'We're always sweeping the streets, washing the floors, operating lifts. The thing is that the negro in America is militant about improving his position. But not the cockney.'[10]

Back in London, there was militancy on the streets outside Caine's new flat. He had taken a seven-year lease on a five-bedroomed apartment in sight of the American Embassy in Grosvenor Square. In sight, too, of the violent anti-Vietnam war protests that had started while he had been away in Louisiana. Caine, who had thought *Funeral in Berlin* a movie more than usually sympathetic towards the Eastern Bloc,[11] was himself opposed to the war. Not for a moment, though, did he consider joining in the demonstrations on his doorstep.

Vietnam was one of the hinges on which the early sixties swung into the late sixties, and while Caine was and remains one of the decade's central icons, it is its first half he most potently symbolizes. His essential image, the persona he has gone on refining and commenting on throughout his career, was carved from the stone of the early sixties (and, of course, the late fifties). Though thrusting and meritocratic, it was also essentially conservative. Shortly after the move to Grosvenor Square, Caine's accountant rung to tell him that he was now a millionaire. It was good news, especially back then, but not good enough for Caine, who had begun to gripe about what he saw as the Labour government's exorbitant rates of taxation the previous year. And as 1966 wore on, it looked like things would only get worse. International trade had been damaged during the spring by the seamen's strike, and in the summer, not long before that call from Caine's accountant, the government froze wages, prices and dividends in a bid to counter inflation. The British economy was coming to pieces. The response to these death throes of empire, at least among youth and the trendier type of artist, was a bacchanalian frenzy – the party to end all parties. Caine wanted nothing to do with it. The late sixties – the idealistic, lackadaisical sixties of kaftans and cannabis – had nothing to do with him. While his former flatmate Terry Stamp took himself off to India to learn about transcendental meditation – 'He threw it out the window. He didn't need acclaim or money or whatever the hell people do this business for'[12] – Caine knuckled down to the slog of more and more work.

Slated at the time of its release, *Billion Dollar Brain* (1967), the third and final Harry Palmer movie of the sixties, is now often cited as the most satisfying movie of the trilogy. Certainly Ken Russell's picture – the *reductio ad absurdum* of the spy genre – looks better and better with each passing year.

Russell had been recommended for the job by no less than Caine and Dennis Selinger. 'Harry Saltzman's attention was drawn to the Debussy film by Dennis Selinger who was trying to win me away from my old agents to join him at CMA . . . Michael Caine had also seen the Debussy film and liked it. He knew another Harry Palmer film was on the stocks and that Saltzman was looking around for a new director and since Mike is like a son to Harry and Dennis is very friendly with both of them, the job was mine for the asking.'[13]

Palmer, who has quit the secret service when the movie opens but is quickly inveigled back in by Colonel Ross (Guy Doleman, again), travels to Finland to deliver a flask full of deadly viruses to an old friend, Leo Newbigen (Karl Malden). When it turns out that Leo is working for General Midwinter (Ed Begley), a crazed Texan millionaire bent on fomenting a war between America and the Russians, Palmer joins forces with the Eastern Bloc in the shape of Colonel Stok (Oscar Homolka reprising his role from *Funeral in Berlin*) and goes all out to prevent armageddon.

Satisfied with the profits from *Funeral in Berlin*, Harry Saltzman upped the budget once more for the third Palmer movie – this time to £3 million. And though the production designer of the first two movies, Ken Adam (who was too busy working on the astonishing sets he built for *You Only Live Twice* [1967]), was not on board, nonetheless, *Billion Dollar Brain* is the most ritzily stylish of the trilogy. With its mammoth stainless-steel and blonde wood sets, with its wittily graphic Maurice Binder title sequence, with its satirically overblown orchestral score by

Richard Rodney Bennett, and with its megalomaniacal villain hell-bent on world domination, *Billion Dollar Brain* was the closest the Harry Palmer movies came to apeing Bond. And yet the film is as unlike any of the Bonds as it could be.

Partly this is down to Russell, who lacked any interest in the spy movie as a form. It is hard to disagree with Russell's suggestion that Len Deighton's original novel 'had no rationality whatsoever',[14] but any idea that a lack of story might throw this director off his stride is a fatuous one. Russell came to the film, after all, following a spell at the BBC making elegant if enervating films on impressionist composers (Debussy and Delius among them). What interested Russell (and what has gone on interesting him) was not story but imagery. Mark Twain once joked that Wagner's music isn't as bad as it sounds. Russell's films, contrariwise, are rarely as good as they look – and *Billion Dollar Brain* looks very good indeed. Much of the action takes place on the icy wastes of the Baltic outside Helsinki, and Russell and his photographer Billy Williams evoke its crispy mistiness supremely well. Those floes and tundra are the only real geographical locations captured with any spiritual fidelity in the Palmer trilogy.

But there are cultural influences at work on Russell's eye, too. As John Russell Taylor pointed out in his review of the movie, 'the conclusion, with Midwinter addressing his men in the snow and then disappearing with all his tanks through the ice, borrows heavily, unwisely and unsuccessfully from [Eisenstein's] *Alexander Nevsky*'.[15] Less remarked on is the Mack Sennett/*Keystone Cops*-style of the film's mid-section, which shows us an uncomfortable Palmer galumphing across the tundra on ill-fitting snow shoes. To underline the point, Richard Rodney Bennett's otherwise grandiloquent score becomes, for these moments of awkward physicality, little more than a series of jokey string plucks. Williams, meanwhile, desaturates his images even more than he has been doing already. Watching Caine's Palmer, still heavily bespectacled but now swathed in a long black coat and matching fur hat, make his way across the snowy vastness, one could almost be looking at a Harold Lloyd black-and-white short. Elsewhere, there is one of Caine's finest close-ups: a shot of Harry all but encased in a globular chair – all stainless steel and pumpkin-coloured fibreglass – puffing on a cigar and blowing smoke at the camera with a wide, hollow, druggy smile. Caine's Palmer seems here to be simultaneously filled with self-regard and solipsistic remorse. Perhaps without Caine's quite realizing it, the alienated puppet of the more intellectual spy fiction was seeping into Palmer's erstwhile robust cockney rebel.

Certainly, while the shot of a red London bus speeding towards the

camera that kicks the movie off suggests that we are stuck in a pre-
swinging London – a notion confirmed by the pan to the seedy offices
from where the HP Detective Agency is run – the Palmer of this film is
just as up-to-date as he had been on his first appearance. *Billion Dollar Brain* was filmed in the spring of 1967, months before the Beatles
unleashed *Sgt Pepper's Lonely Hearts Club Band* on the summer of
love, and Caine, while not having aged overmuch in the two years
since *The Ipcress File*, was showing signs of change. Palmer's hair is
considerably longer at the back than it had been before, and while
his sideburns might not have quite the rococo decadence of those of
Ringo Starr, they have a luxuriance of their own all the same. So too
Palmer's spectacles. Gone are the featureless National Health frames
Harry was sporting in Berlin last year. In their place are a bolder,
sculpted, altogether more stylized pair. And behind them, Caine's eyes
are plastered with mascara. The Palmer of *Billion Dollar Brain* was
no longer the angry young NCO Caine had invented a couple of
years before, but a sly hermaphrodite hipster who'd found a new way
of kicking at the pricks.

Russell's movie plays around, too, with its leading man's actorly status.
In *Alfie* Caine had merely addressed the camera with Olivier-like solilo-
quies. In *Billion Dollar Brain* he actually gets to say one of Olivier's
(courtesy of Shakespeare) most famous lines. The code phrase he has to
use to introduce himself to his undercover contacts in Helsinki is: 'Now
is the winter of our discontent.' Caine says the line while breathing out
steam and hopping from one foot to the other in a frosty telephone box.
Moreover, he contrives to deliver it as meaninglessly as possible: 'Now is
the winter ... of ... our discontent,' he says, pausing to shiver in the
middle and putting the emphasis on the *wrong* word, thus guying the
notion that he is any kind of actor at all.

Ken Russell had no such doubts, though. He was as impressed with
Caine as Caine had been with him.

> 'A recurring fault I've found with actors,' he has said, 'is that their
> reactions take too long. They say a line, *then* they usually follow it
> with a slight change of expression, a sort of exclamation mark –
> which is natural enough because that's the way people behave in
> real life. But on screen it looks unreal. There's no one, except
> Michael Caine and Vanessa Redgrave, to whom I haven't had to
> say at one time or another "Give the facial reaction *at the same
> time* as you say the line." Actors, being egocentric maniacs, think
> you will hang on to the close-up until they've said the line and
> followed it up with their bitter grin or grimace or whatever. But it's

equally important to see the other person's immediate reaction to the statement, which means cutting to him as soon as possible – like immediately after the last word . . . Once you've taught an actor the basic tricks of acting – and people like Elizabeth Taylor know them backwards, which is why they always give the same performance – the rest is mystery. And I think the more you keep them uninformed and maintain an air of mystery so they don't quite know what they're doing, the better they are.'[16]

Certainly, Caine had little idea what was going on most of the time in *Billion Dollar Brain*. By the end of shooting he was worried the movie's plot 'would have befuddled Einstein',[17] though he need not have fretted so. In the end, what distinguishes *Billion Dollar Brain* as the finest of the Palmer trilogy is the wounded look of confusion that plays across Caine's face through much of the movie. Nowhere is this more poignant than in his dealings with Anya (Françoise Dorléac, whose last movie this was before her death in a car crash), Newbigen's lover, for whom Harry falls head-over-heels. There is a genuine tenderness in their scenes together, a sense that this would have to be Palmer's last movie because he is so clearly going to abandon international espionage, marry Anya and make babies with her. Alas, Anya turns out to be a double agent working for the Russians and leaves Palmer high and dry at the movie's end.

Or does she? As they exchange looks for the last time there is a depth of feeling communicated that few of the great romantic movies get near. If *The Ipcress File* had given us the spy as working-class nobody and *Funeral in Berlin* had played with the idea of the spy as superstar sex god, then *Billion Dollar Brain* serves up the spy as sensitive soul stumbling through a world he can't make sense of. Slack-jawed and wide-eyed, Caine's Palmer is dragged from one expository scene to another, a party to the audience's bafflement as the plot twists and thickens until he's not sure which side anyone is on and, more subversively, whether either side has any more to recommend it than the other. At one point Palmer even drinks to Lenin. Indeed, Russell has suggested that the film, in dealing with the question of America's interfering in areas outside its concern, is a parable about the Vietnam war.[18] This may be stretching things a bit. Nonetheless, *Billion Dollar Brain* is a considerably more sensitive and intelligent movie than most entries in the spy genre.

Until he returned to the part more than a quarter of a century later, however, in a couple of cheap nineties action flicks, *Billion Dollar Brain* was the last we saw of Caine as Palmer. The critical reaction to the film was the most negative any of the trilogy had had, and while Saltzman had plans to film Deighton's next Palmer novel, *Horse Under Water*, Caine was adamant (rightly enough, as it turned out) that he had done everything he could with the character. 'I hope some new actor can give his interpretation of Harry,' said Caine, 'but after three films I don't think the Palmer character holds anything for me any more.'[19] Saltzman did look around for another actor – 'We don't want anyone who looks like Mike and he probably won't even wear spectacles or even be a cockney,' he said[20] – but nothing ever came of the idea. Since Saltzman was talking during the period of Sean Connery's absence from the Bond series, when the part was taken over – disastrously, as far as the box office was concerned – by George Lazenby, he had good reason to change his mind and let the series go.

So had Caine. *Billion Dollar Brain* was the last film on which he did his own stunts. The scenes on the ice, with Harry jumping from floe to floe, are for real, and Caine found out too late that he hadn't even been given any ice knives with which to save himself should disaster strike. Strike it almost did. 'The Coast Guard came down,' remembers Ken Russell, 'and said "If you're not done by tomorrow, forget it". As he left he said "Drive back with your doors open". "Why?" "Well, if your car sinks through the ice you might be able to get out". We *just* did it. The next day it would have been hopeless.'[21]

Perhaps unsurprisingly, Caine jumped at the chance to jet off to Paris to film a small cameo in Shirley MacLaine's latest movie.

He was robbed: Caine in *Deadfall*. © British Film Institute

Almost every man wastes part of his life in attempts to display
qualities which he does not possess, and to gain applause which he
cannot keep.
Samuel Johnson[1]

The last time Caine had been in Paris, shortly after the break-up of his marriage a decade or so earlier, he had been a virtual down and out, living hand to mouth, finding work where he could. This time, he was booked into a suite at the George V hotel. It was all a world away from the icy wastes of Finland. Not that Paris was all that much warmer than the frozen north. Indeed, the episode of *Woman Times Seven* (1967) Caine appears in is called 'Snow'.

A Maugham-esque collocation of stories which had in common only the actress who took the leading role, *Woman Times Seven* was designed to showcase the various talents of Shirley MacLaine. In the event, all it did was show the world MacLaine's lack of variety. Vivacity and high spirits, the movie demonstrates, is all she can do.

To be fair to MacLaine, she may not have been helped by the fact that the movie was being directed by Vittorio De Sica. De Sica had made his name a couple of decades earlier as one of the leading directors of the Italian neo-realist movement, but his work had always been compromised by sentimentality and a fondness for histrionics.[2] De Sica had been an actor before he took to directing, and something in him always seemed willing to forgive whatever his stars wanted to do in front of the camera. And so *Woman Times Seven*, in which a host of international stars – Alan Arkin, Lex Barker, Patrick Wymark, Rossano Brazzi, Robert Morley, Peter Sellers, *et al.* – battle it out with Shirley MacLaine for dominance of the screen, is less a collection of short stories than a series of hamming contests. Surprisingly, perhaps, given De Sica's predilection for overpriming his scenes with emotion, Caine has said he admired the Italian's work. 'I did this [movie] as a favour to Shirley, in return for the one she had done me by taking me to Hollywood for the first time,' Caine has remembered. 'I also did it for other reasons, like the chance to do something, no matter how small, with de Sica, a man I admired so much.'[3]

Lucky for Caine, then, that the part he had been given was a silent one. All he had to do was look shyly love-struck (he has a 'little lost boy look working for him', Anita Ekberg says at one point) while following MacLaine through the city streets to her apartment. On the other hand, just to make sure we get the point, De Sica encourages

Caine to indulge in the broadest mugging of his career so far – droopy eyes, self-regarding smiles, astonished passion. Fortunately, Caine never lets such emotional shorthand do his thinking for him. He might spend a lot of his time on screen hopping and flapping and warming his hands, but unlike pretty much everyone else in the movie, he keeps his cool. Even in his big silent scene, pressed up against MacLaine on the Metro, Caine reins himself in. The two of them examine each other's faces quizzically, but Caine gives away nothing while doing so. He avoids the opportunity the movie affords him either to leer or to lurch. Nobody could make great claims for their work on *Woman Times Seven*, but Caine has undeniably suffered the least damage when the credits roll.

Much the same could be said of Caine's appearance in *Deadfall* (1968), an overambitious caper movie that, like *Gambit*, had been written (and was being directed) by Bryan Forbes. Unlike the earlier picture, though – which had gone through multiple rewrites and casts – *Deadfall* was conceived from the outset as a vehicle for its leading man.

Caine plays Henry Clarke, a jewel thief so dedicated to his work that when the movie opens he is in a sanatorium recovering from alcoholism. Henry, we learn, has brought the disease upon himself in order that he might get near to a genuine alcoholic, the multimillionaire Salinas (David Buck), whose house he plans to burgle. Just before his release, Henry is visited by another thief, Fe Carbonell de Rodriguez Moreau (Giovanna Ralli), who suggests that he join forces with herself and her husband Richard (Eric Portman) to take on Salinas. Smitten with Fe, Henry agrees and, after the team's first successful robbery together, asks Richard to grant her a divorce. Richard refuses, telling Henry that as well as being his wife, Fe is also his daughter. Distraught, Henry decides to rob the Salinas mansion himself, falling to his death as Fe, by now apprised of her real identity, rushes to be with him. Fe is arrested, while back at home Richard commits suicide.

As might be plain from even that brutal summary, *Deadfall* was a disaster waiting to happen. Desmond Cory's 1965 novel, on which Forbes's screenplay was very closely based, was a thriller ashamed of its genre's lowly status in the critical pecking order. Hence Cory's overblown, bombastic prose, which worked desperately to imbue the story it told with a profundity it thought absent from its subject. Here is Cory on the novel's first gymnastic robbery:

> Then suddenly, etched into that blinding Giotto's circle of swinging
> light, bisecting it with the pure and untouchable beauty of
> Euclidean geometry, a falling figure; a body freed suddenly and

unforgettably from all the trammels of the earth, surrendered to
the binding law of the universe, a diving body pure and of itself,
arching downnwards with an unbelievable slowness, knees
together, arms swung out wide, dropping feet first into infinity; a
moment of a beauty so clear and undistilled that Moreau gasped
aloud, numbed into aweness as he might have been by the impact
of Gauguin's colour or a cadence of Mozart.4

Forbes himself seems to have been numbed into awe by Cory's more
purple passages. Nowhere is this more apparent than in the movie's
twenty-three-minute robbery sequence, which Forbes daringly but disastrously cross-cuts with footage of the concert the robbery's victims
are attending. Just as Cory had compared his hero's acrobatics with
Euclidean geometry, so does Forbes attempt to parallel Henry's metic-
ulously organized break-in with a conductor's marshalling of his
orchestra. As the conductor (John Barry, who actually wrote the score
for the movie) lifts his baton, so does Richard lift his torch to light
Henry's scaling of a wall; as the soloist plucks delicately at her guitar
strings, so does Henry snip neatly through an alarm wire. Jewel thieves,
the movie would have us believe, are just as professional, as artistic,
even, as musicians.

Whole chunks of *Deadfall*'s dialogue are similarly portentous –
Beyond Good and Evil sifted through Mills and Boon. The bulk of the
movie's second hour is given over to Henry and Richard discoursing on
the nature of love. When Fe interrupts them, telling them that they're
'talking too much philosophy and not enough business', she speaks for
the entire audience. *Deadfall* is a thriller that forgets to thrill. Caine's
only achievement in the movie is to refuse to endorse Henry's tragic
sententiousness. Knowing that to inflect all this stuff about love and
pity would be to heighten its ludicrousness, Caine summons a laconic
flatness of tone that takes the wind out of the dialogue's sails.

The result, unfortunately, is that Caine's Henry becomes unreadable,
an enigma. Though Forbes has said that the figure of Henry 'was more
sophisticated than some of [Caine's] earlier roles', and that he wanted
to take him away from 'the cockney Jack the lad [roles] that established
him',5 *Deadfall* would have made a lot more sense had Caine been
allowed to play the part as a crooked class warrior. When Richard asks
Henry why the jewel thief is the only type of criminal the public are
fond of, Henry says it's because of 'the Robin Hood element – robbing
the rich to feed the poor'. The trouble is that Caine's Henry is so
eminently well-fed and well-read: his burglaries seem less an exercise
in socialist redistribution than in Nietszchean self-definition. Forbes's

ambition to dispense with the iconography of low-born rakery that had accreted about his old friend during the previous three or four years was understandable, yet there is no denying that the movie would have made a lot more sense had Caine been allowed to trade on his image and give us a cool cockney crook bent on revenge on the upper classes – a Riff-Raffles if you will. By refusing to let Caine play to his strengths, *Deadfall* fell flat on its face.

Shot on Majorca during the autumn of 1967, the film was Caine's first all-out failure. Though he had hitherto occasionally chosen parts unwisely, *Deadfall* finally showed to the world a Caine who could not rise above his material. He had done his best to subvert the picture's clever-clever chit-chat, but his hypersensitive control of his effects meant that he ended up looking as if he had no idea what his character was meant to be doing. As the anonymous critic of the *Monthly Film Bulletin* noted at the time, Caine's tight-reined performance 'directly bel[ied] the emotional excesses attributed to him in the script'.[6] Other reviewers were no less harsh.

Caine and Forbes have never worked together again, though this is not, says Forbes, for want of trying on his part.[7] Nor is there any need to suspect Caine of being disappointed in Forbes's work. 'Something important got lost,'[8] he comments of *Deadfall* in his autobiography, but he apportions no blame. He had by now made enough movies to know the truth about them: good or bad, they are always essentially accidental achievements. 'Making films is such a complicated business it's a miracle you can win any of them,'[9] Caine relaxedly ruminated in late 1968, a month or two after the opening of *Deadfall*. And anyway, the movie had not been his choice. Following *Gambit*, Caine had signed a two-picture deal with Twentieth Century Fox – a deal which gave him no say on the movies the company deemed suitable for him. The second picture was to prove even more disastrous than *Deadfall*.

If Caine had looked bemused by *Deadfall*'s passionate excesses, then he looked downright baffled by his part in *The Magus* (1968). Adapted by John Fowles from his own best-selling 600-page novel, the movie – set in Greece but actually filmed on Majorca – complicated an already gnomic tale, first by throwing out large chunks of its back story, and second by remoulding its protagonist in the shape of Michael Caine. Fowles's observation that his leading man was 'a natural bastard, so I suppose he's a sort of natural casting'[10] aside, Caine bore no resemblance to the Nicholas Urfe of the novel. Fowles's Urfe was a thick-skinned public-school bully, fresh out of Cambridge and with pretensions to aestheticism. The movie's Urfe, on the other hand, is described in the film by a friend as 'one of the new élite. Impeccable background: his father was a bus driver . . . huge chip on his shoulder. Now classless, rootless . . .' The quintessential Caine figure, in other words. Given such a change of emphasis, though, it is hardly surprising that the movie largely abandons the novel's ham-fisted existentialism to become a kind of post kitchen-sink/prototype hippie retread of *Alfie* – Caine playing the feckless young gadabout sowing his seed wherever he fancies until a beautiful girl and a sage old man teach him the meaning of true love.

Green tragedy: Caine with Anna Karina in *The Magus*. © British Film Institute

Intriguingly, though, Fowles *had* seen a kind of Urfe figure in Caine when the two had met during the Cannes film festival of 1965, just a few weeks before he sent the manuscript of *The Magus* off to his publisher. Fowles, who was in Cannes to help publicize William Wyler's film of his first book, *The Collector* (1965, with Terry Stamp in the titular role), had this to say about the star of *The Ipcress File*: 'Mike Caine. A Cockney boy made good – Terry's friend. He can't act, but takes himself very seriously: hot for birds, for the *dolce vita*, for prestige. Very ugly, these new ultra-hard young princes of limelight.'[11] Oxbridge artiness aside, that is essentially the Urfe of Fowles's novel.

Caine, meanwhile, had loved Wyler's version of *The Collector* and told its producers John Kohn and Jud Kinberg that he wanted to appear in a movie of Fowles's next novel, 'no matter what it is'.[12] Once Caine had read the book he was, he said, 'absolutely fascinated by it . . . what I feel it's about [is] if we could only live our lives knowing what we know now . . .'[13] Twenty years later, knowing what he knew then, Caine's ardour had cooled considerably: 'I always think a writer must be great if I don't understand his or her work and if the critics say s/he is great . . . John fell into this category: I was told he was great, and did not understand him, so he must be so. Of all his novels . . . *The Magus* was the most obscure.'[14] Thus has Caine subsequently washed his hands of the movie, an understandable enough cleansing given the terrible reception it received from critics and public alike. Woody Allen summed the drubbing up when he remarked that if he were given the chance to live his life over again he wouldn't change a thing – except skip *The Magus*. As so often, Caine was the best thing in Guy Green's movie, but just as his naturalistic compression had undermined *Deadfall*'s Henry, so here it pulled the rug from beneath his character's melodramatic conversion to love. Caine's toothy, getting-of-wisdom laugh as he reads Eliot's 'Four Quartets' at the movie's end is among the most misjudged moments of his entire career. Perhaps unsurprisingly, it was almost two years after the cameras stopped rolling before the picture opened in cinemas at the end of 1969.

'If one wants to make international impact,' Dennis Selinger had always insisted to his clients, 'the surest system is to make as many movies as possible.'[15] Caine had long been the man who best understood his agent's philosophy, but even so, to construct a chronology of Caine's activities during the late sixties is to be amazed at his fecundity. He can hardly ever have stopped working for more than a couple of weeks at a time. Though he wintered in London as 1967 became 1968, he was not impressed with the changes he saw – the drug-taking hippy culture had swept through the city – and he was happy to go back to work early in the new year.

After two movies made back to back on Majorca, Caine found himself in mainland Spain, in Almeria to be precise. The location for Sergio Leone and Clint Eastwood's spaghetti westerns, Almeria was at the time playing host to Sean Connery's misguided horse opera *Shalako* (1968). The two stars took time out from their respective shoots for socializing, during which Caine made a failed play for Connery's co-star, Brigitte Bardot. In truth, Caine was probably just fooling around. According to his then friend and minder, Johnny Morris, Caine was far more interested in booze than he was birds. 'He used to repeat himself,' Morris said many years later. 'He was drinking a lot . . . used to tell the same stories. I heard well-known actors saying, "I hope he's not going to tell us that story again." '16

In such light, Caine's finely calibrated performance in the movie he was making at the time is all the more astonishing. It was a war picture called *Play Dirty* (1968) and it was to be directed by the highly regarded French film-maker René Clément – a prospect that delighted Caine. Understandably then, Caine was alarmed when, on the second day of shooting, rumours began to circulate that Clément, who could not get on with the producer Harry Saltzman, was about to quit. In the event, Clément lasted two weeks, a period during which Caine's high hopes had dissipated somewhat. 'I don't really know what film he was making,' Caine told an interviewer the following year.17 According to the man who took over the picture, though, the fact that Caine missed his opportunity with Clément has rankled him ever since. Caine was, said André de Toth, 'A climber, he wanted a credit, a picture – good, bad or indifferent – with *the* René Clément.'18 Possibly this is so, though it has to be said that de Toth, a pragmatic Hollywood pro with several brooding *films noirs* to his name (and the Executive Producer credit on *Billion Dollar Brain*), was far more in keeping with Caine's idea of a good director. Though Caine has described *Play Dirty* as a 'mediocrity',19 he puts the blame for this on the late changes made to the script rather than de Toth's direction.

The director was equally happy with Caine's work, even though he thinks 'he felt uncomfortable, insecure in the film without Clément'.20 For de Toth, Caine was,

> probably more disappointed than I, and I understood him and his resentment of the film . . . [It makes] his portrayal in *Play Dirty* so remarkable . . . since both he and the character he portrayed were out of the safety of their rocking chair. My respect for his professionalism only grew as we drilled on under not the clearest Almeria sky . . . Caine was a trouper.21

De Toth is being too hard on himself here because *Play Dirty*, which was intelligently if windily scripted by Melvyn Bragg, is far from being a mediocre picture. Perhaps because of its title, the movie was reviewed as if it were some kind of cash-in on the success of Robert Aldrich's then recent gung-ho blockbuster *The Dirty Dozen* (1967). In fact, there is a world of difference between the two pictures, chief among them the mordant, cynical intelligence of *Play Dirty*. Aldrich's movie had patted itself on the back for its ironic take on heroism and criminality. Essentially, that picture says, the men we choose to honour in war are mighty similar to the men we choose to castigate in polite society. In de Toth's picture, though, there is *no* heroism. War, *Play Dirty* suggests, is no more than a series of cock-ups, cock-ups that lead to catastrophes – and nobody is ever around to take the blame.

Cakes and ale: Caine celebrates his 35th birthday on the *Play Dirty* shoot. © British Film Institute

Ostensibly in charge, though, is Caine's Captain Douglas, a chess-playing dandy with a mission to blow up Rommel's fuel supplies in the north African desert. To help him fulfil his task he is given an admittedly *Dirty Dozen*-ish team of men. Among its number are a pair of homosexuals, a couple of crooked no-goods, and Leech, a chippy second-in-command who knows (as Douglas knows) that he ought to be first-in-command.

Leech is played by Nigel Davenport and he brings to the role a burly sarcasm – all bulging eyes and scrunched lips – that under-cuts Douglas's fey incompetence beautifully. Nonetheless, the movie would have been better had Leech been played by the man who was originally cast in the part: Richard Harris. Unfortunately, Harris had arrived on *Play Dirty*'s Almeria set in mid-February 1968 to find that the script had been altered in ways he didn't like. 'The script I was given and the script I accepted in London earlier were totally different,' he said at the time.[22]

Why does one so regret the loss of Harris on *Play Dirty*? Because the movie's essential conflict would then have been an ontological phenomenon just waiting to be captured on celluloid. Bluntly, Harris and Caine simply would not have got on: the clash between Douglas and his subordinate Leech would have taken place for real – in front of the camera. For Caine and Harris approached their job from very different perspectives. Throughout his career Caine has insisted that professionalism and craftsmanship are the first requisites of the actor. Harris, on the other hand, was a performer who relied on brimstone and bravura, on the heat of the moment, on the intoxicating gust of inspiration. 'I wasn't going to play second fiddle to Caine,' Harris remembered a little while later. 'That was a royal fuck-up because Saltzman lied to me ... [I] had a clause in my contracts saying an offered role could not be tampered with once I'd accepted. Saltzman signed that contract. But then, when I arrived in Spain, I was given thirty new pages, with four of my main scenes cut to ribbons ... I told Saltzman, "You are a contemptible, low-life fucker" and I walked off.'[23]

Still, with or without Harris, *Play Dirty* is far from being the wash-out it has too long been characterized as. To be sure, the movie flags at times, as if de Toth, whose last movie as director this was, has forgotten that you should always leave a scene as early as possible. But there is still much to treasure here, and Caine in particular has some wonderful moments. Near the start of the movie, Caine's Captain Douglas is summoned to see Brigadier Blore (Harry Andrews). To get to the meeting Caine has to do no more than walk across an office, but in three or four seconds of film (and in distant medium close-up, too) he manages to convey smugness, diffidence, panic, casual lust (as a secretary breezes by) and, finally, a kind of pensive irony.

Later on in the action, Douglas, whose authority over his men has never been in anything but question, orders his team to bury the bodies of a group of Arabs they have just massacred. The men look at him with the same ill-disguised insolence they have exhibited throughout the movie, and Douglas is forced to pick up his gun and bark the order once more. Davenport's Leech, after much sarcastic soul-searching, tells the men, 'I think he means it,' and they get down to digging some graves. A slackness in de Toth's editing here, a depressurizing slowness in the cut from Caine to Davenport, is all that prevents this scene from achieving greatness. Watching it again, one marvels anew at the lack of control in Caine's Douglas, the way he lets his voice break as he tries to retain command. There is a whining strain to his last order – 'Bury them!' – which tells us not only that Douglas is unconvincing but, worse, that he knows it. Any illusions about Douglas's finally earning the respect of the troublesome troop he has been put in charge of are utterly dispelled by Caine's fearful despair. *Play Dirty* may not be a masterpiece, may not be *Apocalypse Now* (1979), but it is one of the more thoughtful, even sensitive, entries in the war-movie genre that sprung back to life towards the end of the sixties as America invaded Vietnam. As the years go by it looks better and better.

Not so *The Battle of Britain*, Caine's (and Saltzman's) second war movie of 1969. What was Saltzman playing at, producing a furiously sensitive anti-war film one month and a £5-million rabble-rouser the next? Perhaps we should remember that only four years before he had created the insubordinate Harry Palmer as an insurance policy against the imperial fantasy of the Bond movies turning sour. Like any smart financier, he was running with the hare and the hounds.

Fortunately for Caine, he had little to do in the movie. He smokes cigarettes in one scene and gets gunned down in another. It sounds like he'd chosen a bad part, but nobody in the movie (and everybody was in the movie, from Laurence Olivier to Trevor Howard, from Christopher Plummer to Kenneth More) got to do anything more interesting. Director Guy Hamilton seemed interested solely in sub-pornographic footage of the movie's hardware – all those Spitfires whizzing over Kent.

The movie was released around the time of the twenty-ninth anniversary of the real Battle of Britain, but it did little business and proved to be Saltzman's first big loser. Was this failure due to the fall-out from the Vietnam war? After the summer of love, were the public no longer interested in movies about our brave boys taking on the might of Europe and thrashing them? Tempting to think so, but the temptation should probably be resisted. It is nearer the truth to say that the problem with Saltzman's movie (which was made without any American finance, and for which its stars were paid far less than their going rates) was its emphasis on spectacle at the expense of story. Only a churl could fail to thrill at the movie's recreation of an airborne dogfight twixt Brits and Krauts over southern England. Only a chump, though, could want to watch another and another and another. The movie was a bore, and a bore that went on far too long. In that, if in nothing else, it looked forward rather than backward, to the pop-eyed blockbusters of the post-Spielberg era, to *1941* (1979) and *Pearl Harbor* (2001).

11 1969–70

We used to wonder where war lived, what it was that made it so vile. And now we realise that we know where it lives, that it is inside ourselves.
    Albert Camus[1]

Euro-sceptics: *The Italian Job*. © The Kobal Collection

To walk along an average street in the Britain of the late sixties was to be given the chance to read one or other or both of two slogans. 'I'm Backing Britain,' said the stickers adorning many a car window. 'Watch out, there's a thief about,' proclaimed their house-window coevals. *The Italian Job* (1969), the movie that, after a string of flops, put Caine back on winning box-office form at the end of the sixties, can be read as a braying demonstration of those two slogans. Along with *Alfie* and *The Ipcress File*, *The Italian Job* is one of Caine's – indeed, British cinema's – most canonical movies of the decade. And yet, in many ways, the movie is a goodbye to the idea of the sixties. Hysterically overdetermined, the picture is so keen to prove that, despite hippies and hashish, Britain can still punch above its international weight that it collapses into a kind of camp entropy.

At heart, it was a very old-fashioned picture. Troy Kennedy Martin, whose script and original idea the movie was, had cut his teeth on *Z Cars*, a kitchen-sink cop show he had dreamed up for the BBC back in 1962. And for all its Portobello Road, flower-power flash and flurry, *The Italian Job* is essentially a fifties-style cops-and-robbers satire. Indeed, it bears a striking resemblance to the Peter Sellers comedy heist movie *Two-Way Stretch* (1960). In that film, three men break out of jail and carry out a daring robbery masterminded by a pal on the outside, before returning to their cells to ensure the perfect alibi. *The Italian Job* simply reverses the terms. Caine's Charlie Croker breaks *into* prison in order to be briefed on his latest job by Mr Bridger (Noel Coward). From there on, the detail (though not the scale) is very similar: bullion trucks, car chases, chaos. And yet, and yet. There is an essential difference between the two movies. Whereas *Two-Way Stretch* is as feelgood as British comedy comes, *The Italian Job*, for all its bright-eyed braggadocio, leaves a nasty taste in the viewer's mouth.

Partly this is to do with violence. The movie was made only a couple of years after Britain's World Cup win of 1966, but though Caine's Croker and his gang travel to Italy in the guise of football supporters, the emphasis is, somewhat presciently, on the hooligan qualities of soccer fans. For the movie's first half, Caine's Croker and his team of joking cockney jack-the-lads are not far removed from Sellers and his gang of likeable, incompetent villains. But during the robbery, dressed in matching boiler suits and wire-visaged crash helmets and carrying matching white clubs, the self-styled self-preservation society is a disturbing sight – fascist stormtroopers who take as much pleasure in bloodshed as they do in bullion.

There is fascism, too, in the movie's xenophobia.[2] Anybody who isn't British, the picture says, is a buffoon. Indeed, *The Italian Job* can most profitably be understood as a film about Britain's relations with the European Common Market (whose doors De Gaulle had closed to Britain for the second time in 1967, the year before the movie was shot). Essentially, the movie is a fantasy about Britain's not needing to sign up to the Common Market because we are so much better than the rest of its members. Our villains – mere rogues and rascals – are far more likeable than Italy's mafia; our computer programmers far cleverer than those bearded European boffins; our (state-manufactured) Minis run rings round those silly (state-manufactured) Fiats.

Little surprise, perhaps, that *The Italian Job* offered Caine his most aggressive role to date. Indeed, he spends most of the movie shouting. Alas, he has little else to do. Just as with the *Battle of Britain*, the hardware – in this case those Mini Coopers – takes centre stage. This might not have mattered if Caine had been allowed to coast through the movie on charm, but the emphasis on brutality denied him the chance.

Crucially, what Caine most needed were more scenes opposite Noël Coward's Mr Bridger. Though Coward and Caine dined together frequently during filming, they spend only a couple of minutes together on screen. Here, the movie would have you believe, is a vision of the British class system in miniature. On the one hand, Caine's uppity sixties cockney; on the other, Coward's thirties cocktail charmer. What gives their few scenes together extra spark, though, is the knowledge that Coward wasn't, in fact, much higher born than Caine. Like him, he hailed from south London, where he had grown up in shabby gentility in Edwardian Twickenham. Coward's class, then, was as much of an act as Caine's pretending to be Sir Charles Croker when he books into a Mayfair hotel. As with *Zulu* and *Gambit* before it, Caine's presence in *The Italian Job* subconsciously reminds us that Britishness is always at some level a charade.

Above and beyond that, Caine's and Coward's scenes together suggest that the social revolution of the fifties and sixties (which had created Caine and crippled Coward) had been all very well, but that now Britain must unite in a classless war against the real enemy: Europe. For all its cosiness – the casting of Benny Hill, Irene Handl, John Le Mesurier, Quincy Jones's schmaltzy theme tune, the Alpine footage – *The Italian Job* is a deeply troubled film, and what troubles it is Britain's uncertain place in the world. With its Europhobia and 'grab what you can and sod everyone else' attitude, this seemingly harmless caper movie can be read as a blueprint for the Thatcher revolution of ten years later.

Little wonder, perhaps, that the film did next to no business in America. It was, though, a box-office smash in Britain and is still one of Caine's most famous movies.[3] Three decades after its original release it was back in British cinemas – to rapturous receptions from the masculinity-in-crisis culture of the nineties. In 2003, moreover, the movie was remade for Hollywood, with Mark Wahlberg in the Caine role. *The Italian Job* has no small purchase on the popular imagination.

Class tension: Caine with Noel Coward in *The Italian Job*. © British Film
Institute

That said, the movie is far from being one of Caine's best, although
the performance he gave in it did point the way towards some of his
most important work. Charlie Croker's ignorant viciousness would be
put to rather more intelligent use a couple of years later when Caine
came to construct the titular lead of *Get Carter*, while his vacuous
patriotism would be subtly called into question in *The Man Who
Would Be King*. But though Caine has subsequently sung his praises,
the movie's director, the late Peter Collinson, was never going to be the
man who would tease any malicious subtleties from his star.

Fortunately, Caine was booked next to work with Robert Aldrich,
one of the cinema's most gratuitously truthful analysers of masculinity.
Caine had had his commercial success; now, perhaps, for the critical one.

Certainly, Caine felt he had the right to expect something good to
come out of the *Too Late the Hero* (1970) shoot – by some measure
the most miserable of his career. Filming took place over twenty-two
weeks in the Philippine jungle. Temperatures regularly reached 120°F,
mosquitoes plagued the cast and crew, and the food, especially to a man
of Caine's delicate stomach, was inedible. In a bid to establish some kind

of sanity, Aldrich agreed with his team that they should work long days and long weeks – and then reward themselves with long weekends: fourteen days on, five days off. The result, as Aldrich had no doubt been hoping, was a high-pressure shoot similar in spirit, if not in actual worries, to the terrible tedium of military existence.

In that, *Too Late the Hero* bore more than a passing resemblance to *The Long and the Short and the Tall*. Caine's Private 'Tosh' Hearne drinks from the same well as the Bamforth of the earlier play. Like Bamforth, Tosh is never short of a cynical wisecrack; like Bamforth, Tosh is always talking back. Unlike Bamforth, though, Tosh's insubordinate impulse seems to stem less from individual psychology than from a kind of stylized impudence. Crop-haired and crabby, Caine's Tosh is effectively Harry Palmer before he was demobbed.

Indeed, the movie allows Tosh the scene Palmer was never granted – the one where he gets to rant angrily at his superior before being put on a charge. What's most remarkable about this moment is that it all comes out of nowhere. One moment Tosh is asleep, the next he is being roused to his duties and stumbling about the camp in a daze. Then one of the men asks him for a light, and in obliging Tosh realizes that the cigarette in question is one from a packet he gave to another man in the troupe who is now dead. Tosh erupts at what he sees as theft and a fight ensues. 'Stop this grubby little display,' barks Captain Hornsby (Denholm Elliott), and one knows instinctively that it is that snobbish little 'grubby' that goads Tosh into further action. He turns on Hornsby and harangues him for his incompetence and cowardice – and as he does so, Caine almost imperceptibly switches the round-shouldered stoop Tosh has affected throughout much of the movie's preceding hour for a skyscraper-straight spine and shoulders thrusting backwards. There is something of the horror movie about this change, of Jekyll becoming Hyde. Baring his teeth and licking his lips, Tosh is Caine's most outrageously vulpine class warrior yet – a soldier who stands in the correct manner only when *challenging* a superior officer.

As such, Caine had a lot to thank Aldrich for. A couple of years earlier, it will be remembered, Aldrich had offered up to the world the perhaps self-indulgently grimy *The Dirty Dozen*; a couple of years later he would treat it to that mordant anti-Vietnam western, *Ulzana's Raid* (1972). Aldrich was never, in short, a man to side with received opinion or the well-connected. He and Caine might have been made for one another, and it is one of the minor tragedies of both men's careers that they only got to work together this once. *Too Late the Hero* played host to Caine's most delicate insolence in years. The picture isn't a tenth as much fun as *The Dirty Dozen*, but in abjuring the earlier movie's pyrotechnic high jinks in favour of character and debate, it comes out on top.

Set during World War II on an island in the South Pacific run at one end by the Allies and at the other by the Japanese (with a vast no-man's jungle in-between them), the movie tells the story of a troupe of disconsolate no-hopers sent on a desperate mission. Their job is to deliver a decoy message to the Japanese in order that they might take their eye off a fleet of American ships that is due to pass by. In other words, this is *A Hill in Korea* all over again, though *A Hill in Vietnam* might be more fitting. Like *Billion Dollar Brain*, *Too Late the Hero* was one of the earliest entries in Hollywood's anti-Vietnam cycle. For unlike, say, the men in *A Hill in Korea*, nobody in Tosh's troupe believes in the necessity, let alone the virtue, of his task. Even the movie's major military figurehead, Captain John G. Nolan (Henry Fonda), sees it as no more than a pointless suicide mission.

One of the best things about the movie is that Caine isn't, as he had recently too often been, the only distinguished performer on display. Andrew Sarris has described Aldrich's direction of actors as spreading 'a subtle frenzy on the screen',[4] and there is indeed more going on in any one scene of *Too Late the Hero* than in whole movies made by other people. The film allows everyone their moment. Denholm Elliott's effetely ineffective Hornsby, for instance, while conceived and written as the cliché-spouting public-school booby of the piece, is allowed his dignity by both Aldrich and Caine. Indeed, one of Caine's big achievements in the movie is to quietly dominate every scene without lording it as the star of the show. Everyone from Ian Bannen to Ronald Fraser is allowed their moment in the limelight, and at such moments Caine doesn't so much fade away (as usual, it is impossible to take your eyes off him) as have the very un-English actorly confidence to do nothing but just be.

Interestingly, it is Cliff Robertson's Lieutenant Lawson, created in his customarily mechanical Method style, that suffers most alongside Caine's less self-conscious naturalism. Almost unique among Hollywood stars, Robertson had the ability to appear more ineffectual than any of the British actors in his pictures. This wispy intangibility means that the ending of *Too Late the Hero* goes badly awry. With most of the troupe now dead, Aldrich tries to up the tension by having us wonder who will survive: Caine's uppity Brit or Robertson's nervy but competent Yank. The trouble is that Robertson's half-hearted Lawson has so rigged the deck in Caine's favour that it is no surprise – though still a big deal – when Tosh comes out on top.

Away from the set, however, Robertson proved himself enough of a man to impress his co-star. During a break in filming several members of the cast and crew chartered a plane to take them to Hong Kong. Fifteen thousand feet up a cabin door burst open and an icy stratospheric rush cut through the plane. Panic all round. Except for Robertson, who told Caine to grab him by the back of his belt while he calmly lent out into the air and pulled the door to. If only something of that mutual macho reliance had come over on the screen *Too Late the Hero* might have been an all-out men-without-women masterpiece.

Outside the confines of Aldrich's narrative, of course, there were more than enough girls to go round. Carousing with the crew in a bar in Olangapo, Caine was propositioned by one of the local whores when she dipped a breast in his drink. Caine thought better of taking her up on her offer, though he was by no means entirely averse to the light entertainment offered by the local girls. In Taiwan one night, he bedded a young lovely who turned out to be the daughter of a local VIP. Caine only found this information out, alas, when he was roused from his sleep late in the night by a bunch of gun-toting cops demanding to see his papers. Thankfully one of the policemen recognized him – 'You are Alfie' – and, the girl having already left for the night, let things lie.5

A few weeks further into the shoot, though, Caine became involved rather more seriously with a woman. Minda Feliciano was the daughter of the Philippines' former Secretary of Public Works, José Feliciano. They were introduced at a bar in Manila and the habitually unreadable Caine could be read like a book. 'Michael was knocked back,' said his stuntman cum minder Johnny Morris. 'He couldn't stop talking about her afterwards.'6 When, after the Aldrich shoot, Caine returned home to Grosvenor Square, Minda moved in with him. She stayed there for the best part of two years, during which time Caine finally satisfied part of the dream he had been nurturing since being evacuated to Norfolk all those years ago. He bought a country manor.

Purchased early in 1970, around the time Feliciano obtained a decree nisi against her publisher husband, the Queen Anne-style Mill House in sight of Windsor Castle on the Thames cost Caine £60,000.7 For the next couple of years there, he and Feliciano hosted parties and weekend lunches for their friends and admirers. But for all its comparative duration – longer than any affair since Caine's marriage – the relationship with Minda was far from stable. How could it have been otherwise? During their three or so years together Caine made five or six pictures, not all of them in England. The couple rubbed along with each other on a day-to-day basis, in other words, far less than most couples. The relationship had always been stormy, too: Caine, for all his vaguely progressive thoughts on class mobility, was an out and out dinosaur when it came to sexual politics. Even during this, the age of what was then called women's lib, he maintained that a woman's place was wherever her man told her it was. So it was that when one night in October 1971 Feliciano locked herself in the Mill House and refused to come out, he wasted no time wondering how to talk her round. Johnny Morris was despatched to Windsor to deal with the problem.

Nobody has ever come totally clean on how that problem was dealt with, though Morris did get Feliciano out of the house as required.[8] Minda herself was curiously reticent on the end of the affair, too: 'I don't want to say anything about what happened between Michael and me,' she told a reporter in June 1972. 'Just that it was a terrible shock and a terrible time for me. Now I'm over it and, I think, a new person. I gave myself completely, but I wanted to and I was happy to.'[9]

After the briefest of shoots on (and appearances in) *Simon Simon* (1970) – a half-hour silent comedy directed by Graham Stark that called on the talents of, among others, Peter Sellers, Tony Blackburn, David Hemmings, Eric Morecambe and Bob Monkhouse – Caine was off to Austria to play an honourable mercenary in James Clavell's *The Last Valley* (1971). Shot over a three-month period at the end of 1969, the movie ended up being released in April 1971 – four weeks *after* the release of *Get Carter. The Magus* aside, such long delays had been unusual in Caine's career, though this one did have the benefit of throwing his performance in *Carter* into relief.

Despite their vastly different stories, settings and periods, there are intriguing similarities (and huge differences) between the two pictures. Crucially, both of Caine's characters are hired killers who have come in different ways to see the error of their ways. But where Carter can see further killing as the only way out of his predicament, the Captain (Caine's character is otherwise unnamed) of *The Last Valley* has a rather more cerebral take on his quandary. A mercenary during the Thirty-Year War, the Captain has come to the conclusion that since all religion is nonsense all fighting about religion is even bigger nonsense. Hence when, one day, he and his band of men stumble on a beautiful, pasture-landed village in a hitherto undiscovered valley, he takes the decision that they shall hide out here until the war is over.

Discursive, slow-moving and argumentative, *The Last Valley* was a more serious picture than seasoned Caine watchers had got used to seeing their hero in. 'I chose it deliberately,' Caine said during the shoot. 'It's a much harder character than I've ever played before . . . I was in danger of being thought a lightweight actor. So it's quite a change.'[10] Indeed it was.

As his anonymous status might suggest, Caine's Captain is meant, on one level at least, as an allegorical figure – the man of action who is intelligent enough, given the circumstances, to see through the vain-glory of war. One of the reasons Caine agreed to the movie is because he thought its story of the chaos of religious warfare paralleled the troubles in Northern Ireland.[11] In August 1969, just before shooting began on *The Last Valley*, British army troops were sent into Northern Ireland as violence in the region escalated. When the movie came out, eighteen months later, at least one reviewer found in it parallels with the Vietnam war.[12]

Historical analogies do not a movie make, of course, especially when so much of said movie is working to undermine its 'moral'. *The Last Valley* might mean well, but Clavell's camera enjoys the depiction of violence rather too much for the movie's anti-war message to be taken wholly seriously. All mist and blood, gallows and sackcloth, *The Last Valley* is shot like a big-budget Hammer horror picture.[13] There is even an example of that most Hammer-ish of images, the close-up of the stake that has penetrated a heart and is now covered in blood. But it was not such contradictions that led to the movie's bombing at the box office. For all its good intentions, *The Last Valley* is a work of fustian dullness.

As so often with Caine's movies, the best reason to see it is his per-formance, one for which his $750,000 salary (at that point his highest ever) seems entirely merited. It is doubtful any other actor could have given as much to the film as Caine did. Indeed, as Pauline Kael pointed out, it is he 'who holds most of the movie together'.[14] With his rusty bronze beard and regimented walk, the Captain is a world away from the parts that had made Caine's name. Surrounded by a bunch of mwah-ha-ha-ing caricaturists, Caine makes his Captain a man of stoic stillness, a contained soul who seems increasingly laden down with the leather and iron of his armour. Stiff of shoulder and stooped of back and with his arms hanging unnaturally away from his trunk, Caine's Captain has about him an air of unbending virtue – but also the knowledge that virtues that will not bend tend to get snapped. *The Last Valley* offered Caine his first shot at playing an intellectual, and he rose to the challenge magnificently. With no more than the flick of an eye or the adjustment of a lip, he manages to suggest the thought processes of a man struggling to come to terms with what is in effect a mid-life crisis: that of the soldier of fortune who wants to change his ways.

Insisting that his accent must be absolutely convincing, Caine bor-rowed recordings of German dialects from a shop in the Strand for the purpose of careful study. The result was one of the finest imitation

German accents ever committed to celluloid. Not only does Caine
eschew the (admittedly hilarious) camp whining of a Peter Sellers joke
turn, he avoids too the overebullient theatricality of, say, Laurence
Olivier's Nazi villain in *The Boys from Brazil* (1978). 'It is a performance of which I am particularly proud,' Caine has said, with no small
justification.[15] 'I was trying to destroy an image – the bird-pulling
Cockney boy.'[16] Unfortunately, he destroyed the image so well that it
gave even his most fervent admirers an excuse not to see the picture –
and Caine an excuse to cease caring about what he appeared in. Even
though *Films and Filming* magazine voted him their Actor of the Year
for *The Last Valley*, Caine has since all but disowned the movie. 'It
was such hard work,' he has said, 'and all to no avail. I knew the day
we finished it was not going to work.'[17]

It was, then, an unusually depressed Michael Caine who returned to
London from *The Last Valley* shoot at the end of 1969. Over the previous couple of years, after all, he had not always chosen his movies
wisely. Indeed, he had, he said, agreed to do one movie merely to
escape the noise at home. 'They're building a new hotel next door,' he
had said in his Grosvenor Square flat a year or so earlier. 'I almost
took a film this year just to get away. . . "Don't you want to know
who's directing it?" they asked. "Never mind all that," I said. "I'll
do it." '[18] Doubtless he was joking, but was he *just* joking? *Hurry
Sundown, Deadfall, Woman Times Seven, Battle of Britain* – the badly
received flops had lined themselves up in short order these past few
years. *The Last Valley*, he was convinced, was all set to go the same
way. And now the sixties were drawing to a close. Who could have
refused Michael Caine the right to worry that his star was about to die
alongside the decade that had made him?

I am determined to prove a villain.
    Richard III[1]

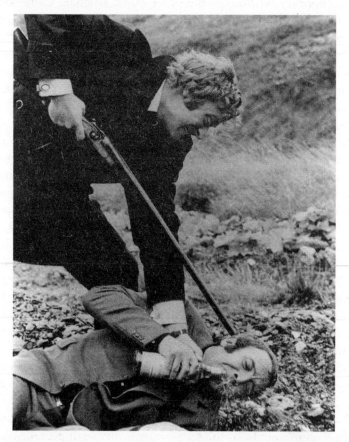

Loaded: Caine's role in *Get Carter* was reversed by the new-lad generation of the 1990s. © British Film Institute

Seventies cinema and television, Christopher Booker argued in a history of the decade, chose to dwell 'on the charm of almost every time except our own'.[2] *Upstairs Downstairs, The Onedin Line, Barry Lyndon* (1976), Caine's own *The Last Valley, Kidnapped* and *The Man Who Would Be King*: it isn't hard to picture the movies and shows Booker had in mind. The seventies were obsessed with the past.

As the decade grew old, and the post-*Star Wars* (1977) cinema became dominated by science fiction, things looked like they were changing, but this was just an illusion. *Star Wars* and its imitators weren't so much visions of the future as retreads of the out-of-this-world fantasies of the fifties. Ridley Scott's *Alien* (1979) aside, it wouldn't be until the eighties that the genre really began to get to grips with the contemporary world. On the other hand, Michael Caine kicked the decade off with a movie that was brutally alive to the texture of the times: *Get Carter* (1971). Here is a picture which nails Britain's realization not only that the sixties' dream was over but also that it had always been the merest fantasy.

The movie is set in and around Newcastle-upon-Tyne, a British city that had seen as much change as any since the Second World War. And so, along with the shots of serried back-to-back terraced houses so familiar from those kitchen-sink dramas of ten years earlier, we get to see the all-new concrete and asphalt high-rises post-war urban planners had wished on the place. But while the movie clearly thinks little of these new developments, neither does it have any faith in the redeeming powers of the more traditional working-class housing. When, halfway through Jack Clayton's movie of *Room at the Top*, Laurence Harvey's Joe Lampton returns home to the terraced back-to-back he had grown up in, the film asks us to believe that such places have a nobility and pride that Joe's newer, glitzier surrounds lack. Not so *Get Carter*. The old-fashioned terraces we see here are as fly-blown and flocculent as the East End of *Oliver Twist*. As Graham Fuller has suggested, the Newcastle of *Get Carter* is imbued with 'the same mood that Robert Towne captured in *Chinatown* (1974)'.[3]

Which is one of the reasons why Caine came into his own in this picture. Even what ought to be the glaring problem of his casting – that he is playing a *Geordie* gangster who returns home to Newcastle from London – can be easily overlooked because the accretions of meaning Caine brought to the part override any such pedantries. *Get Carter*, while being the best British gangster picture ever made, functions also as a condenser of film and history. In its sending of Caine back to his kitchen-sink roots and having him discover that they have shrivelled away into violence and urban decay, the movie presaged the seventies' post-mortem on the sixties. There had been one hell of a party, but the party, it turned out, had been a wake.

The earlier kitchen-sink movies had found a spurious romance in the grit and grime of their settings,[4] and by and large their heroes were, if not exactly admirable, then at least likeable. The string of villains Caine had played through the sixties had all been armoured in

Mean streets: Caine joked that he had thought he was working class until he arrived in Newcastle for the *Get Carter* shoot. © The Kobal Collection

charm – the charm bestowed by the decade's faith in the Robin Hood myth. The sixties had worshipped bad guys. Even the Kray twins, those malevolent East End gangsters, had been held up as icons of the day (indeed, had been among Caine's bedfellows in David Bailey's *Box of Pin-Ups*). The vaporous flirting with egalitarian politics that condensed first around the angry young men and then around the counterculture meant that crime could be regarded as just another form of rebellion. Who but a party pooper could have disapproved of what Charlie Croker and the lads got up to in *The Italian Job*, or Harry Dean in *Gambit*? Isn't it only enlightened, post-feminist hindsight that makes the character of *Alfie* seem so reprehensible?

Jack Carter was different. As Alexander Walker astutely pointed out, 'Carter is the hard man who might have had Alfie as his weakling brother.'[5] He might also have had any number of western heroes as his more admirable brother. For *Get Carter* is essentially a western, though one with the morality taken out of it. 'I never thought that someone like Michael Caine would play such a shit,'[6] the director Mike Hodges has said, surprised by his star's willingness to undercut the lowly charm with which he had made his name. 'I must be truthful and say that I'd always seen Ian Hendry in the role.'[7] Instead, Caine seized at the opportunity to investigate the reality behind the fantasies he had loved to watch as a child. When, early on in the movie, Carter is seen in a train carriage reading a copy of Raymond Chandler's *Farewell My Lovely*, you wonder for a moment whether he is to be an avenging angel, a knight of old engaged on a moral mission. But Carter's black trenchcoat – a devilish version of Bogart/Marlowe's stone-coloured number – gives the lie to any such notion. Carter's only moral code is kill or be killed.

Based on the 1970 novel *Jack's Return Home* by Ted Lewis, *Get Carter* is a revenger's tragedy in which Caine's London gangster Jack Carter travels to Newcastle to look into his brother Frank's mysterious death. In doing so, he uncovers a pornography ring into which Frank's teenage daughter Doreen (who may, it is suggested, actually be Jack's daughter) has been inveigled. Sickened and angered, Carter kills anyone in his way as he determines to do away with the wealthy local villain who is running the show, Cyril Kinnear (John Osborne). Before he can do so, though, Kinnear's own assassin guns Carter down.

Pretty much everybody dies, then, in this bleak, near heartless movie that Caine, perhaps sensing the country's mood swing, had leapt at the chance to make. (The project had been suggested to him by Michael Klinger, with whom Caine teamed up to form a production company for the film.) Yet Caine had aesthetic as well as socio-cultural reasons for wanting to appear in *Get Carter*. As we have seen, he had been annoyed through his early days of movie-going by the blatant unreality of the British film industry's depiction of class. But as a young Elephant and Castle tough, though, he had been equally irked by the cinema's fantasy take on the world of crime. Only in *Brighton Rock* (1947) – the Boulting Brothers' adaptation of the Graham Greene novel starring a young Richard Attenborough – had Caine discerned anything of the vital realism he sought in the movies. *Get Carter*, he thought, would be his chance to strike another blow for reality. And indeed, three decades and hundreds of violent movies later, the low-life violence served up in *Get Carter* is still shocking to watch. This is not, though, because the movie shows us sights more gruesome than any other picture does. Rather, it is because of the exorbitant lack of human feeling Caine's Carter exhibits throughout the picture's 112 minutes. Jack Carter is as cold a character as Caine has created – and he might have been created in order to highlight the understated calm of his creator.

Ian Hendry (who ended up playing one of Carter's victims, Eric Paice) never forgave Caine for having usurped him in the role he had thought might restore him to the fame he had enjoyed in the early sixties. Indeed, Hodges has said that relations between the two actors during the shoot were often fraught. Hendry, a drunk who romanticized his trade, had no time for what he saw as the mechanized banality of the untrained Caine.[8] But even if Hendry had judged Caine's worth correctly, he would still have been wrong to believe he would have made the better Carter. A Hendry Carter would have been steeped in tragic grandeur, in the big gestures and declamatory urgency this actor so loved. Hendry would have made Carter an off-white knight, throwing the movie off its axis by making the character too readily comprehensible. Caine's Carter, by contrast, is a nigh unreadable avenger.

Caine's narrow, slash-like eyes move motivelessly throughout the movie, but that tic aside Carter is devoid of grace notes. The movie was shot in the autumn of 1970, when Caine was thirty-seven – a year younger than the hero of Lewis's book – although he looks far older. Carter's face seems weathered by more than just the movie's bleak northern light, and his body seems more and more laden as the movie progresses, his slightly stiff walk eloquent of time and its depredations. Caine's speaking is similarly broken-backed. On repeated occasions he asks a character whether they know of another character: 'Do you ... know a man called ...' Caine puts the emphasis on the phrase's first two words and their subsequent purposeless pause, an emphasis that lends these otherwise banal lines a sinister edge. It's as if Caine's Carter is now so unrelated to the world he is struggling to find a way around that he has to translate the half-formed ideas in his head into something comprehensible to it. And so, seemingly unsure of the structure of English sentences, Carter's every line in the movie is pregnant with threat, heavy with dread. It is Caine's old Pinteresque trick of making the quotidian gnomic again, of course, but in *Get Carter* the fantasy gangland of Pinter's *The Homecoming* becomes naked and real.

To direct their first co-production Klinger and Caine chose Mike Hodges, a television director whose début behind the movie camera this was to be. They had been impressed by *Rumour*, a play he had written, produced and directed for Thames Television in 1970, which had painted the world of Fleet Street journalism in dark tones. Hodges retained this sombre palette for *Get Carter* and used it to coax from Caine a performance that investigated the vicious turpitude behind his slack-mouthed blankness. But then, Hodges' low-key direction is every-where of a piece with Caine's casual naturalism. His camera is forever lingering motivelessly: on a group of majorettes marching; on a nosy neighbour (spied in distant long shot through a telephoto lens); on a man betting in the bookies' Carter has already walked out of. The effect is to remind us that the world in which Jack is going about his business is a real one, not merely something got up for him to do his scenes in.

Yet the realism is undercut by the movie's casting of John Osborne as Kinnear. Osborne, of course, was one of the men responsible for Michael Caine's fame as an actor. There would have been no Harry Palmer, no Alfie Elkins, not even any Charlie Croker had Osborne not looked back in anger. Now, though, Osborne's Kinnear was looking forward in entrepreneurial, dictatorial malevolence. Far from being some brave young freedom fighter, Kinnear is the movie's chief emblem of the institutionalized corruption and pornography it sees as endemic in the Britain Osborne had helped liberate from austerity and repression. Consciously or not, then, the movie becomes a comment on the whole artistic and socio-cultural dream that had spawned Caine, and how, with the realization that the party spirit of the sixties was not one of post-Reichian liberation but little more than the last decadent gasp of Empire, that dream had turned sour. *Get Carter* has retained its power because of the way it understands that the socio-cultural tradition that had given us Michael Caine was over.

Not that Caine himself needed to worry overmuch about his iconic status as the new decade got into its stride. Nonetheless, it must have been reassuring to have Alfred Hitchcock suggest he take the lead in his latest project. Hitchcock was working on an adaptation of Arthur LaBern's tale of a maniac sex killer haunting central London, *Goodbye Piccadilly, Farewell Leicester Square*. Caine would have played Bob Rusk (a part eventually taken by the physically very similar Barry Foster), a sadistic wholesale greengrocer with an inability to commit to a relationship, primarily because before the relationship has had a chance to get going he has strangled its other half with his necktie.

Was there ever a wittier casting director than Hitchcock? Anthony Perkins, be it remembered, had played a succession of apple pie mommy's boys before he took on the part of *Psycho*'s (1960) Norman Bates, inaugurating in the process the modern horror movie's location of evil as *within* the family. So too the casting of Caine in what came to be called *Frenzy* (1972) would have been an inspiration. Who better to play a sex-crazed psychopath in sagging London than the man who had incarnated a sex-crazed sociopath in the city's swinging predecessor? Alas, Caine had cold feet about the part, finding it 'loathsome', though he lacked the courage to turn Hitchcock down to his face. Instead, he left the job to his agent. Hitchcock made a point of never speaking to Caine again.[9]

In the event, though, Caine had probably made the right decision. *Frenzy* turned out to be Hitchcock's last great movie, but its greatness lies in its turning rape and murder into black comedy – comedy so black that Barry Foster was for ever afterwards tarred with it. One does not know whether Foster harboured ambitions of attaining Caine-esque star status, but the fact is that despite a bleakly witty performance in the movie his film career never subsequently took off. Marvellous as it would have been to see what Hitchcock could have done with his flip amorality, Caine was sensible to see that being cast as a monstrous sex killer was not his best opportunity at the time.

Instead, he got back into period costume for *Kidnapped* (1971), filmed atop the hills and on the loch shores of Scotland. The movie was his second to be adapted from a Robert Louis Stevenson story (the other being *The Wrong Box*), and though Caine might not leap to mind when one thinks of the swashbuckling genre, nonetheless he acquits himself very well as Stevenson's Alan Breck. A Scots loyalist devoted to the overthrow of English rule, Stevenson's Breck (in reality a murderous thug) was a kind of Scarlet Pimpernel in reverse: instead of rescuing the gentry from the guillotine he rescues common folk from the marauding English. Caine has claimed that he made the film in order that his daughter might get to see her father on the big screen, and there is no need to disbelieve him. (Dominique was not yet fourteen and thus deemed too young to see her father's many X-certificated releases.) Nonetheless, the role of Breck could hardly have been unattractive to him, representing as it did the latest in his lengthening line of class-warrior parts.

The director, Delbert Mann (most famous for his sentimental American working-class movie *Marty* [1955], starring Ernest Borgnine), gives Caine the big star build-up, and we do not get to meet Breck until the movie is almost twenty minutes old. But despite the relaxed strength and amiable subtlety of Caine's performance – at one point in the movie he eats a meal as well as any actor has ever carried out this difficult task – it is the second leads, chief among them Trevor Howard and Freddie Jones, who take the honours. This is largely because Howard's Lord Grant and Jones's Cluny get all the best lines and all the best wigs. *Kidnapped* is full of bellowing, strutting, peruke-pulling fops, and it is rather a shame that Caine, who wears his hair in the then fashionable shoulder-length style and his moustache in seventies wide cut, doesn't get the chance to posture and pontificate a little more than he does.

Instead, he gets the chance to demonstrate again his unease with certain accents. Sean Connery's seems to have been the model for the voice here, but though Caine's Breck pronounces many of his words with a wry Scots drawl, he pronounces few entire sentences with it. At one point sliding down the country into Yorkshire, before veering wildly westerly to drop into the bumpkin rasp he would put to good use a year later in *Sleuth*, Caine's pronunciation is less than convincing.

He does, though, make good use of the air of throwaway brutality he had perfected for *Get Carter*. Midway through the movie, Caine crosses swords with a couple of English soldiers, and the glint of satisfaction in his eye as he runs first one, then the other through has the gleeful chill of conviction. What Caine doesn't manage to suggest is the growing fondness the script requires him to feel for his young sidekick David Balfour (Lawrence Douglas). Douglas, to be sure, was a callow and clumsy actor, but Caine must shoulder some of the responsibility for the fact that so little in their relationship rings true. In too many of their surrogate father/surrogate son scenes the two actors seem almost not to be in the same shot together – as if Caine has his mind on other things.

Which he may well have done. Midway through the filming of *Kidnapped*, the production ran out of money. Apart from a small percentage on profits, Caine got paid nothing for the three months he had spent in the Scottish Highlands that summer of 1971. 'It was an absolute and utter disaster from beginning to end,' he said several years later,[10] though he had not treated the movie like that while unpaid filming was still going on. Indeed, according to the movie's producer, Fred Brogger, Caine did more than most to ensure things were kept on an even keel through the difficult days: 'Nobody was paid fully . . . Mike was a key figure to get us through it. The stuntmen were threatening mayhem . . . rebelling every day. Mike kept soothing them over.'[11] In other words, even when not being paid properly, Caine was still the consummate professional devoted to his craft and unwilling to accept that anyone else involved should be any the less devoted.

Kidnapped may not have been the most satisfying of productions for Caine, but the bucolic nature of its shoot stayed with him when he returned to London in the late summer of 1971. While the tabloids were happy to continue whipping up the frenzy of Caine the party animal, the man himself took to spending more and more time at Mill House. On the horizon loomed his fortieth birthday. He had the bachelor pads, he had the country house, he had the money, and he had all the work he could handle. He had more than his share of women, too, but none of those relationships had amounted to very much. For the first time since his divorce of fifteen years earlier, Caine began to wonder about settling down.

He played a married man – his first ever – in his next film.[12] *Zee & Co* (1972; *X, Y and Zee* in the United States) was the first film Caine had appeared in in seven years in which he didn't get top billing. That honour went to Elizabeth Taylor (Caine would play second fiddle again later that same year – to Laurence Olivier in *Sleuth*). Never one to deny herself the trappings of stardom, Liz said that while everyone else involved on the movie's fourteen-hours-a-day shoot could start work at 8.30 in the morning, she would not be turning up until 10 a.m. For the first hour and a half of each day, then, Caine had to act with a continuity girl. Accordingly, there is little sense of continuity in Caine's and Taylor's scenes together – and since the movie is largely made up of scenes featuring Caine and Taylor, it is hardly surprising that the movie makes so little sense.

Caine plays Robert Blakeley, an architect heavily reliant on, yet discontentedly married to, the tempestuous Zee (Taylor). One of the chief virtues of Caine's performance lies in the way it keeps on finding new ways of suggesting that, even after many years together, Robert is still somehow surprised that he ended up with Zee. A small adjustment of his thick-rimmed spectacles, a slight movement of his jaw – Caine contrives to make such minutiae the stuff of drama. Essentially a retread of Taylor's noisy mid-sixties hit, *Who's Afraid of Virginia Woolf?* (1966), what story there is in *Zee & Co* centres around Stella (Susannah York), a seamstress whom Robert meets at a party and pursues with the kind of eager rapacity he has hitherto reserved for the tiffs and turmoil that constitute the bulk of his relations with Zee. As with her character in *Woolf*, though, Taylor's Zee is utterly dependent on being able to harangue Robert – without him she might go *really* crazy. And so, after at first taking some small ironic delight in his infidelity, she determines to wreck the affair.

Based on a short novel by Edna O'Brien (a novel so short it isn't much different to the screenplay she turned it into), *Zee & Co* must have looked mighty good on paper. O'Brien's dialogue bubbles along nicely, but always underneath it there is the sense of threat. The trouble is that Caine, Taylor and York were instructed (by director Brian G. Hutton) to rant *all* their lines. Hutton – a measure of whose cack-handed narrative skills can be gained from the impenetrable coilings of his *Where Eagles Dare* (1969) – turns a Rattigan-style study of the complexities of marriage into little more than a shouting match. And since Liz wasn't there for the first part of the working day, Caine had nothing but air to shout at – a fact that, despite the fine calibrations of his performance, shows. The movie's main distinction, then, comes in its quieter moments, chief among them the scenes showing Caine's stoic acceptance of his fate. At the end of the picture, his relationship with Stella wrecked by Zee's fiendish machinations, Caine's features seem to flatten and his eyes swim out of focus as he returns to Zee and embraces his doom. 'I'm still your baby,' says Zee, and Caine manages to look at once dubious and acquiescent as he lies his assent.

Impossible, though, to watch *Zee & Co* without a dreadful sense of opportunities missed, promises unfulfilled. Despite a warm review from *The New Yorker*'s Pauline Kael,[13] the movie did little business, and O'Brien went on the record and declared herself angry and heart-broken at the damage she considered Hutton to have inflicted on her script. Caine, however, got the good reviews he has never quite grown accustomed to: *Zee & Co* was a mess, but it had at least the virtue of suggesting that Caine could play more than bolshy Privates and cockneys on the make.

And because the Liz Taylor entourage included her then husband Richard Burton, the making of the movie had the virtue of showing Caine what too much drink could do to an actor. Spiky and paranoid, Burton made reference to 'Little Mickey Caine' in his notebooks of the time,[14] and there is other evidence that he felt challenged somewhat by Caine's presence. Swollen with liquor, Burton was a stumbling advertisement for the problems sudden wealth could bestow on a lower-class boy made good. At the movie's end-of-shoot party in mid-December 1971, Caine took his farewells and wished Burton a happy Christmas. 'Why don't you go and fuck yourself?' the Welshman rasped back. Caine has admitted to being bemused, baffled even, by Burton's hostility, though the facts of the matter are plain enough to an outsider's eye. Burton must have seen something of himself in Caine. Like Caine, after all, Burton had been the bright boy in an impoverished family. Like Caine, he had risen to fame on the back of the bloodless post-war cultural revolution (indeed, Burton had actually played John Osborne's ranting solipsist Jimmy Porter in the movie version of *Look Back in Anger* [1959]). Unlike Caine, though, Burton had proved unable to capitalize on his cinematic fame. His Hollywood performances were all overblown and orotund, and by the late sixties his career was in the doldrums. To Burton's jaundiced, bloodshot eyes Caine must have looked like the working-class boy who really was going to make good. And not because he had the greater talent (Burton was a far more varied and incandescent actor than Caine), but simply because he had the willingness to keep pushing himself on.

The best answer Caine could have made to Burton's somewhat unseasonal suggestion, then, was that he was far too busy working to have time for anything like that. Burton, on the other hand, had shown himself time and time again to be more than willing not only to fuck himself, but to fuck himself over. Michael Caine wasn't going to allow such a fate to overtake him.

Specs appeal: Caine with his wife Shakira. © British Film Institute

Man is a gaming animal. He must always be trying to get the better
in something or other.
    Charles Lamb[1]

Not that everything was fine and dandy for Caine. As Johnny Morris
had remarked of the *Play Dirty* shoot, Caine had a tendency to bore
people with the same old stories. And on Caine's own testimony he
was knocking vodka back at a prodigal rate as he approached the
classic age for a midlife crisis. Sometimes, he said, he was getting
through three bottles a day – not a record, perhaps, but certainly sufficient to have given Richard Burton and his like pause. Cocaine,
Robin Williams once quipped, is God's way of telling you you've got
too much money. Cocaine, of course, was not the drug of choice in the
early seventies, especially for a working-class lad made good. Had
Michael Caine been born ten years later, then drugs might have been
more his line. But for a man of his generation, booze was still the way
of staving off boredom and the blues. And as Caine's near namesake,
Charles Foster Kane, knew, boredom and the blues are an almost
inevitable by-product of success. After half a decade in the limelight,
Caine was beginning to wonder whether having everything was the
same as having what you wanted.

A possible answer to that problem hove into view one night as he
sat in his Grosvenor Square apartment nursing another drink. Hove
into view in, of all places, an ad for instant coffee that, like all ads for
instant coffee, like all ads for anything, centred on a drop-dead gor-
geous woman. Just like James Stewart with Kim Novak in *Vertigo*
(1958), Caine fell for her big time and determined to track her down.
Assuming, since she was appearing in a coffee ad, that she was a
Brazilian, he was all set to fly down to Rio in search of her, when Nigel
Politzer, a friend with advertising contacts, put him right. Her name
was Shakira Baksh. She was an Indian model who had come third in
the 1967 Miss World competition. But now she lived in London,
somewhere on the Fulham Road. Give him a few hours, said Politzer,
and he would mention Caine's name to her. A few hours after that
Caine was talking to her himself. A few days later they were dating.

Contacting a former beauty queen and asking her for a date might
sound ludicrously glamorous, but it's nothing out of the ordinary for
a big-time movie actor. Most people like to brag about any contact
they have had with the famous; for a Miss World runner-up the eti-

quette of PR all but dictates that she respond positively to an approach from an international movie star. So far, so run of the mill for a dual celebrity courtship. What was unusual about the courtship between Caine and Shakira is that it grew into a relationship and then a marriage. More than three decades on, the couple are still together and during all that time there hasn't been as much as a whisper that all has not been right between them. Caine took up with Shakira at a time when he was wondering, rather like Alfie in that movie's theme song, what it was all about. Through Shakira he came to realize that what it was all about, at least for him, was committing himself to someone else and sticking by that commitment. This was, of course, something he had signally failed to do with Patricia Haines and their daughter Dominique. Back then he had been too eager to get on, too much of a job-chaser to pay much attention to the politics of romance. This time around his career was simmering very nicely: no need for any boiling over in a relationship. It is not in any way to denigrate Caine's love of Shakira to say that it can be seen as another side of his professionalism, his seriousness about his work. Had he not married her, it is quite probable that his career would have gone awry, as so many British movie stars' careers did in the seventies.

So when the lease on his Grosvenor Square apartment ran out, Caine didn't bother to look for another place in town. Instead, he and Shakira, who had been shacked up in the Mayfair flat almost since they had met, decamped to Mill House and a life of rural domesticity on the Thames. They parted only when Caine had to fly off to Malta to make *Pulp* – the second and, as it turned out, final project of the Hodges/Klinger/Caine triumvirate. A week into making the movie, though, Shakira herself arrived in Malta and since then the couple have rarely been apart.

Caine's more laddish worshippers might like to think that Shakira tamed Caine, but that would be to overlook the fact that Caine was desperate to be tamed. 'It got to the stage where it wasn't fun anymore,'[2] he said of his old bachelor days, eighteen months or so after meeting Shakira. It hadn't, of course, got to the stage where the fun and games were affecting his work, but Caine was chary enough to know that such a stage might one day come. Richard Burton's injunction that Caine go fuck himself had precisely the reverse effect. He sorted himself out instead. Over the course of his past few movies, an incipient beer belly might have been seen cleaving to his once lean form. Caine didn't exactly slim down as the seventies wore on, but the weight he carried after taking up with Shakira was a product more of the Sunday lunches he would rustle up at home than of any post-shoot

drink-ups. Anyway, Caine worked off any excess eating in their exten-
sive grounds. From that day to this, he has remained a keen amateur
gardener. Two years before the oil crisis that finally put the mockers on
the sixties dream of casual revolution, Caine brought his own revels to
an end, finding inner peace with the flowers and trees in his garden at
Mill House.

There were few horticultural pleasures to be had on the island of
Malta, where Caine flew for the winter of 1971–2 to make *Pulp*
(1972). Indeed, asked by the BBC World Service during the shoot
what he liked best about Malta, Caine replied: 'The plane home.'[3]
Later, back home, Caine amplified the point: 'I adore trees and gardens, and Malta is the only land I've ever been to that has no trees. It
drove me bananas.'[4]

Perhaps it did, though Caine's discomfort and boredom clearly
came in handy while making the movie. Mickey King, Caine's character in *Pulp*, spends the bulk of the movie's ninety-odd minutes in a
state of amused bafflement, Caine spiking the mix with a twist of deli-
ciously louche indolence. *Pulp* is a leisurely movie, and Caine is almost
dogmatically relaxed throughout it, shambling and shuffling along,
perpetually two steps behind the narrative. While at first glance shape-
less, *Pulp* is in fact a tightly constructed little comedy thriller. Mike
Hodges worked on the script for more than six months, ending up, as
he himself admits, with a virtual retelling of *Get Carter*. Once again, a
girl has been raped and killed. Once again, the villains turn out to be
the local big-time mobsters all covering up for each other. If anything,
though, things are even more complicated this time around.

Caine's Mickey King is a writer from the school of Mickey Spillane,
holed up in the Mediterranean for purposes of tax evasion, who is
asked by his agent to ghostwrite the memoirs of former Hollywood
gangster-movie star, Preston Gilbert (Mickey Rooney), who now lives
in secluded secrecy nearby. On a coach journey during which he is to
make contact with one of Gilbert's companions, Mickey meets a camp
Lewis Carroll-quoting Mysterious Englishman (Dennis Price) and the
cross-dressing thriller fan Miller (Al Lettieri). Convinced that Miller is
his contact, Mickey goes to his room only to find him dead in a bath
streaked with blood. Eventually, someone does approach Mickey, Liz
Adams (Nadia Cassini), and finally he is introduced to the man whose
biography he is to write. No sooner is the book finished, though, than
a priest shoots Gilbert dead at a party and only narrowly misses killing
Mickey. Mickey turns detective and finds out that, years before, Gilbert
and a local politician had been involved in a sex and murder scandal

that they had succeeded in covering up. Now the politician, Prince Cippola (Victor Mercieca), fearing that Gilbert has told the story in his memoir, wants Mickey dead, too. But Mickey manages to kill the murderous priest, who turns out to be Miller in disguise, though not before taking a bullet in the leg. The movie ends with Mickey, his leg in plaster, dictating a new novel while being kept luxurious prisoner by Cippola and his wife (Lizabeth Scott).

If *Pulp*'s ending seems to evoke that of Evelyn Waugh's great 1934 novel *A Handful of Dust*, we should not be surprised. In Waugh's book, Tony Last is last seen the captive of a Dickens-loving loon, condemned endlessly to read *The Old Curiosity Shop* out loud to him. For Waugh, the book was a parable about civilization and barbarism: 'I wanted to discover how the prisoner got there,' he once said, 'and eventually the thing grew into a study of other sorts of savages at home and the civilized man's helpless plight amongst them.'5 He might have been describing *Pulp* or even, of course, *Get Carter*. Silly to pretend that Jack Carter was the last civilized man; nonetheless, like Waugh's hero, Carter is the only man within the confines of his narrative who can tell right from wrong. So, too, Mickey King. Mickey may turn out semi-pornographic thrillers with titles like *My Gun Is Long* and *The Organ Grinder* under pseudonyms such as Les Behan, but he is at least aware of the books' slipshod immorality. Caine's voice-over leaves us in no doubt as to the wry irony with which King looks on his hack status. Mickey is doing bad work, the words Caine has to say make clear, but the languorous, ironic drawl in which they are intoned makes it clear that he *knows* it is bad work.

In other words, Mickey King is a jokey update on the figure of the upright but compromised private eye of the great novels and *films noirs* of the forties. *Pulp* was the first of a trilogy of seventies movies that investigated the conventions of noir in the light of the new cynicism. Like Roman Polanski's *Chinatown* (1974), like Robert Altman's *The Long Goodbye* (1975), *Pulp* suggested that the honourable white knight of classic noir, the noble warrior cutting a moral swathe through the immoral swamp of capitalism, was now no more than a fantasy figure. After Vietnam, after Watergate, nobody believed in uncomplicated good guys any more.

Like *The Ipcress File*, then, *Pulp* offered Caine another chance to pay tribute to and comment on his fascination with Bogart. The presence of Bogie's some time co-star Lizabeth Scott,6 in her first movie appearance for fifteen years, can only have helped sway his decision to make the film. Instead of Bogart's wised-up scepticism, though, Caine's King has an air of naive goodness about him. *Pulp* was Caine's first movie in which he gets to smile and laugh without even a hint of malice. Though there is a knowing sexiness about the glint in his eye and the flash of his teeth, Caine's Mickey King is almost gleeful in his dumbness. The amiable stupidity Caine created for *Pulp* was to have a big influence on the way Sean Connery played many of his post-Bond parts. Unfortunately, it predicted little about what was to happen in Caine's career over the next few years. *Pulp* bombed at the box office, Mike Hodges moved more towards the straight Hollywood genres (*The Terminal Man* [1974], *Flash Gordon* [1980]), and for a good few years Caine let his gift for light comedy go hang.

Yet Caine's King is a masterpiece of gentle fun. Long-haired and big-jacketed and wearing spectacles the size of TV screens, Caine ambles through this movie of car crashes and murderous priests – Hodges has admitted to having been influenced greatly by that other soufflé of wit, John Huston's *Beat the Devil* (1954)[7] – the only straight man amid a gaggle of gigglers. At one point he has to repeat a joke from the Peter Sellers/Bryan Forbes movie *Only Two Can Play* (1962) and deliberately spill the contents of a ritzy cigarette box. But where Sellers went into panicky overdrive, Caine is content to motor along in second gear, a look of contented confusion playing across his features. The story *Pulp* tells, in other words, is no more than a McGuffin devised by Hodges to let Caine have some semi-somnolent fun in front of the camera. Given what they achieved here, it is a crying shame they have never worked together again. All the great stars need an occasional movie in which they can cool down and play gently, almost self-mockingly, to the camera. Robert Redford's career is made up almost entirely of such pictures. In a sense, *Pulp* takes us as near as anything Caine has ever done to the figure he bodies forth in interviews and on chat shows – the laid-back raconteur who somehow contrives to never miss a trick. Had the movie been a bigger hit, his subsequent career might have looked very different. As it was, it had at least the effect of making known to even the most doubtful observer that Caine was not going to be shackled by his past achievements. In the sixties he had been thought of, indeed, had wanted to be thought of, as a star. As the seventies got into their stride he made it clear that he was actually that rarer thing – a star who is also a character actor.

Indeed, Caine was cast in *Sleuth* (1972) at the suggestion of Sir Laurence Olivier. Albert Finney and Alan Bates were also under consideration for the part of the chippy, hairdressing upstart Milo Tindle, but in the event Caine was a shoo-in. Finney was deemed too portly and Bates thought the part beneath him. Sent by the producer Morton

Gottlieb to see the play on which the movie was based, Bates walked
out at the interval (by which time Milo appears to be dead) believing
such a small part unbecoming for an actor of his stature.[8] In fact, the
role is as wordy a one as exists in the English-speaking theatre, though
it is matched in volubility by the show's other character, Andrew
Wyke. Neither he nor Milo ever shuts up.

Class war: Caine and Laurence Olivier on the set of *Sleuth*. © British Film
Institute

A writer of old-fashioned country-house detective fiction, Wyke
might have been invented to bear out Christopher Booker's aforementioned suggestion that the seventies were a time for nostalgia.[9] For
Wyke, thirties' Britain was a golden age after which everything has
gone wrong. A huge hit in London's West End, on Broadway, and subsequently all over the world, *Sleuth* is – its creator Anthony Shaffer
once said – 'a metaphor for the huge distinctions between pre-war and
post-war Britain . . . in a way an aria for a lost, traditional Britain'.[10]
It is also a drama about the destructive gamesmanship inherent in
masculinity. But then Shaffer, who had written the screenplay for
Frenzy (the Hitchcock movie Caine had turned down) and was working on *The Wicker Man* (1973) while Sleuth was being shot, was a

consummate gamesman himself. His black comedies are constantly upsetting their audiences' preconceptions.

Sleuth takes place in just the kind of isolated country house in which Wyke sets his own thrillers. Wiltshire is referred to in the course of the action – though the movie's exteriors were actually shot down the road in Dorset's Athelhampton House – and Wyke has every inch cast himself as the local Lord of the Manor. His guest for the evening is Milo Tindle, a young London hairdresser who has recently rented himself a weekend cottage in the neighbourhood. Preliminary drinks and politenesses over, Wyke informs Tindle that he knows he is having an affair with his wife. Which is fine, so long as he has the money to take her off his hands properly; the last thing Wyke wants is for her to come back to him a few months down the line. Hence, he explains, his cunning plan: Tindle should 'steal' the jewellery Wyke has given his wife over the years. Tindle can then sell it to raise cash, while Wyke claims the insurance: everybody wins. Alas for Milo, the great detective novelist has a more cunning plan than that. The 'robbery' has in fact been staged to give Wyke a motive for shooting Tindle: he will tell the police that he was merely defending his property against intruders. As the curtain goes down at the end of Act I, Milo is lying dead on the floor of Wyke's manor house.

In Act II (and the movie is shot with all the strictures of the theatrical in place; there is no doubt about the break in the drama) a policeman, Inspector Doppler (Alec Cawthorne), calls on Wyke to ascertain the whereabouts of the now-missing Tindle. Wyke is mystified. He didn't really kill him, he explains, merely fired a blank, whereupon he fainted. When the inspector finds Tindle's clothes in Wyke's cellar, though, Wyke panics, and Doppler, just before arresting his prey . . . tears off his disguise to reveal that he is Milo exacting his revenge. At which point Wyke *really does* shoot Tindle and the police *really do* show up.

All very complicated, though doubtless very satisfactorily so on stage. On the movie screen, however, *Sleuth* – directed by Hollywood veteran Joseph Mankiewicz – lumbers along, laden down with expository dialogue. So much expository dialogue that Lord Olivier found it hard to remember his lines. During the filming of one scene, set around Wyke's billiard table, for instance, Olivier took great care to pot the balls but failed to say which one he was going to pot (as the script required him to do). Nor was this an isolated instance made difficult by Olivier's concentration on the snooker.[11] Throughout the shoot Olivier was forever halting takes with an 'Oh, shit' or a 'Sorry, Joe.' According to one observer, such dry-ups 'became agonising for the crew members, who, as the takes dragged on, tended to drift away from the set or turned their heads in embarrassment'.[12] 'His memory was not at its best,' Anthony Shaffer wrote in his autobiography, 'and takes often went into the twenties and thirties.'[13] The problem was that, used to the long rehearsal process of the theatre, Olivier found it hard to keep up with the compressions of movie-making. Asking Caine for help with his lines, Olivier was told by his co-star to 'forget about yesterday's and tomorrow's, and just concentrate on the pages we're shooting today'.[14] Within days of commencing, however, the production fell a week behind its projected ten-week shooting schedule.

Caine had bigger problems with Olivier than his forgetting his lines, though. While Olivier had chosen Caine to play opposite him, it quickly became clear he had done so in the hope of besting him. Olivier had a habit of picking the optimal spot on the set for any given scene and then just standing there so that Caine had to act around him. If any line of Caine's interfered with Olivier's move, on the other hand, His Lordship would ask Mankiewicz to cut it. During one two-shot – a medium close-up of Olivier's and Caine's profiles talking to one another – Olivier contrived to move slightly upstage, forcing Caine to have to turn his back half to the camera. 'When he's not at your feet,' Caine griped to Mankiewicz, 'he's at your throat.'[15] The director, though, told Caine not to worry. He knew what was going on and would be able to sort everything out in the editing room.

Deliberate or not, this was the best direction Mankiewicz could have given Caine. Caine's constant fear of being tricked and upstaged by Olivier chimes perfectly with the movie's central dramatic dynamic, lending an otherwise stilted and silly melodrama a patina of realism it desperately needs. In that light, Olivier's off-screen teasing of Caine that when he held his head in a certain way he looked 'like the late lamented Leslie Howard' made aesthetic sense too. Caine's response, at least according to Shaffer, went like this: 'Oh, 'im, 'e always looked as though butter wouldn't melt in 'is mouth, but I can tell you 'e 'ad all 'is leading ladies whoppo straight up.' Then, says Shaffer, Caine used his forearm to make a phallic gesture. At which point Olivier sneered: 'Not, I believe, in *Gone with the Wind*.' 'Not 'er, of course,' gabbled Caine, remembering that Vivien Leigh – Olivier's wife at the time – had been the star of that movie. 'Of course it wouldn't be 'er. Nah, there was nothing like that! . . . Not with Vivien.'[16] That could be the Wyke and Tindle of *Sleuth*'s first act awkwardly discussing their mutual bedfellow.

The casting of Olivier and Caine crystallizes, too, the tension between old-style British gent and nouveau arriviste at the heart of the drama. Wyke really does think things were better back in the thirties. Tindle sees things rather differently. The son of a first-generation Italian immigrant who fled the Nazis only to wash up in a depression-hit Britain, he has carved out a career for himself in that entrepreneurial emblem of the Swinging Sixties, hairdressing.[17] Compare that with the real lives of Olivier and Caine. On the one hand, we have the public-school beauty who during the thirties made his reputation as the great romantic lead of his day. On the other, we have the fish porter's son whose memories of the same decade are of poverty and gangster movies.

Sleuth, then, makes most sense not in terms of narrative but rather in terms of a clash of acting techniques and generations: the throwback Shakespearean rhetorician against the up-to-the-minute cinematic realist. Olivier's initial response to the dramatic revolution that had ushered in Caine and his like had been to star in John Osborne's successor to *Look Back in Anger, The Entertainer*. Olivier played Archie Rice, a music-hall entertainer convinced that England used to be a good country but that everything went wrong some time in the recent past. Olivier's first major post-angry young man role, in other words, was a hymn to everything the angries were deemed to have destroyed. In a sense, *Sleuth*'s Andrew Wyke is no more than an update of this role, although his romanticism is rather more active than Archie's: Wyke is determined that things shall actually *be* as they once were.

The casting of Olivier and Caine in *Sleuth* deepened Shaffer's callow theatrical contrivance, turning the movie into an examination of what the likes of Michael Caine had done to the theatre and the cinema and, by extension, Britain as a whole. Mankiewicz has said that he 'wanted to bring more emphasis to the class struggle that . . . was implicit in the play'[18] and feared that critics missed the subtlety with which Caine's Tindle lapses at times of terror from the received pronunciation he has taught himself into the strangulated cockney he grew up speaking. Olivier caught this tension perfectly when, shortly before rehearsals began in April 1972, he wrote to Caine suggesting that when they meet 'I shall be the Lord Olivier and you Mr Caine.'[19] The wind having been knocked out of Caine's sails, Olivier went on to insist that subsequently they would, of course, simply address one another as Larry and Michael. It sounds generous and thoughtful, but can more fruitfully be read as a sign of Olivier's dedication to his work. Even before rehearsals had begun, Olivier was getting into his part as the haughty aristocrat determined to put the young upstart in his place. It was, in a sense, a Method actor's approach to his work. Like Brando, like De Niro, Olivier was sousing himself in his role for the duration. (As such, it throws into relief Olivier's treatment of that other Method actor Dustin Hoffmann when the two of them were shooting *Marathon Man* [1976]. Hoffmann, who played a runner who undergoes some non-anaesthetised dental work at Olivier's hands, insisted on getting into part both by training every morning and having some fillings removed to understand the pain his character would have to endure. 'My dear boy,' Olivier said to a jaw-clutching Hoffmann one day, 'why don't you try acting.')

Caine, on the other hand, was the relaxed professional he always was, determined not to be fazed by the older, honoured, Shakespearean. Nor was he; perhaps because, despite Shaffer's intentions, it is only the part of Milo Tindle that requires any real acting. Tindle has to break down tearily in the face of his own imminent and sudden death, has to get angry at his humiliation and the whole structure of class relations behind it, has, indeed, to become someone else for a large part of the second half of the movie. The part of Wyke, meanwhile, requires little more than some delicate posturing and mimicry. As Mankiewicz said of Olivier, 'There is no actor in the world who can do as much, from all his work in Restoration comedy, with a peruke and snuff box as Larry.[20]' Which is all very well, though the fact remains that marvellous as such moments in *Sleuth* are, they are as rarefied as Archie Rice's music-hall turn. Olivier's fireworks – rare are his utterances in the movie that fail to scale and descend an octave and a half – are a joy to behold, but it is Caine who sets things ablaze. It would be foolish to claim that the movie stretched Caine as an actor, but *Sleuth* had the virtue of demonstrating that there was still plenty in him to stretch. Whether he would ever get a chance to prove the point was to look more and more unlikely as the seventies wore on.

A good name is rather to be chosen than great riches.
Proverbs[1]

Type-cast: Joseph Losey directs Caine on the set of *The Romantic Englishwoman.*
© British Film Institute

By the time *Sleuth*'s grinding sixteen-week shoot at Pinewood Studios finally wrapped towards the end of August 1972, Caine had decided to give himself his first break of any real duration in the best part of a decade. His fortieth birthday was little more than six months away and it was, perhaps, time to take stock. His relationship with Shakira had had the most stabilizing influence on him of anything since the

success of *The Ipcress File*. After she and Caine had moved into
Mill House full-time, he had, he said, become 'something of a home
body . . . when I'm not working in the garden . . . I'm watching telly'.[2]
The house having some seven acres of land, he had plenty of work to
do. 'I love pottering around . . . digging up things and pruning. The
gardener has to hide the shears from me. It's that bad. Incapability
Brown they call me.'[3]

Stabilizing as Shakira was on him, though, Caine had no plans to
marry again. If a desire for fame had wrecked his first marriage, then
the satisfaction of that desire had wrecked any romantic ideas he
might have had about long-term relationships in general. 'The single
me is a very happy man,' he said. 'The married me is a very uptight
one.'[4] Warming to the theme a few weeks later he admitted that 'the
problem with me and women, and it *is* a problem, is that, basically,
someone in my position doesn't know whether they want you for
yourself, or what you represent.'[5] He was, though, honest enough to
admit that his philosophy was as much pragmatic as it was idealist: 'I
would [get married again] if the world had stopped still around 1945.
But with the new morality in which perfectly respectable girls don't
mind living with a man they aren't married to – it doesn't seem necessary.'[6] That new morality was about to be tested, though – tested and
found wanting, moreover, by Caine's instinctive small-c conservatism.
Little more than a month after he had uttered those words, Shakira
told Caine she was pregnant. Little more than three months after that,
the couple were married and were rarely apart for the duration of the
pregnancy. The memories Caine had of his abandonment of his first
child weighed heavy on him still, it would seem.

Sleuth was scheduled to open in the US just before Christmas (in
time to be considered for the Academy Awards nominations; the
movie was not released in the UK until the autumn of 1973) and Caine
took the opportunity of adding a small holiday on to the attendant
publicity tour. And so, on 8 January 1973, nine weeks before he
turned forty, Caine and Shakira snuck off to Nevada for a Vegas wedding. 'It was like one of those weddings you see in a corny movie,' he
remembered many years later. 'My best man was my press agent and
my agent gave the bride away. The agent paid for the wedding: 180
bucks. They gave you orchids to wear, which cost six bucks each, but
if you gave them back they gave you a buck each, so in the end it was
only $174. I think it was a pretty good bargain. I come from a very
happy family and history repeats itself.'[7]

It repeated itself at the Academy Awards, too. Caine's performance in
Sleuth had been nominated for a Best Actor Oscar (as had Olivier's),

though once again he fell at the last fence. The award was taken by Marlon Brando for his part in *The Godfather* (1972). Caine, who was accompanied to the ceremony by the now fifteen-year-old Dominique, was upset, though less at his not having won than at Brando's refusing to pick up his prize in protest at what he saw as the plight of the American Indians. Ever the professional, ever the craftsman, Caine just couldn't see what politics had to do with matters show-business.

Something of Brando's Don Corleone, however, seems to have rubbed off on Caine. Though he had plans to name the impending baby, should it be a boy, Richard ('after Ricu Blaine, the part Humphrey Bogart played in *Casablanca*'[8]), his basic fantasy at the time derived from Francis Ford Coppola's movie. 'I fanc[y] myself living in a big house, surrounded by adoring children,' he said. 'A sort of peaceful godfather.'[9] A few weeks later, on 15 July 1973, the peaceful godfather's wife gave birth to a daughter, Natasha Halima. The Caines' happiness was not, unfortunately, to last long. Later that same day one of Natasha's lungs collapsed and for the next two or three weeks the couple were on tenterhooks as to whether or not their baby would live. Unfortunately for him, Caine was also on set again, and perhaps for the first time in his career his personal life had an effect on his professional one. Though Natasha did in the end pull through, the same cannot be said of the movie Caine had begun work on.

Strangely enough, *The Black Windmill* (1974) was Caine's first film in which he plays a father.[10] Moreover, he plays a father who is in danger of losing his child – though not to ill health, but to a gang of gun-runners. Caine plays Major John Tarrant in Don Siegel's crisp little espionage thriller, filmed largely around London, Britain's south coast and Paris. When Tarrant's son David (Paul Moss) is kidnapped, the ransom demand is for half a million pounds of uncut diamonds. By curious coincidence, Tarrant's boss, Cedric Harper (Donald Pleasence), has just taken delivery of precisely that amount of jewels, but he and his superior, Sir Edward Julyan (Joseph O'Connor), refuse to sanction the use of the stones and Tarrant is forced to take matters into his own hands.

The Black Windmill is essentially the story of Tarrant's maturing as a father and a husband. At the start of the movie he is separated from his wife Alex (Janet Suzman) and son and living a life of indolent bachelordom. David's kidnapping serves to wake Tarrant up to the real joys in his life, to make him realize what is important. In effect, the movie is a mishmash of two of Hitchcock's fifties masterpieces. Like Cary Grant's Roger Thornhill in *North by Northwest* (1959),

Tarrant is wrung through the mechanisms of the thriller in order that he might be humanized. As with the James Stewart of *The Man Who Knew Too Much* (1956), Tarrant's son is kidnapped and this crisis affords a reappraisal of his life, his work, his marriage. Throw in a Paris car chase, a daring robbery and a shoot-out at an isolated windmill and you have all the ingredients of a top-notch thriller. One, moreover, iced with the chance for Caine to do some real acting as Tarrant moves from being a secret-service automaton ('Isn't that what I'm trained to do – hide my feelings?') to a full-blooded human being. Somewhere along the way, though, something went wrong, and it has to be said that for the first time in his ten years as a star the something that went wrong was Caine.

Don Siegel, an old Hollywood pro who had sealed his reputation in recent years by defining the essential Clint Eastwood persona in movies as different as *Coogan's Bluff* (1968), *Two Mules for Sister Sara* (1970) and *Dirty Harry* (1971), had wanted Caine from day one. Though Siegel's boss, Lew Wasserman, had his eye on Edward Fox (whose glinting cool had served him so well in *The Day of the Jackal* [1973]), Siegel held out for Caine's rather more enigmatic charms. 'There are other actors who are tougher, more handsome, more emotive,' he was quoted in the movie's press book, 'but there was only one with a centre solid enough to convey the very complex undertones of this role.'

The problem was that while Siegel, as his work with Eastwood showed, favoured the kind of steely underplaying Caine had spent years perfecting, he may have actually encouraged his star to do too little here. Caine doesn't so much underplay Tarrant as undercut him. At one point, arguing with his bosses when they refuse to give him the diamonds, Caine's Tarrant has to explode: 'All I can think about now is my son!' Quite so, though Caine's reading of the line, flat and uninterested as a bus conductor's 'Where to?', suggests contrariwise that he has rather a lot of other stuff on his mind, all of it taking precedence over his getting his inflections right.

Which, of course, he did. '*The Black Windmill* . . . all passed in rather a blur,' Caine has said.[11] '[It's] a movie that I remember almost nothing about.'[12] A movie that nobody else can remember a thing about either, thanks in large part to Caine's lacklustre performance. As such, this was Caine's first big missed opportunity – a serious thriller that would have allowed him the chance to scrape away at the affectless carapace he had worn for the best part of the past decade. But with Siegel less than committed to the project,[13] and with Caine's mind elsewhere, *The Black Windmill* was always likely to spin off its axis. It was a mistake for which Caine was to pay heavily. Had this movie (and his performance in it) worked out, it might have saved him from so much of the dross that was to constitute the bulk of his mid-to-late seventies output. As things were, though, they were about to go from bad to worse.

If The *Black Windmill* had looked good on paper, *The Marseille Contract* (1974) must have looked lousy from the moment it hit Caine's doormat. Or rather it would have done had Caine bothered to read it. Instead he read the location dates – a 1973–4 winter shoot on the French Riviera – and agreed on the basis of the more agreeable weather he would likely encounter there. 'I was offered a part which started in Nice, went on to Cannes, then St Tropez, Marseilles and ended up in Paris. They said "will you do it," I said "Yes," they said "we'll send you a script," I said, "don't bother." '14 Hard not to smile when one hears such off-the-cuff repartee, but hard not to shake one's head, too. Reputations, after all, are lost much more easily than they are won.

Part of the problem with the movie, it has to be admitted, is that Caine was hardly moving into mid-life gracefully. As freelance hitman Johnny Deray, a man of state-of-the-art stereos and slash-cut leather jerkins, Caine is clearly meant to cut something of a dash. But with that once incipient, now all too present, pot belly straining at his leathers, Caine looks less a mercenary killer than an ageing rock star. Even that salty old ham Anthony Quinn, whom Caine had run rings around in *The Magus* only five years earlier, comes better out of *The Marseille Contract* than its ostensible leading man.

Whether it was Robert Parrish's direction or Caine's gamely trying to send the movie up, the decision to play Deray – putatively the most lethal assassin of his age – as a lascivious winker and grinner was a mistaken one. Signing up for the movie's titular contract – which calls for Deray to put a bullet in James Mason's befuddled drug-runner Jacques Brizard – Caine is all laughing eyes and flashing teeth: its the day of cackle. Yes, the wintry south of France locations do look lovely, so Caine got what he wanted, but like Deray (who writes his own Marseille contract while the first movement of Beethoven's fifth symphony – the one about the entrance of death, wouldn't you know – plays on his stereo) he ought never to have signed on the bottom line. None of us likes to turn work down, but there is some work that has to be turned down if we want to carry on going up.

Then there is the work we are drawn to for the wrong reasons. And Caine accepted his role in his next movie, a South African-set thriller called *The Wilby Conspiracy* (1975), on utterly erroneous grounds.

Caine's heart, like that of this vigorously anti-apartheid picture, was in the right place. The trouble was that the rest of *The Wilby Conspiracy*'s broken-backed body was all over the place. Caine took on the movie because, while shooting *Zulu* in Africa a decade earlier, he had grown to hate the segregation of blacks and whites. Subsequently, his marriage to Shakira (who accompanied him to Kenya for the shoot; the South African authorities refused permission for the movie to be made in their country) had only made firmer his opposition. But a personal moral code is one thing. Making movies whose basic intention is to thrust that moral code down the throats of its audience quite another.

If you want to send a message, they say in Hollywood, call Western Union. This time around they called Ralph Nelson and Sidney Poitier. Nelson, who had directed the original American version of *Requiem for a Heavyweight* (Caine, it will be remembered, played opposite Sean Connery in the British TV remake) and the anti-Vietnam western *Soldier Blue* (1970), had made a name for himself as a cinematic liberal. *The Wilby Conspiracy* ought to have been a fast-moving chase thriller that just happens to have things to say about relations between the races. In Nelson's hands, however, it turned into a clunking slice of agitprop that not even the combined efforts of Caine and Poitier could breathe life into.

As Olivier had done a couple of years before, Poitier took top billing off Caine, though there was some justice to this. Although Poitier has far the easier part to play, he plays it with rather greater aplomb than Caine does his. Poitier is Shack Twala, a black-rights activist just released from ten years in prison who pals up with mining engineer Jim Keogh (Caine) when he is assaulted by a pair of racist cops. Cue the standard Huck and Nigger Jim cross-country chase as Twala and Keogh flee the forces of oppression. Caine is at his best in these early scenes with Poitier, blustering and bellowing and generally playing the mismatched buddies routine for laughs. The problem is that good as Caine is at cranking up the fun quotient, Nelson keeps on hitting the serious brake. The desired effect may be a tonally various drama, but the actual result is confusion. Is Nicol Williamson's State Security honcho Major Horn, for instance, a fascist demon or a figure of fun? Nelson can't make up his mind, and even the best actors are useless with a directionless director at the helm.

Caine, though, took the wrong lesson from the experience. When *The Wilby Conspiracy* bombed at the box office he regarded it as proof that making anti-racist movies was a waste of time because racist people won't go and see them. Rightly perceiving that the film 'fell between every stool you could possibly have', he went on to wrongly conclude that 'the mass of people agree with apartheid because they didn't bother to see [the film]'.[15] It may be, of course, that the mass of people did agree with apartheid, though you could neither prove nor disprove the proposition from the takings of a movie. All you could conclude from the fact that people fought shy of seeing *The Wilby Conspiracy* was that audiences tend to stay away from movies that can't decide whether they are thrillers or comedies or comedy thrillers. The movie's 'message' is neither here nor there, since according to Caine's logic people only go and see films that concur with their core beliefs. By that measure, had *The Wilby Conspiracy* garnered a bigger audience, that audience would have had to have been made up of people already in tune with the movie's anti-apartheid sentiment. It would, therefore, have been preaching to the converted – and accordingly just as much a waste of everyone's time as it was in Caine's own scenario.

The picture's interiors were shot at Pinewood Studios, and during their weeks there together, Sidney Poitier and his wife Joanna often accompanied Caine and Shakira to dinner. Poitier's favourite restaurant in London was a place called Odin's just off the Marylebone High Street where, on one occasion, the Caine/Poitier table was accosted by a slobbering drunk – a slobbering drunk who turned out to know Poitier very well. It was Peter Langan, the owner of the joint and the man with whom a couple of years later Caine would team up to open a new restaurant – Langan's. Caine, who invested £25,000 in the venture, had visions of opening London's answer to one of Paris's most famous restaurants, La Coupole. Grand and yet utterly without airs, La Coupole is the kind of restaurant London is now full of but three decades ago was not.

In looking to diversify his interests, Caine was sensible of the way the British economy was heading as the seventies moved into their middle period. Inflation had been rising steadily for a few years, taxes likewise, and wealthy Britons like Caine were seeing the bulk of their income being taken away from them by the pre-monetarist Labour government of 1974–5. 'I've no idea what I'm personally worth,' he said shortly after *The Wilby Conspiracy* had wrapped, 'but I intend to remain worth it.'[16] What was causing him particular grievance at the time was the government's projected Wealth Tax on possessions and investments. Yet though Caine talked of leaving England for America as early as 1974, it was to be another five years before he eventually made the move. Instead, he stayed at home in the countryside he loved, taking whatever work came his way and spending his earnings on the art-deco pieces he both admired and had long-term investment hopes for.

Not that money was his sole guide. He took the part of Lewis Fielding in Joseph Losey's *The Romantic Englishwoman* (1975), for instance, because he despised the character. Fielding was a top-selling novelist ('Ten thousand in hardback') with a swish house in the Surrey stockbroker belt, a big car and a beautiful wife Elizabeth (Glenda Jackson), who kick-starts the movie by setting off for Baden Baden, there to find herself. Instead, she finds Thomas Hursa (Helmut Berger), a perpetually bescarfed gigolo who kisses her in the elevator on his way to the hotel roof, where he plans to conceal the drugs he is smuggling. Or does he? The viewer is never sure how much of the action is actually going on and how much of it is the product of Fielding's wilfully excited imagination. Fielding, you see, is working on his own film script, and it is about a marriage that is coming apart. So when, shortly after Elizabeth's return home, Thomas turns up on the couple's doorstep, it is Fielding himself who invites him in and offers him a job: he needs this young interloper around to fire his imagination and help him set up scenes of eternal triangulation.

All very Losey-like. Even the most dedicatedly anti-auteurist critic, after all, could hardly fail to spot that the recurrent motif in Losey's movies is that of the stranger who interrupts the status quo of the central couple. It is right there from his earliest days in Hollywood – *The Prowler* (1951) – through his blacklisted days in England – *The Sleeping Tiger* (1954) – and on to his late masterpieces – *The Servant* (1963) and *Accident* (1967); the very title of *The Go-Between* (1970) delineates precisely Losey's chief thematic concern. For *The Romantic Englishwoman*, though, Losey appears to have conceived of his favourite subject in both a figurative and a metaphoric way. The stranger was to intrude on the Fieldings' marriage in Losey's habitual way, but he was to stand, too, as an emblem of the way that art invades the artist and infects his relations with the real world. Concretizing this last – dangerously abstract – notion was the difficult task that fell to Caine.

It is a task that he has subsequently characterized as pointless and wasteful, calling the movie 'my first (and hopefully last) foray into the realms of "artistic films" '.[17] And yet the film, which commenced shooting in Weybridge on 21 October 1974,[18] is not without its strengths. Chief among them is Caine's performance itself, his most delicately modulated since *Pulp* and *Get Carter* under Mike Hodges. A Brechtian Marxist dedicated to pulling the rug from under the feet of the bourgeoisie, Losey was rather more of an intellectual director than Caine was accustomed to. Yet though Caine's class-consciousness had never been vaguely leftist, and though Losey had all the humourlessness of the die-hard radical (Caine lost a bet that he could make

Losey laugh while they were working together), the two men were fond enough of each other's company.

'The book [by Thomas Wiseman] was about a man who thinks that he is an important writer,' Losey has said. 'From the beginning I thought that the only way it works is that this writer is a non-writer – he's a wealthy man that's made his money out of shit. And he's constantly sucking other people dry to try and make his shit less shitty, more real.'[19] Caine's Fielding is the puppet master of a shallow little show, in other words, and the chief virtue of the film is Caine's rendition of a man shrinking into himself as the poison he spreads around him begins to seep into his own system. Early on in the movie he has a marvellous scene in which he harangues Elizabeth's journalist friend Isabel (Kate Nelligan) for thinking in what he sees as feminist clichés. Caine begins the scene by selecting and lighting an enormous cigar, as if to stoke up his manhood, and he even contrives to find a way of sitting cross-legged that suggests suppressed violence. He stands up, though, to deliver himself of some of his more objectionable opinions ('washing men's underpants is what you were meant to do') and at this point the performance takes on a new mantle of theatricality. Roving round the room between his wife and her friend, Caine's Fielding becomes a kind of brained-up version of Stanley Kowalski, a point-scoring strutter toying with the feelings of others in a bid to add weight to the fictional creations in his study upstairs. Caine's bigger achievement in the movie, though, is to suggest the pain and the anger behind this tough-guy façade, the sense of a man whose struggle with his creativity is really a struggle with his soul. Pallid and immobile, Caine's face in *The Romantic Englishwoman* has all the chill calculation of Jack Carter's, but with an added air of self-lacerating despair. For all his doubts about the movie after it was finished, Caine had none about his own role in it: 'I thoroughly enjoyed playing it,' he said.[20]

The bad reviews were stacking up again. Though *Sleuth* had been much discussed, four years had passed since Caine had had a really good notice. And *Peeper* (1975), a pastiche cum parody of the forties private-eye movie he had actually shot before *The Romantic Englishwoman* but which was not released until several months after that picture, did nothing to change things. The movie was so nondescript it merits not one mention in Caine's autobiography.

When Peter Hyams' script turned up at Mill House, though, it must have looked like a dream come true. Caine was finally getting the chance to play the role he had fantasized about since his youth – that of the Humphrey Bogart figure in *The Big Sleep*. Alas, things did not work out quite like that. For one thing, Caine had not Lauren Bacall but Natalie Wood to work with. Wood was a woman of more than ample charms (for the purposes of the movie she had gone on an 800-calorie-a-day diet so that she might regain the 22-inch waist she had boasted before taking time out to have children) – a doe-eyed, dark-eyed Russian temptress with cheekbones you could cut yourself on. But beyond a kind of despairing passion she was unable to communicate any emotion.

The production for the movie, however, was sumptuous. Every period detail was in its place, the whole photographed by Earl Rath with a warm but narrow desaturated palette that gave *Peeper* the look of a monochrome picture that had been subtly colourized. It burned with nostalgia. Certainly, Hyams (director as well as writer) had no interest in interrogating the genre he was working in. Unlike *Chinatown* and *The Long Goodbye* (those *noir* deconstructions on which we have already touched), *Peeper* offered no more than an unquestioning, affectionate look back to an era it romantically perceived as a simpler and more honest one.

Caine has a great time grafting his own essentially chippy persona on to the instinctive insurrection of the private eye. His accent in the movie is his most stridently cockney since *Alfie*, while he manages to make the dialogue sound like Chandler sieved through John Osborne: 'The place looked like it hadn't been occupied for months,' says Caine's Leslie Tucker at one point, 'although with rich people you can never tell.' The problem is that while Caine is having a high old time of it, the audience is struggling to maintain interest in what is meant to be passing for the action. *Peeper* turned out to be just another embarrassment on the Caine CV.

Certainly he changed his mind about the fun the movie had been when he saw the reviews. The seventies were halfway over and Caine's career, like the British economy, was heading south. Fortunately for him, the ghost of Bogart was coming his way again, and this time it was going to be a help rather than a hindrance.

Better to be king for a day than a schmuck for a whole lifetime.
  The King of Comedy[1]

Crowning glory: Caine with Sean Connery & Christopher Plummer in *The Man Who Would Be King*. © British Film Institute

John Huston had written his original script for *The Man Who Would Be King* in the early fifties. Adapting from a short story by Rudyard Kipling, his mind's eye cast in the lead parts two of his favourite stars from Hollywood's golden age: Clark Gable and Humphrey Bogart. Shown the script, the two actors agreed to the project, but before any work could commence on the movie Bogart died. A few years later, while they were filming *The Misfits* (1961), Gable suggested to Huston that they dust the script off and film it with someone else. Huston agreed, but then Gable died.

Another decade on, while Huston was filming the Paul Newman private-eye thriller *The Mackintosh Man* (1973), the producer John Foreman came across Huston's sketches for the fifties production that never was and had an idea. Foreman had been the man behind the late sixties runaway hit *Butch Cassidy and the Sundance Kid* (1969), a movie whose blockbuster status stemmed chiefly from the marvellous relationship between its two stars: Newman and Robert Redford. Indeed, as soon as *The Mackintosh Man* wrapped, Newman was off to shoot another movie with Redford – *The Sting* (1973). Why not, Foreman asked Huston, cast the two men opposite each other a third time, this time in *The Man Who Would Be King*?

Newman took a look at Huston's original script, complete with suggestions for the alterations necessary for the new stars, and nodded his head in agreement. Accordingly, Huston went off with the screen-writer Gladys Hill to cuff a new screenplay into shape. But when Newman saw this one, though he still liked it tremendously, he decid-ed to opt out. Wouldn't it be better, he suggested to Huston, if this movie about Victorian imperialism starred a couple of British actors? In fact, he thought he knew the two British actors who'd be perfect for Huston's project. 'For Christ's sake, John,' Huston remembers Newman telling him, 'get Connery and Caine.'[2] Foreman having sub-sequently delivered himself of the opinion that Caine 'really is one of the most underestimated actors',[3] Britain's two biggest stars of the sixties – and the only two to have sustained their careers through into the next decade – were finally cast in *The Man Who Would Be King* (1975). And what a piece of casting it was. As Huston was to say just months before he died: 'I believe Connery and Caine gave better per-formances than either Bogart or Gable could have, because they are the real thing. They are those characters.'[4] Indeed, when, a couple of years after the movie's release, Caine and Connery visited Huston in hospital, he greeted them as Danny and Peachy.[5]

Huston had called Caine while he and Shakira were staying on what they called one of their mini-honeymoons in Paris. Huston, it tran-spired, was staying in the hotel next door. Would Caine care to pop round? Since Huston was one of the directors Caine had long wanted to work with, he was on his way in a flash.[6] And as soon as Huston told Caine he had him in mind for the role Bogart was originally to have played, Caine accepted on the spot. After all those years of hero wor-ship, after all those years of playing imitations or parodies of Bogart, he was finally getting the chance to incarnate a character that had been created with the man himself in mind. Caine went back to Shakira with a spring in his step. It was, he later said, 'a marvellous role for me, humour, a good change of pace, a real gift'.7

During the making of the movie, which commenced shooting in the second week of January 1975, Caine and Connery finally cemented their friendship. They had been friendly enough for the best part of twenty years, of course, but only on *The Man Who Would Be King*'s fourteen-week shoot in the hills around Marrakesh did they really get to know one another. What drew them together was their mutual professionalism.

At least since the making of *Sleuth*, Caine had had qualms about appearing on screen opposite other big stars. Olivier had used every trick in his huge book to wrongfoot Caine during production of that movie, and Caine had vowed never to let anyone try anything similar with him again. He need not, though, have had any such fears about Connery. Throughout Connery's long career, the most oft-heard comment made about him is that for an international star – an international star, moreover, famed for his great beauty – he is a man curiously lacking in vanity. No sooner had he sloughed off the restrictive skin of James Bond, for instance, than he was willing to appear on screen minus his hairpiece, revealing his bald pate to one and all. Thirty years ago, in the age of the comb-over and the toupee, this was unusual behaviour. But it was more unusual still in the movie world. One need think only of the tortuous tonsorial teasings of Roger Moore – Connery's successor as 007 – to see how rare such physical candour is.

But Connery's lack of ego extended to the acting process itself. Not for him the secret desire to do his co-star down in every shot. As Caine has remembered:

We used to block the scenes ourselves before John Huston ever saw them. What we did is, if he said I'm not going to cut on this, I'm going to do six pages [of continuous shooting of the screenplay], we would arrange the movements so that we worked each other round so that each time you got the best bit of your part you'd be facing the camera. Unlike a lot of actors who'd have tried to hog it. It's very easy with Sean. He'd say, well I'll do the back of my head and we can see you over my shoulder, and then we'd turn round and do it the other way. He's very co-operative. There's no sense of evil intent in his acting. A lot of actors spend a great deal of time working out how to screw the other actor, which of course, screws the scene, usually screws the picture but definitely screws them.8

Caine is talking about his co-star here, of course, but the description fits his own method of working perfectly, too. For the ultra-professional Caine, the picture always comes first.

It is largely thanks to this generosity of spirit on the part of both his stars that Huston's picture works. Reviewing the movie in *The New Yorker*, Pauline Kael suggested that it was more than the deaths of its two original stars that had kept *The Man Who Would Be King* off the screens for so long. Kipling's original story, Kael argued, convincingly enough, was so naively jingoistic, so steeped in casual racism, that it could have been made into a movie in the sixties only had it been treated with massively distancing irony. As she puts it: 'The film doesn't dare give us the empathic identification with what's going on inside the heroes which we had with Gary Cooper and Franchot Tone in *Bengal Lancer*.'[9] As usual, Kael has a point, though one with which the seasoned Caine watcher feels obliged to take issue. Huston's movie, in fact, does allow us to identify with the unthinking racism and effortless western superiority of its two leading characters, but at the same time these attitudes are undercut by the very actors incarnating them. Connery's and, even more so, Caine's status as working-class lads made good exposes the impotent paranoia behind the brutality and xenophobia of Kipling's original vision by allowing us to grasp that such brutality and xenophobia was the inevitable by-product of a class system that insisted on the subjugation of so many of its own countrymen at home. What Connery and Caine's characters get up to throughout much of the movie is reprehensible, but it is made *comprehensible* by the two actors' emblematic presences. Even the lowliest orders of the British imperial army, the salty Caine and slovenly Connery suggest, would seek to impose themselves on those further down the scale *because* of their own lowly status. Bogart's relaxed insolence, in other words, becomes in Caine's later anglicized reading of it a deeply political statement, one that changes utterly the meaning of Kipling's original.[10]

As befits an adaptation of a short story, the plot of *The Man Who Would Be King* is simplicity itself. Peachy Carnehan (Caine) and Daniel Dravot (Connery) are a couple of essentially good-hearted on-the-make rogues hanging about in India long after their days with the army are over. They meet up with Rudyard Kipling (Christopher Plummer), and after a run-in with a rebarbative District Commissioner (Jack May) decide to make good their plan to travel to the distant province of Kafiristan, conquer the locals, set themselves up as kings and loot the place. Kipling laughs at the cheek of it, but cannot quite bring himself to condemn the notion. It is left to Huston, whose heroes are all Icarus-like over-reachers (one thinks of Bogart and Walter Brennan in

The Treasure of the Sierra Madre [1948], of Jeff Bridges in *Fat City* [1972], of Gregory Peck's Ahab in *Moby Dick* [1956]), to bring the plan crashing down around them.

The Kafiristanis having been conquered, Peachy and Danny take them in hand and transform a motley crew into something approaching a proper fighting army. But when, during one battle, Danny is hit by an arrow (which actually lands safely in his leather harness) and seems miraculously uninjured, failing even to bleed, he is taken for a god. Danny is about to explain the tribesmen's mistake when the wilier Peachy suggests that they use the Kafiristanis' primitive religious ignorance against them: Danny must play the role of god for all it is worth. Great riches are theirs, then, but when Danny announces that he plans to take himself a wife, Roxanne (Shakira Caine), she literally bites back – drawing all-too human blood from his cheek. At which point the tribe realize they have been conned and set in motion a terrible revenge.

Looked at from the tribesmen's point of view, of course, that revenge is less terrible than merely just. They have, after all, been gulled by a pair of con artists who took advantage of their primitivism. The problem with Huston's movie is that it doesn't play things that even-handedly. As I have argued, Caine (especially) and Connery (rather less so) create performances that seek to explain, if not explain away, their working-class characters' insouciant racism and belief in their own superiority. But overall, Huston's picture is rather less subtle than its stars' gentle didactics. From the start of the movie, one is in the presence of a director all too easily seduced by the spectacle of things. The opening few minutes of *The Man Who Would Be King* grant us close-up views of the wonders of India – men who put scorpions in their mouths, men who drink boiling water from a kettle – and we are meant to take these images of noble savagery as emblematic of a culture, a continent, that while marvellous to look at is also plainly uncivilizable. Huston can never quite bring himself to condemn his heroes' mission of mini-imperialism, so that despite the felicities of casting, the picture ends up rather more confused than Kipling's original story.

None of which is to deny that *The Man Who Would Be King* is one of Caine's most enjoyable movies. A large part of the pleasure of watching the picture lies in the easy, relaxed fun Caine and Connery have with one another when they are on screen together (and they are on screen together throughout most of its 129 minutes). The dialogue is shared pretty evenly, and between them Caine and Connery work out any number of ways of balancing out the other's more off-the-leash moments. The effect is of two men utterly happy to be working as a team, of two men as knowledgeable about what the other is going to do as a trapeze act. 'Occasionally, there's an actor who likes to talk about his role,' Huston said after work on the movie was finished, 'so I'll talk with him. But that doesn't happen very often. In fact, with Sean Connery and Michael Caine, there was not one conversation between us. They just did it themselves.'[11]

Caine has admitted to having worried about Huston's *laissez faire* direction: 'At first I didn't know what was going on . . . I'd do a scene with Sean, and we'd finish it, and John would say "cut", and then we'd do the next scene on the first take as well. I never thought the movie would work. And then I saw the movie. It was wonderful. Most directors today don't know what they want – so they shoot everything they can think of. They use the camera like a machine gun. John uses it like a sniper.'[12]

All the effort Caine and Connery put into blocking out their scenes together worked wonders, so that unlike Redford and Newman in *Butch Cassidy* or *The Sting*, one never feels there is any competition between the two men. Part of the fun of those Newman/Redford pictures lay in the two leads' gentle sparring over a girl – usually a girl they would end up sharing. But in *The Man Who Would Be King* there is no such tussle and no such sharing. When Connery's Danny decides he wants to take a wife, Caine's Peachy begrudges him not at all, a point emphasized by the fact that the woman playing Connery's betrothed is in fact Shakira Caine.[13] What looks at first like a sly in-joke (the part had been originally promised to Tessa Dahl, the daughter of children's author Roald and Patricia Neal) is in fact a deepening of the movie's theme of mutual trust and dependency.

At times, of course, Connery or Caine cuts his partner some slack and lets him run with the ball they spend most of the movie lazily tossing to one another. There is a marvellous scene early on in the movie when Peachy and Danny are arraigned before an inflamed District Commissioner who is furious at the two men's criminal activities:

DISTRICT COMMISSIONER: You men are not under arrest. Thanks to Mr Kipling here, who happens to be a genuine correspondent for the *Northern Star*. But both of you richly deserve to be in jail. I have your records before me. There's everything in them from smuggling to swindling to receiving stolen goods to barefaced blackmail.

PEACHY: Sir, I resent the accusation of blackmail. It is blackmail to obtain money by threats of publishing information in a newspaper, but what blackmail is there in accepting a small retainer for keeping it out of a newspaper?

DISTRICT COMMISSIONER: And how did you propose to keep it out?

PEACHY [*smirking*]: By telling the editor what I know about his sister and a certain government official, in these parts.

DANNY: Let him put that in his paper if he has need of news.

DISTRICT COMMISSIONER [*discomfited*]: It would have been wiser if you had both gone home at the end of your service.

PEACHY: Home to what? A porter's uniform for outside a restaurant? And tanner tips from Belgian civilians for closing cab doors on them and their blousy women?

DANNY: Not for us, thank you. Not after watching the Afghans come howling down out of the hills, and taking battlefield command when all the officers had copped it.

PEACHY: Well said, brother Dravot.

DISTRICT COMMISSIONER: There may be no criminal charges against you, but I'll see these files reach Calcutta with the recommendation that you be deported as political undesirables. Detriments to the dignity of Empire and the *izzat* of the Raj.

PEACHY: Detriments you call us? Detriments? Well, I want to remind you that it was detriments like us that built this bloody empire and the *izzat* of the bloody Raj. Hats on. About turn. By the left, and quick march. Left turn . . .

The scene is worth quoting at length not just for its hilarity but for demonstrating the way its rapid shifts and about-turns allow Caine and Connery to play off one another's strengths. What one misses in the transcription, of course, is the effortless segues from Peachy's ranting to Danny's rather more controlled wisecracks. At first, Connery's Danny seems almost willing to stand there and take the barracking, but Caine's Peachy is having none of it. Glint-eyed and slant-lipped, he becomes a rip-roaring version of the rhetorical raconteur audiences have got used to seeing on chat shows over the years.[14] Connery puts on a wonderful display of wide-eyed dumbness, while Caine, all glee-ful, calculating avarice, simply barks orders at the Commissioner before marching himself and Connery out of his offices. One's impres-sion is of having watched a tennis doubles match in which one side has been deprived of half its constituent members. The script makes clear that the District Commissioner's disdain for what he sees as two ragamuffin upstarts is class-based. The joke is that they outclass him as soon as they walk into his office. Plummer's Kipling might well look on from a corner, dumbstruck and giggly.

There's a sense in this scene that Caine is playing himself. Caine's Peachy is quick-witted and sceptical, yet always able to see the funny side of things. But underneath that bluff good humour there beats the heart of a martinet. When Caine's Peachy first meets Kipling, on a train journey, they are interrupted by the arrival of a friendly, charming, melon-eating Indian. His friendliness and filthy eating habits soon irk the irascible Peachy, though, who proceeds to throw him off the train. Huston, who filmed the whole scene in a medium shot, clearly conceived of it as a moment of throwaway humour. But Caine, who gives his voice a harsh, cawing quality throughout the movie so that his habitually grating cockney whine is freighted with even more aggressive weight than usual, refuses to sugar-coat the scene and play things for laughs. Caine has admitted to hero-worshipping Huston (he has claimed that he saw *The Treasure of the Sierra Madre* six times in as many days upon the movie's release in 1948), but his worship did not extend to accepting everything the director said with uncritical veneration. Caine knows, even if Huston doesn't, that Peachy is not very funny and mighty far from being a hero.

But for all its jingoism and racism, *The Man Who Would Be King* is bursting with high-spirited good humour. The movie was well received by pretty much all the critics, giving Caine a success he badly needed. Indeed, he said of it that 'of all the films I've done, [the one which] would survive in the archives . . . would be *The Man Who Would Be King*'.[15] This is hyperbole, but only because Caine has made more than one movie that will be remembered. Nonetheless, simply by virtue of its sheer vitality, Huston's movie is certainly among Caine's greatest achievements. Orson Welles thought of movies as accidents, and *The Man Who Would Be King* is one of the happiest accidents the cinema has ever given us. It's impossible to watch the film without coming away a little cheered – not because it shows us the perfect life, but because by showing us that all dreams of a perfect life are destined for the dustbin of history, it allows us to relinquish our fantasies.

And yet, and yet. The movie does serve up a kind of perfection too, for there *is* something untouchable about the machine-tooled precision of the Caine/Connery double act. Huston himself described them as 'polished . . . everything on cue and with perfect timing'.[16] It is not much of an exaggeration to say that Caine's timing was going to be out for the rest of the seventies.

Certainly, there was every reason for Caine to steer clear of mentioning *Harry and Walter Go to New York* (1976) in his memoir. A luxuriant 1890s period piece (the picture looks as if it was shot and designed by Thomas Eakins), it's a comedy heist picture clearly intended to cash in on the success of *The Sting* a couple of years earlier. In place of Newman and Redford, though, *Harry and Walter* has James Caan and Elliott Gould, redoubtable actors both, though neither of them capable of the ironic self-regard that sounded the bass note of Newman and Redford's work together. The movies have little to offer that is more grindingly embarrassing, more self-consciously amateurish than the sight of Caan and Gould hammily clowning it up as a couple of tuneless song-and-dance men who stumble into becoming bank robbers.

As with Laurel and Hardy (with whom the director, Mark Rydell, absurdly compared his leading men), Harry and Walter's gags are all painstakingly set up. But the pay-offs never pay off, not because you can see them coming from a mile away (there are, remember, no surprises in the ritual humiliations handed out to Stan and Ollie), but because our two heroes have no dignity to be taken away from them. Harry and Walter are clumsy and inane from the moment we meet them; they have no airs and graces. Little wonder, perhaps, that the movie effectively put an end to its two leads' promising careers. Gould, who has never really lived up to his full potential, spent the rest of the seventies in potboilers and cheapie thrillers. Caan, who had been Oscar-nominated for his role as Sonny in *The Godfather* only a couple of years earlier, all but disappeared from sight. He made a partial comeback in the early nineties as the second lead in *Misery* (1990), but otherwise he has been nowhere.

Lucky for Caine, then, that the movie never calls on him to sing or dance. Instead, for most of its two-hour running time Caine's Adam Worth has merely to glow and preen, here smoothing a finger over his Gable-esque moustache, there cutting a swathe through cinematographer Laszlo Kovacs' near monochrome palette of toffee and peanuts in his dove-grey tail coat and stove-pipe hat. Against Harry and Walter's fumblings and shabby tweeds are set Worth's lazy grace and cut-on-the-bias *je ne sais quoi*.

In short, Caine's Worth is the movie's bit of class. Ten years on from Harry Palmer, Hollywood was using Caine as a George Sanders-style dashing knave. Seizing his opportunity, he dignifies an otherwise ham-fisted comedy not by elevating it to the empyrean of Hollywood's golden age, but by bringing it down to the rather more earthy levels of British pantomime. The only one of the movie's four leads – Diane Keaton is as mannered and maltreated as Caan and Gould – who gives anything like a performance that understands what is going on around him, Caine's subtle comic imperialism pulls the rug from under the picture. It wasn't much to be proud of, though having bested the likes of Gould and Keaton cannot but have helped make Caine wonder whether he ought not be plying his trade full-time in Tinseltown.

War of the Roses: Caine with Maggie Smith on *California Suite*. © British Film Institute

No *wind serves him who addresses his voyage to no certain port.*
Michel de Montaigne[1]

The English countryside, though, still captivated Caine. For him, the garden at Mill House was as proud an achievement as any of the movies he had made, though he saw a lot less of it than he would have liked. He had spent the best part of 1975 working away from home, thereby missing one of the loveliest summers of the century in England. Happily, the next year's turned out even more glorious, and this time around Caine was lucky enough to be working from home for its duration.

John Sturges's *The Eagle Has Landed* was shot over twelve weeks that summer of 1976, and though the bulk of the movie is set in Norfolk, it was filmed in Berkshire – in a village called Mapledurham, about fifteen minutes' drive from Mill House. 'If I'm not needed on the set,' Caine remarked at the time, 'I can pop home and play with Natasha or simply potter round my garden looking after the rhubarb and roses.'[2] For once, Caine had the chance of earning his living while cultivating his garden.

Earning his living is just about all he was doing in this movie, though. Sturges, whose hits numbered among them *The Magnificent Seven* (1960) and that moralizing insult to prisoners-of-war *The Great Escape* (1963), had never been anything other than workmanlike. Andrew Sarris plants him alongside Bryan Forbes in the 'Strained Seriousness' section of his book *The American Cinema*, though seriousness seems not quite the right word for Sturges's insolent melodramatics. Nowhere in his oeuvre was there evidence that he knew how to handle actors (though plenty that his stars could do whatever they wanted), not a thing to suggest that he had any capacity for dealing with characters who are other than numbly heroic. And so, although *The Eagle Has Landed* gave Caine another chance to play around with Germanic accents, it handed him precious few other opportunities.

It is 1943, and a bunch of crack German paratroopers, led by Caine's Colonel Steiner, make a night-time landing in England. Their mission: to kidnap Winston Churchill and thus win a huge propaganda coup for the Nazis. Sketched out like that it is not hard to track the influences at work on *The Eagle Has Landed*. Adapted from a book by Jack Higgins, the movie mixed elements from Alberto Cavalcanti's tale of the Nazi takeover of an English village, *Went the Day Well?* (1942), with the hyper-realist fantasies of Frederick Forsyth's best-seller *The Day of the*

Jackal. As with Forsyth's novel, the movie's biggest potential problem was the audience's suspension of disbelief. This is something any story has to surmount, of course, but it was magnified here – not because what people were being asked to treat as realistic was too fantastical to believe, but because even the most ignorant moviegoer was likely to know that nothing like what happens in the story ever really went on. Churchill was never taken captive by the Nazis, just as De Gaulle was not the victim of an assassin's bullet.

Forsyth's solution in his novel had been to outdo even Ian Fleming's James Bond books in slavishly itemizing – fetishizing, even – the banalities of evil. Indeed, so realistic was the book that Forsyth's chapters documenting how the Jackal goes about obtaining a passport under a false name led to a change in the application regulations. Higgins's solution was less rigorous, though perhaps more inspired. When, at the end of Sturges's movie, it is revealed that the Churchill who has just been shot dead by Caine's Steiner was really just an actor impersonating the great leader for fear of just such an assassination attempt, few people in the audience can deny momentarily having their breath taken away.[3]

Caine's solution to all this implausibility, meanwhile, was to employ not one but *two* German accents for different parts of the movie. Whilst talking to his fellow Nazis, Caine speaks his (English) dialogue with the gentle Germanic precision he had perfected for *The Last Valley*. Whilst talking to the English people in the village he and his men, disguised as British officers, have invaded, however, Caine's English is laden over with the clipped officer tones of war movie cliché. To hear him switch, sometimes in mid-sentence, from one voice to the other is to be treated to a variety show *à la* the Olivier of *Sleuth*. Bravura stuff, in other words, though whether that brand of bravura was called for was another matter.

Donald Sutherland, for instance, has a lot of fun with his turn as Liam Devlin, an IRA freedom fighter turned Nazi helpmate. Sutherland's Devlin is the bog country blockhead of a thousand jokes, a moist-eyed romantic buffoon who does to the movie what Caine did to *Harry and Walter* – which is to say, leer at it archly. Caine's problem was that Sutherland's decision to rib Sturges's macho histrionics turned out to be far more fitting than his own desperate attempts to plug Higgins's preposterous story into some kind of reality. While the likes of Donald Pleasence, Anthony Quayle and even Robert Duvall content themselves with smirkily floating along on the surface of the vast practical joke they find themselves marooned in, Caine flaps and flounders in his own naturalistic backwaters.

To be fair, Caine's role is the toughest in the movie, since Steiner is the only character who is not a stereotype. Early on in the story, he has a big scene in which he harangues a bunch of SS officers for being wilfully wicked to some Jewish prisoners under their command. Steiner may be a Nazi, the movie wants us to understand, but he is not a thug. Caine works wonders here, at suggesting a man not quite rigidified by ideology. His movement from surly calm to paranoid hortatory, though plainly calculated to the nth degree, is well nigh imperceptible. But no sooner has he so beautifully established the confusions and ambiguities of his character than he becomes the robotic killer the machinations of the plot demand. By the end of the movie, his men mostly dead and his mission in tatters, Steiner has been transformed into a one-man death squad, determined to revenge his men by gunning Churchill down in cold blood.

For all its inanities, however, Lew Grade, whose company Associated General Films produced the movie, was happy enough with it: 'The Eagle Has Landed made quite a lot of money,' he remembered a few years after its release.[4] Maybe so, though the critics thought it risible and over the years Caine has performed one of his about-faces on the movie's director (whose last picture it turned out to be). At first, he admitted to a liking for Sturges's no-nonsense professionalism: 'He's inclined to think "Take One", which I like. He told me The Magnificent Seven was entirely Take One.'[5] Later on, though, Caine criticized Sturges for not having been sufficiently interested in finishing the movie properly. 'He informed me,' Caine said in 1992, shortly after Sturges's death, '[that] he only ever worked to get the money to go fishing . . . The moment the picture finished he took the money and went. Jack Wiener [one of the movie's co-producers] later told me that he never came back for the editing nor for any of the other post-production sessions that are where a director does some of his most important work. The picture wasn't bad, but I still get angry when I think what it could have been with the right director.'[6]

Caine was back on location within days of the wrap on The Eagle Has Landed. Back in uniform, too, though this time the uniform was English and the character Caine was playing was a real one – so real he was still alive and on set as a military consultant. The movie was Richard Attenborough's A Bridge Too Far (1977), the officer Brigadier Joe Vandeleur. Thirty-three years earlier, then a humble Lieutenant Colonel, Vandeleur had been the commander of a tank regiment trying to rescue a parachute troop trapped behind enemy lines at Arnhem. Pleased to be being played by what he described as a 'taller . . . and funnier'7 man, Vandeleur proved a willing helper in Caine's attempts at making his portrayal as realistic as possible, even going so far as to tell the actor the exact words he used when ordering his battalion to get going.

Alas, their efforts were of little use. Yes, Attenborough was brave enough and honest enough not to try and disguise the fact that Operation Market Garden was General Montgomery's one big failure in the Second World War. On the other hand, the conventions and clichés of the true-Brit war pictures Attenborough had made his name with distort whatever pretensions the movie has to telling the truth. It was all very well for Michael Caine to utter precisely the same words his real-life counterpart had done thirty-three years earlier, but how to get round the fact that the rest of the movie's characters utter only platitudes or plot exposition? How, moreover, to get round the fact that your fictional army is almost entirely peopled by the biggest and brightest stars of mid-seventies' cinema?

Attenborough has subsequently claimed that the reason for the presence of all those stars was that they made a difficult story easy to follow.8 Because each strand of the narrative was being headed up by a famous face, the audience would find it far easier to work out who was doing what and to whom. It's a nice conceit, though one predicated on a falsehood: the story A Bridge Too Far tells is anything but complicated. The allies, under General Montgomery's instructions, dropped three divisions of paratroopers and gliders (two British and one American) deep behind German lines in an attempt to gain a bridgehead over the Rhine. Unfortunately, Montgomery hadn't counted on there being any German troops in the area; there were, it turned out, plenty of them. What was planned as a walkover turned out to be a bloodbath. Eventually, the few surviving allied troops were evacuated. End of story.

The problem with Attenborough's all-the-stars-in-the-heavens approach to the movie, then, was that it resulted in a suicidal double whammy. The cross-cutting from one big actor to another not only caused needless narrative convolution but also disappointment for the fans of each individual star. Whomever you wanted to see, you ended up seeing very little of. Here is Dirk Bogarde posturing, there Larry Olivier (with a most un-Cainely German accent). Here is Robert Redford grinning beatifically under a mid-seventies hairdo, while over there is Tony Hopkins overenunciating. For the rest of those present, the movie was a chance to serve up no more than the kind of glib heroics Attenborough doubtless believed he was rising above with his spectacular shots of darkened skies punctured by moonlit parachutes and battlefield smoke rising majestically into the setting sun. A couple of years later, with *Apocalypse Now* (1979), Francis Ford Coppola was to make of the Vietnam war a similarly chaotic spectacle. Chaos, though, was the point of Coppola's movie – a movie quite aware, unlike Attenborough's, that there was a question as to how moral it is to treat war as an opportunity for visual pyrotechnics.

The screenwriter William Goldman, to whom fell the task of weaving the tangled strands into some kind of coherent web, has described the problems he had structuring the movie.[9] What Goldman has never quite brought himself to say is that *A Bridge Too Far* might have done a lot better – and would certainly have made a lot more sense – had it focused on just one or two officers and their men. As it is, only Sean Connery as Major-General Urquhart comes away with any honours, simply because he is the only actor in the movie whose character is required not to play things dumbly gung-ho but to look askance at what he has been asked to do. Caine himself has no more to do than bark a couple of orders from behind a cravat. With his waxed moustache and jaunty beret he looks dapper and dandy, but he looks bored too, like a man who has spent a long time waiting to say not very much.

Caine has subsequently claimed that he never had any faith in the movie's being a success. How, he reasoned, could a film about failure be anything other than a failure itself? The logic is not quite watertight – as Caine himself would prove a few years later in *Educating Rita* – but he had a point nonetheless, thus demonstrating rather more box-office awareness than either Attenborough or the producer Joseph E. Levine, whose brainchild the picture was.[10] So convinced of the success of his baby was Levine that the movie was actually in production before ever a writer had put pen to paper. Indeed, he was so sure *A Bridge Too Far* was going to make him a fortune, or, rather, another fortune, that it was all his own money on the line – $22 million of it.[11]

Caine read the runes well when he predicted that the movie would be a flop, though he may not have been so much prescient as merely observant. Dull but tawdry and shot through with glorious incompetence, *A Bridge Too Far* can be most profitably seen as a parable on seventies Britain – that strike-torn bedlam of shirking, incompetence and deceit. For a movie star, Caine has always been startlingly aware of what is going on in the world around him. You might not always agree with the conclusions he draws from what he sees, but only a fool could deny that for an actor he is unusually wised-up about life outside his immediate sphere. In a Britain falling to pieces, a movie about a military campaign doing likewise was perhaps not best placed to clean up.

Certainly, Caine saw Britain in the seventies as a losers' paradise. He had hated the old pre-war Britain of class boundaries and snobbery, of course, but after three decades of the left's brave new Blighty of bounty and egalitarianism he was no longer sure that theirs was the right solution either. Spending increasing amounts of his time working abroad and losing increasing amounts of the money he earned there in taxes at home, Caine chafed some more when the Chancellor of the Exchequer, Denis Healey, announced he was going to tax the rich 'until the pips squeaked'. Was it, Caine began wondering again, time to get out? The problem was, his accountant told him, that even if he did decide to make the move to Hollywood, he hadn't the money to do so.

Hence *Silver Bears* (1978), a tale of high financial finagling Caine took on with the sole aim of stashing some money away to buy a property in Los Angeles. One tries to sympathize, though after labouring through this sorry mess the task is made all the more difficult. Essentially a comedy heist movie wrapped up in the wheeler-dealer shenanigans of corporate finance, *Silver Bears* is so impenetrable it would have baffled Keynes, let alone Caine, who wanders through proceedings like a mourner at his own funeral. Occasionally he manages to give Peter (*Charade* [1964]) Stone's lightly bantering dialogue an edge, but the movie is so clotted that Caine's wit never really cuts through. Had he not been one of the busiest actors in the world, Caine might have been able to put *Silver Bears* down to inexperience. The trouble was he didn't put it down to *experience* either. Like Peter Cook, Caine has learned from his mistakes – he could make them all again.

The Swarm (1978), for instance, was a rerun of *The Eagle Has Landed*, at least in terms of Caine's failure to grasp what was going on around him. The tale of a flock of deadly African killer bees, *The Swarm* was producer/director Irwin Allen's follow-up to his blockbusting tale of a skyscraper on fire, *The Towering Inferno* (1974). Both pictures were disaster movies, members of that loud but listless mini-genre that flourished in mid-seventies Hollywood before the reassuring back-to-the-future fantasies of George Lucas and Steven Spielberg came to soothe America's fevered brow. Not that the disaster movies weren't themselves reassuring. *Earthquake* (1974), *Airport 1975* (1974), *The Poseidon Adventure* (1972) – all bespoke of an America on the brink of disintegration, but an America that could be rescued by a return to its old values. Hence the presence in these pictures of some of the greying stars of Hollywood's golden age: Ava Gardner, Fred Astaire, and – in *The Swarm* – Henry Fonda, Olivia de Havilland, Ben Johnson and Fred MacMurray.

Why the need for reassurance? After the twin crises of Vietnam and Watergate, the US was in a state of shock: the cowboys, Vietnam had taught Americans, were no longer necessarily the good guys; the Indians not axiomatically bad. Vietnam, moreover, was a war that America, at ruinous cost, lost. As such, it threw a spanner into the works of the American dream of manifest destiny. The country's central ideal of continuing progress lost its power to enthral. An era of anxious moral relativism utterly alien to the way the country had hitherto conceived of itself was ushered in.

Filmed in the summer of 1977, *The Swarm* was a somewhat late response to this sense of social breakdown. Nonetheless, response it was – and a rather more interesting one than most of the movies on whose template it was based. For one thing, its golden-age stars do not 'pull through' (De Havilland, Johnson and MacMurray are killed in a train crash; Fonda dies testing a dodgy bee-sting antidote he has knocked up). For another, the movie puts its faith in the figure of the scientist – an unusual move in a genre for which macho histrionics are usually more than enough to cut the mustard. The boffin in the disaster picture generally functions as a locus of indolent evil. By placing its faith in enlightenment, then, *The Swarm* is uncharacteristically progressive for its genre, a fact underlined by the casting of Caine in the role of redemptive scientist. English actors in such movies, after all, are usually there to look effete and cowardly and get bumped off at the end of the first act. Caine's Crane may wear what Richard Widmark's General Slater sees as a counter-cultural suede jerkin, but he is still the man who gets the job done.

Caine himself, though, is the man who goes under. While everyone else in the picture had decided to play things for laughs, Caine stood alone for the forces of thespian integrity as if he really did believe there was something going on in the movie other than the desire to shill the rubes of a few quick bucks. And so while Widmark and Fonda, MacMurray and De Havilland have a high old time overplaying their various hands, Caine, who had that house purchase in LA to think about, looks a lot less easy. He spends the bulk of the movie with his hands behind his back, as if the aristo-style mannerisms he had adopted for *Zulu* ten years earlier might drum some discipline into proceedings. The movie's only saving grace is that Caine got one of his best one-liners out of it. 'It was all the bees' fault,' he said shortly after the picture was released to a unanimous drubbing. 'I always knew they couldn't act.'[12]

Caine got better reviews for his part in *California Suite* (1978). Indeed, he and his co-star, Maggie Smith (who won an Oscar for her part in the picture), garnered all the best critical comments. Nor is there any gainsaying the professionalism with which Caine's bisexual antique dealer Sidney Cochran and Smith's histrionic thespian Diana

Barrie work their way through what Herbert Ross's picture takes to be emotional tumult. Nonetheless, to look at the movie today is to see that Caine had done all it required of him – and with rather more aplomb – in *Zee & Co.*

Like that movie, the segment of *California Suite* in which Caine appears (the movie, adapted by Neil Simon from his own play, is composed of four almost discrete one-act dramas) documents a couple of days in the life of a rather unhappily married couple. The problem is that while Simon's script is as stuffed full of one-liners as you'd imagine, there isn't that much meat to go with the stuffing. Dandyish when it thinks itself biting, sentimental when it thinks itself moving, it's all rather like sitting in on a rehearsal of *Who's Afraid of Virginia Woolf?* as directed by Noël Coward. As Pauline Kael remarked at the time, 'part of the hell of filming stage material is that it usually has nothing but foreground'.[13]

Watching Caine and Smith go for one another over and over again with what is intended as rapier wit is a dispiriting exercise – not because they aren't up to the job, but because you can hear in their broken-backed line-readings their realization that the job isn't up to them. That said, Caine and Smith do manage, at times, to make what they have been given to say sound as if it had been written by someone who had spent at least part of his life listening to how other people talk. They look, too, like a genuine couple – in some shots, indeed, look like two people growing to resemble one another. Only a churl could pronounce himself utterly unmoved when, at the end of their story, Sidney and Diana are reconciled once more. But the uplift derives entirely from the miraculous tug of Smith's and Caine's performances and not at all from the putative drama their characters have just been dragged through.

Towards the end of April 1978, Caine began work on what he has variously described as the only 'film I've ever done for the money alone',[14] and 'the worst, most wretched film I ever made'.[15] Such verdicts are a little tough on *Ashanti* (1979), and not only because one finds it hard to believe that Caine had gone into, say, *A Bridge Too Far* with noble aesthetic intent. For while Richard Fleischer's study of the slave trade in modern-day Africa is no masterpiece, it is still a perfectly competent chase movie. Yes, Fleischer never quite makes up his mind whether he is directing a drama or a comedy. Yes, the movie is badly edited, jumping haphazardly from scene to scene, sometimes cutting away too early, too often staying around way too long (*Ashanti* actually opens with a scene in which Caine effectively teaches the audience how to erect a foldout table). And yes, Fleischer, like many a director before him, lets Peter Ustinov get away with, well, being Peter Ustinov. But all that said, this is nobody's nadir.

Caine plays Dr David Linderby, who, together with his black wife Anansa (Beverly Johnson), another doctor, are tending to the sick of West Africa on behalf of the World Health Organisation. But when Anansa is kidnapped by the slave-trader Suleiman (Ustinov), Linderby and another of Suleiman's victims, Malik (Kabir Bedi), give chase. To be precise, they give chase for 3,000 miles or so, all the way to the Red Sea. And one of the best things about the movie is that Caine, by now a paunchy and puffed out forty-five, was a little too old for its action scenes. There is a lovely moment involving Linderby dropping from a helicopter into a crocodile-infested river, but a jump cut takes us to the city days later, where our hero looks unscathed though perhaps a little warier. To watch Caine's Linderby ruminate on the absurd adventures the machinations of the plot required is to watch one of the cinema's most convincing studies of confused middle age.

More than that, Caine has a few moments in the movie that call for his soul to be spilled, and in at least one of them he delivers. The scene in the desert in which Caine's Linderby has to tell a group of slave children that he cannot help them because he has his wife to rescue is perhaps his finest piece of work since *Get Carter* eight years earlier. Caine's angry, teary face looks like the friable front of a man genuinely in two minds – we can see Linderby *thinking* about what he is saying even as he is saying it. It may be that such intensity of vision was no more than a bodying forth of Caine's own nagging doubts about what he was doing on 'the worst, most wretched film' of his career, but that does nothing to gainsay its power.

Good though Caine had been in *California Suite* and *Ashanti*, however, he was going to have to find better parts if he was really to make the Hollywood A-list. And that was the thought increasingly on his mind in the late seventies, as Britain's economy went further and further down the pan. For the past decade he had been a big fish in a comparatively small pool. Of the generation of British stars who had come to prominence in the sixties, only Caine and Sean Connery had maintained momentum into the seventies. Burton, Finney, Courtenay, O'Toole . . . all of them had floundered and then sunk as the decade wore on. But if things went on as they were, there would soon be no pool to swim in, big fish or little. As Caine pointed out on more than one occasion during the seventies, the British film industry put most of its industry into getting the hell out of Britain. 'John Boorman lives in Ireland. Lewis

Gilbert lives in France. John Schlesinger makes more films abroad than he does in England . . . everyone who made films in Britain was driven away by government regulations.'[16] The time was approaching when Caine would have to decide whether he went too. It was a tough call, but Caine was helped to make it by a local electrician . . .

Part Three
LA

Have regard for your name, since it will remain for you longer than a great store of gold.
  Apocrypha, Ecclesiasticus, 41: 12

We're in the mess that we're in because the working classes have, well
– this nasty word 'class', but how else can you describe a man who
works in a factory and brings home a wage? He's got the unions to
talk for him, and big industry has got the CBI and various other
bodies. Who do we have in the middle to talk about our plight unless
we do it ourselves? And this is just what we haven't been doing.
    The Writing on the Wall[1]

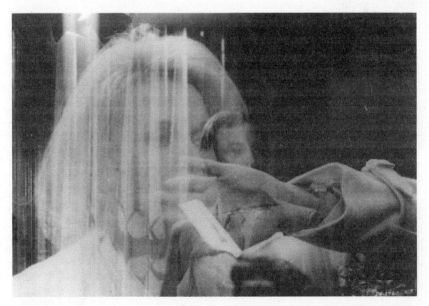

Double trouble: Caine and Angie Dickinson in *Dressed to Kill*. © British Film
Institute

Caine wanted some electrical modifications carried out at Mill House,
but when the workman turned up he took a look around and refused
the job. Why not? asked Caine. 'I am a communist,' said the electrician, 'and it is my belief that nobody should live in such luxury.'
At which point he climbed back into his van and drove off. Caine,

meanwhile, told Shakira to pack their bags: they were moving to Los Angeles.[2]

It's a nice story, the kind of story Caine has amused chat-show audiences with these past three decades, though how much truth there is to it one wouldn't like to say. Doubtless a wealthy man like Michael Caine, an actor used to people being at his beck and call on the movie set, did find certain workmen's practices of the seventies needlessly bureaucratic and/or self-indulgent. Doubtless he had had, as had many other people, run-ins with the greedy and the lazy. Nonetheless, even in the comparatively left-wing Britain of the mid–late seventies, were electricians – who tend to be self-employed – really communist in their leanings? The story might ring truer if the job Caine had needed doing had been to do with his telephone system. Back then, the telecoms industry was a monopoly, and that monopoly was subject to another monopoly in the form of a trade union. But a self-employed electrician is just the kind of amorphous, anonymous figure you need for a story like this. There are no bigger interests behind that figure to take issue with Caine's claims.

Whatever the truth, the late seventies certainly seem to have crystallized Caine's political vision of his home country. Forty years earlier, when he had been growing up, Caine had thought the country held back by the determination of the upper classes to stifle the ambitions of anyone further down the scale. Now, he believed, the situation had been reversed. The working classes were running the country, and they were running it into the ground. Backed by a supine socialist government, the unions and their members were, Caine thought, bringing his country to its knees. It was time to get out.

He had been threatening to leave for the best part of half a decade. As early as the summer of 1974, five months after Harold Wilson's Labour government had been returned to power, Caine was making noises about quitting the country. 'I could live quite happily in America,' he said, 'but I don't want to . . . I love my country, and I want to live in it, but I have no intention of standing by and watching everything I've worked for taken away from me.'[3] What was particularly goading Caine was Denis Healey's projected Wealth Tax, under which people would be taxed not only on their earnings but on what they had already earned, too.

> I've got nothing against taxes as long as they are fair, but the idea of being taxed on my possessions and on what I have in the bank, as well as on what I earn, is outrageous . . . I wouldn't have minded being born poor and dying poor, but being poor and

then working my way out of it . . . I'm totally disinterested [*sic*] in politics, except where it affects me.4

If proof had ever been needed, then, here it was: despite the spurious romance with which sixties intellectuals had endowed anyone from the working class, Michael Caine was not – and never had been – committed to the idea of political revolution. He had never been committed to anything but working hard and improving his lot. And he had no faith in any political party's abilities to actively help him along the way. Two decades earlier, of course, politics had played a big, if unconscious, part in licensing the kind of stardom Caine incarnated. Without the radical hopes of the generation that came to maturity after the Second World War, there would have been no *Look Back in Anger*, no *Alfie*, no Harry Palmer.

Not that Caine saw things that way. As far as he was concerned he was an utterly self-made man. Indeed, since he had managed to fight his way through the tangle of his restrictive roots, how could he be held to account for the fact that so many of his fellows were still caught up in it? For the class system had become a far more malleable thing as he had worked his way up it. As he remarked midway through the protracted will I/won't I move to Hollywood debate, 'It is the working class who perpetuate the class distinctions. They want the upper classes to take care of them. Nobody wants responsibility anymore, so they keep voting in the socialists.'5 And by doing this, thought Caine, they were effectively cutting their own throats: 'The class system on one side has led to resentment, which has led to a real Socialist cloth-cap attitude. On the other side, the class society that we have has led the working people from being the serf for the rich to being the serf for the government.'6

According to Caine, the fact that he had become a serf for the government explained his unbelievably high workload. 'If you do three films,' he said, 'two would be for the Government – and one for yourself.'7 Hence the high ratio of dull or actively bad work he put his name to: 'The thing about being any kind of an artist, particularly in this business, is that you have such a short life. You have to make all the money you can while you're still in demand.'8 Thus *The Marseille Contract* and *Harry and Walter Go to New York*, thus *The Swarm* and *Beyond the Poseidon Adventure*. What's amazing, when you look at Caine's seventies CV, is not that he wanted to move to Hollywood, but that Hollywood was willing to have him. When, on 3 January 1979, the plane carrying the Caine family finally touched down in Los Angeles, its patriarch was a decidedly less than A-list bankable star.

Ironically, Caine had finally left Britain within weeks of a general election that would usher in the kind of government he had, perhaps always, wanted. Margaret Thatcher's victory at the polls in May 1979 (followed by that of Ronald Reagan as US President at the end of the year) brought in an era of so-called small government and tax cuts for the rich. Self-made men like Caine were just the kind that Thatcher favoured, though Caine worried that she would not be long for the job: 'I don't think the trade unions will let Mrs Thatcher last more than 18 months,' he said. 'I don't think any Tory Government at the moment could outlive the wrath of the unions ... the climate in Britain is not about to change in the next few months.'9 Much less was it about to change in his own career.

But before Caine began work while actually living in America he was given pause to wonder about whether he had done the right thing in moving. Yes, Hollywood's electricians didn't talk back at you and yes, when you told the telephone company you wanted a phone and you wanted it tomorrow then it came tomorrow. On the other hand, there is no free National Health Service to fall back on in the US. When you get ill you get your wallet out – as Caine was about to have made forcibly clear to him.

It happened the same day that he had had the phone installed. Caine had contacted the phone company on the Friday, they'd said they'd be round on the Monday, and he'd said no, he wanted the phone putting in on Saturday. He got his way. That same Saturday night, the Caines had been invited to a little party at the home of the lyricist Leslie Bricusse, whom Caine had known since the Pickwick Club days of the early sixties. During the party, the leather belt Shakira was wearing snapped – an incident that called forth jokes about diets and pregnancies.

But Shakira wasn't putting on weight and nor was she pregnant. In fact, her appendix had burst, though she wouldn't know that until the next morning when she came round in hospital. During the interim, while the Caines were asleep in their new home, she had smashed her husband on the nose and cuffed him about the ear in a desperate, unconscious attempt to rouse him. Because within a few hours of that belt having broken, Shakira was near comatose in peritonitic agony. And it was now, in the middle of the night in those pre-mobile phone days, that Caine was so grateful he had insisted on having a phone installed that Saturday. An ambulance was called and the paramedics did their stuff, saving Shakira's life in the bedroom before transporting her to hospital.

Which is where Caine was brought face to face with the realities of the American health service. It costs. While Shakira was taken off to be prepared for the operating theatre, her husband was sent to see the hospital cashier, who solemnly intoned that Mr Caine's bill came to $5,000. Alas, he didn't have that kind of money on him. Didn't, in fact, have *any* money on him. As soon as he knew his wife was OK, though, and he had got himself home, he would send them a cheque. But no. They needed the money up front. No payment, no operation. Caine was just about to hare off home when the cashier suggested that since he was an international star he was surely a member of the Screen Actors Guild. Caine acknowledged that he was. Then everything was OK, the Guild would cover all the medical bills. All he had to do was sign on the dotted line.

Shakira having been successfully operated on and her husband having been told that she was out of danger, Caine went home and reassured Natasha. Then, doubtless, he got to pondering what had happened and how it might have happened differently in the country of his birth. In England, there would have been no arguments about bills and cheques, though, contrariwise, nor would there have been any getting a phone fitted exactly when you wanted. Shakira would have qualified for free medical treatment in England, but she might not have got it because her husband wouldn't have been able to contact the ambulance services as immediately as might have been necessary.

Few people who have interviewed Caine since his wife's near-death experience have not been able to draw him on to political matters. The incident got him thinking about how societies organize themselves. And in the society he had chosen to move to, you needed lots of money if you were to live, let alone live well. Coupled with that was the fact that the Caines' new home in Beverly Hills had eaten up all but a tiny amount of the family capital: he needed to start earning. Switching off his already less-than-reliable bullshit detector, Caine leapt at whatever came his way.

To start with, he got lucky. *The Island* (1980), shot in the summer of 1979, was a promising opening to Caine's Stateside career. The $650,000 he got for the movie was cause enough for satisfaction, but Caine put in good work, too, and was rewarded with the kind of reviews he had become accustomed to over the years: the movie stank but its star came out smelling of roses.

In fact, Peter Benchley's own adaptation of his follow-up novel to *Jaws*, while no masterpiece, doesn't really deserve the opprobrium that has been dumped on it over the years. Caine plays Blair Maynard, an Englishman who works in New York as an investigative journalist. Accompanied by his son Justin (Jeffrey Frank), Maynard sets out to learn what has happened to the 2,000 people and 600 boats that have gone missing in that area of the Caribbean known as the Bermuda Triangle over the previous three years. What has happened to them is that the people have been slain and the boats sunk by a bunch of marauding brigands who are holed up on an island which civilization has passed by. As Dr Windsor (Frank Middlemass) – who rents Maynard a boat (but turns out to be in league with the pirates) – says, 'they're an anthropologist's dream. You're witnessing the seventeenth century.' Alas, Maynard is witness too to the kidnapping and brainwashing of his son, who takes to the degenerate piratical lifestyle with counter-cultural abandon and is soon hell-bent on doing away with his dad.

All very fantastical, and the fantasy is filled out with director Michael Ritchie's customary verve. So it is testimony to Caine's performance that he manages to carry out the hackneyed action-man duties Benchley's script allots him with dignity and aplomb. The bulk of the movie consists of shots of fine British stage actors – David Warner, Dudley Sutton, Frank Middlemass – gurning and grinning in fright wigs and hosiery ('a bunch of arseholes playing Long John Silver,' as Caine's Maynard nicely caricatures them). So there is no gainsaying the import of Caine's decision, taken with director Michael Ritchie's consent, to play his own part for real. As he said at the time: 'It's a modern pirate story, and when the pirates appear the situation becomes very delicate. It's my job to control what the audience thinks about the pirates because I'm really the only representative of the audience . . . in the film.'[10] So he was, and what power The Island has derives from its juxtaposition of Caine's naturalistic withdrawal with the fantastical dreamworld he finds himself dumped in. Though Blair and Justin have only banalities to mouth at one another in their early scenes together, Caine and Ritchie work up a convincing portrait of a father and son relationship that is plainly fragile.

Caine's achievement in The Island was to 'earth' the movie, to propel its ludicrous leathers and leers fantasy by granting it something solid to kick against. The result is a genuinely spooky movie – a slice of Poe, perhaps, or Hawthorne – that is let down only by its conventionally heroic ending: a helicopter version of the cavalry riding to the rescue. Caine's performance slides into fervid fury in this denouement, but the result has a sweaty inanity everywhere at odds with what has gone before.

Movies, though, are not their endings, and there is much for Caine to be proud of in The Island. Despite sterling work from Sutton and Warner and the movie's many other saltily theatrical cohorts, it is

Caine's restraint that dominates and controls the picture. His short sequence in *California Suite* aside, this was his best work since *The Man Who Would Be King* five years earlier.

Even better was his performance in *Dressed to Kill* (1980). Not that Caine was actually in Brian De Palma's movie all that much. He plays Dr Robert Elliott, a New York psychiatrist, one of whose patients, Kate Miller (Angie Dickinson), complains of her husband's incompetent love-making and suggests they have sex. Elliott says no, so Kate allows herself to be casually picked up in an art gallery. Upon leaving her lover's apartment, however, she is hacked to death by a blonde woman with a cut-throat razor. The police interview Elliott, suggesting that one of his patients is responsible for the murder. This is a possibility lent force by a message left on his answering machine from his patient, Bobbi, who says he stole Elliott's razor and killed Kate. But Bobbi, it transpires, exists only in the psychiatrist's mind and is, in fact, Elliott in drag. Elliott, we learn in an explanatory coda, is a transsexual determined to do away with any woman who arouses his heterosexual desires.

Dressed to Kill was, in other words, another entry in Brian De Palma's ever-lengthening filmography of reworkings of Hitchcock. His 1976 movie *Obsession* was a virtual remake of *Vertigo* (1958). *Blow Out* (1981), the follow-up to *Dressed to Kill*, was De Palma's take on *Rear Window* (1954). But *Dressed to Kill* is perhaps De Palma's ultimate Hitchcock homage cum parody for it takes its cue from so many of the master of suspense's movies. It's *Psycho* (1960) cum *Vertigo* cum *Marnie* (1963) cum *Frenzy* cum *Rear Window*. It is easy to admit to the polish and sheer technical bravura of De Palma's movies, but their calculated attempts at buffing up the Hitchcock legacy have a habit of leaving one cold.

Caine leaves one cold, too, in *Dressed to Kill*, though his performance was designed deliberately to do so. His chief job in the movie, after all, was to appear as unobtrusive as possible so that audiences would not suspect him of being the murderer. Accordingly, Caine's Elliott is a lesson in nondescript repression. As Stephen Schiff pointed out in his review of the picture, Caine plays Elliott 'beautifully: arms held stiffly by his sides, mouth crinkling in feigned jollity; eyes lit by a twinkle that's much too carefully controlled'.[11] Stiff, feigned, controlled . . . this was a brave and generous turn from a man whose essential goal at the time, we should remember, was to really impress himself on the Hollywood consciousness. But for Caine the movie itself always comes first. As Pauline Kael remarked at the time,

'He does no reaching for sympathy, and he never turns on the charm,'[12] choosing instead to let his co-stars shine. Indeed, Elliott is one of Caine's most taciturn performances, a study in quiet dignity. Caine really does take a back seat and let the rest of the movie go on around him, the still centre of De Palma's pyrotechnic storm. Even in the movie's few shots of Caine dragged up as Bobbi (most of the shots of Bobbi are, in fact, of a female stand-in) – when we all know exactly what has been going on – he refuses to acknowledge the masquerade.

The movie was well received by pretty much everyone save the more militant feminists of northern England. *Dressed to Kill* was released midway through the Yorkshire Ripper's five-year reign of terror, and the local women's movement thought the picture a disgrace. During one screening, at a cinema in Bradford, they went so far as to throw a bucket of animal blood at the screen. Yet De Palma's movie hardly argues for the murder of women. Indeed, in focusing on the repression that makes Elliott's life so uncomfortable, he and Caine were effectively making a plea *for* liberation – the liberation not just of women, but of everybody, man and woman alike. The over-rigid walk Caine gave Elliott speaks volumes about the psychiatrist's troubled desires, about the terrible burden the restrictions of bourgeois sexuality inflict. Though he has subsequently let it be known how little he enjoyed the mechanics of transvestism – lipstick, tights, leg-shaving and the like – Caine's Elliott was nonetheless an essentially feminist creation. As such, *Dressed to Kill* was Caine's most socially significant movie since *Get Carter*. Whereas during the sixties and seventies he had been an emblem of class war, in the eighties, as leftist politics fractured and variegated, Caine more than once represented the era's increasing emphasis on sexual politics.

Back home in class-torn Britain, Caine had always been happy to be ferried around by a chauffeur. Now resident in the US, though, he felt uncomfortable with such hierarchical practices. No matter how wealthy it was, the democratic, egalitarian thrust of his new neighbourhood made him uneasy with being driven around. The idea of a chauffeur here was a bit show-offy, a bit, well, English. The problem was that unless Shakira were to take the wheel, Caine was effectively housebound. Not only was there no public transport, but the man who had barked orders at his team of crack racing drivers in *The Italian Job* had no idea how to handle a motor. Though, as we have seen, he had bought his first Rolls-Royce – indeed, his first car – more than a decade ago, he had never learned to drive. And so, shortly after setting up home in Los Angeles, Caine decided to sign up for instruction and take the test in the brand new gold Rolls-Royce he had treated himself to. He passed after just six lessons – not bad for a man approaching fifty whose experience behind the wheel had been limited to turning the ignition key for the purposes of a movie close-up. Now he could dot about town as and when he pleased and not be thought to be pulling any kind of rank while doing so.

Like a poet determined to test himself against every verse form, Caine decided to take the lead in *The Hand* (1981) because, *Dressed to Kill* nothwithstanding, he believed he had never appeared in a genuine horror movie. Not for Caine the narrow furrow ploughed by so many contemporary movie stars. Like the actors of classical Hollywood's studio days (who for the most part were simply allotted roles when they were deemed to have time), Caine is a star who has been stretched; stretched rather more than most of his contemporaries, who tend to play things safe and choose roles that fit their image. In an age that prizes similarity over shock, predictability over constant 'prentice work, the sheer variety of character types Caine has played is remarkable. Let us, then, remark upon it: Michael Caine is an actor who pushes himself in order to keep learning and improving his craft.

Quite what he learned on the set of *The Hand* is a moot point, though. Oliver Stone's movie is regarded by many people as the worst movie of his career.[13] This is, though, sweet nonsense. To be sure, *The Hand* is overblown, bombastic, humourless. But how much more knowledge of and sympathy for men (though emphatically not for women – a trait it shares with all Stone's other work) there is here than in, say, *Natural Born Killers* (1994) or even Stone's maudlin take on Vietnam, *Platoon* (1986). What faults *The Hand* has are those of its genre. Despite the efforts of certain high-minded moralist critics,[14] most people find it hard to accord horror movies any more seriousness than the purely sociological. Instead, we laugh at them. We laugh at them, those Freudian moralists lecture us, because really we are scared by them. The truth is rather more prosaic. We laugh at horror movies because (the more intelligent examples aside – *Psycho*, for instance) they are so desperate *not* to be laughed at.

And it would take a man with a heart of stone not to laugh at *The Hand*. For one thing, Caine sports the craziest coiffure of his career in it. Perhaps the Samson myth was washing around Stone's consciousness as work on the movie proceeded, because Caine's character gets wilder in tandem with his hair exploding. By the end of the movie he is as uncontrollable as hiccups. Caine's big achievement in the role is to suggest that underneath this hairy, wig-flipping ape is a human being – an unpleasant human being, a human being wounded by his unpleasantness, but a human being nonetheless. Given Stone's love of bombast and melodrama – both elements to the fore in the movie – this is no small achievement.

Caine plays Jon Lansdale, a cartoonist living in the peachy sunlit quietness of Vermont with his wife Anne (Andrea Marcovicci) and their daughter Lizzie (Mara Hobel). However, for all the rosy weather that forms its backdrop, the Lansdale's marriage is a stormy one and Anne has decided she wants a trial separation. The couple are debating the idea on a drive into town when Lansdale *does* get separated – from his right hand. It gets scythed off by a truck that passes the car just as Lansdale is pointing his finger out of the window. Gone is the hand with which Lansdale draws the cartoons that pay the family's way – the hand that comes, in the movie's Freudian structure, to stand for his patriarchal power. Symbolically castrated, Lansdale goes from mere misery to mental turmoil, and things get worse for him when, reduced to accepting a teaching post on the west coast, Anne tells him she and Lizzie will not be joining him.

From here on in, the movie pans out in precisely the way seasoned horror watchers would predict. Lansdale's hand, mysteriously missing after the accident, goes walkabout, terrorizing and then throttling all the people who have conspired to make its former owner's life a misery. The hand is, in other words, a physical embodiment of Lansdale's, if not unconscious, then at least suppressed desires – the id to his superego. Unsurprisingly, of course, it turns out that the hand is no more real than the sham of the Lansdales' marriage. Lansdale has, in fact, been blacking out and committing the murders he has been ascribing to his missing limb. A retelling of *Psycho*, in other words, though the applause for Stone's movie was rather more muted than it was for Hitchcock's.

Given the limitations of the form, though, Caine pulls off some sterling work here. As a study in psychic damage and derangement, Jon Lansdale joins a long list of Caine characters wounded in inaction. Lansdale's eyes are haunted by lost possibilities long before his hand goes missing. And as his world falls further apart, Caine's Lansdale retreats more and more into himself, his movements more contained and constrained by the frame. Lecturing his students on the art of the cartoonist, Lansdale analyses an illustration and says it gets across an 'entire series of emotions with the minimum of expressiveness'. It is a line that might have been written about Caine himself. As the movie grinds on and the exigencies of the plot require Lansdale to get wilder and wilder, Caine manages simultaneously to suggest a creature withdrawing into its shell.

There is a marvellous moment when one of Lansdale's beddable young students strips off and propositions him and Stone cuts to a close-up of Lansdale's face, a study in wondrous, nervous glee. Like Sean Connery, Caine is always on the lookout for any comic potential in a scene, and here he serves up not the ribald cackle one might expect from a middle-aged washout but a wry astonished chuckle at his good luck. Even at the end of the movie – Lansdale by now a blood-lusting crazy with a hairdo like an upholstery accident – Caine manages to imbue the character with far more dignity than Stone's picture deserves. Far from looking motivelessly malignant, Caine's Lansdale suggests, rather, a man in the grip of a fierce breakdown. Strapped into a psychiatrist's chair with wires coming out of his head, he looks not like the caged monster of cliché but like Harry Palmer refusing to crack under interrogation at the end of *The Ipcress File*. He looks, if you like, like an angry young man refusing to apologize for being angry. Had Stone been willing to take his cue from such iconic accretions and low-key playing, he would have ended up with a rather more interesting movie. Caine aside, though, the picture merits no more than the sound of one hand clapping.

There is probably no sensitive heterosexual alive who is not preoccupied with his latent homosexuality.
Norman Mailer[1]

Cut above: Caine with Julie Walters in *Educating Rita*. © British Film Institute

Though by no means a well man, John Huston had long since checked out of the hospital where Caine and Connery had made what they thought was a deathbed visit to the director in 1977. Tired and emphysemic as he was, Huston was still managing to work and had even managed to act in – as well as direct – *Wise Blood* (1979). Nonetheless, as he approached his seventy-fifth birthday, Huston would have been few financiers' first choice to helm a major production. Indeed, he was not the man Freddie Fields first approached to direct *Escape to Victory* (1981; US: *Victory*). That honour went to Brian G. Hutton, the man who had directed Caine in *Zee & Co* a decade earlier. The choice was vetoed, though, by the movie's star, Sylvester Stallone, who wanted to work with a director he could learn from. At a cost of an extra $250,000 in health insurance, Huston was hired for the production.

As Caine, who was the movie's second lead, could have told Stallone, though, Huston was not a director given to passing on advice. He wasn't even a director given to direction. A couple of weeks into the shoot, when a baffled Stallone asked Caine why he wasn't getting any pointers from Huston, Caine suggested he ask the man himself. Huston told the director *manqué* exactly what he had told Caine on the set of *The Man Who Would Be King*: that good casting all but negated the need for direction. Caine, of course, was reassured by such quiet professionalism; the rather less confident Stallone seems to have taken it as a barbed comment on his abilities as an actor.[2] The result was one of Stallone's uneasiest performances in a movie that before it needed anything needed the insouciant bravado of actors knowing they are taking part in a bit of nonsense.

Escape to Victory is essentially *Stalag 17* (1953) with soccer – a prisoner-of-war movie that centres on the football pitch. Caine was cast as John Colby, a former England player incarcerated at a German prison camp within whose barbed-wire fences he manages a soccer team. After the team is watched on the field one day by Major Von Steiner (Max von Sydow), Colby is asked to play his men against a team of German troops in a Paris stadium. With a promise of proper rations and kit for his men, Colby agrees, at which point the escape committee suggests he turn the event into a break for freedom.

Even after two decades of blockheaded blockbusters, the concept of *Escape to Victory* sounds risible, and matters were not helped, as more than one critic pointed out, by the fact that Caine's footballing manager would have been at least two stones overweight for the most friendly of five-a-side knockabouts. Why was he cast? Partly, of course, because he and Huston had got along so well on the set of *The Man Who Would Be King*. And partly because *Escape to Victory* airs debates around meritocracy that, while utterly ahistorical (nobody questioned the class system in real German prison camps), are familiar components in the Caine oeuvre. At one point in the movie Caine's Colby gets to tell his superior officers that if they insist on lumbering him with a bunch of no-good nobs rather than let him choose a team best equipped to beat the Nazis he will literally not play ball. 'If it's confined to officers,' he rasps, storming around their quarters like a bear in a net, 'I'm not bloody playing. I want a decent team . . . I want the lads . . . your escaping is just some bloody upper-crust game.' Twenty-odd years before his first film, it seemed, Harry Palmer was alive and well and banged up in a German prison camp.

In need of a hero to set against its anti-hero, the movie calls on the talents of Stallone. He plays Hatch, an uppity Canadian who would try to bust out of the camp every day if only the escape committee would let him. And if only they would, for Stallone's presence drags the picture down into levels of inanity the original scenarists must have marvelled at. Screenwriter Yabo Yablonsky had based his idea for the movie on a true story of a group of prisoners of war that did play the Germans at football – and won, for which efforts the Nazis gunned them down. That first scenario had been drafted in the mid-seventies, when downbeat endings were *de rigueur* in Hollywood movies. By the eighties, though, reassurance was the order of the day and Yablonsky's story was restructured accordingly. With its mass liberation denouement, war movies don't come with happier endings than that of *Escape to Victory*. Hence the presence of Stallone, who isn't just in that prison camp for the benefit of an American audience dumbfounded by the rules of English soccer. He is there to portray once more the character he had been playing since *Rocky* (1977): the plucky underdog who comes good in the end.

Caine, meanwhile, is there to give the movie its only moments of dignity. Indeed, he and Huston construct one scene that is masterly in its grim economy. Hatch, having tried to escape once too often, has been placed in solitary confinement. Since he knows the whereabouts of the Parisian resistance, though, he is vital to the escape plan and must be part of Colby's team. But if he has to be in, then somebody else has to be out, and it falls to Colby to tell his hapless goalkeeper Tony (Kevin O'Calloghan) not only that he is out of the team but also that he is going to have to have his arm broken in order that the Nazis cannot insist he play. Huston shoots the build-up to the breaking of Tony's arm in a succession of close-ups. We see Caine's Colby sweaty and pensive, a tight shot of Tony's arm, a closer shot of Colby doubtful and dread-ridden, his eyes pregnant with tears as he bows his head – and then, at the moment of impact, Huston cuts away refusing the chance to sentimentalize the moment.

Alas, this is the only scene carrying anything approaching genuine emotional freight in Huston's movie, whose problems are not merely silliness but those attaching to any picture about sport. Sport is often talked about as a kind of drama, but movies centring on it usually end

up reminding you that sport has, in fact, none of the shape and control of drama. If you want drama in your sport movie, you can't be
very sporting with your sport. You have to bend it out of shape in
order to accommodate both the needs of the narrative and the needs
of your stars. A meritocratic rebel like Caine's Colby, for instance,
would never have allowed his sick team member Fernandez (Pelé) to
play against the Nazis on the day he has a temperature and a stomach
bug, but the exigencies of story and casting mean Fernandez has both
to play and score. Such tomfoolery makes a mockery of any sense
Escape to Victory might be said to have, as does the transformation of
Colby from prototype Harry Palmer to the idealized noble squaddie
Caine had spent his working life trying to undermine.

The picture's escapism may have suited the Stallone image, then, but
Caine, now puffy and pouchy and no longer so easily amused by himself, gave the appearance of having sloughed off the ire and envy of his
youth and staggered into a middle age more suited to embodying post-
war Britain's acceptance of the management of decline. Acquiescent
in his own failures, the Caine figure (whatever the man behind that
figure thought of the Britain of the eighties) became an increasingly
voluble rebuke to the Thatcherite dream.

Nearly two decades after Joe Levine had told Caine that the camera
made him look like a homosexual, offers and ideas for movies in which
Caine would play gay kept coming. At a dinner party at Billy Wilder's
home, Wilder – who had directed the cinema's cross-dressing classic
Some Like It Hot (1959) – told Caine how much he had admired his
performance in *Dressed to Kill* and hoped that they might one day work
together. Characteristically, what Wilder most liked about Caine's transsexual psychiatrist was its attention to detail. 'The gestures,' said Wilder,
'were all right.'[3] Given the dearth of quality Caine product in the
eighties – and certainly of quality Caine comedy product – given, too,
Caine's refusal ever to sugar a part, how one regrets that he and that
arch cynic Wilder never managed to work together.

How one regrets, too, the fact that Caine and Orson Welles failed
to make a movie together, despite various attempts on both sides. The
last project Welles suggested to Caine was, in fact, the only one they
agreed would suit both of them down to the ground. The problem was,
Caine had to tell Welles, that he knew that a movie version of Ronald
Harwood's play *The Dresser* had already been cast. Albert Finney was
to play the show's grand old thespian (the part Welles had seen himself
in) and Tom Courtenay his wildly camp dresser. Absurd to suggest that
Welles and Caine would have made for a better bickering double act

than what turned out to be the movie's Finney/Courtenay wizardry, but they would have found new tensions in the movie's dynamic. Finney and Courtenay knew each other of old; long before the picture went before the cameras each would have had a rough idea of what the other would do in any given scene. Not so Welles and Caine, mutual admirers both, but utterly virginal as to the other's working practices. What would Caine have done to calm and quieten Welles's habitually thunderous scene-stealing? How would the strident tenor have tried to silence the pitch-perfect baritone? Ten years earlier Caine had been raised to new aesthetic heights by the threat of an on-screen besting by Larry Olivier. Having to mince and pout opposite Welles's Nietzschean grandiloquence could well have shifted Caine up another gear.

Instead of the Wellesian Übermensch, though, Caine took on a rather more worldly superhero in his next picture. Having run rings around Sylvester *Rocky* Stallone in *Escape to Victory*, he found himself up against Christopher *Superman* Reeve in *Deathtrap* (1982) – literally up against him. Once again, Caine was playing a bisexual. This time, though, he was playing a bisexual who had to kiss another bisexual in front of the camera. What Joe Levine made of this scene is not on record, though what Caine made of it is plain for all to see: he made it a masterclass in cinematic acting technique.

Caine has said that both he and Reeve were nervous on the day the kissing scene was shot, a nervousness doubtless compounded by the fact that the scene was scheduled for late in the day. To ease the tension, the two men drank their way through the best part of a bottle of brandy in the hours leading up the shoot. Astonishingly, then, the kiss – surely the longest seen on screen since Cary Grant and Ingrid Bergman all but dined out on one another in Hitchcock's *Notorious* (1946) – looks neither nervy nor drunken. It is, in fact, the highlight of a movie rather too bogged down in wry self-referentiality.

More cunningly plotted even than *Sleuth*, Jay Presson Allen's screenplay of Ira Levin's Broadway hit is a series of Brechtian booby traps desperate to go off. Caine plays Sidney Bruhl, a burnt-out mystery playwright who tells his wife Myra (Dyan Cannon) that he is going to steal a new play from the guest they are expecting to dinner – his former student, Clifford Anderson (Reeve). Myra thinks he is joking, but shortly after Clifford arrives Sidney strangles him and buries him in the garden. In bed later that night, the couple are woken by an irate Clifford, who bludgeons Sidney and scares Myra – who has a heart condition – to death. At which point Sidney comes round, the two men congratulate each other on having put into practice their brilliant plan to bump off Myra, and kiss . . .

There are more twists and turns to come before the movie is over, of course, but nothing in *Deathtrap* is as intriguing as that kiss – transformed as it is by Caine into a textbook example of what the movies can do that the theatre can't. What, one wonders every time one watches the film, can the stage actor playing Bruhl have done *after* the kiss? Because Caine, in the five or ten seconds that follow the embrace, gives Sidney Lumet's camera a marvellously compressed exposition of character under emotional pressure. We watch as Caine's Bruhl looks at his dead wife with the utmost tenderness, see his face shade first into thoughtfulness and then more deeply into rue as he picks up the phone and calls for an ambulance. And then, the call over, he snaps straight out of his despair and starts barking orders at Reeve's Anderson. It's a marvellously modernist moment in an already self-conscious movie – Caine giving his audience not quite acting lessons but, rather, lessons in the decision-making process, the engineering if you will, that goes into acting – and all this while keeping the plot moving along.

Sadly, *Deathtrap* has little else that need detain us. Caine is marvellous throughout the picture – watch him stumble drunkenly off a train near the opening of the film – which is a way of saying he was far too good for it. Lumet chose to film much of the story in theatrical long-takes, a decision that slows things down rather. Moreover, that modernist kiss aside, Caine's naturalistic instincts sat uneasy with the archness of Levin's plotting, which is essentially just *Sleuth* without the earlier picture's interest in class. Nonetheless, the tics and twitches of Caine's Bruhl, his Cowardesque handling of the movie's often beguiling dialogue served to pump life into a character that barely existed on the page. 'You just look at what the character does and says and then try to figure out what kind of person he is,' Caine told one interviewer during the movie's East Harlem shoot in the spring of 1981. 'What came out for me . . . was that my character was simply criminally insane. . . But I also try to play this insane character as a real person with human quirks.'[4]

Deservedly, Caine won many a good review for his work in the movie. Nonetheless, there was still a sense that the move to Hollywood and Caine's concomitant decision to trade on his abilities as a character actor rather than on his iconic star persona was resulting in his being stretched less rather than more. Finding new facets of Michael Caine-ness, he was discovering, had been far more testing work than building up from scratch the antique dealers and psychiatrists and investigative journalists he was now being asked to play. Moreover, since none of the movies he had made while resident in Hollywood had made any play with the tensions and torsions that had animated his most vital creations, a slackening ennui began to undermine Caine's self-image. 'He's been under terrific pressure from society because he was once a successful playwright and has now written a lot of flops, and the pressure has brought out things that were already in him but were under more control until separated failures turn him more and more into a desperate character. It's a study of a menopausal nut case.'⁵ Nobody is calling Caine a nut case, but try reading his description of *Deathtrap*'s Sidney Bruhl again, substituting 'actor' for 'playwright' and 'starred in' for 'written'.

Perhaps unsurprisingly, Caine took the rest of 1981 and the first half of 1982 off and began to tend his new nest. One of the first things Caine had done on arriving in Los Angeles was to take out an international subscription to *Country Life* magazine. Though he loved the Californian climate, it was the damp, verdant, lush pastures of England that remained his emblems of the good life. In Beverly Hills, he joked, he spent the bulk of his spare time watering his naturally arid garden. So it was with perhaps more than the usual joy that Caine received the news from the then twenty-four-year-old Dominique that she was to marry her horse-riding boyfriend Roland Fernyhough that November. May would have been nicer, or September – grey, sodden, darkened, mulchy November (not April) is the cruellest month in the British calendar – but Caine was happy just to have an excuse to go home for a few weeks to help plan and organize the wedding.

During the lull between movies Caine became something of a staple on the LA social scene, too. By now an accomplished raconteur (as long ago as the filming of *Play Dirty*, André de Toth had referred to the 'joking, witty and bright Michael Caine – always competing with the David Niven image'⁶), Caine could be relied on to entertain at any dinner table or cocktail party. When Princess Michael of Kent visited Hollywood it was Caine who gave a dinner for her at the fashionable restaurant Morton's. And when, a while later, the Queen came to visit, it was Caine whom she called on to entertain her when the car-dealer she had been sitting next to failed to come up with the goods. They spent the rest of the evening exchanging jokes.⁷ What Caine wanted now, he decided, was a little humour in his working life, too. 'The thing I really enjoy doing is comedy,' he had said on the set of *Deathtrap*, 'but nobody gives anything to me that's funny.'⁸ Not for much longer they didn't.

One of the grander ironies of Caine's Hollywood sojourn is that while he went there with the aim of making bigger and better films, his best work during the period was actually done in British movies. To be sure, Caine got to work on some superior product while resident in Los Angeles, but his two stand-out performances of the first half of the eighties were in movies that originated in his home country – *Educating Rita* and *Mona Lisa*. Why so? Largely because both movies reflected on and bounced off Michael Caine the starry icon. When Caine accepted his part in *Educating Rita* plenty of wise Hollywood heads cast doubt on his decision. Caine had, after all, turned down a role opposite Sally Field to make this small British picture. Field had recently won the Best Actress Oscar for her role in Martin Ritt's *Norma Rae* (1979). What was Caine playing at?

To be fair, the doubters had a point. *Educating Rita*, which had been a massive hit on the London stage, first at the Royal Shakespeare Company's small theatre and then in the West End, was, as its title suggests, a play about a woman. Whatever Caine was going to do in the movie version he was definitely going to be doing so as the second lead. Caine, on the other hand, could have retorted that much the same would obtain in whatever the producers had planned for him with Sally Field. Moreover, Field was an established actress – especially with that Oscar behind her – while Julie Walters – the woman Caine was going to play opposite in *Educating Rita* – was making her screen début. On top of that, the movie was to be directed by his old friend Lewis Gilbert, the man who had sealed Caine's reputation when they had made *Alfie* together a decade and a half earlier. Second fiddle or not, there was every chance Caine could dominate proceedings in *Educating Rita*.

The movie offered, after all, a return to the vaguely class-conscious British drama that had made Caine's name. *Educating Rita* is essentially a reworking of Shaw's *Pygmalion*, though there is something of *Frankenstein* in its plot, too. Caine's English don Frank Bryant falls unrequitedly in love with Rita (Julie Walters), a working-class Open University student in his charge. But as Rita abandons her familial roots and gains in social confidence through being able to discuss the likes of Blake and Forster, Frank comes to believe that he has created a monster. Where once she was an authentic model of integrity and truth, now Rita merely spouts the received ideas of middle-class blather.

The movie, in other words, investigates the crossing of precisely those social boundaries Caine himself had had to traverse in order to prosper. As conceived in Willy Russell's original play and subsequent screenplay, Frank Bryant is little short of a caricature – the etiolated academic of a thousand ivory-tower satires. As played by Caine, though, he becomes a man withered as much by what is inside him as by what goes on outside. Caine makes Frank's disillusionment with

Rita (as this ugly duckling transmutes into an elegant swan) a projec-
tion of his own turbid feelings, his own doubts about the trajectory
his life has taken. By deepening and thickening Frank's emotional
undertow, Caine not only roots Russell's otherwise schematic drama
within a more general historic movement – the emancipation and
betterment of the working class – but also does what he had been
adamant he would: he steals the thunder from Walters' vivacious but
one-dimensional Rita.

Just as Caine had wiped the floor with the old stager Olivier in
Sleuth, so here he burns Walters' fireworks off the screen. To watch
Caine's Frank watch Rita and wonder what he has done to her – to see
his eyes film over with shame and ennui – is to watch an object lesson
in screen dramatics. Or rather, as Pauline Kael remarked at the time, in
the lack of them: 'The goal of Caine's technique seems to be to dissolve
all vestiges of "technique". He lets nothing get between you and the
character he plays. You don't observe his acting; you just experience
the character's emotions. He may be in acting terms something like
what Jean Renoir was in directing terms.'[9]

Caine himself has cited another European influence for his conception
of Frank: Josef von Sternberg. Abandoning the *Pygmalion* parallels, he
chose instead to focus on the similarities Frank bore to the character
played by Emil Jannings in von Sternberg's *Der Blaue Engel* (*The Blue
Angel*, 1930). In that movie, Jannings's middle-class schoolteacher falls
head over heels for low-rent hooker Lola (Marlene Dietrich) and finds
himself gradually being dragged down to her level. But whatever the
inventory of influences on Caine's Frank, what amazes about the conception is its seamlessness, its sense of life merely being lived in front
of the lens. Always a calm actor, Caine here seems more laid-back
than ever, and he visibly relaxes even more whenever Walters takes
centre stage (impossible, despite Russell and Gilbert's 'opening out' of
the original play, to talk about *Rita* in non-theatrical terms).

Educating Rita gave Caine (who put on thirty pounds for the role)
another chance to strut his drunken stuff, and there is a wondrously
genial bafflement behind his ruddy, bleary eyes and Neptune beard as
he stumbles around the groves of academe. Whether Caine convinces as
a drunken *professor*, however, is another question. Caine has claimed
that while filming the movie (it was shot in the summer of 1982, not in
the Liverpool of its setting, but in Dublin – advantageously for Caine
since he didn't have to pay tax there) he met a similarly bearded and
beer-stained tweedy type and asked him whether he was a lecturer in
English, to which the answer was, apparently, yes.[10] Well, it's a nice
showbiz anecdote, and it might even be true – middle-aged humanities

professors do tend to go for country fustian. But the point is that how-ever well-read we know Caine to be, he never quite cuts it as a man who has the whole of the English canon at his fingertips, much less as a man who used to be a poet. Joyous creation that Caine's Frank is – see him clown drunkenly on a dance floor, or stumble Lucky Jim-style around the lecture hall, cap askew, gown at half mast – he is really *only* a drunk. That said, he is one of the best drunks the movies have ever had and Lewis Gilbert was justified in predicting to Caine as the production wrapped that both he and Walters would be nominated for Oscars.

While *Rita* offered more evidence of Caine's delight in variety and versatility, it pointed up, too, a common link between many of the characters Caine was now being asked to play. Thirty years after he had been bawled out on that Horsham repertory stage for hammily acting drunkenness, Caine had developed a reputation for being one of the screen's finest portrayers of alcoholism. Partly this was down to that early lesson about how a drunk is a man trying to act sober. But partly it was down to the fact that unlike, say, Sean Connery, Caine hadn't eased into middle age with anything like grace. In 1980, when Connery hit fifty, he still looked a preternaturally handsome specimen of manhood. Indeed, there was a case for saying (and many people have said it) that the still admirably lean Connery was getting better looking the older he got. Not so Caine, whose waist had begun to swell almost as soon as his bank account had and whose face had been, if not ravaged, then at least rumpled by the years. By the time he hit fifty, in 1983, he had a strong-arm hold on those roles that called for a kind of dilapidated reserve, a sense of dissolute shame, an air of talent gone to waste. (This may be why Caine himself is habitually thought of in those terms in profiles and interviews: he becomes his parts so well that his parts subsequently become him.)

As if to hammer the point home, Caine found himself up against the whiplash beauty of Richard Gere in his next movie, *The Honorary Consul* (1983). More than a decade later, Gere would play opposite Connery in *First Knight* (1995), a movie that consisted largely of the two actors joshing each other about their respective sex-symbol status. In *The Honorary Consul*, however, Gere had no such competition. Caine's Charley Fortnum, the movie's titular civil servant, is a sagging, slobbering wreck of a man – 'pitiably small beer', as a colleague describes him.

Caine, though, was putting away rather a lot of booze on the shoot. Not, it should be stressed, in order to get drunk, but in a bid to steer clear of the dysentery that everyone else on the movie had come down with no sooner had they arrived in Mexico. Long a victim of upset stomachs on out-of-the-way shoots, Caine had learned the hard way the kind of preventative measures that worked for him. And prefacing every meal with neat vodka, accompanying every mouthful of the meal with a mouthful of wine and rounding things off with neat brandy, Caine did indeed manage to avoid the bug. Whether he avoided hangovers is another matter, but fortunately for him Charley Fortnum always had a hangover.

With his hair dyed grey and his straggly, Flaubertian moustache similarly whitened, Caine's Fortnum was a study in sybaritic dissipation. Fortnum's walk came with a built-in stumble and his speech patterns were similarly entropic. He can barely get a sentence out without slurring. Yet somehow, this sad sack has contrived to win himself a stunningly beautiful young wife – a beautiful young wife who works part-time in the local whorehouse. Welcome to Graham Greeneland, a country in whose moral quagmires and quandaries Caine has gone on finding himself very much at home. When Fortnum's wife gets mixed up with Gere's Dr Eduardo Plarr and Plarr gets mixed up with the local radical theological terrorists and they get mixed up with Fortnum to the extent that they mistakenly kidnap him, the plot has thickened in ways that only Greene can stir.

Certainly the director, John Mackenzie, never really gets to grips with these complexities. Mackenzie, who had made a name for himself a few years earlier with *The Long Good Friday* (1979), was an action man first and last, and hence an unhappy choice to helm a cerebral movie like this. *The Honorary Consul* takes for ever to get going, and then seems over almost before it has begun. There is no time for any of the actors to round out their characters and even Caine, for whom his part might have been made,[11] turns in something of a shorthand performance.

The movie was chiefly memorable, then, for introducing Caine to Bob Hoskins, a young pretender on the block to celebrity cockney status. The two men became firm friends, after Caine first took time to advise Hoskins on what he called ' 'ow to look after your money'.[12] They have subsequently appeared together in several other movies, though here they are on screen together so infrequently that they have little chance to play off one another. Moreover, when they do get to rub up against one another, Hoskins' chief of police, Colonel Perez, affects a Hispanic accent of cartoonish absurdity that undercuts any potential drama.

There is, though, no gainsaying the power of the scenes Caine and Gere share. 'You sonofabitch,' Gere is said to have uttered when Caine arrived on location some weeks into the shoot. 'You come down here and I've been busting my ass in this horrid slime-hog backwater. You're going to come waltzing in here for a few weeks and steal this movie.'[13] On the contrary, however, Gere has never been better than when he is up against Caine in *The Honorary Consul*. Watch Gere's Plarr come to realize his complicity in the terrorist violence the movie comes to centre upon. His face – that study in suety blankness that has so often made whole pictures unreadable – seems to take on meaning merely by dint of Mackenzie's cutting between it and Caine's own features, wracked with ironic self-reproach. The result was not a great movie, though at the time it had some claim to being the best film treatment Graham Greene had ever received – save, of course, for Carol Reed's *The Third Man* (1949). Twenty years and thirty-odd films later, though, Caine would star in the best Greene adaptation the movies have yet given us.

Failure is lovable and what is lovable is commercial.
V. S. Pritchett[1]

Sister act: Caine with Mia Farrow in *Hannah and Her Sisters*. © British Film Institute

In 1984, just as Lewis Gilbert had predicted, Caine was again nomin-ated for a Best Actor Oscar – for his role as Frank Bryant in *Educating Rita*. Proud of the work he had done in that film, believing it, indeed, to be not only the best he had ever done but perhaps the best he would ever do, Caine at first thought he had a real chance of winning. When he saw who the other contenders for the title were, though, he began to have second thoughts. Albert Finney and Tom Courtenay were both up for *The Dresser*; Robert Duvall for *Tender Mercies*; and Tom Conti for *Reuben, Reuben*.

Seasoned Academy Award watchers shared Caine's doubts. Frank Bryant simply wasn't the kind of role that won Oscars. The 'natural' potential Oscar-winning role in *Educating Rita*, after all, was that of Rita herself. The movie had called on Julie Walters' character to do what all Academy Award-winning characters have to do – go through a life-changing drama and emerge at the other side as a better person. And indeed, Walters was herself nominated for a Best Actress award. Still, she was no shoo-in. Caine's precision-detailed Frank Bryant had so overshadowed Rita's own dramatic arc that Walters had effectively become the movie's second lead. Whatever their chances, though, Caine went along with the pretence – or pretended to go along with the pretence – of believing he was a potential winner. In fact, other, rather more pressing matters were concerning him.

Caine, as we have seen, had left England at precisely the time that the country was about to change into something rather more like the homeland he had long dreamed of. Within weeks of his departure the new Conservative government under Margaret Thatcher had slashed the higher rates of income tax and (among many other liberations) freed up the capital markets that movie production depended on. Had Caine stuck things out just a few months longer, he could have found living in England a lot easier than he had done throughout the seventies – could even, perhaps, have managed to live well while doing less work.

Perhaps simply because of this accident of bad timing, Caine had never been entirely happy living in Hollywood. In the five years he had been there he hadn't been short of parts, but even his most undiscerning fan would be hard-pressed to argue that his roles had improved during that time. Indeed, the part that had garnered him the most critical interest in that half decade had been *Educating Rita*, a British film made in Ireland. And so, during the build-up to the 1984 Academy Awards ceremony, he and Shakira made a promise to themselves: if he didn't win the Oscar this time around they would pack their bags and return home to England.

In the event, the Oscar went to Robert Duvall for *Tender Mercies* – a terrific Bruce Beresford movie in which Duvall gives one of the best performances of his career. There was nothing to be ashamed of in losing out to a movie that good, as Cary Grant all but said to Caine at an after-ceremony party hosted by Irving Lazar. 'You were a winner here, Michael,' Grant whispered in Caine's ear.[2] Understandably, Caine was much moved, though perhaps there was something about

Grant's use of the past tense that ought to have given him pause. The next two years were going to prove very lean indeed.

Certainly lean was the word for *Blame It on Rio* (1984), Caine's next project, for which he had rapidly to shed the weight he had so assiduously put on for *Educating Rita*. Over the course of just six weeks, Caine lost the best part of three stones on a diet composed of equal parts pineapple and water. Though the resultant new figure was hardly that of Cary Grant at fifty-one (the age at which Grant had still been convincingly incarnating cat burglars on the French Riviera for Alfred Hitchcock), nonetheless Caine looked pretty good. The problem was, he really did need to look like Cary Grant for this movie. Had it been made twenty years earlier, *Blame It on Rio* might well have been written with Grant in mind. Its story of a middle-aged man being attracted to and seduced by his best friend's teenage daughter was (minus any actual seduction, of course) classic Grant territory. Younger women had thrown themselves at Grant throughout his career and nobody in the audience ever batted an eyelid because nobody in the world could begin to conceive of any woman ever turning Cary Grant down. As Audrey Hepburn had said to him in *Charade* (1963), 'You know what the matter with you is? Nothing.' Grant's debonair classlessness worked the same trick on everyone. Caine, though, could never pretend to (would never want to pretend to) classlessness. Even playing a rock solid middle-class type, as he does in *Blame It on Rio*, the wrinkles on his shirt, the wondrous inelegance of his gait, betray his parvenu status.

The movie was directed by Stanley Donen (the man who, twenty years earlier, had made *Charade*). Donen had also helmed some of the great post-war musicals – *On the Town* (1949), *Singin' in the Rain* (1952), *It's Always Fair Weather* (1955), *Funny Face* (1957) – so there was hope that he might bring a little élan to the movie. Instead, he brought an old man's semi-comprehension of contemporary mores; rather than guying the whole set-up, he took it on its own tawdry terms. Whenever in doubt about what to do, Donen simply had Caine's teenage amour take her top off. It was an ugly sight, not because the teenager in question – Michelle Johnson – was unattractive, but because directors with a light touch are few and far between, and having been blessed with lightness they ought not come on hot and heavy. Caine pretty much made this point to Donen on set (and made others off set, telling one paper, 'I don't like to be with bare-breasted women on screen because no one is looking at me for a start! I'm wasting my time. Even the women are looking at her tits to see how they compare to their own!'[3]), though the director was having none of it. Not for the first time in his career, Caine gave the lie to those who would have it that he will be in anything so long as he can take the money and run. He will be in anything so long as he can moan about it in a corner, and then take the money and run.

The real sadness, though, is that there need not have been anything to moan about. With Donen on board, Caine had sufficient reason to feel comfortable with the project. On top of that, the script had been co-written by Larry Gelbart, who, after the cack-handed work he had done on *The Wrong Box* back in the mid-sixties, had proved himself one of the snappiest wisecrackers around. Gelbart, who had written the scripts for the TV series *M*A*S*H*, knew how to build to a gag, as well as how to build on top of one. Caine had every right to expect a winning light comedy. Add to that a three-month shoot in Rio de Janeiro and it looked like he was on to a winner. As he told *Screen International*: 'Stanley knew I wanted to do a comedy as I haven't done that many. The film is no great political or social thing, it's just a romantic comedy in a lush place. It's completely escapist entertainment. You should come out of it laughing.'⁴ Never was a wish more father to a thought.

Fortunately for him, you couldn't blame it on Caine. As Chris Peachment pointed out in his *Time Out* review: the 'sole reason to catch it would be to monitor one more step of Caine's increasing excellence as middle age overtakes him'.⁵ Donen, who had pioneered the Hollywood cinema's use of the split-screen image, makes ample use of that Brechtian device in the movie, along with the similarly distancing straight-to-camera scenes familiar to Caine from *Alfie*. Once again, Caine's marvellous *faux* intimacy towards the camera works miracles, but there is no denying that these are the only vital scenes in the movie's sorry 100 minutes. Backed by a song of platonic awfulness, *Blame It on Rio* is possibly Caine's worst picture ever, and is certainly his most undistinguished.

Then again, what about *The Jigsaw Man* (1984), a lame spy thriller taken by Bond director Terence Young from a lame novel written by his wife Dorothea Bennett? Impenetrable and implausible by equal measure, the movie told the story of one Sir Philip Kimberley (Caine), a British spy who defected to the Russians in the sixties and has subsequently degenerated into a hopeless drunk. Unimpressed with their catch, the Russians hatch a plan to surgically alter this washed-up Englishman's face and send him home, there to get his hands on a list of Soviet double agents. Before long, though, the new-look Kimberley has become something of a double agent himself, playing his Russian minders off against the British secret service and exposing a high-ranking traitor into the bargain. It all ends happily, with Kimberley reunited with his estranged daughter Penny (Susan George) and joining forces with his would-be English nemesis Admiral Scaith (Laurence Olivier) to sell their secrets to the highest bidder.

So much, at least, can be pieced together from several viewings of the film and a reading of the original novel. Like too many jigsaws, *The Jigsaw Man* was missing several of its pieces. And there was good reason for this lackadaisical construction. The movie had been being put together on a hand-to-mouth basis for the best part of a decade, Young firming up one financier only to have him pull out as another one momentarily signed up. Caine himself had been talking excitedly about a project in which he would play Kim Philby since as long ago as 1976, although Philby himself was rumoured to be less than delighted by the casting. For all his putatively egalitarian leanings, Philby – who had turned to communism while at Cambridge in the thirties and was probably the most successful Soviet double agent of the Cold War era – was a thoroughgoing snob, and he declared himself appalled at the prospect of being played by what he saw as 'nothing more than a jumped-up milkman'.[6] 'Which shows just what a great communist *he* is,'[7] quipped Caine – and if only some of this class tension had strung its way through the movie, *The Jigsaw Man* might have proved more interesting. As it is, the movie was another low point for Caine – one for which he almost didn't get paid.

The picture had finally begun shooting in the spring of 1982, but by June of that year the project had been shut down due to cash-flow problems. Laurence Olivier had walked off set following legal advice that he was unlikely ever to see any money for the project and it was left to the doggedly professional Caine to hold things together. He went on working without the promise of any real money for a while, but six weeks into the shoot the plug was finally pulled. At which point he discovered that the Concorde ticket he had been issued with to fly him over to England from LA was only one-way: he had to pay his own fare back home.

Subsequently, of course, Caine put on the near three stones required for the part of *Educating Rita*, which was shot, as we have seen, in the second half of 1982. As that movie came to a close at Shepperton Studios, Caine was approached once more by Terence Young, whose producer Benjamin Fisz had granted him another £4 million in order to wrap *The Jigsaw Man*. On the proviso that he would finally get his agreed fee of $900,000, Caine agreed to stay on and finish the movie.

Such a crooked time scheme perhaps explains to the hapless viewer why the Jigsaw Man is more of a Yo-Yo Man. Has any actor's size and weight fluctuated so visibly during the course of a single movie? The switchback course of Caine's weight is the most interesting thing about this unfathomable mix of cliché and cack-handedness. Even Caine's accents fail him. Neither the Russian he adopts for the bulk of the movie nor the deep southern Yankee voice he puts on for several key scenes are actively bad, but the movie gives him so little to do with them that they become mere technical exercises. Caine might have bested Olivier a decade earlier on the set of *Sleuth*, but merely by walking off the set of *The Jigsaw Man* Olivier had put himself back on top in their little tussle. And things were going to get much worse for Caine before they started to get better.

Water (1985) was written by Dick Clement and Ian La Frenais, the sitcom whizzkids who had created *The Likely Lads* off the back of the Angry Young Man revolution of the sixties and had so precisely anatomized eighties Britain in the huge hit TV series of 1983, *Auf Wiedersehen, Pet*. They had never, though, had a big success in the movies and *Water* did nothing to alter that. This attempt at transplanting the ethos of Ealing comedy to the cynical self-regarding eighties had disaster written all over it from the start. Not that Caine thought so. Perhaps it was the prospect of a lengthy shoot in the Caribbean followed by a final week's work on the Devon coast that decided him. But within hours of receiving a first draft of the script, he had given La Frenais the thumbs up at a Hollywood party.

Caine played Baxter Thwaites, the English governor of Cascara, a Caribbean island that Margaret Thatcher, apparently forgetful of her extravagant spending on the Falklands War of a couple of years earlier, has decided to wash her country's hands of. No sooner is Thwaites told, however, than mineral water is discovered on the island and the British government decides to change its mind. By now, though, there are other parties interested in getting their hands on Cascara and it is left to Thwaites to play the bureaucrats off against one another so that he might maintain autonomous control for the island and the inhabitants he adores.

Caine has a lot of fun as the kind-hearted and caring governor Thwaites – as decent a character as he has ever played. (The part would have been a natural for Maurice Denham or John Le Mesurier in the glory days of British film comedy twenty or thirty years earlier.) Raffish yet dishevelled, Thwaites reminds you that no actor has ever embraced the slump of middle age so wholeheartedly as Caine. Not for him the girdles and wigs one giggles at on so many stars of a certain age. Alas, the movie gives him far too little to do. Caine and

Fulton Mackay (who had made his name on television in Clement and
La Frenais's *Porridge*) play nicely off one another, but Billy Connolly's
troubadour-style revolutionary, a misplaced farceur who drags the
movie down into inanity, is given all the best opportunities. Ever the
professional, Caine knew things were going awry. 'If they go broke on
this they're not going to give me any more work,' he said ominously
on set towards the end of the shoot.[8]

Turbid as *Water* turned out, though, its star need not have worried.
Within three days of the movie's wrapping he was back on set for John
Frankenheimer's *The Holcroft Covenant* (1985). Even for an actor
as prodigiously productive as Caine, this inter-movie turnover was
uncustomarily speedy, though the reasons for it were not at all panic-
fuelled – were, indeed, mundane in the extreme. James Caan had
dropped out of the picture just as the cameras were set to roll and
Frankenheimer needed a replacement as quickly as possible. Caine,
meanwhile, had always wanted to work with the director of *The
Manchurian Candidate* (1962).[9]

Perhaps unsurprisingly, star and director hit it off from the first.
So much so that Frankenheimer took to praising Caan for having
dropped out of the movie: 'I will be forever grateful to him,' he said,
'because he gave me the greatest gift that anyone has ever given me
which is Michael Caine and I must say that Michael Caine is the best
actor that I have *ever* worked with.'[10] What Frankenheimer adored
about Caine was his unstinting professionalism, his relaxed dedication
to the job in hand. Gene Kelly once said of dancing that if it looked
like you were working, you weren't working hard enough. Frankenheimer spoke of Caine's acting in the same terms: 'He does it so – on
the surface – easily, yet he works his tail off. He brings so much to the
part. He brings not only expert professionalism and total dedication
but he makes my job so much easier, he gives me exactly what I want
and you can't ask for anything more than that.'[11] Frankenheimer was
so in tune with Caine's philosophy of work that he understood his
seeming need to be in anything: 'That's all terrific but on top of all that
is this enormous talent and craftsmanship, and that doesn't come from
doing one movie; that comes from doing fifty movies, which is what
he's done.'[12]

Caine later responded to all this praise with the ironic cool that has
never gone down well in his native country: 'He did say that [I was the
best actor he had ever worked with] . . . with the exception of Freddie
March . . . I think it is because he's also worked with a lot of troublesome actors and I am the least troublesome of actors to work with on
a movie set. I just do it and get in a car and go home.'[13] Over the years,

Caine has frequently griped about the treatment he gets in the news-papers of his home country, but this is simply because by and large the British take people at their own valuation. By refusing to dramatize and sentimentalize what he would call his craftsmanship and what his critics would like him to call his artistry, Caine's valuation of himself has always seemed to be that of the materialist pragmatist. By abjur-ing the indexes of romantic rebellion and adhering instead to a code of calm, classical efficiency, Caine has allowed people to believe that he is no more than an ice-cold clock-watcher.[14]

All that said, *The Holcroft Covenant* was never going to do any-thing to raise his reputation. Adapted from a dull dull dull Robert Ludlum novel, the movie was Caine's fourth clunker in a row. He spends the bulk of the film looking flustered and flabbergasted – as well he might since he is given little to do other than fly around the globe to be filled in on the latest plot development. The only moment of potential frisson comes when Caine's Noel Holcroft meets Anthony Andrews's haughty Johann Tennyson. Andrews had made a name for himself a couple of years earlier with a wondrously languorous, effort-lessly snobby part in the TV adaptation of Evelyn Waugh's *Brideshead Revisited*, but any hopes that he might bring some of Waugh's dis-dainful hauteur to the picture and rub Caine's Holcroft up the wrong way are soon dashed.

Having witnessed the releases of *Blame It on Rio* and *The Jigsaw Man* and the filming of *Water* and *The Holcroft Covenant*, 1984 was shap-ing up to be the worst year in Michael Caine's professional life since the dog days of the mid to late fifties. That it didn't quite achieve nadir status was thanks to a post-new-wave pop group called Madness. A bunch of cunningly witty, cod-Dickensian cockneys, Madness had grown up worshipping the example Caine had set the talented but tutorless working class. Now they had written a tribute song to their hero with the banal-sounding title 'Michael Caine'. And great was their joy when the song's subject agreed to take part in the recording, intoning over and over again throughout its thirty-two bars the equally banal-sounding words 'My name [pause] is Michael Caine.' Subsequently, Caine pronounced himself baffled at both the attention and the song, though the now eleven-year-old Natasha loved Madness and was overjoyed that her father should be making music with them.

Rightly so, for nothing Caine worked on in Britain during that year of Orwell's dystopia became him as well as what was eventually another Madness hit single. Indeed, the record has some claim to being the decisive factor in re-registering Caine's iconic status in a country that had got used to seeing him only in semi-anonymous parts in Hollywood flops. Caine's deadpan reading of that one repeated line over Madness's characteristically looping melodic structure served to bolster and buff a dilapidated image that had been in danger of falling into permanent disrepair. Certainly Caine's grimly self-referential appearance in Neil Jordan's *Mona Lisa* a year or so later would have been less historically charged, less emblematically suggestive, without the memory of 'Michael Caine'.

Before making that movie, though, Caine had to return to America. His plea for a part in a comedy had paid off – or, rather, half paid off. Even working for half his usual money, though, no actor was going to turn down the chance of appearing in a mid-eighties Woody Allen film. For the previous five years or so Allen had been at the height of his powers, releasing on a near annual basis one masterwork after another. *Manhattan* (1979), *Stardust Memories* (1980), *A Midsummer Night's Sex Comedy* (1982), *Zelig* (1983), *Broadway Danny Rose* (1984), *The Purple Rose of Cairo* (1985) – what can now be called mid-period Allen was almost as prodigiously productive as mid-period Caine. The difference was that Allen's quality control was singularly more reliable.

Certainly, after two years of bargain-basement drivel Caine needed a hit. Needed, moreover, a chance to stretch his actorly muscles in something with a little class. And Allen, the most prolific gag-writer of his generation, who had matured into a sombre anatomist of the workings and weaknesses of the human heart, reeked of class. Little wonder that in the autumn of 1984, when the call came through offering Caine a part in *Hannah and Her Sisters* (1986), he leapt at the chance.

The movie tells the story of a couple of years in the lives of three New York sisters – Hannah (Mia Farrow), Lee (Barbara Hershey) and Holly (Dianne Wiest). Hannah is happily married to Elliot (Caine), though he has been lusting after Lee for years. Lee, meanwhile, is unsatisfactorily hooked up with Frederick (Max von Sydow), a depressive painter who gets most of the movie's best one-liners. Holly is single, though by the end of the movie she is pregnant by Mickey (Allen), a former TV producer turned seeker after religious truth who just happens to once have been married to Hannah.

All that makes for a nicely circular, Ophülsian structure – though a rather grander one than Allen was accustomed to working on. Most of his pre- *Hannah* movies had been either non-stop gag-fests with scant regard for narrative logic, or else slower, sadder, romantic comedies. Here though, as well as working with all the actors already mentioned,

Allen was writing and directing for, among others, Julie Kavner, Sam Waterston, Carrie Fisher, Lloyd Nolan and Maureen O'Sullivan (Farrow's real-life mother). The result is curiously broken-backed – a movie of many marvellous scenes and vignettes, but one that never quite gathers itself into a unified whole. A movie, in other words, that laid itself open to the kind of surreptitious domination Caine had so often made a habit of.

Certainly, he overpowers the picture's titular lead in their every scene together. At the time, of course, Mia Farrow was Allen's real-life girlfriend and Caine has said he felt a mite uncomfortable at being between the sheets with her in her own bedroom while her then lover looked down on them through a camera.[15] Yet for all that unease – and although they had never been any more than show-business acquaintances – Caine manages to suggest a depth to his on-screen relationship with Farrow that isn't really present in Allen's screenplay.

Quite a lot isn't present in that screenplay, though, which has the dreamy quality familiar from Allen's more fantastical movies. Farrow's own part is so underwritten as to be all but gnomic, a problem not ameliorated any by Allen's admittedly characteristic decision to let her underplay even her biggest scenes. Not for one moment does Farrow convince as the star Broadway leading lady who has abandoned her art for family life.

Elliot, meanwhile, swerves wildly from comedy to heartbreak without Caine's managing properly to map a route between the two moods. Possibly this is the result of the heavy edit the movie needed to get it into a semblance of shape (at 107 minutes it was far and away Allen's longest to date), though neither can it be denied that the part is confusingly conceived and written. As Pauline Kael pointed out at the time, Elliot is really something 'out of bedroom farce that [Caine] seems expected to give other dimensions to'.[16] At one point Elliot has to tell his analyst that 'For all my education and so-called wisdom, I can't fathom my own heart.' Unfortunately, neither can Caine nor Allen. Much less, of course, can the audience make sense of him. Allen has said that he wanted to make a movie that took off from Tolstoy's belief that 'life is meaningless'.[17] Tolstoy had a point, of course, though if Allen really wanted to reiterate it why did he insist on changing the ending of Elliot's narrative strand? As things were in the original draft, the movie was to conclude with a chafed and disheartened Elliot still loving Lee from afar and wondering whether to leave Hannah. In the movie as is, however, we get a very unconvincing exculpatory voice-over from Elliot explaining how he had gone a little crazy but is now over it.

If all that sounds a long way from humour, then maybe it is a way of saying that what Elliot needed was a little more lightness – the kind of lightness we know to have been present in the original, far longer movie. One of the scenes that bit the dust, for instance, involved Elliot in a desperate lunge at Lee, which ended with her accidentally stabbing him in the hand with a pair of scissors.[18] In the movie we have, though, Allen gets most of the big laughs while Caine becomes the stand-in (or fall guy, depending on your point of view) for the director's more self-indulgently tenebrous side. The Farrows were known to be a little uneasy at what they saw as a barely veiled dramatic analysis of their collective shenanigans,[19] and Caine's Elliot was, perhaps, one of the ways Allen hoped to take cover from any family flak. Little wonder that when Caine asked Allen if he could wear spectacles for the part (the first time he had worn them throughout a movie since *Peeper*) 'because,' he said, 'I figure I'm playing you,'[20] the director acquiesced.

And yet, and yet. Unlike so many of Allen's leading men (and women) – Kenneth Branagh in *Celebrity* (1998), say, or John Cusack in *Bullets Over Broadway* (1994) – Caine refuses the opportunity to serve up just another Woody impersonation. No whining, no hand-wringing, no self-deprecating mug-pulling here. Indeed, at times Caine is magisterially good in this picture. His voice-over readings are textbook examples of inflection, and he uses to great comic effect the air of uncomprehending fury he had been perfecting over the years. Then there is the flustered, startled look that he had evolved for his previous movies' more slapstick moments, but which is here pressed into service to suggest a middle-aged man suddenly wrong-footed by passions and desires he had contentedly thought long departed.

Caine's achievement in *Hannah and Her Sisters* – and it is the biggest achievement of the movie – was to suggest a human core beneath the essential Allen figure of neurotic highbrow. Submitting to the part's refractive inscrutability, Caine almost managed to overturn its confusions and suggest they were the result not of a fractured narrative but of a fractured personality. Almost, but not quite. Allen's conception of Elliot was so unfocused and diffuse that the dimensions Caine manages to endow him with add up not to a multifaceted personality but to an aesthetic schizophrenia – to the radical inexplicability of life itself. In 1987, he was duly rewarded with another Oscar nomination for Best Supporting Actor.

*The great epochs of our life are the occasions when we gain the
courage to rebaptise our evil qualities as our best qualities.*
   Friedrich Nietzsche[1]

Dirty, nasty, slimy, kinky: Caine with Cathy Tyson in *Mona Lisa*. © British Film
Institute

In October 1985, Caine flew back to London to film a small role for
Neil Jordan's *noir*-ish thriller *Mona Lisa* (1986). 'I wanted him to be as
a man of his age would have been if he had chosen crime rather than
acting,' said Jordan, who was overjoyed at the prospect of having a
bona fide star appear in his third picture. 'I wanted him to return to [the
kind of] characters [he had played] in films like *Alfie* and *Get Carter*.'[2]

And indeed the part of Mona Lisa's Mortwell was something of a return to the kind of class-conscious roughs that had made Caine's name. As one writer has suggested, 'the Thatcherist sleaze of Mortwell, the gangland boss who services the demands of an amorally pleasure-seeking society' can be seen as an emblem of the decaying of the old-style working class Caine had grown up in and then out of.3 With his tawdry leather jackets and sharp but ill-fitting slacks, Caine's Mortwell is a sixties yob made good by the liberating decadence of the Thatcher boom. But he fits as uneasily into the new system's hierarchies as he does into those badly cut hipsters. Mortwell's introduction into the narrative is even presaged by a debate about tea in a snobby hotel. A well-liveried waiter asks Bob Hoskins' George whether he would like Earl Grey or Lapsang Souchong; just tea, comes George's Norman Wisdomesque reply. Later, Caine's Mortwell will tell George that he 'don't want to hear nothing about no tea'. Men like Mortwell, the movie argues, may run Thatcher's brave new England, but the strictures and strains of the old England still run them.

But *Mona Lisa* was a return to Caine's roots in more ways than one. Months before filming began and before he was actually on-board, Caine had a chat about the movie with the already-cast Hoskins at his offices in south London. A very familiar part of south London: the offices turned out to be part of a redevelopment of St Olave's Hospital in Rotherhithe – the hospital where Maurice Micklewhite had been born more than half a century before.

Hoskins had first mentioned the movie to Caine during the summer when they were shooting *Sweet Liberty* (1986), but at the time he had seemed little interested. The pay, after all, was going to be little more than what Hoskins called 'two bob and a lollipop',4 and the part itself was a small one. Certainly, Hoskins was startled when Caine agreed to play Mortwell. Indeed, he remembers how the actor who had had the most profound influence on his own technique approached him on the first day of the shoot. 'I bet you thought I'd never do it, you cunt,'5 said Caine, perhaps getting into character a little earlier than he has often claimed to do.

The small pay cheque aside, appearing in *Mona Lisa* was one of the wiser career moves Caine made during the eighties. He gave per-formances of equal virtue throughout the decade, but *Mona Lisa* was one of Caine's few eighties movies that rose to the challenge he set it. Though he was only present on location for five days and his cumu-lative appearances in the movie bulk up to rather less than ten of its 104 minutes, Caine's Mortwell dominates proceedings. Nor is this merely because he is the locus of evil around which Jordan's narrative revolves. Rather, it is due to the fact that Caine, surrounded by the likes of Hoskins, Cathy Tyson, Perry *EastEnders* Fenwick and Joe Brown, looks like Jimmy Cagney being worshipped by the Dead End kids in *Angels with Dirty Faces* (1938) – or like a professor hosting a tutorial for a group of very gifted pupils. Caine may not be in the movie long, but his influence and example permeates pretty much every scene.

Yet despite being its overarching presence, Caine actually has very little to do in the movie. Like Harvey Keitel's Sport in *Taxi Driver* (1976, a movie whose story *Mona Lisa* is a slightly more lyrical retelling of), Caine is really just there to move the narrative along. Nonetheless, for the part of the Dickensianly-named Mortwell – a low-lifer living the high life on the back of his pimping and porn empire – Caine invented what is probably his most monstrously amoral villain. Fetid and sweaty in even the dankest whorehouse, and baring unusually moist teeth in a mouth that seems to carry on slavering *after* the kill, Caine's Mortwell is all vulpine avarice – supped full with horrors yet hungry for more.

Jordan reserves his harshest, most expressionistically Stygian lighting set-ups for Caine, so that Mortwell, incandescent with ire, seems a product of the darkness that envelops him. To see him bark and spit at Hoskins that he get something 'dirty, nasty, slimy, kinky' on Raschid (Hossein Karimbeik); to see him, a frame later, slide into the arm-round-shoulder politesse of talking with an old friend ('all right then, George?'); and to see him, a frame after that, slink back to his arm-chair like the minotaur in his cave – to see all this is to be reminded that Caine's love of Cary Grant is not merely fathered by a wish to play light comedy. Admittedly, Grant never played a character as amoral as Mortwell, but there was, as critics have pointed out, a dark side to his bonhomie.[6] Here in *Mona Lisa*, though, Caine is working on another level altogether: using the tics and timing of his comedy to suggest not just evil but the grinning, insidious depravity that at the time was being talked of as if it were progress. Even as he prepared to move his family back there, Caine was capable of serving up his grimmest indictment yet of his new-look homeland.

'Alan Alda phones me up and said: "I've got just the part for you – a big-headed movie star". How could I refuse?'[7] Thus Caine on the origins of *Sweet Liberty*, a minor-league, movie-set comedy of little achievement, though of no small interest to Caine scholars. As a reworking of *The Purple Rose of Cairo* (the whining-voiced Alda, who wrote, directed and starred alongside Caine in the movie, clearly worships Woody Allen), *Sweet Liberty* is a failure. But as an investigation of the history and career of its movie-within-a-movie's leading man, it more than repays the price of admission.

Alda plays Michael Burgess, a history professor who specializes in the American War of Independence. So much so that his last book won a big prize and is now being turned into a bigger movie. Such a big movie that Burgess is appalled when he gets sight of the script, which has been cobbled together out of a couple of facts culled from his masterwork. Begging screenwriter Stanley Gould (Bob Hoskins, appearing opposite Caine for the third time in three years) to let him inject some historical accuracy into a rewrite, Burgess finds himself becoming a regular on set. There he falls for the movie's leading lady, Faith Healy (Michelle Pfeiffer), and when she agrees both to work his more realistic material into her performance and to go to bed with him, he becomes convinced that she has fallen for him, too. Alas, when Faith sleeps with her leading man Elliott James (Caine) in order to work some Method-actorly improvements on their scenes of on-screen passion, Burgess realizes he has been living a dream and decides to commit to his girlfriend.

Sweet Liberty is not, perhaps, as sickly as that synopsis might suggest, but it is a pretty syrupy confection nonetheless. The movie lacks bite, a vicious air that ought to be able to descend whenever things get too strained twixt Alda's academic and Saul Rubinek's hack director Bo Hodges. Nonetheless, there is fun to be had here, if only in ticking off the self-referential moments in Elliott James's trot through the action. Reviewing the film in *The New Yorker*, Pauline Kael pointed out that the stand-in used for Caine during the sword-fighting scenes was a rather less than convincing double. Indeed so, though had Caine in fact wielded his own sword things would have been no more credible. As we have seen, Caine's actorly skills had all been learned on the job. Having missed out on stage school, he had never learned how to fence. Similarly, his class roots meant he was a stranger to the riding of horses. Filming *Zulu*, it will be remembered, Caine had actually fallen off his horse and – *for the shots that made his name* – been replaced by a stunt double. *Sweet Liberty* joshes this delicious irony by giving Caine's Elliott a scene that *requires* him to fall from his mount. 'Get the camera on my face,' barks Elliott. 'I want them to see it's me.'

The real joke, though, is that Elliott is emphatically *not* like Caine. Elliott is the kind of actor Caine has always sought not to be: a pouting histrionic cad with a roving eye and hands to match. At one point in their relationship Alda's Burgess has to tell Pfeiffer's Faith that he is having trouble working out who she is: 'I'm trying to get used to how different you are,' he says. 'You're two different people.' Caine's

Elliott, though, wryly undermines this divergence between screen presence and off-screen reality. Elliott and the blackguardly swordsman he incarnates for the movie-within-the-movie are but a cigarette paper apart from one another, and yet they have no connection with Caine himself. In a movie obsessed with the search for authenticity, Caine's presence keeps reminding us of the fruitful friction that must obtain between role and actor if a *real* performance is to be the result. Caine's old adversary, that rebarbative theatrical modernist Joan Littlewood – who had told him that *Educating Rita*'s Frank Bryant had been the 'first fucking performance [he'd] given in 20 years'[8] – ought to have found time to applaud his Brechtian confection in *Sweet Liberty*. Lascivious but leisurely, he deftly steals the thunder from a far from stormy movie.

It had long been one of Caine's defining traits, of course, to give of his best when surrounded by others at their worst. Even in the half-witted *Half Moon Street* (1986), he contrived to haul himself from the wreckage of Bob Swaim's movie with his dignity intact.

The film was adapted from a slim and deeply unsatisfying novel by Paul Theroux – *Doctor Slaughter* – in which we are asked to believe that a beautiful young American economics academic working in London would choose to supplement her meagre income by working as a high-class call girl. On top of this, we are asked to believe that said call girl should fall, whilst going about her business, head over heels in love with a pensionable well-to-do by the name of Lord Bulbeck. And on top of *that*, we are asked to believe that said economics academic, having decided to work as a call girl, can't see that she is being used by the agency as bait to trap Bulbeck, who is organizing a Middle East peace conference.

Understandably, perhaps, Sigourney Weaver puts in a performance of stupefying inanity as Dr Lauren Slaughter, it's an impossible part – an all too typically Therouxian vision of a brainy but horny woman – but Weaver, all pop-eyes and earnest passion, never manages to suggest that she sees anything in Bulbeck (Caine) beyond his status.

The movie's only genuine moments of purchase derive from the links it makes between Theroux's Bulbeck and Caine himself. 'My father sold scrap iron in Limehouse,' the Bulbeck of the original novel tells Lauren. 'I was always a Labour man.'[9] In the film, Bulbeck's father was even more lowly – a docker who owned part of a greyhound; not far removed from a fish porter who liked a bet. As the movie progresses, such parallels multiply and converge. Bulbeck tells Lauren she must never call him by his real name, and they agree on that of Sam Weller – the name of the cockney wit in Dickens's *The*

Pickwick Papers. One evening, Lord Bulbeck takes Dr Slaughter to the Royal Court theatre – three decades earlier the site of the première of Osborne's *Look Back in Anger*. Whether this starry, playful self-referentiality was deliberately woven into *Half Moon Street* we do not know, but who could deny that it is the movie's only conceivable point of interest?

In the spring of 1986, Caine once more returned to England to film *The Fourth Protocol* (1987). The movie was based on a novel by Frederick (*The Day of the Jackal*) Forsyth,[10] and both Forsyth and Caine had a hand in producing. Forsyth, who had also written the screenplay, had invested $1.5 million; Caine around half that sum: $705,000.[11] 'I wouldn't want to be a producer again,' Caine said subsequently, though it is always easy to be wise after the event.[12] For the fact is that though the critics came down hard on *The Fourth Protocol*, the movie is one of Caine's best efforts of the eighties. It might not have the iconoclastic potency of *The Ipcress File*, but the picture is still an interesting analysis of what happened to the Harry Palmer types of two decades earlier.

Caine plays John Preston, as vigorously anonymous a name as that of Harry Palmer. Caine said at the time that he thought of Palmer as a Woody Allen-style secret agent and of Preston as Clint Eastwood,[13] but this is nonsense. Palmer was no bungler and Preston, at least as incarnated by the rather unathletic Caine, is no action man.

Like Palmer, though, Preston is something of a maverick within the secret service. At the start of the movie he is being bawled out for having broken into a fellow agent's apartment without authority. Preston, however, came away from the break-in with the goods, a fact that gives him the opportunity to bawl out his superiors in return. So far so *Ipcress*, although there is a difference. Though his immediate superior Brian Harcourt-Smith (Julian Glover) is appalled by Preston's antics, *his* superior, Sir Nigel Irvine (Ian Richardson) is quietly amused by them. Such amity twixt the upper and lower classes (along with such antagonism to the middle echelons) is evocative less of Palmer's early to mid-sixties than of the late sixties, the post-*Billion Dollar Brain* sixties, when the counter-culture was at its most hierarchical and divisive. Richardson's sly, smirking Irvine is a joy to behold as he pals up to Caine's Preston, while Glover's Harcourt-Smith is left looking as impotent and piqued as Guy Doleman's Colonel Ross was throughout much of the Palmer trilogy.

Nonetheless, Harcourt-Smith gets his way and Preston is demoted to lowly work preventing smuggling. Lowly but important, because soon Preston has arrested a man caught trying to bring a component for an atom bomb into the country. Harcourt-Smith refuses to take Preston seriously, though, and our hero is once again obliged to take matters into his own hands. In doing so, he comes up against Major Petrofsky (Pierce Brosnan), a Russian agent who has rented a house next to a US air base in Suffolk, there to build his bomb and blow the American forces sky-high.

It all sounds a little silly, but nobody ever got rich betting against the tensile strength of Frederick Forsyth's research. Whether writing about the hows and whys of bomb construction or the workings of the Norwegian telephone system, you can be sure he has got his facts straight. But has he got his story straight? Certainly *The Fourth Protocol*'s narrative drive is torsioned out of true by Forsyth's obsession with near naturalistic detail. Most of the interest in the movie centres on matters not of moment but mundanity. Early in the picture, for instance, Caine and his team of crack surveillance experts trail a suspect around the streets and subways of London. It's a riveting scene, largely because Forsyth and the director John Mackenzie – and, of course, Caine – are determined to play things for real. The problem is that as the movie develops, it does nothing to build on such incidents. Instead of escalating conflict, we get more of the same: close, detailed, painstaking surveillance – fun the first time; less so, the fourth.

Which is not to deny that there are pleasures to be had here. John Mackenzie, for instance, who had directed Caine a couple of years earlier in *The Honorary Consul*, finds something fearful in the young Pierce Brosnan; even his cheekbones look like weapons. And like Caine, Brosnan commits to his role with a ruthless realism. When, finally, the two men meet and fight things out, both have put in sufficient legwork to make the scene more than a post-modern joke on Harry Palmer scrapping with the James Bond *manqué*.

Mackenzie pays too little attention to Preston's life away from work, but in the brief moments we are treated to it is good to see Caine acting with a child. Good, too, to see Caine in top quality drunk mode as the movie opens. There is a delicious moment as he stumbles and sways into a swish Mayfair apartment block on New Year's Eve, telling the porter he's on his way to a party. As soon as he is out of the man's sight, though, he snaps erect and alert and goes into action. The ensuing safe-break is a thing of beauty, perhaps the only moment in the movie where *everything* works. We get to see numerous close-ups of the detailed work – the visual equivalent of Forsyth's densely registered prose – that Preston has to carry out on the security system of the flat he has broken into. There is a tense countdown as he patches into the alarm with no more than a stretch of wire and a Duracell battery. And then there is the safe-break itself, which besides the usual plastic explosive calls for a bin-liner full of water. Preston blows the safe as Big Ben tolls midnight and the party elsewhere in the building goes loudly haywire. At which point Preston examines his handiwork and wishes himself a Bond-style 'Happy New Year.'

Such lightnesses of touch are few and far between in a movie that takes itself rather too seriously. Part of the ideological import of the Bond movies, for instance, was their dogged lighthearted decadence, their insistence that before it was anything else espionage was fun. For a moment here – and later, when Caine's Preston quips that he likes to start the new year with a bang, much to the amusement of Sir Nigel Irvine – Forsyth's script (which had been gagged up by George Axelrod) looks like it might yoke the glitter of Bond to the grime of Palmer. Unfortunately, Forsyth's ideological single-mindedness, his commitment to the goodie–baddie opposition that Palmer had done so much to undermine, ensures that things remain resolutely uncomplicated.

Nonetheless, it was unfair of Caine to subsequently complain about the wordiness of Forsyth's script. As joint executive producer he'd had the chance to say things weren't right before the film went in front of the cameras. Anyway, there was no need to be wise after the event. *The Fourth Protocol* was not a bad film. Its problem was that the increasingly infantilized mainstream movie audience was moving away from anything that looked even remotely connected with events in the real world. Though it didn't make much money, it is nonetheless a respectable entry in the CVs of everyone concerned – more than can be said for too many of the films its star was involved with during the eighties.

Asked by a reporter about the parallels between Harry Palmer and John Preston, Caine said he thought 'Harry was a gifted amateur, which is what the British were 15 or 20 years ago. Preston is a top professional, which is what the British have become lately.'[14]

The wish was father to the thought, but the thought was under-standable because all the way through filming *The Fourth Protocol* Caine kept sneaking away to Oxfordshire to check on the progress of his family's new home. He had bought Rectory Farmhouse in the summer of 1984 for the now astonishingly low figure of £380,000. With eight bedrooms and a corresponding amount of land, the house was far from small, but Caine set about having it reworked, losing a fifties extension here, installing an en-suite bathroom there and having a whole new addition to the estate built that was bigger than the original house.

Even with that new spirit of professionalism abroad in the land – and even without *soi-disant* Marxist workmen going out of their way to subvert and delay things – all this work took almost three years to complete. Caine was as regular a visitor to the site as he could be, going so far as to spend some nights of *The Fourth Protocol* shoot sleeping there on a camp bed. But it was not until the summer of 1987, a couple of months after Margaret Thatcher's third consecutive election victory, that the Caine family finally left Los Angeles and moved into their new home.

'I want to believe in England again,' says Caine's Frank Jones sententiously towards the end of his next film, *The Whistle Blower* (1986). The movie was released around the time that Caine finally set up home in England again, but it had been filmed during the bleak midwinter of eighteen months previous. Caine has said Shakira told him it was time they left Beverly Hills for the Home Counties when she caught him watching reruns of *Black Beauty* on TV and sighing at the English countryside. Looking at the dull, suety, grey Britain *The Whistle Blower* serves up, though, even the most devout Anglophile would have to wonder why the Caine family chose to abandon their adopted home.

The movie is set in and around the Government Communications Headquarters (GCHQ) in Cheltenham – at that time the site of one of Mrs Thatcher's more pyrrhic victories. In 1984, she had succeeded, against much opposition from within her government, in preventing staff there from belonging to a trade union.[15] Julian Bond's screenplay hovers around – without actually touching upon – such issues. Nonetheless, its picture of a Britain effectively under American control was mildly seditious at the time of its release. The eighties were the most politically paranoid decade in Britain since the fifties, though in the later period it was the Left rather than the Right that was forever finding thinly veiled threats and treacheries wherever it went.

The Whistle Blower opens with Bob Jones (Nigel Havers), a GCHQ linguistics expert, telling his father Frank (Caine) of his suspicions about the recent deaths of two of his work colleagues. Frank counsels Bob to keep quiet and get on with his work, but a few weeks later, when his son 'commits suicide', Frank changes his mind. Convinced that Bob was murdered by the secret services, Frank, aided by left-wing reporter Bill Pickett (Kenneth Colley), sets out to investigate.

Shortly afterwards, Pickett himself dies in an 'accident'. Frank keeps on digging, though, discovering that his old friend from the Korean war Charles Greig (Barry Foster) organized Bob's 'suicide' because he had discovered the identity of a mole in the security service. This last is Sir Adrian Chapple (John Gielgud), a high-ranking officer whose nefarious activities are known about by British Intelligence but whom they have been unwilling to arrest for fear of further alarming the Americans. Frank, however, inveigles himself into Chapple's home and forces him into writing a confession before shooting him dead.

All of which might hint at the possibility of Caine's returning to the kind of quietly insurrectionary character that had made his name. Alas, *The Whistle Blower* does little with that possibility. The rhymes between Caine's life and Frank's – both served duty during the Korean war; both believe in keeping one's head down and getting on with the job in hand; both bristle at the brutal iniquities of the British class system, though both, most intriguingly, come to doubt the promise of America – are never really made to sing. Frank's anger at his son's death never spills over into anger at the larger forces that had connived at it. Caine, one might say, makes a convincing father but a far from convincing freedom fighter. This is not, though, because of a failure in his performance but rather because of the contradictions and confusions at the movie's heart. Frank's half-hearted undermining of the powers that be echoes one of the key themes of Caine interviews across the decades: the working class's supine acceptance of the fate that has been allotted it. The problem is that while such a reading can be constructed *a posteriori*, watching the movie itself is little fun. The big-screen début of TV director Simon Langton, *The Whistle Blower* is an intriguing and intelligent, but in the end dull, picture – rather like the show that had made Langton's name, the John Le Carré/Alec Guinness/BBC ho-hummer *Smiley's People*.

The movie comes to life only twice: once when Caine's Frank pretends to get drunk with a genuinely sodden Charles Greig in order to get the truth out of him. Barry Foster (the man who had taken the role Alfred Hitchcock offered Caine in *Frenzy*) offers up a loving image of a man becoming progressively more sloshed, but the machinations of the plot call for Caine's Frank to act drunk one moment and sober as a hanging judge the next – a challenge he carries off with an aplomb that never even threatens to descend into actorly self-regard.

The film's other great scene takes place when Gielgud's wondrously snobbish Sir Adrian, helping himself to a glass of malmsey wine, suggests with a regal sneer that Frank might like a 'beer'. The joy of the scene is that Caine manages to keep his class anger in check. Now into his fifties, he is no longer the angry young man but the (effortfully) controlled middle-aged man. Indeed, Caine's control and modulation throughout the picture is a joy to watch (would that Gielgud, that salty ham, had paid it heed). Caine's Frank starts life in the picture as an almost beatific presence, relaxed almost to the point of petrification. He moves with a wondrously judged middle-aged hobble, a gimcrack gait resulting not from tiredness but from an uncertainty of balance. In a world that is ready to wrongfoot him, in other words, Caine's Frank already looks unsteady. As the story moves along, though, Frank's movements become smoother and more certain, just as he becomes a man who knows what he will have to do to restore honour to his family.

Caine's problem is that his mastery of the screen overbalances the movie quite as much as that middle-aged dodder throws his body off kilter. Frank's desperate plea that he wants 'to believe in England again' has little power in a movie whose vision of England is the vision of anti-Thatcherite cliché: downtrodden, forbidding, grey and oppressive. But taken as a comment on the predicament of the actor who utters it, it has a kind of grim truth. Unhappy with the way things had worked out for him while living in Hollywood, Caine was desperate that his return home be seen not as a retreat but as a rethink. He really did want to believe in England again, but such belief could only come about if England returned the compliment.

Part Four
CBE

A prophet is not without honour, save within his own country.
  Matthew, 13: 57

Every parting gives a foretaste of death; every coming together again
a foretaste of the resurrection.
  Arthur Schopenhauer[1]

Master and Servant: Caine with Steve Martin in Dirty Rotten Scoundrels.
© British Film Institute

'I am so glad that you are coming back to this country, Mr Caine.'[2]
The words are those of Margaret Thatcher, the event a reception at the
American Ambassador's house in Regent's Park a day before the wedding of Prince Andrew and Sarah Ferguson, to which the Caines had
been invited. It was July 1986, the best part of a year before Caine and
his family would actually make the move back to Britain, but already
their imminent return was the subject of discussion in his homeland.

Certainly, Mrs Thatcher, the first British Prime Minister to have a near instinctive grasp of the syntax of semiotics, knew what this prodigal's return home meant: that her policy of cutting the higher rates of tax could be seen to be working. It meant that talent could be claimed to be flowing back into the country. More than that, if the likes of Michael Caine, the chippy class warrior who had hung on to his chips despite having hit the mother lode, could be seduced by her Conservative government's radical policies then so could the working class as a whole be kept on board. For Caine was one of the best advertisements there was for Thatcherism. Indeed, it could be argued that he had presaged and predicted the social and economic revolution she ushered in. The brave new classless Britain of the eighties was in theory a far more amenable place to Caine than its heavily demarcated forebear. Nonetheless, Caine has often said that the reason he brought his family home was simply so that Natasha could have an English education. 'I was helping her with her history homework one day and saw a book which said that World War Two started in 1941 when America went to war with Japan,' he told one reporter a few months before the Caines flew home. 'I thought she'd better go back to school in England for a while.'3 On the other hand, he has also said that the night Mrs Thatcher congratulated him for deciding to return home he toyed with asking her to cut his taxes yet further.4

Certainly, money was still a big concern. During the filming of *The Whistle Blower* he had characterized himself as a rather more picky actor than might once have been the case: 'Nowadays I can pick and choose what I do. If someone says to me there's a picture in the Atlantic, it'll take three months, but it's with a director and a co-star I don't like but they guarantee I'll win an Oscar, I say No thanks . . . Now I do parts in films I want to be in, with people I like. I'm too old and too rich to do anything I don't enjoy.'5 A year later, however, Caine was to be found shooting *Jaws: The Revenge* (1987), perhaps the worst-received movie of his career. By now accustomed to critical drubbings, Caine wrote the picture off with his customary bravado: 'I have never seen the film but by all accounts it is terrible. However, I HAVE seen the house that it built, and it is terrific.'6

In point of fact, were Caine to make the effort to see the movie he might find it rather less painful than he has been led to believe. *Jaws: The Revenge* isn't *that* bad. No, it's not a patch on Steven Spielberg's franchise-inaugurating original of twelve years earlier, but it is certainly a more ambitious entry in the series than either of the two intervening movies. Ambition is not achievement, of course, and this *Jaws* bites off rather more than it can chew. Nonetheless, the director Joseph

Sargent and writer Michael de Guzman deserve some credit for at least fooling around with their shark's status as psychosexual emblem. As the tagline on the poster put it, 'This time it's personal' – by which is meant that the vengeful shark of this movie wants to get his own back on the family that did his progenitor in a decade earlier. But it is personal, too, in that *Jaws: The Revenge* at least touches on conventional emotional issues. Just as the new monster of the deep is bent on devouring Ellen Brody (Lorraine Gary) – the woman widowed in *Jaws 2* (1978) – so, too, is the pilot Hoagie (Caine) bent on making her his wife. Ellen's marine biologist son, the Oedipal Michael (Lance Guest), meanwhile, is not sure which threat he considers the greater, which monster he should destroy first.

All of which is a way of saying that while Caine's role in *Revenge* is a comparatively minor one, it is also central to the picture's meaning. Yet what is most marvellous about his performance as Hoagie is its point-blank refusal to play metaphoric pawn in some arty allegory. Instead, Caine scuffs against the symbolic grain of the picture, serving up in his every scene the kind of unruffled naturalism audiences love him for. Indeed, it is *because* of Hoagie's refusal to treat the world as a metaphor that Ellen is drawn to him. As part of a family whose every moment is dominated by the *image* of the shark that killed its husband/ father, she cannot help but be drawn to a man who, on encountering the same beast, talks not of its mythic status, its vagina dentata-like image, it's almost Marcusean desire to overthrow the family, but carps instead about 'the breath on that thing'. Caine's presence, in other words, grounds *Jaws: The Revenge* in something approaching, if not reality, then at least a semblance of it.

Shooting took place from February through May 1987, with the exteriors wrapping at the end of March – just a day too late for Caine to make the trip to Los Angeles for the Academy Awards. Not that he was upset to have missed the ceremony. He had, he figured, trekked out to the ceremony and come away with nothing once too often to worry overmuch about his nomination for *Hannah and Her Sisters*. Though the movie had been one of Woody Allen's comparatively serious films – and therefore more rather than less likely to win some kind of award – Caine was pretty certain he wouldn't be a recipient. The part of Elliot had been an intelligent and sensitive one, but in Oscar terms it couldn't hold a candle to the competitors. The etiolated aesthetics of Denholm Elliott in *A Room with a View*; the sententious heroics of Tom Berenger and Willem Dafoe in *Platoon*; the saccharine theatrics of Dennis Hopper in *Hoosiers*: all these were shoo-ins when compared with Caine's light comic turn. And so the Bahamas shoot

went on even as Caine's name was pulled out of the Tinseltown envelope. Finally, after three near-misses, he had won an Oscar and chosen
to miss the event the better to wrestle a rubber shark.

After a clutch of thrillers, Caine moved into comic territory for the
closing years of the eighties. And the first of these, *Surrender* (1987),
turned out to be the best-written picture – *Hannah and Her Sisters*
excepted, of course – he'd appeared in for years. Happily, moreover,
Caine shows none of the ill-at-ease quality that had threatened to
wreck the Allen movie. *Surrender* was a screwball comedy, and though
it was no *Bringing Up Baby* (1939), it did, at least, do more than bring
home the bacon. Caine has fun in the picture, but his enjoyment does
not come – as it so often can – at the expense of the audience's. That
said, the movie was a flop.

   Why? Mainly, one suspects, because for a romantic comedy *Surrender*
was curiously dark and rancorous. Caine's hack novelist Sean Stein
starts out in the picture as what he would doubtless describe as an
empirical misogynist. So many women – wives, ex-wives, girlfriends,
ex-girlfriends, hookers – have dumped on him that he has taken
against the entire sex. Caine, who looks a nightmare in a succession of
pastel-hued blousons and track pants, was doubtless hoping to imbue
his character with a strain of the malice Cary Grant brought to even
his most charming roles. But the tension is slack and the writer/direc-
tor Jerry Belson lets Caine get away with, if not quite murder, then at
least mayhem. The set-up is decent enough for a rom-com, but there is
a viciousness to Caine's creation that Belson would have been wiser to
tame. Bluntly, Caine's Sean looks like he feels his hatred so much that
his change of heart in the arms of disappointed artist Sally Field never
quite convinces.

And with that, the Hollywood sojourn was over. Caine's first project
once back permanently on his home soil was a half-hour television
lecture on the techniques of film acting. One of a series of three pro-
grammes for the BBC (Jonathan Miller hosted *Acting in Opera*, Simon
Callow *Acting in Restoration Comedy*), *Acting in Film* was something
of a coup for Caine. The show centred on analyses of key scenes from
Alfie, *Educating Rita* and *Deathtrap*, with Caine taking a group of
young actors through the minutiae of his performances. As such, it
came as a poke in the eye to anyone who had ever doubted Caine's
mastery of cinematic technique. None of the scenes he chose to
examine *seemed* to be particularly challenging – no great emotional
range was required, no bravura leaps of actorly imagination. And yet

whenever anyone else (and the actors taking part included troupers as experienced and talented as Celia Imrie and Maria Aitken) was asked to join in they were exposed as rank amateurs by comparison.

Cometh the hour, cometh the man. Caine's brisk, no-nonsense pragmatism, his insistence that craft was of as much import as art, sat mighty easy in the Thatcher decade. Not for Caine the hyperbolic effulgence, the wilting aestheticism contemporaneously being parodied by Nigel Planer in *Nicholas Craig – The Naked Actor*. Instead, Caine abjured the romantic afflatus of 'actor speak' for the cool analytical precision of the classicist. The result was that much of what he pronounced sounded merely commonsensical, though like a lot of commonsensical pronouncements Caine's weren't common until he had pronounced them:

> When you are the on-camera actor in a close-up, never shift
> your focus from one eye to the other. Sounds odd, doesn't it? But
> when you look at something, one of your eyes leads. So during a
> close-up, be especially careful not to change whichever eye you
> are leading with. It's an infinitesimal thing, but noticeable on
> the screen. The camera misses nothing! Another tip from my
> own experience: when it is my close-up being shot, I pick the
> off-camera actor's eye that is closest to the camera and look at it
> with my eye that is furthest from the camera. This turns my face
> squarely toward the camera, so as much of my full face as possible
> is in the shot.[7]

Also made famous in the masterclass was Caine's belief that an actor shouldn't blink unless he wants his character to appear weak. Caine went through a couple of scenes with his 'apprentices', in one take asking the actor to blink while speaking his dialogue, in the second to keep his eyes resolutely open: 'Remember – on film that eye can be eight feet across.'[8]

The show went out on 27 August 1987, mere weeks after the Caines had taken up residence in Oxfordshire, and as such gave a mighty boost to the prodigal's return. When Caine had left England for Hollywood eight years earlier, there had been much carping in the press about his deserting a sinking ship. Many of the movies he had made during his time in Los Angeles had been received very badly, especially by the sniffier Fleet Street critics, and *Acting in Film* served notice that, despite his occasionally errant selection of roles, Caine was still an actor to be taken seriously. Though it would take a few years to filter into the mainstream, Caine's achievement in the show was to make himself heard once more in his home country. Quite as much as any of his subsequent movies proper, *Acting in Film* served to stamp once more Caine's aesthetic authority on the British film industry.

And yet the British-financed *Without a Clue* (1988) – the first movie Caine made while once more an English resident – is another of the pictures that he chose to omit mentioning in his autobiography. The omission is a curious one since, despite the bad press the picture got, Caine had good cause to be proud of his performance. His clueless Sherlock Holmes, a detective who can only survive with the round-the-clock assistance of Dr Watson, is one of the great comic creations of his career.

In truth, the movie is a one-joke affair – the joke being that Holmes was a fictional character invented by Dr Watson (Ben Kingsley) for the purposes of drama in his short stories. Alas, when the public demand-ed to meet Holmes, Watson was forced to hire a womanizing drunk of a ham actor, Reginald Kincaid (Caine), to fill the part. Cue pratfalls and inanity in roughly equal measure.

But Caine's pratfalls and inanity are so wondrously varied that the movie only rarely flags. Though the influence of Peter Sellers' Inspector Clouseau on Caine's Holmes is plain, so too is the fact that Caine knew it was an influence and worked *through* it rather than let it dominate his performance. Watch Kincaid as he sits on Holmes's magnifying glass: Sellers' Clouseau would have erupted at the loss of his dignity; Caine's Kincaid merely makes a silent grimace. Or see him swinging through the air on the curtain ropes of the theatre that plays host to the movie's denouement. Caine plays Kincaid's fear straight, boosting the laugh by undercutting the moment; Sellers could never have grasped the potency of such understatement.

Nobody could make great claims for *Without a Clue*. Enjoyable though it is, the picture is no masterpiece. But its presence in the Caine oeuvre is instructive in that it can stand as representative of the kind of work he takes merely to keep himself working. More than competently written and directed, the movie is exactly the kind of production that Caine might have appeared in in repertory theatre in the pre-movie age. Caine has said he never wanted to be a theatre actor,9 although he had that wish practically forced on him by what Harold Macmillan would have called 'events, dear boy'. Caine learned a lot in rep, and had he been born a few years earlier he would proba-bly have spent his life working in it. Moreover, he has organized his career on lines far more in keeping with those of repertory theatre than with those of the Hollywood independents. Though Caine has been self-employed throughout his career as a star, he has run that career as if he were employed by a studio and taken whatever work came his way. So, too, Reginald Kincaid, who, his last production having bombed at the box office, is only too happy to take on the role of Sherlock Holmes and do whatever Dr Watson tells him. Whether or not he intended it to be, *Without a Clue* is Caine's tip of the hat to his actorly roots; there is far more to this movie than initially meets the eye.

Caine was back in Victorian dress almost immediately for *Jack the Ripper* (1988), a three-hour-plus television drama with a $6-million budget. The acting workshop of the previous year aside, this was Caine's first small-screen foray since the late sixties. The million pounds he got for taking the job must have sweetened the deal. Nonetheless, one has to wonder how Caine felt about going back to the medium he had always regarded as second-class at best. Caine was fifty-five when filming began in the spring of 1988, and though it was only a year since his Oscar win for *Hannah and Her Sisters*, little he had done since the Allen picture had earned him any plaudits. Could it be that Caine, fast approaching the age at which his father had died, was beginning to wonder if the game was up?

If so, he needn't have worried. *Jack the Ripper* was a satisfying enough piece of television drama. In Britain it went out on the ITV network over two consecutive weeks on 11 and 18 October 1988 (the hundredth anniversary of the Ripper's infamous reign), airing a month later on CBS in America. This last was clearly the more important screening for Caine. 'It goes out in November,' he told one on-set reporter, 'in what they call the sweeps, because they tot up the ratings and see what they are going to charge for advertising. It is a very important, prestigious production.'[10] And so it was, though its import for Caine seems to have resided largely in how much impact it would have in the US. Caine might have been back on British television, but he was damned if he was going to do anything there that wouldn't boost his image stateside.

Jack the Ripper was the brainchild of David Wickes, the show's producer and director, who had cut his teeth on that low-life seventies cop show *The Sweeney*. Like that series, *Jack the Ripper* was a Euston Films production, the company that was also responsible for another lyric to London low-life, *Minder*. Euston, in other words, dealt in the kind of genre and iconography that Michael Caine had made possible. With their cockney rhyming slang banter and their delight in exposing the underbelly of the urban beast, Euston's shows were by-products of the *Ipcress* and *Alfie* era. But they were classy by-products. No television show has ever been better written than *Minder*, the closest the small screen has ever got to home-grown poetic drama.

Wickes had researched the Ripper murders for more than a year and was convinced he had finally worked out who was responsible (the case has never, of course, been solved by the police). Refusing to accept the claims put forward in Stephen Knight's well-regarded book *Jack the Ripper: The Final Solution* – itself the basis of a very fine film, Bob Clark's *Murder by Decree* (1979) – that the Ripper was in fact several men, all bar one of them Masons bent on covering up the fact that the Ripper's first murder had been carried out by Prince Albert, Wickes had decided that the murders were the work of only one man: a crazed surgeon using his victims for research into schizophrenia. Well, it's an explanation, though one that unfortunately undermines the rationalist mindset and class-conscious thrust of Wickes's three-hours-long drama. These twin forces are crystallized in the figure of Caine's Inspector Frederick Abberline, the detective said to have been Conan Doyle's inspiration for Sherlock Holmes. However, where *Murder by Decree* deconstructed itself by casting Holmes in the role of solver of the Ripper killings, thereby at once charging the establishment with murder but simultaneously exonerating it through the figure of the gentleman detective, Wickes's version of the tale never quite fulfils its radical impulse.

Abberline is established from the outset as a working-class cop all too wise to the machinations of the bourgeoisie. Using his most strangulatedly cockney tones since *Alfie*, Caine's Abberline reads 'pipers' rather than papers and looks at clocks to tell the 'toym'. 'We came up the hard way,' Abberline's superior tells him at one point as he counsels against his pursuing the Ripper too vehemently. 'We're pawns you and me and shilling whores . . . our sort can't win – you should know that by now.' Later, Sir Charles Warren (Hugh Fraser) tells Abberline he does not want him to come up with a case that will result in 'a crisis that will rock the British empire to its foundations'. The casting of Caine in the role of a radical but rational truth-teller, then, emblematizes the class tensions of Victorian London – a place where the moneyed could get away with murder simply because their victims were deemed so lowly they didn't count. But, having set out its anti-Victorian-values stall, Wickes's production shies away from the conclusion it has made most logical. Instead of deciding that there *was* a high-up conspiracy to prevent the police from finding the real killer(s), the show pins everything on a nutty old Darwinian (i.e. just the kind of rational man Abberline modelled himself on).

Jack the Ripper never outstays its welcome, but nor does it rise to the challenges it sets itself. Its attempts at *Grand Guignol* are undermined by the production's rather too cosy feel, a sensation bolstered by the presence in its cast of so many of Caine's old pals from previous movies (Ray McAnally, Susan George, Michael Gothard). Caine's performance as Abberline is never less than adequate, though that said it is pretty much a one-note affair. Bowled over by his stardom from their first meeting, Wickes seems to have let Caine do just what he pleased. 'I want,' said Caine at the audition, 'to play him fucking *relentless*.' Wickes smiled and told Caine the job was his. 'There was no need to carry on,' he said, 'here was a consummate actor who had grasped the essence of the part in a sentence.'[11] Maybe so, though that did not mean that the role did not need to build if the drama were to have any overall power. Caine's Abberline ought to have started out just as disenfranchised and cynical as his superior, coming only gradually to realize that something was indeed rotten in the state of England. Instead, he goes at things full-tilt from moment one, and though there is much fun to be had from seeing this dogmatic cop lumber around Victorian London, there is no denying that the show could have been a lot more demanding. Despite Caine's rampant professionalism in front of any camera, he may have taken the fact that this was a TV production as an excuse to coast.[12]

Though the finished result boasted one of his best comic performances, Caine coasted somewhat through his next project, too. The main reason he took the part in Frank Oz's *Dirty Rotten Scoundrels* (1988) was the chance it afforded him to spend the summer of 1988 with Shakira and Natasha on the French Riviera. The other reason Caine has said he agreed to the role is that the script, unlike so many of the comedies he had agreed to over the years, was a sure-fire winner. This, of course, is wisdom after the event. Nothing is ever a dead cert in the movies, and with *Dirty Rotten Scoundrels* there was more cause than usual to fear the worst. The movie was a remake of Ralph Levy's *Bedtime Story* (1964), a picture regarded by many as one of the nadirs of the popular cinema. Intriguingly, though, the Caine role in the earlier movie had been incarnated by one of the British cinema's ur-gentlemen. Four decades earlier, David Niven had been one of the stiff-upper-lipped, trimmed-moustache types that the teenage Maurice Micklewhite had felt undermined the realism of too many British movies. Now here he was, the cinema's one-time angry young man, agreeing to reconstruct a part he would once have called a lie.

Except that Caine's presence in *Dirty Rotten Scoundrels'* role of gentleman huckster serves to foreground the character's status as a fiction. Caine has said he considers being called a 'cockney actor' 'that most insulting of epithets',[13] but though he has demonstrated much range and versatility over the years he has never quite escaped origins. (Nor, of course, has he ever wanted to. Caine is very happy to trot out the stories of sarf London impoverishment when they are needed.) On the other hand, many of his roles have had more meaning simply because they have been played by a man whom the audience *knows* to be putting on a performance. When this 'cockney actor' affects a to-the-manor-born air, he does something far more radical than cock a snook at the upper classes. Just as he did in *Zulu*, Caine points up the fact that class is in itself a *performance*. All of which may be thought to have taken us rather a long way from a film that even the most fervent Caine admirer would find hard to argue is more than an effortless piece of frippery. But in its fooling around with disguise and role-playing, *Dirty Rotten Scoundrels*, whilst not Pirandello, is a movie as much about the con of the movies as it is about two con men scamming their way along the French Riviera.

The other man in question is Steve Martin, who was billed above Caine in the opening credits – the first time in many years that Caine had not been deemed a movie's main box-office draw. If it irked, it can't have irked for long. Who needs top billing, after all, when in your every scene together you can pull the rug from under your usurper? *Dirty Rotten Scoundrels*' problems are all to do with Martin: his mugging, his gurning, his polymorphously perverse body movements – all of them designed to get the big laugh, all of them embarrassments next to the snug containment of Caine's performance. Martin's first scene in the movie is a sob story designed to soak a rich lady out of her money. Martin windmills around the scene as if it's high opera, but your eye keeps focusing on Caine, in the back of the shot, who's doing no more than maintain a studious but disinterested look at the action. Such duets have always brought out the best in Caine (Anton Rodgers' phoney Franglais cop points up Caine's subtleties too) – the light, almost airy malevolence that underlies even his sunniest creations. There is a vicious gleam about Caine (never one of the cinema's most graceful types) as he gets to teach the pratfalling Martin the art of walking like a gentleman. Vicious, because Martin, like Cary Grant, like Sean Connery, is one of the movies' great movers – an athletic comic who can make his body do pretty much anything and needs no lessons in gait from Caine.

What Martin can't do, and Caine so beautifully can, is play havoc with his accent. While Martin's Freddy Benson is stuck with a Texan-sieved-through-LA drawl, Caine's Lawrence Jamieson fools master-fully around with a German accent, revisits the deep-southern lilt he had developed for *Hurry Sundown*, and toys with various calibrations of upper-crust English. *Dirty Rotten Scoundrels* was a triumph for

Caine – a triumph that took $40 million at the US box office. More than a decade after its release, in a 2003 poll for Blockbuster Video, Caine and Martin were (absurdly) voted best comic double act of all time. Perhaps unsurprisingly, talk of a sequel has long been on the cards. Should it ever materialize, one wishes it a kinder fate than the Harry Palmer sequels Caine unwisely agreed to in the early nineties.

Their three months on the Riviera over, the Caines repaired to London and their newly purchased apartment at Chelsea Harbour. Though it was little more than a couple of miles on the map, Chelsea was a far cry from the Elephant and Castle, where Caine had grown up half a century earlier. Indeed, he told one TV interviewer at the time, from his balcony he could pick out the Elephant's landmarks across the river, safe in the knowledge that he was never going back there. Momentarily content with his lot, he took his foot off the gas; 1989 was the first year since 1973 in which no Michael Caine movie opened at the cinema. Instead, he spent the autumn and winter relaxing: at one or other theatre in London, cooking for family and friends, beginning work on the garden at Rectory Farmhouse.

Anyone who thought that Caine was preparing to ease up on his workload and glide through the second half of his fifties had the wrong idea, though. A gap in his schedules had allowed Caine the time to take in some of the new Britain he had missed being created as the seventies became the eighties. But it was no more than a gap. By the spring of 1989 he was ready for work again, and the Caines decamped to New York city for the filming of a low-budget comedy thriller, *A Shock to the System*.

Based on an engaging Simon Brett novel set in the suburbs of London, this was a glamour picture trading – like Oliver Stone's then recent movie *Wall Street* (1987) and Brian De Palma's soon-to-be released take on the Tom Wolfe hit novel *The Bonfire of the Vanities* (1990) – on the Wall Street/Madison Avenue corporate glitz of the Reagan/Bush Senior era. Accordingly, Jan Egleson's movie rewrote Brett's original to take in not only Manhattan but also Long Island Sound. In the event, the move across the Atlantic did little damage to the novel's moral comedy of manners, but there is no gainsaying the feeling that had the movie been made in England Caine might have come out of it even better than he did. *A Shock to the System* (1990) is one of the great movies of Caine's middle age. Had it been set in the new London to which he had just spent six months acclimatizing himself, though, it could have been his masterpiece.

Why? Because the picture is, in essence, a retelling of Robert Hamer's *Kind Hearts and Coronets* (1949). No, Caine is not required to disguise himself eight times for the movie (as Alec Guinness was for the Hamer picture; rather than that kaleidoscope of roles, Caine is playing the equivalent of *Kind Hearts'* Dennis Price figure). And no, unlike Price's Louis D'Ascoyne, Caine's Graham Marshall is not explicitly committing murder in the name of class warfare. And yet, and yet. Caine being Caine, a class reading of the movie is nigh impossible not to make. Even at fifty-seven, after all, he still imbues his characters with shades of his angry young man origins. When Marshall, who has just murdered Robert Benham (Peter Riegert), is 'informed' of the man's demise, Benham is referred to as Marshall's 'superior', a term that Marshall is quick to correct: 'No: he was my boss.' Quite the young Jimmy Porter.

Certainly, Marshall shares something of Porter's (and Alfie's and Harry Palmer's) faith in the power of money. 'My father was a London butcher,' he says at one point, 'he told me there's no heaven – but Mayfair is the closest.' Two decades since Caine became an international star he is still mouthing sentiments the Henry Clarke of *Deadfall* might have made. 'What's the point of happiness?', Henry asked. 'You can't buy money with it.' Money Marshall has no problem with; happiness, though – that is in shorter supply. His wife Leslie (Swoosie Kurtz) is a thankless harpy and his bosses have just passed him over for a promotion for which he had thought himself a shoo-in. Homeward bound that evening and angry at the world, Marshall is accosted by a beggar on a subway platform. Half by design, half by accident, he pushes the tramp under the wheels of a train, fleeing the station without anyone having seen what he has done. The shock of the moment over, though, this accidental murder gives him new hope: if he can get away with it once . . .

Caine's big achievement in *A Shock to the System* is to suggest Marshall's Jekyll and Hyde morality without lurching between performative modes. In the voice-overs he is granted, Caine's Marshall talks of himself in the third person, actually saying after that subway incident, 'He wanted to split into two persons – him and the murderer.' And Caine masterfully suggests this split, sliding from bonhomie to bile and back again between breaths. Watch him when he is told that he isn't getting the promotion he had thought was his. Caine's Marshall suggests unruffled calm turning to unfettered chaos with no more than a slide of an eyelid. And he harnesses Marshall's schizophrenia so winningly that it rubs off on the audience. Just as we did with Alfie Elkins, we end up siding with Marshall against people who are rather more likeable than he is.

The only problem with Marshall is that – unlike in Brett's original novel – his character is badly underwritten. While Brett takes time to fill us in on Marshall's life and times, the movie (which clocks in at less than 90 minutes) just plonks him down in Manhattan and tells him to get on with it. Given such limitations, Caine serves up a lesson in character acting, fleshing Marshall out into a man not only with a past but with a present that we understand as having let him down. Caine's Marshall is chock full of regret at what he has become, yet none of this is in the dialogue: it is in the droop of Caine's maw or the flash of an eye. Caine humanizes this midlife sad sack, making of him a man still youthful enough to be disappointed by the world.[14]

Perhaps it was this air of sorrow that meant *A Shock to the System* ended up doing sadly little at the box office. The movie wasn't helped by an uninspired poster and tag line – 'He's having the crime of his life' – nor by its skirting the higher-minded moralizing on corporate greed that was then fashionable. As a fable of the eighties, though, it surpasses *Wall Street* and *The Bonfire of the Vanities* by a long mile, in the process giving Caine one of his best chances ever. Just as Graham Marshall refused to conform to the ageist constrictions of the new economy, so did his creator motor into his fourth decade as a star with the ebullient self-confidence of a man half his age.

22 1990–96

I think that's just another word for a washed-up has-been.
Bob Dylan[1]

Maybe it's because he's a Londoner: Caine as Scrooge in *The Muppet Christmas Carol*. © British Film Institute

As the eighties became the nineties, Michael Caine – at best a marginal figure in British culture for the past decade and more – came to dominate anew his home country and its vision of itself. His performances in *Hannah and Her Sisters*, *Mona Lisa* and *Dirty Rotten Scoundrels* had all in their different ways served to emboss once more Caine's image on the popular consciousness. The acting lesson he had given on national television had bolstered his claims to respect for his craftsmanship and artistry. His frequent appearances on chat shows and in the pages of the more popular newspapers were testimony to his easy charm and relaxed wit. Since the death of David Niven in 1983, Caine had had (and has gone on having) no small claim to the title of cinema's greatest living raconteur.

But it was the death of his three-time co-star Laurence Olivier, on 11 July 1989 at the age of eighty-two, that really worked to embed Caine back into the national iconography. Three months later, on 20 October, a memorial service for Olivier was held in Westminster Abbey and Caine was among the actors chosen to accompany the great man's coffin down the aisle. Walking alongside him were such loftily regarded talents as Peter O'Toole, Paul Scofield, Maggie Smith and Douglas Fairbanks Jr, each of them carrying a memento of Olivier's theatrical and cinematic career. Caine carried Olivier's Oscar for Lifetime Achievement and the screenplay Olivier had written for his movie of *Henry V* (1944). The picture had been a Powell and Pressburger-esque tribute to Englishness, a monument of unsentimental love to its director's homeland, a stirring advertisement for a nation still at war. Carrying the script for that film through the theatrical throng at Westminster Abbey, then, was a moment quite as freighted with meaning for Caine as the creation of Harry Palmer or Lieutenant Gonville Bromhead. 'I'm England, that's all,' Olivier had once claimed. Giving Caine the duty of escorting the *Henry V* script at his funeral was as good as handing that self-designated hon-our on. Whether Olivier meant the passing on to be read at all ironically is a moot point. Certainly, The Lord Olivier (as Larry loved to call him-self) remained until his death an emblem of an England by then long gone. Could his passing of the reins to Caine be read as a sly dig at the younger man who had inaugurated and embodied so much about the new England Olivier had come to loathe? Well, perhaps. Far more likely, though, that Olivier, rightly enough, saw the fifty-six-year-old Caine as quite as much an establishment figure as himself.

Nonetheless, Caine's resurgence as a British icon through the nineties and into the new century was a second wind that blew in two directions. On the leeward side he was feted by the high and mighty he had so long wanted to impress. On the windward, he became one of the key mentors of the new lad culture. During the nineties, Caine was the cover star on as many magazines as he had been during his sixties heyday. Interestingly, the magazines he turned up in (and kept turning up in; one of them – *Loaded* – went so far as to turn the story of *Get Carter* into a cartoon series) were aimed at young men, men too young to have seen him when he had first made his name.[2]

What did they see in him? Primarily, the fact that Caine had never disclaimed his background. Though his accent had modulated ever so slightly upwards over the years, Caine could never be mistaken for anything but a man who had started out as a lower-class Londoner. Four decades earlier, when he had begun the long struggle to extricate himself from his roots, Caine had been something of an oddity. Back then, people knew their place: 'Some of the greatest supporters of the class system are the working classes,' he remembered shortly before his sixtieth birthday. 'They keep it all going with phrases like "ideas above your station". . . When I became an actor nobody gave me any moral support. I became an outcast among my own people, they didn't want to know me. Everybody said: "Who do you think you are?" so I never went back.'[3] In the newly globalized nineties economy, though, everyone was an outcast. Either you were a class migrant or you were nothing. Even the south London of Caine's youth – from whose grimy deprivations young men had for generations followed their forefathers into portering or printing – felt the change. Camberwell kids of the seventies and eighties found themselves either a suit and an office job or a place in the dole queue. Adrift in a world their families and schooling had ill-prepared them for, such youngsters found in Caine an emblem of stability. Caine's down-to-earth upward mobility pointed a way through this new 'classless' chaos. Little wonder, perhaps, that Harry Palmer was to be brought (disastrously) back to life during the decade.

Other characters from the Caine back catalogue returned to haunt the culture too. *The Italian Job* and *Get Carter* were both re-released *and* remade, the latter featuring Caine as one of Carter's enemies. A remake of *Alfie*, with Jude Law in the title role, was released in 2004,[4] and there is talk, too, of *Sleuth*'s being given a make-over, this time with Caine taking on the Olivier role – playing again, in other words, the opponent of the character he originally incarnated.[5] Such about-turns – common enough in the theatre, of course, where actors can return to the same plays many times throughout their careers, refining and commenting on their earlier selves – are largely unheard of in the movies. Thus throughout his sixties and seventies Caine has managed to somehow both rest on his laurels *and* trade on his past glories. You can't get more British than that.

Things have not, of course, always gone swimmingly for him. On 12 December 1989, a few weeks after the Olivier memorial service, Ellen Micklewhite died at the age of eighty-nine. Caine's mother had for several years been a resident at a private nursing home with round-the-clock care from the staff. As a paying resident, though, she had

been able to do as she pleased, and what pleased her more than anything was bacon and eggs, white wine and cigarettes. Such had been
her staple diet, and Caine himself had long been devoted to a very similar one. After Ellen's death, however, he vowed to clean up his act.
Save when a role has required him to pile on the pounds, the Caine of
the nineties and noughties has been a somewhat trimmer, healthier-
looking actor than moviegoers had become accustomed to since the
mid-seventies.

Saddened by his mother's death perhaps even more than he would care
to admit, Caine took the first job that came along. *Bullseye!* (1990),
though, was nowhere near the target. In fact, it was so far off the mark
that Caine's Hollywood press agent, Jerry Pam, tried for perhaps the
first time in their relationship to dissuade him from making a movie. 'I
didn't want him to do it,' Pam has said, 'but he was determined. I
think what he really liked was that it was a chance to work with Roger
Moore.'⁶ The movie also afforded Caine the opportunity of working
with Michael Winner, a director who shares Caine's pile 'em high, sell
'em cheap philosophy, but who has never managed Caine's trick of
making the product in question worth buying in the first place.

   And *Bullseye!*, a comedy thriller written by sitcom stalwarts Laurence
Marks and Maurice Gran and *Goldfinger* lyricist Leslie Bricusse, was
one of Winner's biggest losers. Essentially, the movie is an update of a
Will Hay thirties war comedy – specifically, Basil Dearden's *The Goose
Steps Out* (1942). This time around, though, the Home Office, instead
of asking Hay to impersonate Hitler, asks Caine and Moore, a couple of
lowly London con artists, to impersonate a pair of scientists who have
managed to make cheap energy out of cold fusion. Caine has a lot of
fun with his voice in the movie, particularly with a deliberately bad
American accent. But the gags are weak – not a patch on the picture's
other big influences: Buster Keaton and the John Cleese-scripted *A Fish
Called Wanda* (1987), a surprise Britcom hit of a couple of years earlier
– and the plotting slack. Like Caine, Winner is clearly a man who loves
to work. Unlike Caine, he doesn't work hard enough.
   Indeed, though Caine spent the best part of the next twelve months
away from movie work, he kept himself busy by writing his lengthy
memoir, *What's It All About?* But by the spring of 1991 he was on
set once more, back in Hollywood, for the movie of Michael Frayn's
hit West End and Broadway play *Noises Off.* Directed by Peter
Bogdanovich, the movie was to prove Caine's longest shoot since the
days of *Too Late the Hero* and *Sleuth.* Frayn's play, a miracle of compressed chaos, had been transformed into a script of 225 pages – far

too long for a conventional movie (on which one page of script is roughly equivalent to one minute of screen time). But Bogdanovich, a devotee of Hollywood's fast-moving comedies of the thirties, had decided to have each scene played at such breakneck pace that those 225 pages would translate into a mere 104 minutes of movie time.

Fast scenes call for painstaking rehearsal, of course, and the shoot had only just got into its stride that Friday evening of 11 May, when Caine, relaxing in the Beverly Hills house he had rented from Leslie Bricusse for the duration of the shoot, was called to the telephone. On the other end of the line was a journalist on the British tabloid newspaper the *Sunday People*. Did Caine have any idea, the reporter wanted to know, that he had a sixty-five-year-old half-brother living in a nursing home in Beckenham, Kent? The answer was no. Maurice Micklewhite junior had known as a teenager that his mother visited a sick relative on a weekly basis, but she had told him it was a mentally ill cousin. In fact, she had been going to see David William Burchell, her first son, born 11 July 1925, and resident until just before her death in the asylum which may, as we have seen, inadvertently have inspired her second son's stage name – Cane Hill.

Perhaps the shock of this news explains the slightly diffuse quality of Caine's performance in *Noises Off* (1992). As the irascible director of a theatrical sex farce that keeps going wrong, Caine is clearly enjoying himself, but the movie gives him far too little to do. Flustered but never flabbergasted by the havoc his cast is wreaking on stage, Caine's Lloyd Fellowes steers a steady course from silent fuming in the back row, through front-row harangues and on to backstage hysteria. The problem is that the movie – and Frayn's original stage hit – calls for Caine to go through the routine not once but several times. While the other actors in the show get to run through their pratfalls from *Rashomon*-style variant viewpoints – so that we can see how easily chaos comes again – Caine's Fellowes functions merely as the production's chorus figure. Peter Bogdanovich was on solid ground in believing that Caine does some of his best work in reaction shot. Nonetheless, he would have done well to have given his star a little business of his own to attend to.

Largely because nobody had been able to work out how to translate Frayn's precision-tooled pandemonium from the stage to the screen, *Noises Off* had taken almost a decade to become a movie. Wisely, Bogdanovich opted not to water things down, instead keeping all the business of the original intact. Indeed, he may have made things even busier. Certainly, the movie has something of the frantic energy of Bogdanovich's post-modern screwball masterpiece *What's Up Doc?*

(1972). But unlike that earlier movie, nothing is at stake in *Noises Off* (a problem that doesn't exist in the stage version, the spectacular frivolity of which is always enough to ensure a wonderful show). Caine does his best to make Fellowes look like he is heading for a breakdown both professionally and personally (he is carrying on both with the show's leading lady and its stage manager), but the mechanics of farce end up taking precedence over any emotional truth. Bogdanovich would have done better to loosen Caine's reins and let him go all out for laughs.

For what one misses in Caine's Fellowes is the sense that a theatre director is ever *more* than merely a martinet: that he is, at different times, an inspiration, a lover, an enemy, a friend. Moreover, while Fellowes's cravat and silken blouson gesture towards camp, Caine remains resolutely heterosexual throughout proceedings. Since Christopher Reeve is playing the production's leading man, why didn't Bogdanovich have his two stars reprise their kiss from *Deathtrap? Noises Off* is, after all, such an archly self-regarding play that a little cinematic intertextuality – the kind of stuff that had sealed Bogdanovich's reputation two decades earlier – would have made up for the movie's more leadenly theatrical moments.

Noises Off hit British cinemas in June 1992, just a couple of months before David Burchell died. Thanks to his half-brother's money, the last year and a half of his life had been rather more comfortable than the preceding sixty-odd, and he was at least granted what he would not have had had that Sunday tabloid not come truffling: burial next to his mother in Caine's Thames Valley garden. It was a Dickensian ending to a Dickensian life – and Caine would put this literary example to good working use before the year was out.

Before that, though, there was a CBE to be willingly accepted in the Summer Honours List and a movie called *Blue Ice* (1992) to be unleashed on a far from willing public. Directed by Russell Mulcahy and co-produced by its star, this last has some claim to being one of the dullest movies Caine has ever appeared in. Tediously unexciting, yet never quite awful enough to merit ironic laughter, the movie clunks along at a dilatory pace – a still chubby Caine meant to be the romantic lead to Sean Young, a woman less than half his age.

Caine plays Harry Anders, a one-time spy turned jazz club owner who through becoming involved in a weapons' smuggling plot manages to uncover the fact that his former boss, Sir Hector (Ian Holm), is actually a crook. So far so *Ipcress File*, though Mulcahy's homages – seedy London scenes, a drug-induced hallucination sequence – fail to cut even Sidney J. Furie-style mustard. The movie's only interest is its playing up of Caine's fifty-nine years. Anders's old-fashioned Jaguar car and love of jazz are indexes of his fish-out-of-water status in the luridly drawn Britain Mulcahy is otherwise drawn to. As such, *Blue Ice* points the way towards the Caine of ten years hence, the Caine of *The Quiet American* and *The Statement* – an actor gesturing towards becoming one of the cinema's great old men.

After the Sherlock Holmes of *Without a Clue*, the Inspector Abberline of *Jack the Ripper*, and the titular duet of *Jekyll & Hyde*, there was only one emblematic character of the Victorian capital Caine had left to play – Dickens's Ebenezer Scrooge. The chance came in 1992 when he took on the role for *The Muppet Christmas Carol*, thus completing a unique tetralogy of roles. Maybe it's because he's a Londoner, but no other actor has played every member of this quartet of Victorian London icons. Was it mere coincidence that Caine had been asked to take on these roles *after* his much-trumpeted return to his home country and home town? Probably the answer is yes. Nonetheless, *The Muppet Christmas Carol* (1992) trades heavily on Caine's cockney origins. At one point the movie even treats us to a lingering shot of an old curiosity shop; the name above the store-front is Micklewhite.

For all this archness, Caine plays Scrooge without ham. Given that Rowan Atkinson's guying of history had recently been such a big hit on TV in the series *Blackadder*, the producers could have been forgiven for sending up the whole Victorian curmudgeonly stuff. Instead, they play Dickens's story for real, with Scrooge joining the distinguished list of villains on the Caine CV. For the movie's first hour he gives us a vision of pure malice – a malice made all the more strong by the fact that he is terrorizing not Tiny Tim but tiny animals: Kermit, Miss Piggy, *et al*. Caine's inspiration was as much contemporary as it was Dickensian, though. 'My basic role models for Scrooge . . . came from watching CNN and seeing the trials and tribulations of all the Wall Street cheats and embezzlers,'[7] he said.

In Dickens's original story, Scrooge is a relatively taciturn figure – a man more often spoken of than to. The Scrooge of *The Muppet Christmas Carol*, though, gets to talk a lot more. Caine spends a great deal of the movie exchanging dialogue with the Muppet characters around him – Muppet characters who are not, of course, really there. Hard work for anybody, but especially for an actor like Caine, who has long said that the bulk of his job is in evoking the appropriate reaction to whatever has just been said or done to him. Never once, though, do you doubt that Caine's Scrooge is addressing real beings rather than empty air – an achievement that bolsters his performance at those most challenging moments of any production of *A Christmas Carol*: those in which Scrooge is talking to or being talked to by the ghosts of Christmas Past, Present and Future.

Caine does, though, make a virtue of the physical detachment he has from the movie's other characters, using it to underline Scrooge's detachment from the whole of life. One never feels (as one does with the Scrooge of Alastair Sim) that one is watching a man awaiting humanization by some ghostly intervention. Nor does one feel (as one does with Albert Finney's Scrooge) that the Scrooge of *The Muppet Christmas Carol* is essentially a character actor having a lot of fun playing a niggardly nasty. This Scrooge is as much a victim of his own vileness as any of those he torments. Caine, in other words, creates the most recognizably human of cinematic Scrooges – a triumph in a movie in which there is nothing else remotely human either to contrast himself with or to bounce himself off. Even his rather flat rendition of Paul Williams's song of life-changing epiphany at the movie's denouement seems charged with a kind of willed realism merely for being done so cack-handedly. What a mistake it would have been to have mimed the song or, worse, to have sung it more confidently. Caine was confident enough about his own achievement in the picture, though. 'What you've got,' he said at the time of the movie's release, 'is my performance as Scrooge had I been at the National Theatre.'[8]

The year 1993 was another of those rarities in which no Michael Caine movie opened in cinemas. And though he worked as usual, he also took time out for some charity work. He helped launch a charity called Dine-a-Mite in which for one night of the year restaurants (including his own Langan's in London's Piccadilly) donated half their takings to the homeless. 'I see the homeless every day in the street,' said the man who had grown up in the London of the Depression, 'and it pisses me off. There have always been bums about but I've never seen young people homeless. It upsets me. It really needs some great commitment from the Government but I don't know whether we're going to get it.'[9]

Caine also admitted that he had voted – for the first time in his life – in the 1992 general election. 'I did it because of John Major,' he said. 'I'd never seen a Tory who'd been on the dole. And I wondered if this was a combination that could possibly work.'[10] In the event, of course, it didn't, but that is not to gainsay Major's socio-cultural status. Major, one is tempted to say, would never have been Prime Minister without Caine. Not because Caine voted for him, but because Caine's example can hardly but have been a (perhaps unconscious) spur to the young Major.

For the two men had much in common. Like Caine, Major had been born a south-Londoner. Like Caine, he had grown up in straitened circumstances. Like Caine, Major wore heavy, thick-rimmed spectacles. Like Caine, Major was a tough-guy who looked like a pushover. And like Caine, it was hoped, Major would bring some cross-class appeal to a party that had a reputation for not having much time for the lower orders. 'I voted for John Major because he reminded me of Harry Palmer,' said Caine, 'especially in those pictures of him in the 1960s when he was having that affair.'[11] Lucky the Tory MP who resembles a chippy sixties spy. But was the truth rather more mundane? Hard to suppress the suspicion that all Major really did for caine was finally give him something he had been looking for throughout his life: a licence to vote Conservative without feeling guilty about it.

Caine might not have released any movies in 1993, but that didn't mean he wasn't busy filming. In the spring he found himself in Alaska playing the heavy in Steven Seagal's directorial début *On Deadly Ground* (1994). The début turned out to be Seagal's directorial swan-song too. Just as it should have. Quite how the picture ever got to be made is baffling. Certainly, the picture was a disaster for Caine – so much so that according to Jerry Pam Steven Seagal 'is the only man he would never want to work with again'.[12]

The problem is not that the movie is another slice of the meat-headed kung-fu nonsense Seagal has made his career out of. It is that Seagal, a keen environmentalist, wants what ought to be a no-brain action movie to make serious points about the damage big business is doing to the world. Alas, Seagal is no Nicholas Ray and this is no *Wind Across the Everglades* (1958). Rather, *On Deadly Ground* is a movie that is forever being held back from fulfilling its duty as mindless entertainment by Seagal's preachy dogma. The picture even ends with the star cum director giving us a five-minute lecture on ecological damage. (Small thanks are due to the studio here: as originally written the lecture was going to go on for *fifteen* minutes.)

What was Caine doing in all this? Playing the English bad guy, that's what. For years, Hollywood had depended on what it saw as the hauteur of British actors to serve up the tastiest villains. James Mason had done so with masterly chill in Hitchcock's *North by Northwest* (1959); more recently, Alan Rickman had reinvented the tradition with a wonderfully sneering performance as a German heavy in the first *Die Hard* (1988). Now it was Caine's turn, as tough-nosed industrialist Michael Jennings, a man who'll stop at nothing to make money. 'I've usually played nice guys because I'm a nice guy myself,' Caine said at the time. 'But if you're really a nice guy then secretly in your heart you want to be really obnoxious. As an actor you get a chance to do it. Other people go to psychiatrists; actors just go to work and get paid a lot of money to act out their fantasies.'[13]

Such fantasies not withstanding, Caine has just one good moment in the movie, a scene in which he is preparing to be interviewed for a television documentary on the environmental impact of his oil-drilling project in Alaska. One of his employees makes a suggestion on what he might say, at which point Caine explodes like a grenade in an oil well: 'Listen – you have any great ideas,' he rasps, 'just keep 'em to your fucking self.' And then he turns to the director and says with humble politesse, 'Now, where do I stand?' before going in front of the camera and talking eco-twaddle with disarming charm. Such mercurial changes of mood were familiar from Caine's Mortwell in *Mona Lisa*, but here he brought to them an archly self-conscious note that nicely punctured the wilful earnestness of Seagal's preaching.

Within months of *On Deadly Ground*'s release, Michael Caine CBE was honoured again, this time by Goldsmiths' College in Lewisham. The nearest institute of higher education to the Camberwell and Peckham of his childhood, Goldsmiths' made Caine an honorary fellow for his past services to the arts. The historic note was handy, since Caine's present services to the arts left rather a lot to be desired. After the Seagal debacle came *And Then There Were Giants* (1994), a clumsy TV movie about World War II in which John Lithgow's Franklin D. Roosevelt and Bob Hoskins' Winston Churchill engaged in a gurning contest with Caine's Joseph Stalin. Given Lithgow's and Hoskins' leery caricaturing, Caine's decision to play Stalin with his customary restraint must have looked good on paper. On celluloid it looked rather less good. His Stalin all but disappears under the uniformly honeyed glow of the TV-movie lighting scheme.

Then, thirty years since first playing him, Caine stupidly accepted an offer to resurrect the role of Harry Palmer. In 1970, when he had been lured back to play James Bond one last time, Sean Connery took home what was then the biggest pay-packet in the history of the movies: £1 million. The paycheque cannot, though, have been the main reason behind Caine's decision to reprise the Palmer role. *Bullet to Beijing* (1996), as the new movie was called, was being made for peanuts. The total budget for the picture *and* that of *Midnight in St Petersburg* (1996) – a follow-up to *Bullet* that was actually shot back-to-back with it – was a mere $9 million. To put that in perspective, $9 million is about 7 per cent of the amount spent on the Arnold Schwarzenegger spy thriller *True Lies* (1994), which came out around the time the new Palmers were being shot.[14] For once, Caine wasn't in it for the money.

Certainly, there was an altruistic quality to the remarks he made about his co-star in the two pictures, Sean Connery's son Jason. Talking about what he saw as the problems the British film industry laboured under – its wilful artiness, its obsession with low-life, its lack of interest in the money-spinning Hollywood genres – Caine bemoaned the young British actor's lot and seemed determined to do what he could to improve it. 'For all that,' he said, 'you've got the young kids coming up . . . Ralph Fiennes, Daniel Day-Lewis, Jason Connery – I had Jason's part in my new film written up to push him. He's another youngster sitting on his arse in Earls Court; if he was in America he'd be working his socks off.'[15] Alas, while Fiennes and Day-Lewis have gone on to do great things, the years have not been kind to Connery junior, nor to Caine's belief in his talents. At the time of filming the new Harry Palmer duet, Jason Connery was thirty-one – the same age his father had been when he made *Dr No*.[16] *Bullet to Beijing* did not, though, make him a star.

Much less did it deserve to. Both it and *Midnight in St Petersburg* were turgid to the point of putrefaction. Only the most flowery aesthete could disagree with Caine's belief that the British film industry ought not to be ashamed of having a go at making a thriller. But inserting pointless chases and shoot-outs into a picture that otherwise consists of actors attempting to explain the plot to one another does not a thriller make. 'I'm too old for this,' says Caine's Palmer after leaping on to a moving train in *Bullet to Beijing*. Yes indeed, though we should remember that the earlier Palmer movies had no need of leaps on to moving trains to keep their youthful momentum going.

For the basic thing wrong with *Bullet to Beijing* and *Midnight in St Petersburg* is that they really have nothing to do with Harry Palmer at all. Though Len Deighton gave his blessing to the project (once Caine had agreed to get involved),[17] there was really no need for the producers to let him in on the deal. The hero of these two movies is less Harry Palmer than an antiquated Bond.

Caine's nineties Palmer has none of the cheek and charm of the original, largely because the movies give him nothing to rub up against. Made redundant from the Ministry of Defence, Palmer has joined forces with his one-time enemies in the KGB to wage war on the gangsters of the new Russia. Plenty of opportunity for trouble-making there, but when a Russian conspirator calls Harry 'my capitalist friend',

Palmer doesn't bat an eyelid. Caine's original Palmer was no socialist, of course, but he would have bridled at being called a capitalist. Everything he did he did with subversive intent. The Palmer of *Billion Dollar Brain* loathed the powers that be, whichever side they were on. The Palmer of *Bullet to Beijing* and *Midnight in St Petersburg* looks like a middle-management flop who ought to have been cashiered years ago.

How much better this duet of movies might have been had they been set in nineties Britain. Doubtless the budgets wouldn't stretch to a prolonged London shoot, but Caine's Palmer could have had a high old time of it in John Major's putatively 'classless society'. Instead, large chunks of *Midnight in St Petersburg* are taken up by lectures on the glories of the Hermitage museum – travelogue-style sequences that shame the product placements in even the most nakedly greedy Hollywood blockbuster. As it is, the only thing that makes Palmer bristle throughout the two movies is Nick's (Connery) admission that (like the James Bond of the Ian Fleming novels) he was educated at Eton and that his father worked in British intelligence.

No less bald is the dialogue Caine was given to remind people who his character was. So it is that while being threatened with the chop, Palmer defends his record by reminding his boss 'of the troubles with the Ipcress File, and the funeral . . . in Berlin.' At one point Harry even talks on the phone to the Sue Lloyd/Jean of *The Ipcress File* – although mysteriously, while the pair make a dinner date during their conversation, she never actually appears in the finished movie. Not, at least, in the version released in the UK. To actually see Lloyd's Jean in her nineties cameo you need to buy a copy of the Canadian DVD version of *Bullet to Beijing*. This and other cuts were deemed necessary when the producers belatedly decided not to give the movie a theatrical release. Instead, it premièred on The Movie Channel in the US, before being trimmed and released on video in Britain in 1997, more than two years after having wrapped. A similar fate awaited *Midnight in St Petersburg*.[18]

The new Palmer duet's failure to achieve a theatrical release, while at least ensuring that the movies were never seen by his more bloodthirsty critics, hit Caine hard – and hit him all the harder for following on the heels of the disaster that had been *On Deadly Ground*. Nor did things improve with the TV movies *Mandela and de Klerk* and *20,000 Leagues Under the Sea* (both 1997). Caine put in a measured-to-the-point-of-dullness performance as de Klerk in the former, but his Captain Nemo in the latter lacked the bathetic braggadocio James Mason had brought to the role in the Walt Disney production of the fifties.

But while the movies would always be his bread and butter, Caine had long had other fish to fry. Ever since his first culinary venture with Peter Langan two decades earlier, Caine had been a keen restaurateur. By the mid-nineties he was co-owner of five London diners: The Canteen, Langan's, Langan's Brasserie, Odins and Shepherds. And in early 1996 Caine opened his first US-based restaurant: the South Beach Brasserie in Miami. The opening coincided with Caine's selling his Hollywood home and moving the family's American address to the retirement haven of Florida. Had the movie experiences of the past few years got to him? As his sixty-fifth birthday loomed, were thoughts of retirement pressing on him? Certainly, he seemed to conceive of his culinary ventures in terms of a substitute for show business. 'I think it's live theatre,' said the ever-ebullient Caine of his new restaurant. A more nostalgic air overtook him as he warmed to his theme, though: 'I started out in the live theatre and if you think in terms of similarities it's like opening a play. Will the people like the sets? Will they like the ingredients? Will the critics like it? Will it run? Will it be full? Will it make money? Will it lose money? It's a form of gambling.'[19]

The gambles haven't always come off. On two occasions Caine the restaurateur has fallen out with his co-owners. First with Peter Langan, who ostensibly became annoyed with his partner when he refused to invest in a Los Angeles diner but who had long goaded Caine about his lowly origins. The relationship ended with Langan accusing Caine of having 'a council house mind'.[20]

The second falling out was with Marco Pierre White, who ran the kitchen at The Canteen, a spit from Caine's London base in Chelsea Harbour. The restaurant had launched at the end of 1992 to the accompaniment of much mutual backslapping, but even as the South Beach Brasserie was opening, Caine was paying White off to the tune of £500,000. The Byron-haired chef had walked out after Caine had suggested in less than uncertain terms that they should put fish and chips and bangers and mash on The Canteen's menu. The lowly Leeds-born White, who had joined the huntin', shootin' and fishin' set as soon as he could, wanted nothing to do with such lowly English dishes. As it happened, though, Caine had a keener nose for current tastes than his head chef. The nineties were the decade of 'retro-meals' in London's eateries; no restaurant was complete without its toad-in-the-hole, its steak-and-kidney pudding, its spotted dick and custard. Not for the first time, Caine's 'council house mind' spoke for a wider culture than his would-be rarefied antagonists would have liked.

The fall-out with White came immediately after a similar spat with Richard Harris. The two men had a history, of course. Harris, it will be remembered, had chafed at the idea of 'playing second fiddle to Caine' when he had arrived on the set of *Play Dirty* to find several of his big scenes 'cut to ribbons'.[21] A quarter of a century later, he took exception to comments Caine had made about his drinking in a newspaper interview. 'The British actors were all drunks,' Caine had said, 'O'Toole, Harris, Burton,'[22] a triple character assassination that Harris argued had no basis in fact. 'Peter O'Toole is not an alcoholic or a drunk, neither was I, neither was Richard Burton; I knew them both very well. The point is that it's a cheap shot by an actor I consider not in the same league as Burton or O'Toole or even myself.'[23]

But Harris reserved his real venom for a letter published in reply to the Caine interview. Caine, wrote Harris, had always been 'guilty of self-elevation through association with his peers'. In fact, he was 'an over-fat, flatulent 62-year-old windbag, a master of inconsequence now masquerading as a guru, passing off his vast limitations as pious virtues'. Moreover, 'he was traumatised into petty tantrums of disbelief when Hopkins, McKellen, Jacobi and Stephens were elevated to knighthood ... but ... he did achieve the title he had diligently worked for, "Farceur du Salon" of Beverly Hills – and a lot of people know that.'[24]

It was cruel, but beneath the invective and disdain lay Harris's jealousy for the sustained success that had flowed from Caine's quiet classicism. Flowing of lock and fiery of temper, Harris was a romantic given to the belief that he and his fellow artists must dare to go into 'the wilderness ... [to] face the lion's roar ... [and] smell the breath of their bad habits; a voyage most great actors embarked on where, on occasion, they might touch the Gods to ignite their craft. A safari which the Caines of this world, wishing to be a part of, gracefully absented themselves for the quiet charades of "the movers and shakers in Palm Springs".'[25] Essentially, Harris's problem – like Burton's, like O'Toole's – was not that he couldn't act, but that he couldn't *not* act. Romantic visionaries whether drunk or sober, these men were never not performing. The histrionic undertone in Harris's letter – those ignitions, those voyages, those lion's roars – chimed perfectly with the histrionic overtones that accompanied him all his life.

And yet the fact remains that for all his drunken romanticism, Richard Harris served up no more than a couple of searing, harrowing performances in a movie career made up largely of barnstorming. So too Burton and O'Toole, both of whom were occasionally visited by the muse, both of whom were responsible for some of the movies' worst acting. But neither their good performances nor their bad ones were the result of drunkenness. Their bad performances, like their good ones, were dependent on so many more factors than individual talent and sensibility and sobriety. The essential difference between these movie romantics and movie classicists such as Caine is that the latter are always aware that they are just one factor in any given production. Movies are teamwork and as such no place for romantic individualism. Harris's belief that great actors are all tortured visionaries was as nonsensical as Caine's affected belief that it was merely his time-keeping professionalism – and not his unswerving commitment to improving his craft – that had got him where he was.

There was, on the other hand, no gainsaying that Caine's professionalism had *kept* him where he was these three decades and more. Three decades and more that had brought him close to his home country's statutory age of retirement. No such statutes applied in the self-employed world of acting, of course, but with all those restaurants needing an eye kept on them and all those lousy scripts that had recently come his way, Caine would have been less than human if he hadn't considered throwing in the towel.

Or turning to direction.

The history of art is the history of revivals.
  Samuel Butler[1]

Role reversal: Caine with Jack Nicholson in *Blood and Wine.* © British Film Institute

He was writing a thriller, he said, and had hopes that once it was published he might be given the chance to direct a movie based on it.[2] The best part of a decade on, nothing has come of this project – for which we should probably give much thanks. Even granting Caine his status as one of acting's best living raconteurs, the clunky prose of his autobiography augurs none too well for his talents as a novelist. Moreover, Caine's BBC acting masterclass, while it had pointed up the strengths and virtues of his own technique, had also demonstrated his inability to conceive of any other way of approaching the problems a given script sets an actor. A Caine-directed movie might have ended up looking and sounding as leaden and monotonous as the Caine caricature served up by so many mimics on TV and radio. *Spitting Image*, Rory Bremner, *The Fast Show, Dead Ringers* – each of them had their own take on Caine's seemingly affectless aesthetic, but though their impersonations were capable of raising the occasional laugh, none of them quite captured his deadpan rigour. As we have seen, though, such rigour works well only when set against something baggier, looser, less restrained. A Caine-directed movie would likely be all restraint. In an age when British movie-makers wouldn't know restraint if it wrapped them in a winding sheet, there would be something to be said for Caine the auteur's strictures, but it is usually unwise to try righting a wrong with another wrong.

Meanwhile, Caine had his own acting career to sort out. With *A Shock to the System* his *fin de siècle* had started out so well, but though he had since come up with an oddball winner in *The Muppet Christmas Carol*, the nineties could hardly be said to have gone well for him. It would, perhaps, be overegging things to characterize 1997 as the year of Caine's big fightback. Nonetheless, it was during that year that Caine showed himself, for the first time since the end of the previous decade, capable of roles that required more of him than turning up and accepting his cheque. As if to presage the successes to come, the British Film Institute made Caine a Fellow in February 1997.

A month later, Bob Rafelson's *Blood and Wine* hit British movie screens, and though Caine's role in it was really little more than a cameo, he used it to prove he could still outgun the opposition – even when the opposition in question was Jack Nicholson. Caine's emphysemic safe-cracker Victor Spansky isn't in the picture for more than twenty minutes of its running time, but with his slicked-back dye-dark hair, his trim fifties-style moustache and his beige man-made-fibre wardrobe, he dominates the movie.

Nonetheless, the two leading men were badly cast. Alex Gates, a chiselling smoothie forever failing to realize his big plans, would have been a natural for Caine. No actor since Mitchum has so well embodied the man who cheats himself of his dreams. The sadness of Nicholson's Gates is droopy in comparison. His despair seems metaphysical, entropic, a by-product of body and blood rather than world and wine. How much more fitting to have had Nicholson play Spansky – enervated, breathless, seedy as a bird box, and all the while capable of eruptive violence.

Rafelson himself seems to realize he has cast his leading men wrongly when, halfway through the picture, Nicholson's Gates is called upon to

sweep the contents of a restaurant table to the floor, glasses and cups
shattering loudly around himself and Spansky. Doubtless the scene is
meant to remind us of Nicholson's near iconic moment of eruption in a
diner in Rafelson's *Five Easy Pieces* (1970). Instead, though, Gates's
effusion seems merely out of character and far more the wilfully unpre-
dictable action of a man like Spansky. For Caine is magnificent during
Spansky's outrages, all feline volatility as he pounces out of nowhere on
his victims. One moment he is chatting disinterestedly to them, the next
he is bashing their heads against trees or swinging at them with golf
clubs. Caine brings a dirty passion to these moments of brute realism, an
explicatory depth his dialogue never grants him, but that allows the
viewer to understand what has brought him to this pass. Spansky is not
randomly violent, Caine's finely tuned performance keeps telling us; the
victim of a breathless body, it is almost as if that body wants to take
revenge on the healthier ones it sees around itself.

Given such an achievement, it would be churlish to gripe overmuch about *Blood and Wine* (1996). Even though the movie would
almost certainly have been better had its central casting been reversed,
there is no gainsaying that Caine's performance in it was the best
work he had served up in almost a decade. Although for the rest of the
century he would continue turning in little more than cameos, they
were to be marvellous cameos. Even his slyly Cowardesque ghost in
Peter Yates's abominable *Curtain Call* (1999) crawls grinning from
the movie's wreckage. The same cannot be said for his spectral co-star,
Maggie Smith, whose arch and angular performance suggests she took
the banalities of Todd Alcott's screenplay seriously. Fortunately for
her (and Caine), the movie was never granted a cinematic release,
although it has been known to turn up in the afternoon schedules of
Channel Five.

A similar fate awaited *Shadow Run* (1998). A heist thriller that
looked two decades out of date, the movie marked Caine's third collab-
oration with producer Geoffrey Reeve (*Half Moon Street* and *The
Whistle Blower* had been their first pairings) – and was as ramshackle
and run-up-on-the-cheap as its two predecessors. Playing opposite TV
lightweight Leslie 'Dirty Den' Grantham and a miscast TV heavyweight,
Tim *Auf Wiedersehen, Pet* Healy, Caine never found his rhythm in this
clumsily repetitive, doggedly dull picture. Even the working-class bond
the movie seeks to establish between Caine's elegantly besuited cockney
villain Haskell and Matthew Pochin's put-upon scholarship boy
Edward Joffrey is played ham-fistedly, Caine seemingly confused by
what his character is meant to feel. As well he might be, since Desmond
Lowden's plotting is all over the place. Loyalty to one's old friends is a

fine thing, but *Shadow Run* was yet another instance of Caine's habit of accepting work without properly analysing it beforehand. Again fortunately, then, the movie never managed to find a distributor, and did not even appear on DVD until four years later in September 2001.

And though it didn't feel like it at the time, Caine was more fortunate still when a role he had set his heart on – that of the villain in Jeremiah Chechik's *The Avengers* (1998) – went instead to an old friend. 'It was a huge Hollywood movie with lots of money and a high-profile part that would bring me back in an entirely different persona,' Caine remembered shortly after the picture had opened to unanimously disastrous notices. 'Then Sean Connery came into the frame, and when he does he blows everyone else out of the water . . . I was bitterly disappointed not to get it. As it was, something that seemed like a terrible blow . . . turned into a stroke of luck.'³ Two strokes of luck actually. Not only did *The Avengers* bomb, but the movie Caine made instead turned out to be the kind of CV-polisher he desperately needed.

Caine has subsequently claimed that he was desperate to get the part of Ray Say in Mark Herman's *Little Voice* (1998), though this is probably hindsight talking. Just as Caine's good fortune in *not* getting the part in *The Avengers* wasn't apparent at the time, so his being cast in *Little Voice* – the movie that would restore him to eminence and credibility – can hardly have seemed like a career-rebuilding opportunity. It was a small British picture, a small *regional* British picture, set, like Herman's previous movie, *Brassed Off* (1996), in Yorkshire. The part Caine was up for in this small movie was, moreover, pretty small itself. Though Ray Say had a couple of half-page speeches, his role in the narrative was essentially choric. Caine, in other words, was being asked to try out for another cameo.

Try out, because there was another contender for the role, and one who had not only worked for Herman in *Brassed Off* but also played the part of Ray Say in the West End stage production of Jim Cartwright's original play: Pete Postlethwaite. Since the same actress (Jane Horrocks) who had played the titular lead in the West End was to star in the movie, Caine reasoned that Postlethwaite was a shoo-in. And perhaps he would have been, had Steven Spielberg not cast him in *The Lost World: Jurassic Park* (1997), a movie whose shooting schedule precluded Postlethwaite's appearing in Herman's picture. Instead, Caine got the role, and in October 1997, mere weeks after *Shadow Run* had wrapped, he was on location in Scarborough with Herman, Horrocks and the movie's other stars, Brenda Blethyn, Jim Broadbent and Ewan McGregor. A sterling cast indeed. You have to go back to *Mona Lisa* or even, perhaps, to *Educating Rita* to see Caine up against so much home-grown

One man show: Caine with Jim Broadbent and Brenda Blethyn in *Little Voice*.
© British Film Institute

competition. Yet in the event, it was a walkover. Caine didn't just steal the picture: he made it look like a one-man show.

Ostensibly, the movie belonged to Horrocks. After all, the original play had been inspired by and built around her ability to mimic the leading songstresses of the media age. Garland, Bassey, Monroe – Horrocks could do them all with plangent accuracy, though whether she could do any more is debatable. I can't comment on her West End personation, but it has to be said that despite the soar and swoop of her voice her performance in the movie is a one-note affair.[4] Horrocks's LV spends the entire picture mired in gloom. Not even getting the chance to show off her talent cheers her up, much less a budding relationship with Ewan McGregor's (risibly unconsidered) Billy. Though her character is put through the wringer of the conventional three-act drama, Horrocks modulates her performance not one jot. Now there are criticisms to be levelled at the redemptive clichés of so many movies, but if your movie is redemptively clichéd then you have to be mighty sure of your subversive skills if you're not going to attempt to embody the redemption. Subversion, though, isn't on Horrocks's agenda.

Matters don't improve with LV's mother, Mari (Brenda Blethyn). All rubber gloves and corsetry, Blethyn's foul-tongued Mari is a caricature of working-class womanhood that would have looked unsubtle even in the forties. In its way, the performance is quite as insulting to the working class as any of those that had so affronted the young Maurice Micklewhite at Peckham's Tower Cinema.

Perhaps by way of compensation, Caine's failed but still hopeful showbiz impresario Ray Say is more broadly cockney than any character he has ever created. Quite what this London wide boy is doing on the North Yorkshire coast the movie never makes clear, but let that pass. Observe instead how Caine never once makes a cartoon of Ray. There is no talking down here. Nor, however, is there any looking up. Caine's Ray is drawn with the kind of dense objectivity one finds in only the greatest novels. The movie tells us next to nothing about Ray's back-story, but it is all there in Caine's diffident swagger, in the braggadocio that brightens everyone's eyes but his own. Ray is the only working-class character Caine has ever created who has neither rebellious urges nor fantasies of digging himself out of the place he has been allotted. His dreams of managing an act big enough to take him away from the grotty clubs and bars that are his habitual arena arise not out of a wish to get on in life but rather – as with the titular character of Woody Allen's *Broadway Danny Rose* (1984) – to get the best out of whatever act he is representing. And it is because Caine never asks that we pity Ray – nor, of course, that we laugh at him – that he dignifies his despair. (The movie's big flaw is its failure to take its cue from Caine's ambiguities. It never rises to the challenges he sets it. It's incapable of anything but a condescending adoration for what it plainly regards as the great unwashed.)

Caine has two big scenes in the picture – the one quiet, restrained, modulated to perfect pitch, the other brutally histrionic – both of them object lessons in technique. First up is the scene in which Ray coaxes and cajoles and teases LV into using her talent for singalong mimicry at a concert he has booked her into – an emotional *tour de force* and one of the greatest moments in Caine's career. How gently Caine builds the drama in the scene (there is a very real sense in which it is he and not Herman who is here directing), how sinuously his voice moves from cooing to cawing and back to caressing. Ray's eyes, ruddy and reamed by decades of booze, are at once snakily malevolent and on the edge of tears. He looks as wounded as he does wounding, and there is a teasing urgency about his wish to do well for LV. At the time of its release, Caine said of the movie that it suffered because 'Jane's impersonations are *too* good and everybody thinks she's lip-synching to records, which she isn't.'[5] In fact, it is Caine who throws the movie off-balance, turning a parodic vision of working-class sleaze into an almost Flaubertianly detailed tragic study.

Such tensions are crystallized in Caine's second big scene: Ray's tuneless rendition of Roy Orbison's song 'It's Over'. LV has failed to turn up for the show and Ray, who has staked everything he owns on having her spotted by the London talent scout who's in town for the night, is ruined. 'It's Over' is one of Orbison's most powerfully maudlin numbers, and its despair is made all the more palpable in Ray's foul-mouthed, four-letter rewrite ('It's over, it's faaaaacking over!' 'It's over . . . over? . . . it never fucking started'). Yet Caine undercuts this pathetic frustration by singing the song with vicious pomp. Sweaty and scoured, his hair a rococo explosion of curls and spikes, Caine's Ray looks like the godfather of Johnny Rotten, but a Rotten who has realized that he is himself responsible for the degradation he sees all around him. Caine finds in Ray, in other words, the gleeful nihilism he gave Jack Carter and *Mona Lisa*'s Mortwell, but he turns it back on its proprietor and stares right into the heart of darkness. To watch Caine in *Little Voice* is to be reminded of Turner's (Mick Jagger) Artaudian suggestion in *Performance* (1970) that 'the only performance that makes it, that really makes it, that makes it all the way, is the one that achieves madness'.[6] And by achieving madness, Caine transforms an ill-constructed three-act drama into a blistering analysis of moral compromise and self-disgust. Unsurprisingly, Caine was garlanded with praise for his work on *Little Voice* and was rewarded for his efforts with his second Golden Globe – this time for Best Actor in a Musical or Comedy – and the London Critics' Circle award for Best Supporting Actor.

Caine was back, and as if to hammer the point home, in June 1999, five months after Ray Say hit British cinemas, *Get Carter* was re-released. If *Little Voice* had reminded people what a subtle actor Caine could be, then *Carter* reminded them of his urgent realism. Merely for limning seventies Britain with such prescient accuracy, Mike Hodges' film had grown in stature over the three decades since its début, but its status had been boosted all the more by the then current crop of British gangster pictures. Laughable and lamentable in equal measure, such trivia as Guy Ritchie's *Lock, Stock and Two Smoking Barrels* (1998) only pointed up the squalid integrity of Hodges' picture. Caine's grim-visaged warrior showed up the designer yobbishness of nineties lad culture for the posturing fantasy it was, proving even to those who had hitherto been blind to see it that Ritchie and his cohorts were doing no more than look back in a semblance of anger.

Caine, meanwhile, was getting mellower with the years. Certainly, his role in Lasse Hallström's *The Cider House Rules* (1999) couldn't have been further removed from those that were being cashed in on by the new Britpack. In this warm-hued adaptation of John Irving's 1985 novel, Caine plays arguably the most decent character of his entire career. Caine grants Dr Wilbur Larch, the resident physician of the St Cloud's Orphanage, a Dickensian decency that would have cloyed in a movie less imbued with the romantic spirit. Three decades earlier, in *Alfie*, Caine had given us a man who could both force an abortion on a woman and then bathe in luxuriant guilt over his actions. Caine's Larch, a surgeon who knows that to rid a woman of an unwanted pregnancy is as decent a thing to do as take in a baby orphan and feed and tend to it, has no such sentimental scruples. Larch may be addicted to ether, but there is nothing dreamy about his grip on reality. Caine's first achievement in the role is to suggest that Larch's pragmatic approach to medical ethics is the by-product of his own occasional need to escape the everyday. Paul Newman, who, after reading an early version of the screenplay, had sagely turned down the part, could never have managed this marriage of the quotidian to the fantastic. Too accreted with memories of his days as a romantic lead, Newman could never have given Larch the sombre virtues Caine grants him.

That sombreness ballasts what would otherwise be a rather over-lyrical movie. Everything about *The Cider House Rules* is bathed in a russety glow, from the perpetually autumnal New England landscapes to the strawberry blonde tresses atop Charlize Theron's apple-cheeked Candy. Even Dr Larch's abortion clinic is shot through an increasingly honeyed set of filters – no pallid porcelain and cold steel here – so that as the film progresses the north American seasons move from seeming merely equatorial to near subtropical. Larch's mission, every frame of Hallström's picture reminds us, is not to improve the whole world but to make a small patch of it as perfect as possible. Caine's mission, contrariwise, is to earth this potentially gloopy vision, to give it weight and decorum.

Though he has no big scene – indeed, his biggest scene, when he lies etherized on his bed and dies, is as quietly undemonstrative an ending as any Hollywood character has ever had – and no big change of heart, it is Caine's Larch who rules this Cider House. While a number of English critics – including the present writer – were unconvinced by Caine's New England accent,7 he deservedly won himself a second Oscar for Best Supporting Actor.

He also deserved the Fellowship that the British Academy of Film and Television Arts bestowed on him after the movie's UK release, though whether the audience and critics at the BAFTA ceremony deserved the haranguing they got from Caine at the awards is rather more moot. 'For most of my career,' he told the great and the good of the British film industry on 9 April 2000, 'I've felt like the spy who

Sweet and sombre: Caine in *The Cider House Rules.* © British Film Institute

came in from the cold – that I did not belong in my own country or profession.' The lament was taken as just another instance of the chippy Caine having a go at the class system, though in fact it was rather more than that. It was the complaint of a populist entertainer tired of being overlooked on prize-giving day in favour of something he saw as 'arty' or 'controversial'. 'It's very difficult to win an award round here,' Caine went on. 'They do make some strange choices. Jesus, I've made 85 movies and one only has won [a BAFTA].'[8] There is no need to doubt the statistics, though the sentiment can be less immediately endorsed. By the Caine measure, movie awards organizations have always made strange choices. Caine blamed the British film industry, but had he been born an American he might well have found himself making much the same speech at the same time of life at the Oscars ceremony. The fact is that movie awards, like most awards, tend to be given to the sententious and pretentious, to the wilfully serious. There is nothing wrong with seriousness, of course, but you would have to be seriously muddle-headed to miss the fact that not every picture that sets out to entertain ends up doing no more than that. Seriousness is an end, not a means, and it can be reached by as many routes as there are movie-makers.

Seasoned Caine-watchers, of course, could hardly have been shocked by what he had said at the BAFTA ceremony. In an interview published the day before the awards he had addressed the same issues, talking of the difficulty of winning an award in his home country ('they don't give away stuff that easily'[9]) and of how that home country had never felt much like home ('I've always felt slightly patronised, trivialised, marginalised'[10]). Warming to his theme, he argued that there was a class war implicit in the criticisms so often levelled at him: 'We are not going to let Michael Caine be a real actor – he's got to be a cockney character.'[11] He had a point, though not perhaps the one he thought he was making. Unique in being a character actor who is also a star, Caine has almost brought upon himself the confusions that exist between his ontological presence and the epistemological readings of that presence he has projected on the silver screen. Ever since Harry Palmer and *Alfie*, thirty-five years earlier, Caine had been inviting journalists and interviewers to conflate his on-screen image with his off-screen existence. He had played at being a star whose image meshed perfectly with his inner being, and now the inner being was being taken for the star. 'Celebrity,' as John Updike has said, 'is a mask that eats into the face.'[12]

As if to hammer that point home, his next role, in Stephen Kay's remake of *Get Carter* (2000), was as one of the characters Caine had himself killed off in the original. In the Carter role was Sylvester Stallone, garbed and goateed most elegantly and sporting a shirt that stays white even as blood sprays all around him. For Stallone's Carter, as befits the infantilized Hollywood of our age, was a whiter-than-white white knight. Not for Kay and Sly the moral sadness and sleaze of Hodges' and

Caine's picture. Instead, we have a classic three-act redemptive drama that flies in the face of the original movie's glum compromises.

Nonetheless, this remake of one of Michael Caine's most famous films is not the dog the critics of the time would have had us believe. To be sure, it is not a patch on the original, but there is no gainsaying that as a modern thriller Kay's remodel works very well. The movie has pace and rhythm, and remarkably, for a remake, even manages the odd narrative surprise. Stallone is not, never could be, Caine, though in this movie he is at least at his best, which is to say he is at his most Robert Mitchum-like – and Mitchum was, as we have seen, a key influence on the acting style adopted by Caine from very early on in his career.

Actually, Caine puts in rather less by way of acting here than even Mitchum might have dared attempt, playing Brumby (*Coronation Street*'s Bryan Mosley in the original movie) with his regular London accent. Since he had just made an Oscar-winning appearance in a movie in which he did put on an American voice, there is no question that he could have come up with something more Washington state had he wanted/been asked to. But that is the point. Caine's 'exotic' cockney vowels are as deliberate an emblematic ploy as they were in the original movie (in which, it will be remembered, Caine's Carter had a Geordie family and a cockney accent). The movie wants us to know that it is *Michael Caine* who is reappearing in a remake of one of his most famous movies.[13]

Other than such self-conscious play, the chief virtue of Kay's remake is its uncovering of an America cinema audiences so rarely see. The movie was filmed on location in Seattle, though this is not the Seattle so many of us are familiar with from *Frasier*. If Kay's framing and cutting and use of stardom owe a lot to the in-your-face style of the *nouvelle vague*, his sets and establishing shots and locations – all dinge and dirt and decay – owe everything to the designer dread of the work of David Fincher ([*Alien3*] [1992] *Se7en* [1995], etc.). But this is not mere homage. Kay manages to find in Seattle something of the dying industrial quality that was so essential to Mike Hodges' original take on Newcastle-upon-Tyne.

Caine himself has subsequently disowned the film, claiming that he takes responsibility only for those movies 'where my name's over the title'.[14] There is something of a man being wise after the event here, though, since Caine can never have really believed that a Sly Stallone American remake of a grimy British picture could ever be anything but chalk to the original's cheese. Though America had had its share of recession in the early nineties, when a *Get Carter*-style thriller might have had some purchase on the country's mindset, at the end of the feelgood Clinton era the movie's slightly soiled ambience felt like a put-on that not even Caine's presence could validate. All these caveats aside, though, *Get Carter* Mark Two was a far from insulting end to Caine's twentieth century.

The world doesn't make any heroes any more.
  The Third Man[1]

Welcome to Casablanca: Caine with Brendan Fraser in *The Quiet American*.
© The Kobal Collection

After dusting off one of his most canonic performances to see out the twentieth century, Caine ushered in the twenty-first by brushing up on his Shakespeare. Almost thirty-six years had gone by since his one and only appearance in a production of Shakespeare: as Horatio in the BBC's 1964 version of *Hamlet at Elsinore*. Now, approaching seventy, he was cast as the titular character in a modern-dress version of *King Lear*. Was the arch aesthetic conservative moving into avant-garde territory for the new millennium? Not a bit of it. *Shiner* (2000) was a retelling of Shakespeare's tragedy, set among the vice and villainy of

London's East End. As another in the *Get Carter*-inspired new British gangster genre, then, it gave Caine the perfect opportunity both to comment anew on one of the key roles of his career and to try his strength against one of the theatre's most demanding roles. As he modestly said at the time: 'I thought it's the nearest I'm ever gonna get to play [Lear], so I'm gonna do it.'[2]

Caine plays Billy 'Shiner' Simpson, a cockney bad boy made good whose kingdom, did he but know it, is being stolen from him by his daughters. Meanwhile, Shiner is worried that his boxer son 'Golden Boy' Eddie (Matthew Marsden) has been strong-armed into throwing a fight that could have won him a shot at a world-title encounter. When, within hours of the fight, Eddie is gunned down, Billy convinces himself he is being conspired against by the brutal and moneyed American fight promoter Frank Spedding (Martin Landau) and plots a bloody revenge. Things do not, though, go according to plan.

Nor do they come out all right on the night. *Shiner* – which reunited Caine with producer Geoffrey Reeve (with whom he had worked on *The Whistleblower*, *Half Moon Street* and the still-to-be-released *Shadow Run*) – has an awful lot going for it, but there is no denying that the movie contrives to throw most of its opportunities away. Clumsily structured and paced, and shot like a low-budget television series (the script was written by Scott Cherry, a graduate of ITV's police soap opera *The Bill*), the production seems almost punch-drunk by the fact that it has managed to land Michael Caine in its leading role.

And indeed, Caine is on top form, mapping Shiner's decline into chaos with icy clarity. While he affects an air of relaxed devilry, Caine's Shiner is a man haunted from the off. Though when we first meet him he really does believe that finally, in late middle age, he is going to be given (through his son's forthcoming victory) a shot at the big time, there is a delicate doubt in Caine's moist eyes that hints at ill-suppressed dread. Shiner's self-belief, Caine's microscopically calibrated performance of tics and twitches tells you, is no more than a hysterical fantasy. The man is primed and ready to implode.

Or explode. It might seem odd, given the parallels with *King Lear*, to complain about the gratuitous nastiness of *Shiner*. Nonetheless, the movie is as vile a gangster picture as any the British cinema has yet given us. As Spedding, for instance, that fine Method actor Martin Landau has to tell Caine's Shiner to leave him alone, threatening that if he doesn't 'I'll personally force you to fuck your mother.' A moment later, though, director John Irvin and writer Cherry seem so appalled at what they have done that they have Landau try and ironize the sentiment:

'What?' he rasps at his henchmen. 'Do you think that was too much about his mother?'

But it is Caine who is given the movie's most disgusting moment. Shiner puts his gun to the swollen abdomen of the pregnant wife of one of his own henchmen, threatening to kill both her and the baby unless the man confesses to having set 'Golden Boy' up. Deranged and flailing, Caine is unquestionably magnificent here. But the pressure group Mediawatch UK had a point when it called the scene a disgrace, not because of the brute integrity of Caine's conception, but because Irvin's camera so plainly adores the character wreaking such vile havoc.

Such childish glee, along with cack-handed plotting and confused set-pieces, could hardly but detract from the power of Caine's Lear-like breakdown, and the result is that a great performance ends up seeming merely perfunctory. Ironically, Reeve's and his director John Irvin's faith in Caine's ability to carry their picture ends up sinking it. Movies, as Caine has always acknowledged, are teamwork, and though he is by some stretch the strongest thing in it, *Shiner* is always less than the sum of its parts.

Shiner began shooting in January 2000, around the time the Caine family moved from the Oxfordshire house it had occupied since the late eighties to a new home outside Leatherhead in Surrey. Only three years after buying it, Caine had sold his apartment in Miami and consolidated his property portfolio into the rather more manageable duo of a London apartment and, a mere forty-minute drive away, a 21-acre estate in the wealthiest of the Home Counties. More than ever, Caine had become the country gentleman he had dreamed of being in Norfolk six decades before. It can only have seemed fitting when a letter from Buckingham Palace offering him a knighthood arrived in the post.

Michael Caine became Sir Maurice Micklewhite on Thursday, 16 November 2000. 'I was named after my father, and I was knighted in his name because I love my father,' said Caine after the ceremony. 'I always kept my real name. When I go home, I leave Michael Caine the film star with the costumes, the wigs and the props in the studio.'3 And to be sure, as he approached the Queen and went on bended knee it was seemingly Caine the restaurateur and not Caine the actor who was celebrated by the playing of the song 'Food, Glorious Food' from Lionel Bart's stage show *Oliver!*.4 But the use of the song can also be read more pointedly: as a nod to Caine the victorious Dickensian, the low-life rapscallion who dreamed of being a gentleman and turned out, like Oliver Twist, to have been a member of the middle classes all along. No

Oliver of stage or screen, though, has ever looked more shell-shocked by joy than Caine did on the steps of Buckingham Palace that day.

A month later, Caine was back in British cinemas, playing his second doctor in two years. But while the Dr Royer-Collard of Philip Kaufman's *Quills* (2000) was a worthy follow-up to the Dr Larch of *The Cider House Rules*, the two characters were as far removed as could be. In place of Larch's sunny nobility was Royer-Collard's vigorous insensitivity, a bullying brutishness that owed more to Jack Carter and the Mortwell of *Mona Lisa* than it did to the Hippocratic oath. Given his fondness for institutionalized torture and humiliation, one would call Royer-Collard a sadist were it not for the fact that the man he spends the bulk of his time torturing during the movie's two hours is the Marquis de Sade (Geoffrey Rush).

The movie is set in 1804 at the liberally run Charenton asylum near Paris, where de Sade has been incarcerated. Nonetheless, with the help of a laundress, Madeleine (Kate Winslet), he manages to smuggle out the manuscript of the sexually explicit *Justine* to his publisher. Doubly angered, Napoleon orders Dr Royer-Collard to take over the running of the asylum. Royer-Collard pronounces himself disgusted with de Sade's work, but becomes a victim of it when his marriage to a teenage bride – the orphaned Simone (Amelia Warner), whom he sodomizes on their wedding night – becomes the subject of his charge's next satiric drama. In revenge, Royer-Collard has de Sade subjected to a round of increasingly agonizing 'treatments'. At the movie's end, de Sade dies by choking himself on a crucifix.

Censorship, pornography, sexual hypocrisy – *Quills* makes most sense when set against what was going on in the America of the late nineties. In place of a writer being tortured for attempting to probe the limits of absolute freedom, substitute a President having his private life intruded upon by a gaggle of hectoring nonentities. Emphatically, *Quills* was nowhere near as challenging a work as Peter Weiss's 1964 play *Persecution and Assassination of Jean-Paul Marat as Performed by the Inmates of the Asylum of Charenton Under the Direction of the Marquis de Sade* (made into a film by Peter Brook in 1966). Still, Kaufman's movie had things to say about the culture whence it sprang. Amid the increasingly infantilized product of contemporary Hollywood, that is no small achievement.

Despite the grim beauty of its location shoots (Luton Hoo in Bedfordshire doubling for Charenton), *Quills* – like Weiss's play before it – is essentially a one-set drama, and indeed the movie was adapted by Doug Wright from his own play. Nonetheless, Kaufman and his team rightly decided to play down any theatricality in the picture. 'This has all the makings of a farce,' says de Sade says when he hears that Royer-Collard has taken a teenage bride, but one of the movie's chief virtues lies in its refusal to camp things up.

Caine, of course, is in his element here. As the reactionary alienist whose treatment for any illness is a mix of starvation and water torture, he was given ample opportunity to undercut his instinctive realism with an arched eyebrow or a twitched lip. Instead, he plays Royer-Collard dead straight, with a kind of impatient vindictive glee. Yet despite the absence of camp grace notes, Caine's Royer-Collard mines a seam of grim humour merely by refusing to overtheatricalize. Caine knows that nobody in the audience – especially after the social revolution he had helped usher in three decades earlier – could possibly be on Royer-Collard's side and that therefore, even at his most vicious, he is almost axiomatically a figure of fun. This is not to say that Royer-Collard's sodomizing of his young wife is played for laughs; but it is to say that Caine's snarling maw – a familiar leitmotif from his earlier rough-house roles – lends the scene an ironic air: the good doctor as sex-mad gangster.

Caine's problem is that the movie doesn't allow him to do much else. Royer-Collard is essentially no more than another cameo, and accordingly Caine has nowhere to take the characterization. His best scene comes when Joaquin Phoenix's liberal-minded Abbé Coulmier (who had run Charenton before Napoleon's diktat that Royer-Collard take over) offers to be flogged in place of Madeleine. Caine's Royer-Collard refuses the offer, though he does so with a bored, urbane drawl that slyly undercuts the character's wilful vileness by suggesting that he *is* capable of having a little fun – providing, of course, that it is at the expense of others.

How very different from his next role, playing opposite Sandra Bullock in a light comedy of the sexes. *Miss Congeniality* (2000) was a millennial update on the Pygmalion myth with Bullock as the ugly duckling and Caine as the Svengali who can bring her out.

Caine researched the character of beauty expert Victor Melling by spending some time with a Texan pageant consultant and talking to Shakira (who, remember, had come third in the 1967 Miss World contest). But the joy of Caine's playing is the way his naturalistic subtleties so beautifully abrade the camp-as-Christmas stock type the movie clearly intended to trade on. Victor Melling has a wondrously graceful carriage, backed up by the most uncontrollably posturing arms Caine has ever treated the camera to, yet such elegant high-jinkery is forever being undercut by Caine's off-screen reputation as an unreconstructed male chauvinist.

Caine gives the character a variant on the upper-class English accent
he has been fooling around with since *Zulu*. 'It's always "yes", never
"yeah",' Caine's Melling counsels Bullock's Gracie Hart as he attempts
to smooth down her rough edges and give her a little class. In other
words, the cinema's first master of the cockney glottal stop was now
being used for lectures on received pronunciation. The big change in his
vocal technique, though, came in its volume control. As Ron Moody
has said, Caine is 'very quiet when he's going to kill you. But he shouts
at all other times.'5 The joke was well made, though it was made before
Miss Congeniality, a movie in which Caine's voice is as soft-spoken as
that of Celia Johnson in *Brief Encounter* (1945). Exploring something
of this new-found quietude was to be the big achievement of Caine's
next major project.

'I always knew I'd end up playing my old man,' Caine said of his role as
Jack Dodds in *Last Orders* (2002). And though Jack was a self-employed
butcher, with his own van and shop and none of the job troubles that
Maurice Micklewhite senior had suffered while his sons were growing
up, nonetheless the parallels between the two men are striking. Like
Maurice senior, Jack Dodds has spent the whole of his life in the
Bermondsey area of south-east London. Like Maurice senior, Jack has a
son, Vince, who refuses to come into the family business, preferring
instead to strike out on his own. Like Maurice senior's, Jack's wife Amy
makes weekly trips to see her disabled child. And like Maurice senior,
Jack Dodds dies of cancer in London's St Thomas's Hospital. The parallels are so precise that it is hard to suppress the suspicion that Graham
Swift – himself a south Londoner, and upon whose Booker Prize-winning
novel Fred Schepisi's movie is very closely based – had read about
Michael Caine's recently discovered half-brother during the time the
book was gestating in his subconscious.

Beyond the familial analogies, though, *Last Orders* feels, too, like a
commentary on the history and career of its leading man. Caine may
have joked that he was playing his father; equally, though, there is a very
real sense that he is playing himself. *Last Orders* is plainly a movie about
family life, but it is also a movie about the 'family' of cinematic angry
young men inaugurated by actors such as Caine during the late fifties
and early sixties. Here is Jack Dodd's undertaker friend Vic Tucker,
for instance, and underneath Vic is Tom Courtenay, the imprisoned ath-
lete who refused to try his best just so as to upset his governor in *The
Loneliness of the Long Distance Runner* (1962). Here is Lenny Tate,
the greengrocer Jack has been friends with since childhood, and beneath
him is David Hemmings, the actor who portrayed an alienated swinging

Actors' studio: Caine with Bob Hoskins, Tom Courtenay and David Hemmings in *Last Orders*. © The Kobal Collection

London photographer in Michelangelo Antonioni's *Blow-Up* (1966) as a cock-happy conflation of David Bailey, Terry Stamp and Caine himself.

The movie's other two leads, meanwhile, are both actors who have several times doffed their hats to Caine for being the man who broke the thespian mould, licensing in the process careers such as their own. Bob Hoskins, who has been friendly with Caine since they met on the set of *The Honorary Consul*, plays Ray, the insurance agent cum gambler. And Jack's son Vince is played by Ray Winstone, the former East End boxer who had publicly endorsed Caine's outburst at the snobberies and striations of Britain at the 2000 BAFTA ceremony: 'People say there's no class system,' snapped Winstone. 'Let me tell you, there fucking well is.'[6] Caine, Winstone has said more than once, was one of the few men he looked up to as a youngster: 'Where I came from, if you thought of becoming an actor, if you had any heroes, they [Caine, Courtenay, Hoskins, Hemmings] were it.'[7] *Last Orders*, then, can be seen as a kind of bifurcated family tree – with Michael Caine at the root of both branches.

For all that his presence looms over the whole production, however, Caine's part in the movie is little more than another of the cameos he has largely dealt in since the mid-nineties. *Last Orders* had a nine-week shoot, but Caine was on set for a mere ten days. Jack Dodds is, after all, dead when the narrative commences; and though he is the hub on which

Swift and Schepisi's near Resnaisian flashbacks revolve, in a good percentage of his appearances he is played not by Caine but by J. J. Feild, a rangey young blond actor who incarnates Jack the lad.

Caine has said that as well as basing Jack Dodds on his father, he found inspiration for him, too, in the dozens of duckers and divers he knew while growing up. There is no need to doubt this, though it should be stressed that of all the parts he has ever played, this is the one that comes closest to the essence of the public Michael Caine. A bonhomous raconteur who manages to be both proud of his work and able to cut off from it at the drop of a hat, Jack Dodds is very much the Michael Caine we are allowed access to in interviews and on TV chat shows.

Nonetheless, if the movie has a problem it is that the real Caine – and the personalities behind its other four male leads – is not allowed to shine quite brightly enough during its two hours. Schepisi's tightly constructed adaptation of Swift's already tightly constructed novel boasts barely one line of dialogue that is unmotivated by narrative necessity. Everything that is said moves one or other of the storylines along with classical economy. Such formally tight plotting sits uneasy, however, with the kind of naturalistic busking Caine and his fellow actors are being asked to trade in. The stream-of-consciousness narrative technique feels constricted by the sheer amount of incident it has to pack in, and only once – in the scene where Caine, Hoskins and Courtenay sing along to Roy Orbison's 'Blue Bayou' on the pub jukebox[8] – do you feel a genuine spark of *lived* existence. *Last Orders* feels impoverished for want of improvisation. But this is a minor cavil. Coming on seventy, Caine had every reason to be proud of his work here.

And he had nothing to be ashamed of for his star-turn in *Goldmember* (2002), the third movie in Mike Myers' series of Austin Powers parodies of the swinging sixties-style James Bond hero. As Austin's father, the pensionable spy Nigel Powers, Caine managed the rare feat of having a lot of fun in a nothing part while ensuring that his audience had some fun too.

Elegantly besuited and hilariously bewigged, Caine's Nigel is at once stylish and salty – an oldster trading risibly on the cachet of lost youth. Though Myers' movie gives Caine little to do but look dumbfounded by the socio-sexual changes he had helped usher in, there is no gainsaying the insolent *jouissance* of watching Britain's biggest international star allow himself to be so mercilessly deconstructed.

As we have seen, throughout his career Caine had conceived of himself as an inheritor of (and challenger to) the mood of laconic introspection

minted in Hollywood by Humphrey Bogart. Yet since his success in
The Man Who Would Be King, more than a quarter of a century
before, Caine had had no real chance of again getting to grips with the
Bogart tradition. Early in 2001, however, he was finally given another
shot at the title. Thomas Fowler, the journalist anti-hero of Christopher
Hampton's *The Quiet American* (2002), may be living and working in
fifties Vietnam, but a few years earlier he would have been quite happy
running a gin joint in downtown Casablanca. At one point Caine's
Fowler even gets to say the distinctly Bogartian line, 'I offer no point
of view, I take no action, I just report what I see.' Ostensibly, that is
Fowler's defence of journalism, but it reminds us, too, both of the
'objective' style of acting Bogart and Caine made famous and of one of
Bogie's most famous lines from *Casablanca* (1941). 'I stick my neck out
for nobody,' declaims Bogart's Rick as the Nazis gather to his left and
the Free French cluster to his right. Eventually, though, Blaine and
Fowler will stick their necks out – and for the same reason: a girl.

The girl in question in *The Quiet American* is Phuong (Do Hai Yen),
as inscrutable an easterner as Hollywood has ever served up. As such,
though, she is in good company. In this movie nobody is easily read-
able. Like Caine's *The Honorary Consul, The Quiet American* was
adapted from a Graham Greene novel, and though it fights shy of the
deepest murk and mire of Greene's original, nonetheless the story – at
least for its first half hour – is told so relaxedly that it makes *Funeral
in Berlin* look like a model of clarity. It is 1952, and Thomas Fowler is
The Times's foreign correspondent in Saigon. Fowler has a wife back
home in England, but her memory is as distant and dim to him as the
taste of a pint of bitter. And anyway, he has sweeter tastes to enjoy out
here, chief among them the aforementioned Phuong, a vision in plaits
and silk brassiere. Quite what she sees in Fowler is rather more of a
mystery, one that certainly proves baffling to a new kid in town, Alden
Pyle (Brendan Fraser), who is taken once round the dance floor by
Phuong and declares his undying love. Fowler takes the proposition
on the chin, but there is something ravaged and rueful in Caine's eyes
that suggests he thinks the game is up.

In fact, the game is merely afoot. Pyle, the quiet American of the
movie's title, is an economic aid officer stationed at the US embassy,
though his uncanny knack for turning up at every one of Vietnam's
more pyrotechnic hotspots has you wondering whether there's something he isn't telling us. Fowler's assistant, Hinh (Tzi Ma), knows what
it is. Pyle is actually working for the CIA and he organized the bomb
that blew up outside Fowler's favourite café, killing and maiming innocent people. 'Sooner or later, one has to take sides if one is to remain

human,' says Hinh, and the hitherto disinterested Fowler becomes a man of action, regretfully tipping off the communists so they can send Pyle to a watery grave. Welcome to *Casablanca*.

Except that Fowler is not quite sure he wants to be there. *The Quiet American* is in many ways a better movie than *Casablanca* because it deals in greys as well as blacks and whites. In Michael Curtiz's movie you are never in any doubt as to who the bad guys are. Here, things are a little more complicated – and a lot more complicated than they are in Greene's novel. The Pyle of the book, for instance, is a cardboard cut-out put through the shredder of Greene's anti-Americanism. Brendan Fraser is made of sturdier stuff, though, starting out likeably geeky and do-gooding before gradually shading Pyle into a study in blood-stained guilt. Like Fowler, you're sad to see him go. And like Caine, too, because though this is his movie all the way, it was Fraser's presence opposite him that ensured he raised his game. Not since *The Man Who Would Be King*'s Sean Connery had Caine had to act against someone who really had a chance of taking him on.

What a shame, then, that the director, Phillip Noyce, didn't try and take Caine on, too. Instead, he merely took his cue from Caine's subtlety of gesture and expression, and the result is a movie that can be nigh impossible to read. Until that big explanatory scene between Fowler and his assistant, *The Quiet American* is far too quiet for its own good. For the first hour and more, anyone who hasn't read the book won't have a clue what's going on. Hence the overreliance on dialogue in the movie's closing half hour, with everyone explaining everything to everyone else.

Nonetheless, there are many pleasures to be had here, not least in speculating on what President George W. Bush must have made of the movie (Noyce was unlucky enough to have presented it to his patrons, Miramax, on 10 September 2001 – one day before the felling of the twin towers). Here, after all, is a film that wonders whether America ought to get involved in matters of state outside the States; a film that asks whether our best intentions are always for the best. Most of all, here is a film that, unlike so much contemporary Hollywood product, finds in the blast of a bomb a *moral* turning point. For that alone, it deserved explosive applause.

But it merited attention, too, for the calm, cumulative detail upon which Caine built his finest performance in years. Justifiably proud of the work he had done on *The Quiet American*, Caine entertained serious hopes of finally achieving a Best Actor Oscar. It wasn't to be. In the aftermath of 9/11, Miramax co-chairman Harvey Weinstein had cold feet about releasing what he considered an unpatriotic movie. Though Caine was indeed eventually nominated for the Oscar, Weinstein's doubtful mood infected the judges and they played safe, giving the award to Adrien Brody for his work in Roman Polanski's *The Pianist* (2002).9

Throughout all those politicking shenanigans, though, Caine kept himself as busy as ever. The spring of 2002 found him in Ireland shooting *The Actors*, writer/director Conor McPherson's rather too affectionate tribute cum piss-take to the grandiloquent school of acting Caine has always done so much to subvert. Caine plays Anthony O'Malley, the leering, lascivious lead of a troupe of rep players straight out of the fifties provinces. It isn't much of a part, but the movie does allow Caine the chance finally to give us what he had so insolently promised thirty-five years earlier in *Billion Dollar Brain*: his Richard III. The result is joyous. O'Malley's Richard is a fright-wigged, crook-backed lip-curler who delivers even the most perfunctory of his lines with the rapacious stentorian glee that the likes of the Richards Harris and Burton too easily mistook for art. Caine, in other words, had a high old time of it in *The Actors* (2003), though in doing so he was having rather more fun than the audience. For O'Malley was just another cameo role, and during those long stretches of the movie in which Caine's services weren't required, an air of clumsy tedium rapidly descended.

Tedious, too, was *Secondhand Lions* (2003), which Caine flew to Texas to shoot in the autumn of 2002. Like *The Cider House Rules* and *Hurry Sundown* before it, Tim McCanlies' movie was another for which Caine got hauled over the coals for his putative inability with American accents. Once again, though, the carping was unfair. While Caine's Texas drawl does slip London-ward on a couple of occasions, for the most part it cuts the mustard. As such, it is Caine's only real achievement in the movie. Saddled with a lacklustre, near plotless script, Caine for the first time in his career fails to rise to the challenge he had been set at that Lowestoft repertory theatre four decades earlier: namely, find himself things to do in those scenes that call for nothing specific from him. Though it is nice to see Caine playing opposite Robert Duvall again (they had appeared together in *The Eagle Has Landed*), neither actor finds anything in the other to rub up against and spark off. Not even the presence of Haley Joel Osment, the startlingly gifted child actor who inspired Bruce Willis to more than gurning and strutting in *The Sixth Sense* (1999), coaxed anything from Caine.

But there was rather more nourishment in *The Statement* (2003), Norman Jewison's film version of Brian Moore's penultimate novel. Caine gives one of the best performances of his entire career as Pierre Brossard, a one-time French collaborator being pursued in the present day for the execution of seven Jews during the Second World War. The movie opens in the forties with a young Brossard (George Williams) giving the order to shoot – but with Caine himself doing the voice-over. Caine's voice, though, is so soft-spoken and high-pitched that it takes you a line or two of dialogue to place it – an effect duplicated when he appears on screen in the flesh. Caine, after all, is a rather sprightly seventy-year-old, but the figure he cuts in this movie might be twenty years older. To watch Caine's Brossard dispose of a body is to watch a man humbled and harried by the depredations of time. Life has got to him, yet he retains an insect-like antenna for danger. Withered and nervy, Caine's hunch-shouldered Brossard makes even the act of drinking a beer seem freighted with doom.

For all that paranoiac observation, though, Caine's performance is not at all passive. While Brossard has about him something of the diffidence of *Hannah and Her Sisters'* Elliot, he has, too, the simplistic certainties of Jack Carter. The result is a figure whose confusions make him more chilling than any of Caine's earlier villains, a remarkable study in guilt and shame. Pouchy and sagged, his frequently unreadable face could almost pass muster as the titular character of *The Magus*.[10] Caine is forever finding new ways of suggesting how Brossard is wrongfooted by his consciencelessness: he knows that he ought to feel bad about what he has done . . . but he doesn't; instead, Caine makes him feel bad about not feeling bad.

The Statement's problem is that for too long it veers away from Brossard to focus on the security services on his tail. Caine just isn't around that much, and when he is he is too often alone, with nobody to bounce his swerving emotions off. Ever the Pudovkinian, Caine acknowledged that Brossard's aesthetic isolation meant he was a co-creation: 'It's a performance that will be controlled more by the director and the editor,' he said during the spring 2003 shoot. Brossard was 'so far distanced from everybody. It has been kind of lonely.'[11] Given the limiting effects of such aesthetic isolation, Caine rises to his task with astonishing verve – just as he had done when acting against a blank screen for *The Muppet Christmas Carol*. In that picture, though, Caine had the advantage of guying the kind of glint-eyed malevolence that had made his name. *The Statement*, on the other hand, is nothing if not serious, and while Caine heightens and intensifies his solitary scenes to a rare pitch, the movie can't help but flatten out when he's not around.

Nonetheless, with *The Statement* and *The Quiet American*, Caine had delivered himself of two of the greatest performances of his career a year each side of his seventieth birthday. How to follow them? What ought Michael Caine be doing in his fifth decade as an international star?

Given that over the past few years a host of movie stars – Nicole Kidman, Kenneth Branagh, Kevin Spacey, to name but a few – have turned or returned to the theatre, could we perhaps see Caine back on stage? It would be nice to think so – perhaps in a production of Pinter's *The Homecoming* (what an impotent patriarch he would make) or *The Caretaker* (all self-pitying viciousness), or even as Shylock in *The Merchant of Venice*. In fact, Caine was recently offered a part on Broadway, in Neil Simon's follow-up to *California Suite, London Suite*. Alas, Caine pleaded stage fright ('I said, Neil, I can't do it because from the minute I put the phone down I'd be having a nervous breakdown'[12]), though it is likely he was as afeared of boredom as of stage jitters. No man who keeps himself as busy as Caine can much relish the repetitive strain injuries attendant on putting the same show on night after night.

Because Caine seems incapable of ever merely going through the emotions. Roger Moore's joshing suggestion that Caine will open any envelope that comes his way because it might contain a cheque doubtless has some truth to it, though it is equally true that Caine cannot see an envelope without wanting to push it. Perhaps he *will* do anything for the money, but while doing anything he will do *everything* to make the anything something. Film acting – like film directing, like writing verse or sculpting bronze – is a craft rather more frequently than it is an art. Caine has been an artist on screen more often than most, but even his most devoted fan would have to concede that he has been a craftsman far more often than he has been an artist. In an age when everyone believes himself an artist, though, a craftsman is no small thing to be. "What's it all about?", asks *Alfie* (a question subsequently pressed into service as the title of his autobiography); his creator has too often done himself a disservice by saying it is all about the money.

Notes

Introduction

1 David Sylvester, *London Recordings* (London: Chatto and Windus, 2003), p. 69.
2 *Sunday Telegraph*, 11 October 1992.
3 *Sunday Times Magazine*, 12 March 2000, p. 20.
4 *Premiere*, January 1999, p. 42.
5 See *The Time Out Book of Interviews*, Ed. Frank Broughton, Penguin, 1998, p. 248.
6 New York: Da Capo Press, 1979 (revised edn).
7 Born 1930.
8 Born 1936.
9 *Signs and Meaning in the Cinema* (London: Secker and Warburg/ BFI, 1969), pp. 74–115.
10 Michael Caine, *What's It All About?* (London: Century, 1992), unnumbered predatory page.
11 William Hall, *Raising Caine* (London: Sidgwick & Jackson, 1981). Subsequently, the book has been republished with a couple of extra chapters as *Arise, Sir Michael Caine* (London: John Blake, 2000), and again, with a couple of extra pages, as *70 Not Out* (London: John Blake, 2003).
12 Michael Freedland, *Michael Caine* (London: Orion, 1999).
13 Anne Billson, *My Name Is Michael Caine* (London: Muller, 1991).
14 David Bishop, *Starring Michael Caine* (London: Reynolds and Hearn, 2003).

Chapter 1

1 Charles Dickens, *Great Expectations* (London: Penguin 1965 edn), p. 92.
2 *Daily Mail*, 15 October 2003.
3 Michael Caine, interviewed by Peter Evans, *News of the World*, 24 April 1983.
4 Michael Caine interviewed on Sky television, date unknown.
5 Michael Caine, *What's It All About?* (London: Century, 1992), p. 525.
6 John Updike, introduction to *Early Stories* (London: Hamish Hamilton, 2004), p. xiv.

7 quoted in Ephraim Katz, *The Macmillan International Film Encyclopaedia* (London: Macmillan, 1994), p. 205.

8 W. H. Auden, 'September 1, 1939', *Selected Poems* (London: Faber, 1979), p. 86.

9 Christopher Lee, *This Sceptred Isle: Twentieth Century* (London: Penguin, 1999), p. 180.

10 Quoted by D. J. Taylor, *Orwell: The Life* (London: Chatto & Windus, 2003), p. 118.

11 Astonishingly, his son describes him as being thirty-six in his autobiography; Caine op. cit., p. 6.

12 See Orwell's 'Hop-Picking Diary', in *Volume X* of his complete works, Ed. Peter Davison (London: Secker and Warburg, 1998), p. 228.

13 *Ibid.*, p. 229.

14 Caine, *op. cit.*, p. 28.

15 Caine interviewed on *Parkinson*, BBC1, 30 November 2002.

16 Caine, *op. cit.*, p. 50.

17 quoted in William Hall, *Arise Sir Michael Caine* (London: John Blake, 2000), p. 11.

18 Caine interviewed in *The Times*, 19 December 1992.

19 See Caine's interview in the *Daily Mirror*, 13 May 1991.

20 Interestingly, another south London boy made good, David Bowie, had a half-brother who ended up in Cane Hill. For more, see Peter and Leni Gilman, *Alias David Bowie* (London: Hodder & Stoughton, 1986), p. 184 *et passim*.

21 Quoted in the *Daily Mirror*, 13 May 1991.

22 George Orwell, *Down and Out in Paris and London* (London: Penguin, 1974), p. 118.

23 Bryan Magee, *Clouds of Glory* (London: Jonathan Cape, 2003), p. 114.

24 *Ibid.*

25 V. S. Pritchett, *A Cab at the Door* (Chatto & Windus, 1968), p. 67.

26 Quoted in Roy Porter, *London: A Social History* (London: Hamish Hamilton), p. 307.

27 quoted in Hall, *op. cit.*, p. 9.

28 Caine, *op. cit.*, p. 12.

Chapter 2

1 Ralph Waldo Emerson, 'War', *Miscellanies*, 1884.

2 Norman Longmate, *How We Lived Then* (London: Hutchinson, 1971), p. 3.
3 Peter Ackroyd, *Dickens* (London: Sinclair-Stevenson, 1990), p. 63.
4 And Sam Weller is the pseudonym Caine's Lord Bulbeck gives himself in order that he might conduct an affair in *Half Moon Street* (1986).
5 Caine, *op. cit.*, p. 17.
6 Quoted in the *Eastern Daily Press*, 14 March 2003.
7 *Ibid.*
8 Quoted by Peter Evans, *Daily Express*, 30 January 1964.
9 *Eastern Daily Press, op. cit.*
10 *Ibid.*
11 When it closed, Hackney Downs School, as it was then called, was no longer a grammar school but a comprehensive.
12 The school even had four 'Houses'; Caine was allotted a place in Kelly. (Norman Tucker, email to the author, 12 February 2003.)
13 Brian Masters, *The Swinging Sixties* (London: Constable, 1985), p. 135.
14 Mattingly interviewed in the documentary *The Real Michael Caine* (Channel 4, 23 December 2002).
15 Quoted by Henri Gris, *Sunday Citizen*, 12 March 1967.
16 Caine, *op. cit.*, p. 32.
17 *Spectator*, 26 June 1959.
18 Caine interviewed on BBC News 24 by Tom Carver, 23 May 2003.
19 Caine, *op. cit.*, p. 46.

Chapter 3

1 Samuel Johnson, quoted in Boswell's *Life of Samuel Johnson*.
2 Quoted in Piers Brendon, *Dark Valley: A Panorama of the 1930s* (London: Jonathan Cape, 2000), p. 160.
3 Caine, *op. cit.*, p. 45.
4 Caine interviewed by Tom Carver (BBC News 24, 23 May 2003)
5 *The Real Michael Caine* (Channel 4, 23 December 2002).
6 Caine, *op. cit.*, p. 46.
7 David Lodge, Afterword to *Ginger, You're Barmy* (London: Penguin, 1984), p. 212.
8 Two tasks Caine was allotted while in the Queen's Royal Regiment at Guildford barracks. Princess Margaret was visiting and it was thought that (a) the heap of dirty black fuel might offend her gaze

and that (b) its being autumn, a leaf might fall during her visit, thus offending some other unstated aspect of her belief system.

9 I should like to acknowledge a large debt to Callum MacDonald's short but excellent book *Britain and the Korean War* (London: Basil Blackwell, 1990) for much of the information presented here.

10 Peter Hennessey, *Never Again* (London: Jonathan Cape, 1992), p 406.

11 Quoted in Hall, *op. cit.*, p. 42.

12 Lodge, *op. cit.*, p. 175.

13 Caine, *op. cit.*, p. 71.

14 Richard Hoggart, *A Sort of Clowning, Life and Times: 1940–59* (London: Chatto and Windus, 1990), p. 198.

15 Caine, *op. cit.*, p. 81.

16 Caine, *op. cit.*, p. 88.

17 *The Economist*, 2 February 1952, pp. 218–9.

Chapter 4

1 Ian Fleming, *Diamonds Are Forever* (London: Pan, 1958), p. 162.

2 This version comes from Elaine Gallagher and Ian Macdonald, *Candidly Caine* (London: Robson, 1990), p. 18.

3 See Caine, *op. cit.*, p. 91 and Hall, *op. cit.*, p. 50.

4 See Jonathan Aitken, *The Young Meteors* (London: Secker and Warburg, 1967), p. 237.

5 'The average wage in 1950 (£6.8s.0d) [£6.40] had almost doubled by 1959 (£11.2s.6d) [£11.12]': see Peter Lewis, *The Fifties* (London: Heinemann, 1978), p. 32.

6 Gallagher and Macdonald, *op. cit.*, p. 20.

7 *West Sussex County Times*, 10 July 1953.

8 *Ibid.*, 7 August 1953.

9 Hall, *op. cit.*, p. 52.

10 Terence Stamp, *Coming Attractions* (London: Bloomsbury, 1988), p. 211.

11 *Ibid.*

12 Eric Lax, *Woody Allen* (London: Jonathan Cape, 1991), p. 302.

13 Caine, *op. cit.*, p. 100.

14 A decade or so later she would come third in the First International Bread Pudding Competition at the Playboy Club.

15 Caine, *op. cit.*, p. 104.

16 *Ibid.*, p. 105.

17 Hall, *op. cit.*, p. 58.

18 Lewis, *op. cit.*, p. 42.

19 *Ibid.*, pp. 42–3.

20 *Ibid.*, p. 44.

21 See Terry Coleman's interview with Caine, *Guardian*, 23 November 1985.

22 Quoted by Gris, *op. cit.*

23 See Mark Garnett and Richard Wright, *The A–Z Guide to Modern British History* (London: Jonathan Cape, 2003), p. 494.

24 Her film and television appearances catalogued at www.imdb.com suggest she did indeed have little luck: no entries appear for her until the early sixties.

25 See Robert Hewison, *In Anger* (London: Weidenfeld and Nicolson, 1981), p. 145.

26 *Ibid.*, p. 143.

27 Caine, *op. cit.*, p. 128.

28 Hall, *op. cit.*, p. 69.

Chapter 5

1 Cyril Connolly, *Enemies of Promise* (London: Routledge, 1938); reprinted in *The Selected Works of Cyril Connolly, Volume One: The Modern Movement*, Ed. Matthew Connolly (London: Picador, 2002), p. 120.

2 *Look Back in Anger*, Act 3, Scene 1 (London: Faber, 1957), p 84–5.

3 Caine interviewed by Victoria McKee, *The Times*, 19 December 1992.

4 Peter Vansittart, *In the Fifties* (London: John Murray, 1995), p. 229.

5 See *Ibid.*, p. 231.

6 As Lynn Barber does in a profile of Caine for *Vanity Fair*, December 1999.

7 See the Caine interview with Kevin O'Sullivan in the *Daily Mirror*, 8 April 2000, for the magnum opus of this kind of nonsensical wish-fulfilment.

8 See Corinna Honan's 'The Class War of Michael Caine', *Mail on Sunday*, 20 September 1992.

9 Hall, *op. cit.*, pp. 66–7.

10 Caine, *op. cit.*, p. 110.

11 Cubby Broccoli with Donald Zec, *When the Snow Melts: The Autobiography* (London: Boxtree, 1998), p. 125.

12 Caine, *op. cit.*, p. 140.

13 The figure comes from Michael Freedland, *Michael Caine* (London: Orion, 1999), p. 76; Shawn Levy in *Ready, Steady, Go! – Swinging London and the Invention of Cool* (London: Fourth Estate, 2002), p. 62, says Stamp was paid £12 a week.

14 See Terence Stamp, *Coming Attractions* (London: Bloomsbury, 1988), p. 160.

15 Harris quoted in Michael Feeney Callan, *Richard Harris, Sex, Death and the Movies: An Intimate Biography* (London: Robson, 2003), p. 187.

16 Michael Caine, *Acting in Film – An Actor's Take on Movie Acting* (New York: Applause, 1997; revised edn), p. 17.

17 See David Austen's 'Playing Dirty', *Films and Filming*, April 1969.

18 Alan Brien, *Sunday Telegraph*, 28 February 1963.

Chapter 6

1 Terence Rattigan, *Separate Tables* (1954).

2 Stamp, *Double Feature* (London: Bloomsbury, 1989), p. 85.

3 *The Real Michael Caine*, Channel 4, *op. cit.*

4 Hall, *op. cit.*, p. 3.

5 For all its pretensions to radicalism, in fact, the movie is deeply racist and can be read as a story about British working-class tensions over the large-scale immigration of the fifties. For Rorke's Drift in 1879, read Notting Hill in 1959.

6 quoted by Anthony Storey in *Stanley Baker: Portrait of an Actor* (London: W. H. Allen, 1977), p. 82.

7 Alexander Walker, *Hollywood UK* (New York: Stein and Day, 1974), p. 304.

8 This happy phrase is from Patrick Gibbs' review of *Zulu, Daily Telegraph*, 24 January 1964.

9 Quoted in Freedland, *op. cit.*, p. 81.

10 Quoted in Levy, *op. cit.*, p. 66.

11 Estimated from data given in Arthur Marwick, *The Sixties – Cultural Revolution in Britain, France, Italy, and the United States, c.1958–c.1974* (Oxford: Oxford University Press), p. 257.

12 Levy, *op. cit.*, p. 69.

13 Quoted in *Glenda Jackson: A Study in Fire and Ice*, Ian Woodward (London: Weidenfeld & Nicholson, 1985), p. 37.

14 Caine quoted by Peter Evans, *Daily Express*, 30 January 1964.

15 *Ibid.*

Chapter 7

1 Kingsley Amis, *The James Bond Dossier* (London: Jonathan Cape, 1965), p. 14.
2 In *Declaration*, quoted in Christopher Booker, *The Neophiliacs* (London: Collins, 1969), p. 120.
3 Quoted in Michael Feeney Callan, *Sean Connery* (London: Virgin, 1993), p. 111.
4 Quoted in Mandrake column, *Sunday Telegraph*, 13 October 1985. This may, of course, be hindsight talking. Prior to the filming of *The Ipcress File* Caine was not a star and it is unlikely any novelist would have thought of him for any part.
5 See Lindsay Anderson, *The Diaries*, ed. Paul Sutton (London: Methuen, 2004), p. 86.
6 Quoted in John Parker, *Sean Connery* (London: Gollancz, 1993), p. 157.
7 See Caine, *op. cit.*, pp. 195–6, and Hall, *op. cit.*, pp. 120–2.
8 By the summer of 1964 Barry was doing very well indeed for himself, holed up in a Cadogan Square apartment that brought on some of the *Daily Mail*'s most breathless prose: 'The Barry living-room scheme is essentially modern with strong Rensaissance overtones. Walls are white, the carpeting avocado green and the dramatic curtains are in a cerise linen weave. John Barry is fascinated by early antiques, and although his armchairs and luxurious four-seater settee are modern . . . they are upholstered in antique gold suede.' Quite the little Frasier Crane! Lucky Caine, then, who slept in Barry's spare room for a couple of weeks in the autumn of 1964 while waiting for his own new apartment to be made ready for occupation. (*Daily Mail* quoted in Eddi Fiegel, *John Barry – A Sixties Theme* [London: Constable, 1998], p. 131.)
9 See Andrew Rissik, *The James Bond Man – The Films of Sean Connery* (London: Elm Tree, 1983), p. 79.
10 As Caine not quite joked thirty years later: 'It was the first day of the new socialist government and I thought, this is my first big money and I've got to give it away. Bloody hell. Just my luck.' Quoted in the *Sunday Times* magazine, 23 July 1995.
11 Quoted in Booker, *op. cit.*, p. 243.
12 Unlike the 007 of Fleming's novels, whose love of Queen and country and, indeed, of his boss, M, borders on the pathological.
13 Indeed, Len Deighton admitted that Bogart was the only man he would rather have had to play his hero. (Bogart had, of course,

been dead for the best part of a decade.) See the *Sunday Telegraph*, 29 November 1964.

14 Plots whose logic even their author, Raymond Chandler, could never convincingly explain.

15 Len Deighton, *The Ipcress File* (London: Hodder and Stoughton, 1962); quoted from Panther edition of 1964, p. 13.

16 *Sight and Sound*, Summer 1965, p. 150.

17 Not that Caine was as confident as he appeared. On the first day of filming *The Ipcress File* he had his chauffeur fired because the chap told him that he hadn't understood Len Deighton's original novel and consequently didn't think much of it nor of its chances as a movie. Every actor is entitled to first-night nerves, of course, but Harry Palmer plainly had prima donna tendencies. See Caine, *op. cit.*, pp. 208–9.

18 See the *Sunday Telegraph*, 29 November 1964.

19 Quoted by 'Arkadin', *Sight and Sound*, Winter 1964–5, p. 34.

20 *Sight & Sound*, Summer 1965, p 150.

21 Caine, *op. cit.*, pp. 300–1.

22 Deighton, *op. cit.*, p. 60.

23 Quoted in the *Sunday Express*, 13 February 1966.

24 *Sight & Sound*, Summer 1965, p 150.

25 *Daily Telegraph*, 19 March 1965.

26 *Sunday Telegraph*, 21 March 1965

27 Both quoted in Gallagher and Macdonald, *op. cit.*, p. 81.

28 Caine, quoted in *Films and Filming*, April 1969, p. 8.

29 *Sunday Telegraph*, 8 August 1965.

30 Quoted in Levy, *op. cit.*, pp. 166–7.

31 Stamp, *op. cit.*, p. 137.

Chapter 8

1 Cody Jarrett's (James Cagney) catchphrase in Raoul Walsh's *White Heat* (1949; screenplay: Ivan Goff and Ben Roberts).

2 Hall, *op. cit.*, p. 85.

3 Bill Naughton, *Alfie*, 1966 (London: Panther, 1966), p. 7.

4 Quoted in the *Guardian*, Friday 4 May 2001.

5 *Ibid*. It was, incidentally, a very cheap movie as far as Caine was concerned. Lewis Gilbert offered him either a one-off fee of £75,000 or a percentage of the profits. Caine opted for the one-off payment, 'and that cost me about $3M', he said in 1981 (Hall, *op. cit.*, p. 143).

6 Caine, *op. cit.*, p. 213.

7 Indeed, William Hall believes that Alfie is the character people think of when they think of Michael Caine. I am not so sure. Yes, *Alfie* proved Caine could act. But it was the role of Harry Palmer that had proved, and would prove again, that he could simply be.

8 *Film Quarterly*, Spring 1967, p. 44.

9 *Ibid.*

10 Quoted on *The Real Michael Caine*, Channel 4, *op. cit.*

11 *Spectator*, 1 April 1966.

12 *Sunday Express*, 25 July 1965.

13 *Ibid.*

14 Bailey/Wyndham, *op. cit.*

15 Caine quoted by David Lewin, *Daily Mirror*, 25 February 1967.

16 See *Films and Filming*, *op. cit.*, p. 8.

17 Robert Murphy, *Sixties British Cinema* (London: British Film Institute, 1992), p. 246.

18 The phrase is Andrew Sarris's. See *The American Cinema* (New York: Dutton, 1968), pp. 192–3.

19 Quite literally: as Tom Milne pointed out in his review of the movie, the credits even manage to misspell the name of Wilfrid Lawson. See the *Monthly Film Bulletin*, May 1966.

20 *Sunday Times*, 29 May 1966.

21 It was, though, destined to be the flavour of the month a year or two hence, when the summer of love hippies sought to undermine the iconography of what they saw as late-nineteenth-century repressiveness.

22 Bryan Forbes: undated letter to the author.

23 See Graham McCann's *Cary Grant* (London: Fourth Estate, 1997) for a wonderfully subtle analysis of the Grant persona.

24 Quoted in the *Sunday Telegraph*, 29 November 1964.

25 See Ronald Neame with Barbara Roisman Cooper, *Straight From the Horse's Mouth: An Autobiography* (New York: Scarecrow Press, 2003), p 210.

26 *Ibid.*, p. 211.

27 *Ibid.*, p. 214.

28 *Ibid.*, pp. 209–10.

29 *Ibid.*, p. 210.

30 *Ibid.* quoted in *Films and Filming*, *op. cit.*, p. 8.

31 See the *Sunday Express*, 3 January 1967.

32 Quoted in the *Sunday Express*, 13 February 1966.

Chapter 9

1 Georges Braque, quoted in John Russell, *Braque* (London: Phaidon, 1959), p. 9.
2 Caine, *op. cit.*, p. 266.
3 *Monthly Film Bulletin*, April 1967, p. 56.
4 See Cameron Crowe, *Conversations with Wilder* (London: Faber, 1999), p. 149.
5 Quoted by Willi Frischauer, *Behind the Scenes of Otto Preminger* (London: Michael Joseph, 1973), p. 18.
6 Caine, *op. cit.*, p. 275.
7 Quoted by David Lewin, *Daily Mail*, 8 August 1966.
8 Hall, *op. cit.*, p. 174.
9 Lewin, *op. cit.*
10 Quoted in anonymous interview, *Time*, 17 February 1967.
11 Caine, *op. cit.*, pp. 162–3.
12 Caine interviewed by Nick Roddick, *Stills*, October 1984, p. 29.
13 Quoted in John Baxter, *Ken Russell: An Appalling Talent* (London: Michael Joseph, 1973), p. 152.
14 *Ibid.*, p. 154.
15 *Monthly Film Bulletin*, January 1968, p. 3.
16 Quoted in Baxter, *op. cit.*, p. 190.
17 Caine, *op. cit.*, p. 283.
18 Baxter, *op. cit.*, p. 154.
19 Quoted in the *Daily Mirror*, 3 December 1968.
20 *Ibid.*
21 Baxter, *op. cit.*, p. 158.

Chapter 10

1 Samuel Johnson, *The Rambler* (London, 1750–1752), p. 189.
2 Peter Sellers is said to have based the phoney, over the top, whirling dervish of a film director he pretends to be in *After the Fox* (1966) on De Sica (who was directing Sellers in the movie). See Roger Lewis's *The Life and Death of Peter Sellers* (London: Century, 1994), pp. 526–7.
3 Caine, *op. cit.*, p. 283.
4 Desmond Cory, *Deadfall* (London: Corgi movie tie-in edn, 1968), p. 98.
5 Undated letter to the author.

6 *Monthly Film Bulletin*, November 1968, p. 178.

7 Forbes's letter, *op. cit.*

8 Caine, *op. cit.*, p. 284.

9 *Sunday Express*, 10 November 1968.

10 Quoted in Eileen Warburton, *John Fowles – A Life in Two Worlds* (London: Jonathan Cape, 2004), p. 297.

11 *John Fowles, The Journals: Volume 1* (London: Jonathan Cape, 2003), p. 630.

12 Caine interviewed in *Films and Filming*, May 1969, p. 18.

13 *Ibid.*

14 Caine, *op. cit.*, p. 294.

15 Quoted in Michael Feeney Callan, *Sean Connery* (London: Virgin, 1993), p. 169.

16 Morris interviewed for *The Real Michael Caine*, Channel 4, *op. cit.*

17 Caine interviewed in *Films and Filming*, April 1969, p. 4.

18 See André de Toth, *Fragments: Portraits from the Inside* (London: Faber, 1994), p. 441.

19 Caine, *op. cit.*, p. 288.

20 De Toth, *op. cit.*, p. 446.

21 *Ibid.*

22 See the *Daily Telegraph*, 27 February 1968.

23 See Michael Feeney Callan, *Richard Harris, Sex, Death and the Movies: An Intimate Biography* (London: Robson, 2003), p. 187. The episode clearly played on Harris's mind for the rest of his life. See Chapter 23 for how it achieved closure.

Chapter 11

1 Albert Camus, *Notebooks 1935–1942*, trans. Philip Thody (Hamish Hamilton, 1962), p. 3.

2 Nor was xenophobia confined to the film itself: during shooting, the British crew would regularly order bacon sandwiches from England for consumption in Italy. See Matthew Field, *The Making of The Italian Job* (London: Batsford, 2001), p. 42.

3 In 2003 a snatch of Caine's dialogue – 'You're only supposed to blow the bloody doors off!' – was voted the greatest one-liner in cinema history by the readers of *Empire* magazine.

4 Sarris, *op. cit.*, p. 85.

5 Caine, *op. cit.*, p. 308.

6 Quoted in the *Daily Mail*, 28 August 2002.

7 See *Daily Express*, 4 March 1970.

8 See *Daily Mail*, 28 August 2002.

9 Quoted in *Sunday Express*, 11 June 1972.

10 Quoted in *Sunday Express*, 12 October 1969.

11 Hall, *op. cit.*, p. 217.

12 See Pauline Kael, *The New Yorker*, 13 February 1971, reprinted in *Deeper into Movies* (London: Calder & Boyars, 1975), p. 249.

13 Indeed, the British Board of Film Censors insisted on the excision of some of its more pornogaphic violence.

14 Kael, *op. cit.*

15 Quoted in Hall, *op. cit.*, p. 217.

16 Quoted in Hall, *op. cit.*, p. 216.

17 Caine, *op. cit.*, p. 321.

18 See *Sunday Express*, 10 November 1968.

Chapter 12

1 William Shakespeare, *Richard III* (Act One, Scene 1).

2 Christopher Booker, *The Seventies: Portrait of a Decade* (London: Allen Lane, 1980, p. 4.

3 'Brute Force', *Film Comment*, Sept/Oct 2000, p. 36.

4 But as Terry Collier says in the movie version of the Newcastle-set sitcom *The Likely Lads* (1976), 'There's not much poetry paddling down to an outside bog on a freezing cold night.' When, shortly after *Get Carter* opened, Caine ran into Ian La Frenais, the half of the *Likely Lads* writing team who came from Newcastle, he joked that he had always thought of himself as working class until he made *Get Carter*, when he realized he was middle class. See Gallagher and Macdonald, *op. cit.*, p. 129.

5 Alexander Walker, *National Heroes: British Cinema in the Seventies and Eighties* (London: Harrap, 1985), p. 25.

6 Quoted in Mark Adams, *Mike Hodges* (Harpenden: Pocket Essentials, 2001), p. 24.

7 See 'Mike Hodges discusses *Get Carter* with an audience at the National Film Theatre, September 23, 1997'. Reproduced in Steve Chibnall and Robert Murphy (Eds), *British Crime Cinema* (London: Routledge, 1999), p. 117.

8 See Clark Collis, 'Number One Gangster', *Empire*, December 2000, p. 129.

9 Caine, interviewed on BBC News 24, 23 May 2003.

10 Quoted in Hall, *op. cit.*, p. 227.

11 *Ibid.*, p 228.

12 *Zee & Co* was filmed after *Kidnapped*, though released before it.

13 *The New Yorker*, 12 February 1972; reprinted in *Deeper into Movies* (London: Calder & Boyars), pp. 405–9.

14 Quoted in Melvyn Bragg, *Rich: The Life of Richard Burton* (London: Hodder and Stoughton, 1988), p. 553.

Chapter 13

1 Charles Lamb, 'Mrs Battle's Opinions on Whist', *Essays of Elia* (London, 1823).

2 Quoted in *Sunday Express*, 10 June 1973.

3 Quoted in Steven Paul Davies, *Get Carter and Beyond*, (London: Batsford, 2002), p. 64.

4 Quoted in Hall, *op. cit.*, p. 238.

5 Quoted in *The Reader's Companion to the Twentieth Century Novel* (London: Fourth Estate, 1994), p. 181

6 She appeared opposite Bogart in *Dead Reckoning* (1947).

7 See Mark Adams, *op. cit.*, p. 32.

8 See Anthony Shaffer, *So What Did You Expect: A Memoir* (London: Picador, 2001), p. 74.

9 Booker, *op. cit.*, *passim.*

10 Quoted in Alan Strachan's Obituary of Shaffer, *Independent*, 8 November 2001.

11 Which he had no need to concentrate on anyway: the shots were all inserts provided later by a professional snooker player. See Kenneth L. Geist, *Pictures Will Talk: The Life and Films of Joseph L. Mankiewicz* (New York: Scribners, 1978), p. 378.

12 *Ibid.*

13 Shaffer, *op. cit.*, p. 79.

14 Quoted in Geist, *op. cit.*, p. 380.

15 *Ibid.*

16 Shaffer, *op. cit.*, p. 78.

17 In the original play, Tindle was a travel agent – a career with fifties rather than sixties connotations.

18 Geist, *op. cit.*, p. 393.

19 See Caine, *op. cit.*, p. 351.

20 Quoted in Geist, *op. cit.*, p. 379.

Chapter 14

1 Proverbs 22: 1.
2 Quoted in the *Sunday Express*, 27 August 1972.
3 Quoted in the *Sunday Express*, 10 June 1973.
4 Quoted in the *Sun*, 12 August 1972.
5 Quoted in the *Sunday Express*, 27 August 1972.
6 *Ibid.*
7 Quoted in the *Sunday Times Magazine*, 12 March 2000, p. 18.
8 Quoted in the *Sunday Express*, 10 June 1973.
9 *Ibid.*
10 Strictly, the Mickey King of *Pulp* was the first father Caine ever played, but since he is divorced and we never see any of his family I think the point stands.
11 Caine, *op. cit.*, p. 371.
12 *Ibid.*, p. 366.
13 For more on the director's discontent see Don Siegel, *A Siegel Film* (London: Faber and Faber, 1993), p. 407 *et passim*.
14 Quoted in Gallagher and Macdonald, *op. cit.*, p. 147.
15 *Ibid.*, p. 149.
16 Quoted in the *Daily Mail*, 18 July 1974.
17 Caine, *op. cit.*, p. 383. Losey is no less disparaging of the movie: 'I have no reason to be ashamed of it as a craftsman, although I think it is a piece of junk,' he told one biographer. See David Caute, *Joseph Losey: A Revenge on Life* (London: Faber and Faber, 1994), p. 375.
18 Caute, *op. cit.*, p. 377.
19 Quoted in Michel Ciment, *Conversations with Losey* (London: Methuen, 1985), p. 341.
20 Quoted in Hall, *op. cit.*, p. 255.

Chapter 15

1 From *The King of Comedy*, Martin Scorsese, 1983.
2 Quoted in Rissik, *op. cit.*, p. 143.
3 See *Films Illustrated*, December 1975, p. 142.
4 Huston interviewed in *Rolling Stone*, 19 February 1981; reprinted in *John Huston Interviews* (University of Mississipi Press, 2001), p. 104.

5 See Lawrence Grobel, *The Hustons* (London: Bloomsbury, 1990), p. 705.

6 See Caine, *op. cit.*, p. 389.

7 Quoted in Axel Madsen, *John Huston: A Biography* (London: Robson, 1979), p. 246.

8 Quoted in Rissik, *op. cit.*, p. 151.

9 *The New Yorker*, 5 January 1976; reprinted in Pauline Kael, *When the Lights Go Down* (New York: Holt Rinehart Winston, 1980), p. 108.

10 The character of Peachy as written for Caine was altered considerably from that of the dullard in the original story.

11 Quoted in Stuart Kaminsky, *John Huston: Maker of Magic* (London: Angus & Robertson, 1978), p. 202.

12 *John Huston Interviews, op. cit.*, p. 101.

13 Her first and last movie performance.

14 Astonishingly, the scene was largely ad-libbed, Caine told Michael Parkinson on his chat show, BBC1, November 2002.

15 Quoted in *Stills*, October 1984, p. 30.

16 Grobel, *op. cit.*, p. 684.

Chapter 16

1 Michel de Montaigne, Essays (1580–88).

2 Quoted in the *Sunday Express*, 11 July 1976.

3 Though the more cine-literate may also find themselves being reminded of Will Hay's wartime masterpiece *The Goose Steps Out* (1941), in which a suitably moustachioed Hay is parachuted into Germany, there to impersonate the Führer.

4 Quoted in Walker, 1985, *op. cit.*, p. 197.

5 Quoted in Hall, *op. cit.*, p. 265.

6 Caine, *op. cit.*, pp. 407–8.

7 Caine, *ibid.*, p. 415.

8 See Gallagher and Macdonald, *op. cit.*, p. 164.

9 See William Goldman, *Adventures in the Screen Trade* (London: Futura, 1985), p. 274 *et passim*.

10 Levine, it will be remembered, was the man who produced *Zulu* and subsequently told Caine that he was never going to make it.

11 Goldman, *op. cit.*, p. 274.

12 Quoted in the *Sunday Express*, 3 September 1978.

13 *The New Yorker*, 8 January 1979; reprinted in Kael, 1980, *op. cit.*, p. 529.

14 Quoted in *Film Comment*, July/August 1980, p. 20.

15 Caine, *op. cit.*, p. 440.

16 *Film Comment, op. cit.*, p. 21.

Chapter 17

1 Anonymous matron on the 1974 TV show *The Mangling of the Middle Class*, quoted in Philip Whitehead, *The Writing on the Wall* (London: Michael Joseph, 1985), p. 210.

2 Caine, *op. cit.*, pp. 421–2.

3 Caine quoted in the *Daily Mail*, 18 July 1974

4 *Ibid.*

5 Caine quoted in the *Daily Mail*, 19 September 1977.

6 Caine quoted in the *Daily Mail*, 21 September 1977.

7 *Ibid.*

8 *Daily Mail*, 18 July 1974.

9 *Ibid.*

10 *Film Comment*, July/August 1980, p. 19.

11 *Boston Phoenix*, 29 July 1980; reprinted in *Love and Hisses: The National Society of Film Critics Sound Off on the Hottest Movie Controversies* (San Francisco: Mercury House, 1992), p. 40.

12 Pauline Kael, *The New Yorker*, 4 August 1980; reprinted in *Taking It All In* (London: Arrow, 1987), p. 38.

13 It is also a popular nominee for Michael Caine's worst movie. When I began this book *The Hand* was one of the few Caine pictures I had not seen. More than one friend advised me that when I had made good that shortfall I would want to abandon the project.

14 The Leavisian turned Freudian Marxist Robin Wood, for instance. See *Hollywood from Vietnam to Reagan . . . and Beyond* (New York: Columbia University Press, 2003).

Chapter 18

1 Norman Mailer, 'The Homosexual Villain', in *Advertisements for Myself* (1959).

2 See Caine, *op. cit.*, pp. 451–2.

3 Quoted in Freedland, *op. cit.*, p. 209.

4 Quoted in the *Guardian*, 11 August 1981.

5 *Ibid.*

6 See André de Toth, *Fragments: Portraits From the Inside* (London: Faber, 1994), p. 442.

7 Caine, *op. cit.*, pp. 467–8.

8 The *Guardian,* op cit.

9 See Pauline Kael, *The New Yorker,* 14 November 1983; reprinted in *State of the Art* (London: Arrow, 1987), p. 85.

10 Caine, *op. cit.*, p. 471.

11 Though, in fact, during the decade or so it took to actually get the movie made, various drafts were written with actors as varied as Trevor Howard, Richard Burton and Orson Welles being considered for the part. See Chapter 12 of Quentin Falk's *Travels in Greeneland* (London: Quartet, 1984).

12 Quoted in Karen Moline, *Bob Hoskins: An Unlikely Hero* (London: Sphere, 1988), p. 171.

13 *Ibid.*, p. 172.

Chapter 19

1 V. S. Pritchett, 'Quixote's Translators', *The Complete Essays* (London: Chatto and Windus, 1991), p. 699.

2 See Caine, *op. cit.*, p. 478.

3 Quoted in Gallagher and Macdonald, *op. cit.*, p. 211.

4 Quoted in Bishop, *op. cit.*, p. 41.

5 Reprinted in John Pym (Ed.), *Time Out Film Guide 11* (London: Penguin, 2002), p. 125.

6 Quoted in the *Daily Express,* 11 July 1977.

7 Quoted in the *Sunday Telegraph Magazine,* 19 December 1976.

8 Quoted in the *Guardian,* 14 July 1984.

9 See Caine interviewed in *Stills,* October 1984, p. 28.

10 Quoted in *Films and Filming,* February 1985, p. 17.

11 *Ibid.*

12 *Ibid.*

13 Quoted in *Films and Filming,* January 1985, p. 31.

14 A similar tussle twixt romanticism and classicism was contemporaneously being played out on the snooker table between Alex Higgins, the drunken Celtic instinctive, and Steve Davis, the rock-solid hard worker. Higgins won the country's hearts, but Davis won the tournaments, the money and the place in the history books. He has never quite been forgiven.

15 A relationship which Caine had been instrumental in bringing about: Caine had met Farrow during the numerous parties that accompanied the *Gambit* shoot; many years later, while dining in Allen's favourite restaurant, Elaine's, in late 1979, he had introduced Farrow to Allen. See Marion Meade, *The Unruly Life of Woody Allen* (London: Weidenfeld & Nicolson, 2000), pp. 134–5.

16 *The New Yorker*, 24 February 1986; reprinted in *Hooked* (London: Marion Boyars, 1990), p. 114.

17 See Stig Björkman (Ed.), *Woody Allen on Woody Allen* (London: Faber, 1994), p. 156.

18 See Stephen J. Spignesi (Ed.), *The Woody Allen Companion* (London: Plexus, 1994), p. 216. We do, of course, get to see one lunge, in Frederick's studio, which results in a Bach record being scratched.

19 See Meade, *op. cit.*, p. 178.

20 Caine interviewed by the *Boston Herald* in 1986, quoted in Spignesi, *op. cit.*, p. 216.

Chapter 20

1 Friedrich Nietzsche, *Beyond Good and Evil* (trans: R. J. Hollingdale, London: Penguin, 1973), p. 79.

2 Quoted in Gallagher and Macdonald, *op. cit.*, p. 223.

3 See Geoff Eley, 'Distant Voices, Still Lives – The Family Is a Dangerous Place: Memory, Gender, and the Image of the Working Class', in Robert A. Rosenstone (Ed.), *Revisioning History: Film and the Construction of a New Past* (New York: Princeton University Press, 1995), p. 23.

4 See Moline, *op. cit.*, p. 220.

5 *Ibid.*

6 See David Thomson, *The New Biographical Dictionary of Film* (London: Little Brown, 2002), pp. 351–2, and Graham McCann, *op. cit., passim.*

7 Quoted in *Films and Filming*, June 1986.

8 Quoted in the *Observer Magazine*, 7 September 1986, p. 24.

9 Paul Theroux, *Doctor Slaughter* (London: Penguin, 1985), p. 74.

10 Asked about her literary tastes on the *Russell Harty Show* (BBC, 23 July 1987), Margaret Thatcher once said she was *re*-reading *The Fourth Protocol*.

11 See Freedland, *op. cit.*, p. 227.

12 Quoted in Gallagher and Macdonald, *op. cit.*, p. 234.

13 See the documentary on the special edition DVD of *The Fourth Protocol*, Carlton Visual Entertainment, 2003.

14 Quoted in the *New York Times*, 14 August 1987.

15 See John Campbell, *Margaret Thatcher – Volume 2: The Iron Lady* (London: Jonathan Cape, 2003), pp. 353–4, for a fuller account of these events.

Chapter 21

1 Arthur Schopenhauer, *Parerga and Paralipomena* (1851), reprinted in *Essays and Aphorisms* (trans: R. J. Hollingdale, Penguin, 1970), p. 167.

2 Caine, *op. cit.*, p. 522.

3 Quoted in the *Sunday Express Magazine*, 4 December 1986.

4 Caine, op. cit, p 522.

5 Quoted in the *Daily Mirror*, 1 February 1986.

6 Caine, *op. cit.*, p. 525.

7 Michael Caine, *Acting in Film: An Actor's Take on Movie Making* (New York: Applause, 1997), pp. 59–61.

8 *Ibid.*

9 'To me . . . the stage was like being in love with a tarty broad who couldn't care less if I lived or died.' By contrast, 'movies are like being in love with a woman who cooks, washes your socks and is great in bed . . . and television is a very beautiful one-night stand who also cooks a very good breakfast.' Quoted in the *Mail on Sunday*, 2 October 1988.

10 Quoted in *Arena*, Autumn 1988, p. 46.

11 Quoted in Gallagher and Macdonald, *op. cit.*, p. 243.

12 Whatever its flaws, *Jack the Ripper* was a considerably grander achievement than the Wickes/Caine follow-up of *Jekyll & Hyde*, which aired on British TV just over a year later on 6 January 1990. The class tensions Caine had managed to tauten Abberline with were nowhere apparent in his Dr Henry Jekyll, an arch bourgeois hero whose problems start when the potion he has knocked up in his lab turns him into a lusty, blood-crazed plebeian bent on carnage in the same Victorian London his predecessor the Ripper had had so much fun in. Caine, as we have seen, has spent a significant amount of his working life in substandard rubbish, but *Jekyll &*

Hyde is almost unique in his oeuvre in that he never rises above the limitations of the material. Thankfully, he would achieve much more in this line in *A Shock to the System*.

13 Caine, *op. cit.*, p. 426.

14 The Marshall of Brett's novel (London: Macmillan, 1984) is forty-one. Caine's Marshall is in his late fifties and looks it – and the movie's biggest problem lies in its asking us to believe that lovely young Stella Anderson (Elizabeth McGovern) could fall for him.

Chapter 22

1 Bob Dylan on what it is like to be an icon, quoted in the *Mail on Sunday*, 18 January 1998.

2 In more ironic vein, Caine's influence could also be detected in the figure of Jarvis Cocker, the lead singer of the Britpop group Pulp. Geeky and bespectacled and more effete than even the Harry Palmer of *Billion Dollar Brain*, Cocker's music acknowledged a debt to the music of Caine's old friend John Barry. But it was in Pulp's song 'Common People' (from the album *Different Class*) that the Caine connection was truly made: 'I want to live like common people/I want to do whatever common people do/I want to sleep with common people/I want to sleep with common people like you.'

3 Quoted in the *Mail on Sunday*, 20 September 1992.

4 A disaster – as anyone with the meanest knowledge of history could have predicted.

5 And Hugh Grant – *Hugh Grant*(!) – in the Caine role.

6 Quoted in Freedland, *op. cit.*, p. 229.

7 Quoted in publicity material for the movie.

8 Quoted in *Empire*, January 1992.

9 Quoted in the *Sunday Express Magazine*, 6 February 1994.

10 *Ibid.*

11 Quoted in the *Sunday Times Magazine*, 23 July 1995.

12 Quoted in Freedland, *op. cit.*, p. 235.

13 Quoted in the *Sunday Express Magazine*, 6 February 1994.

14 The estimated final cost of *True Lies* was $120 million. See Nigel Andrews, *True Myths: The Life and Times of Arnold Schwarzenegger* (London: Bloomsbury, 1995), p. 225.

15 Quoted in the *Sunday Times Magazine*, 23 July 1995.

16 And the same age as Caine when he made *The Ipcress File*.

17 See the *Sunday Times Magazine*, 23 July 1995.

18 Both movies have subsequently been broadcast in the UK on Channel 5.

19 Quoted in *Empire*, April 1997, p. 100.

20 Quoted in the *Sun*, 18 March 1986.

21 Quoted in Michael Feeney Callan, *Richard Harris – Sex, Death and the Movies: An Intimate Biography* (London: Robson, 2003), p. 187.

22 Quoted in the *Sunday Times Magazine*, 23 July 1995.

23 Quoted in the *Sunday Times*, 6 August 1995.

24 Letter from Richard Harris to the *Sunday Times*, 6 August 1995.

25 *Ibid.*

Chapter 23

1 Samuel Butler, 'Handel and Music: Anachronism', *The Notebooks*, Ed. Henry Festing Jones (London: A. C. Fifield, 1912), p. 130.

2 See the *Sunday Times Magazine*, 23 July 1905.

3 Quoted in the *Sun*, 22 December 1998.

4 Just like her performance in Mike Leigh's otherwise marvellous *Life Is Sweet* (1990).

5 *Film Review*, February 1999, p. 61.

6 *Performance*, Donald Cammell, Ed. Colin MacCabe (London: Faber and Faber, 2001), pp. 99–100.

7 The problem arises, I suspect, because Caine's voice is now such an index of Englishness that his fellow countrymen can't help but *listen* out for it.

8 Quoted in the *Guardian*, 10 April 2000.

9 Quoted in the *Daily Mirror*, 8 April 2000.

10 *Ibid.*

11 *Ibid.*

12 John Updike, *Self-Consciousness* (Knopf, 1989), p. 241.

13 In that light, even Brumby's seemingly throwaway line to Carter, 'Not many people know about it,' becomes a moment of supreme modernist self-awareness. For the one line that every Michael Caine impersonator knows is the Peter Sellers-invented 'Not a lot of people know that.'

14 Quoted in *Empire*, October 2001.

Chapter 24

1 Major Calloway (Trevor Howard) in *The Third Man* (screenplay: Graham Greene, 1950).

2 See the *Times Magazine*, 15 September 2001.

3 Quoted in *Hello!* 28 November 2000.

4 See Hall, *op. cit.*, pp. 339–40.

5 Quoted by Freedland, *op. cit.*, p. 236

6 Quoted in the *Guardian*, 14 April 2000.

7 Winstone interviewed on the set of *Last Orders*; available on the extras menu of the *Last Orders* DVD.

8 The second time in five years Caine had sung Orbison; the reader will recall his magnificently mannered rendition of 'It's Over' in the closing stages of *Little Voice*.

9 An anti-war movie in which America just happened to be on the right side.

10 Another film about Nazi collaborators.

11 Quoted in the *Independent*, 28 November 2003.

12 Lesley White, *op. cit.*

13 In Caine's next picture, Christopher Nolan's *Batman Begins* (2005).

Filmography

The order of the films is that of release and not of production. The director's name follows the title. Specific dates refer to a movie's first public screening in London; any help ascertaining missing dates will be thankfully received. If a movie failed to gain a UK theatrical release the word 'unreleased' follows its year of production. VHS means that a movie exists, though is not necessarily available on video; DVD that it is presently, at least, available on DVD. MC is, of course, Michael Caine.

SAILOR BEWARE
1956
Gordon Parry, 86 minutes.
Producer: Jack Clayton; Screenplay: Philip King, Falkland L. Cary, from their own play; Photography: Douglas Slocombe; Editor: Stan Hawkes; Music: Peter Akister.
Cast: Emma Hornett, Peggy Mount; Henry Hornett, Cyril Smith; Shirley, Shirley Eaton; Albert, Ronald Lewis; Mrs Lack, Thora Hird; Edie Hornett, Esma Cannon; Carnoustie Bligh, Gordon Jackson; uncredited, MC.

A HILL IN KOREA (UK: 21 September 1956)
1956
Julian Amyes, 81 minutes; VHS.
Producer: Anthony Squire; Screenplay: Ian Dalrymple, Anthony Squire, Ronald Spencer, from the novel by Max Catto; Photography: Freddie Francis; Editor: Peter Hunt; Music: Malcolm Arnold.
Cast: Lt Butler, George Baker; Sgt Payne, Harry Andrews; Cpl Ryker, Stanley Baker; Pte Docker, Michael Medwin; Pte Wyatt, Ronald Lewis; Pte Sims, Stephen Boyd; Pte Lindop, Victor Maddern; Pte Rabin, Harry Landis; Pte Lockyer, MC.

THE STEEL BAYONET
1957
Michael Carreras, 85 minutes.
Producer: Michael Carreras; Screenplay: Howard Clewes; Photography: Jack Asher; Editor: Bill Lenny; Music: Leonard Salzedo.
Cast: Maj Gerrard, Leo Genn; Capt Mead, Kieron Moore; Lt Vernon, Michael Medwin; Sgt Major Gill, Robert Brown; Pte Middleditch, Michael Ripper; uncredited, MC.

HOW TO MURDER A RICH UNCLE
1957
Nigel Patrick, 80 minutes.
Executive Producer: John Paxton; Producer: Ronald Kinnoch; Screenplay: John Paxton; Music: Kenneth V. Jones.
Cast: Sir Henry, Nigel Patrick; Uncle George, Charles Coburn; Edith, Wendy Hiller; Aunt Alice, Katie Johnson; Edward, Anthony Newley; Grannie, Athene Seyler; Aunt, Marjorie Noel Hood; Albert, Kenneth Fortescue; Constance, Patricia Webster; Gilrony, MC.

THE KEY
1958
Carol Reed, 134 minutes.
Producer: Carl Foreman; Screenplay: Carl Foreman; Photography: Oswald
Morris; Editor: Bert Bates; Music: Malcolm Arnold.
Cast: Stella, Sophia Loren; Capt Ford, Trevor Howard; David Ross,
William Holden; Capt Van Dam, Oscar Homolka; Weaver, Bryan Forbes;
uncredited, MC.

CARVE HER NAME WITH PRIDE
1958
Lewis Gilbert, 119 minutes.
Producer: Daniel M. Angel; Screenplay: Vernon Harris, Lewis Gilbert;
Photography: John Wilcox; Editor: John Shirley; Music: William Alwyn.
Cast: Violette Szabo, Virginia McKenna; Tony Fraser, Paul Scofield; Mr Bushell,
Jack Warner; Mrs Bushell, Denise Grey; Etienne Szabo, Alain Saury; POW,
MC (uncredited).

A WOMAN OF MYSTERY
1958
Ernest Morris, 71 minutes.
Producers: Edward J. Danziger, Harry Lee Danziger; Screenplay: Brian
Clemens, Eldon Howard; Photography: Jimmy Wilson; Editor: Maurice
Rootes.
Cast: Ray Savage, Dermot Walsh; Joy Grant, Hazel Court; Ruby Ames, Jennifer
Jayne; André, Ferdy Mayne; Harvey, Ernest Clark; uncredited, MC.

BLIND SPOT
1958
Peter Maxwell, 71 minutes.
Producer: Monty Berman; Screenplay: Kenneth Hayles, from an original story
by Robert S. Baker; Photography: Arthur Graham; Editor: Jim Connock.
Cast: Dan, Robert Mackenzie; Yvonne, Delphi Lawrence; Chalky, Gordon
Jackson; June, Anne Sharp; Brent, John Le Mesurier; uncredited, MC.

THE TWO-HEADED SPY
1958
André de Toth, 93 minutes.
Producer: Bill Kirby; Screenplay: James O'Donnell, from a story by J. Alvin
Kugelntass; Photography: Ted Scaife; Editor: Raymond Poulton, Music:
Bernard Schurmann.
Cast: General Schottland, Jack Hawkins; Lili, Gia Scala; Reinisch, Erik
Schumann; Gestapo Leader Mueller, Alexander Knox; Cornaz, Felix Aylmer;
uncredited, Donald Pleasence, MC.

PASSPORT TO SHAME
1958
Alvin Rakoff, 91 minutes.
Producer: John Klein; Screenplay: Patrick Alexander; Photography: Jack Asher;
Editor: Lee Doig; Music: Ken Jones.

Cast: Vicki, Diana Dors; Johnny, Eddie Constantine; Nick, Herbert Lom; Malou, Odile Versois; Aggie, Brenda de Banzie; uncredited, Joan Sims, MC.

DANGER WITHIN
1959
Don Chaffey, 101 minutes.
Producer: Colin Lesslie; Screenplay: Bryan Forbes, Frank Harvey; Photography: Arthur Grant; Editor: John Trumper; Music: Francis Chagrin.
Cast: Lt-Col David Baird, Richard Todd; Lt-Col Huxley, Bernard Lee; Major Charles Marquand, Michael Wilding; Capt Bunter Phillips, Richard Attenborough; Capt Rupert Callender, Dennis Price; uncredited, MC.

THE BULLDOG BREED
1960
Robert Asher, 98 minutes.
Executive Producer: Earl St John; Producer: Hugh Stewart; Screenplay: Jack Davies, Henry Blyth, Norman Wisdom; Photography: Robert Asher; Editor: Gerry Hambling; Music: Philip Green.
Cast: Norman Puckle, Norman Wisdom; Admiral Sir Bryanston Blyth, Ian Hunter; Chief Petty Officer Knowles, David Lodge; Commander Clayton, Robert Urquhart; Philpots, Edward Chapman; uncredited, Oliver Reed, MC, Johnny Briggs, Glyn Houston, Sheila Hancock.

A FOXHOLE IN CAIRO
1961
John Moxey, 80 minutes.
Producers: Steven Pallos, Donald Taylor; Screenplay: Leonard Mosley, Donald Taylor, from the book *The Cat and the Mice* by Leonard Mosley; Photography: Desmond Dickinson; Editor: Oswald Hafenrichter; Music: Wolfram Rohrig, Douglas Gamley, Ken Jones.
Cast: Capt Robertson, James Robertson Justice; John Eppler, Adrian Hoven; Radek, Niall MacGinnis; Count Almaszy, Peter van Eyck; Major Wilson, Robert Urquhart; Sandy, Neil McCallum; Yvette, Fenella Fielding; Amina, Gloria Mestre; Rommel, Albert Lieven; Weber, MC.

THE DAY THE EARTH CAUGHT FIRE
1961
Val Guest, 99 minutes; DVD.
Producer: Val Guest; Screenplay: Wolf Mankowitz, Val Guest; Photography: Harry Waxman; Editor: Bill Lenny; Music: Monty Norman.
Cast: Peter Stenning, Edward Judd; Jeannie, Janet Munro; Bill Maguire, Leo McKern; Night Editor: Michael Goodliffe; News Editor: Bernard Braden; Policeman, uncredited, MC.

SOLO FOR SPARROW
1962
Gordon Flemyng, 56 minutes.
Producer: Jack Greenwood; Screenplay: Roger Marshall.
Cast: Mr Reynolds, Anthony Newlands; Inspector Sparrow, Glyn Houston; Mrs Reynolds, Nadja Regin; 'Pin' Norman, Michael Coles; Chief Supt

Symington, Allan Cuthbertson; Baker, Ken Wayne; Lewis, Jerry Stovin; Inspector Hudson, Jack May; Larkin, Murray Melvin; Mooney, MC.

THE WRONG ARM OF THE LAW
1963
Cliff Owen, 94 minutes; VHS.
Producer: Aubrey Baring, Cliff Owen; Screenplay: John Warren, Len Heath; Photography: Ernest Stewart; Music: Richard Rodney Bennett.
Cast: Pearly Gates, Peter Sellers; Inspector Parker, Lionel Jeffries; Nervous O'Toole, Bernard Cribbins; Trainer King, Davy Kave; Valerie, Nanette Newman; Jack Coombes, Bill Kerr; Bluey May, Ed Devereaux; Reg Denton, Reg Lye; Asst Commissioner, John Le Mesurier; Sid Cooper, Graham Stark; Supt Forest, Martin Boddey; uncredited, MC.

ZULU (UK: 23 January 1964)
1964
Cy Endfield, 135 minutes; DVD.
Producers: Stanley Baker, Cy Endfield; Screenplay: John Prebble, Cy Endfield, from an original story by John Prebble; Photography: Stephen Dade; Editor: John Jympson; Music: John Barry.
Cast: Lt John Chard, Stanley Baker; Rev Otto Witt, Jack Hawkins; Margaretha Witt, Ulla Jacobson; Pte Henry Hook, James Booth; Lt Gonville Bromhead, MC; Col Sgt Bourne, Nigel Green; Pte Owen, Ivor Emmanuel; Sgt Maxfeld, Paul Daneman; Cpl Allen, Glynn Edwards; Pte Thomas, Neil McCarthy.

THE IPCRESS FILE (UK: 18 March 1965)
1965
Sidney J. Furie, 109 minutes; DVD.
Executive Producer: Charles Kasher; Producer: Harry Saltzman; Screenplay: Bill Canaway, James Doran; from the Len Deighton novel, Photography: Otto Heller; Editor: Peter Hunt; Music: John Barry.
Cast: Harry Palmer, MC; Dalby, Nigel Green; Ross, Guy Doleman; Jean, Sue Lloyd; Carswell, Gordon Jackson.

ALFIE (UK: 24 March 1966)
1966
Lewis Gilbert, 114 minutes; DVD.
Producer: Lewis Gilbert; Associate Producer: John Gilbert; Screenplay: Bill Naughton, from his own play; Photography: Otto Heller; Editor: Thelma Cornell; Music: Sonny Rollins.
Cast: Alfie, MC; Ruby, Shelley Winters; Siddie, Millicent Martin; Gilda, Julia Foster; Annie, Jane Asher; Carla, Shirley Anne Field; Lily, Vivien Merchant; Doctor, Eleanor Bron; Abortionist, Denholm Elliott; Harry, Alfie Bass.

THE WRONG BOX (UK: 26 May 1966)
1966
Bryan Forbes, 110 minutes; VHS.
Producer: Bryan Forbes; Co-Producers: Larry Gelbart, Bert Shevelove; Screenplay: Larry Gelbart, Bert Shevelove, from the novel by R. L. Stevenson and Lloyd Osbourne; Photography: Gerry Turpin; Music: John Barry.

Cast: Joseph Finsbury, Ralph Richardson; Masterman Finsbury, John Mills; Michael Finsbury, MC; Morris, Peter Cook; John, Dudley Moore; Juli, Nanette Newman; Dr Pratt, Peter Sellers; The Detective, Tony Hancock; Peacock, Wilfred Lawson; Lawyer Patience, Thorley Walters.

GAMBIT (UK: 22 December 1966)
1966
Ronald Neame, 109 minutes; VHS.
Producer: Leo Fuchs; Screenplay: from a story by Sidney Carroll, Jack Davies, Alvin Sargent; Photography: Clifford Stine; Editor: Alma MacRorie; Music: Maurice Jarre.
Cast: Nicole, Shirley MacLaine; Harry, MC; Shahbandar, Herbert Lom.

FUNERAL IN BERLIN (UK: 23 February 1967)
1966
Guy Hamilton, 102 minutes; DVD.
Producer: Charles Kasher; Screenplay: Evan Jones; Photography: Otto Heller; Editor: John Bloom; Music: Konrad Elfers.
Cast: Harry Palmer, MC; Samantha Steel, Eva Renzi; Johnny Vulkan, Paul Hubschmid; Col Stok, Oscar Homolka; Ross, Guy Doleman; Mrs Ross, Rachel Gurney.

HURRY SUNDOWN (UK: 24 August 1967)
1967
Otto Preminger, 146 minutes.
Producer: Otto Preminger; Screenplay: Thomas C. Ryan, Horton Foote; Photography: Milton Krasner, Loyal Griggs; Editors, Louis R. Loeffler, James D. Wells; Music: Hugh Montenegro.
Cast: Henry Warren, MC; Julie Ann Warren, Jane Fonda; Rad McDowell, John Phillip Law; Reeve Scott, Robert Hooks; Vivian Thurlow, Diahann Carroll; Judge Purcell, Burgess Meredith; Lou McDowell, Faye Dunaway; Rose Scott, Beah Richards; Sheriff Coombs, George Kennedy.

BILLION DOLLAR BRAIN (UK: 16 November 1967)
1967
Ken Russell, 111 minutes; DVD.
Executive Producer: André de Toth; Producer: Harry Saltzman; Assistant Director: Jack Causey; Screenplay: John McGrath; Photography: Billy Williams; Editor: Alan Osbiston; Music: Richard Rodney Bennett.
Cast: Harry Palmer, MC; Leo Newbegin, Karl Malden; Anya, Françoise Dorléac; Col Stok, Oscar Homolka; Gen Midwinter, Ed Begley; Col Ross, Guy Doleman; Dr Eiwort, Vladek Scheybal; Basil, Milo Sperber; Birkinshaw, Mark Elwes; GPO delivery man, Stanley Caine.

WOMAN TIMES SEVEN (UK: 9 May 1968)
1967
Vittorio De Sica, 99 minutes; VHS
Executive Producer: Joseph F. Levine. Producer: Arthur Cohn; Screenplay: Cesare Zavattini; Photography: Christian Matras; Editors, Teddy Darvas,

Victoria Mercanton; Music: Riz Ortolani.
Cast: Paulette/Maria Teresa/Linda/Edith/Eve/Marie/Jeanne, Shirley MacLaine;
Jean, Peter Sellers; Giorgio, Rossano Brazzi; Cenci, Vittorio Gassman; Fred, Alan
Arkin; Young man, MC; Claudie, Anita Ekberg; Victor, Philippe Noiret.

DEADFALL (UK: 17 October 1968)
1968
Bryan Forbes, 120 minutes.
Producer: Paul Monash; Associate Producer: Jack Rix; Screenplay: Bryan Forbes;
Photography: Gerry Turpin; Editor: John Jympson; Music: John Barry.
Cast: Henry Clarke, MC; Fé Moreau, Giovanna Ralli; Richard Moreau, Eric
Portman; Girl, Nanette Newman; Salinas, David Buck.

PLAY DIRTY (UK: 2 January 1969)
1968
André de Toth, 117 minutes; VHS.
Producer: Harry Saltzman; Assistant Director: Roger Good; Screenplay: Lotte
Colin, Melvyn Bragg; Story, George Marton; Photography: Edward Scaife;
Editor: Alan Osbiston; Music: Michael Legrand.
Cast: Capt Douglas, MC; Cyril Leech, Nigel Davenport; Col Masters, Nigel
Green; Brig Blore, Harry Andrews.

THE ITALIAN JOB (UK: 5 June 1969)
1969
Peter Collinson, 100 minutes; DVD.
Producer: Michael Deeley; Associate Producer: Bob Porter; Screenplay: Troy
Kennedy Martin; Photography: Douglas Slocombe; Editor: John Trumper;
Music: Quincy Jones.
Cast: Charlie Croker, MC; Mr Bridger, Noel Coward; Professor Peach, Benny
Hill; Altabani, Raf Vallone; Camp Freddie, Tony Beckley; Beckerman, Rossano
Brazzi; Lorna, Maggie Blye; Miss Peach, Irene Handl; Governor, John Le
Mesurier.

THE BATTLE OF BRITAIN (UK: 17 September 1969)
1969
Guy Hamilton, 131 minutes; DVD.
Producers: Harry Saltzman, S. Benjamin Fisz, Guy Hamilton; Associate
Producer: John Palmer; Screenplay: James Kennaway, Wilfred Greatorex, based
partly on the book *The Narrow Margin* by Derek Wood and Derek Dempster;
Photography: Derek Young; Editor: Berr Bates.
Cast: Air Chief Marshal Sir Hugh Dowding, Laurence Olivier; Sqn Leader
Skipper, Robert Shaw; Sgn Leader Colin Harvey, Christopher Plummer; Section
Officer Maggie Harvey, Susannah York; Sgt Pilot Andy, Ian McShane; Sgn
Leader Canfield, MC; Group Capt Baker, Kenneth More; Air Vice Marshal Keith
Park, Trevor Howard; Air Vice Marshal Trafford Leigh-Mallory, Patrick
Wymark; British Minister in Switzerland, Ralph Richardson.

THE MAGUS (UK: 13 November 1969)
1968
Guy Green, 116 minutes.
Producers: John Kohn, Jud Kinberg; Screenplay: John Fowles; Photography:
Billy Williams; Editor: Max Benedict; Music: John Dankworth.
Cast: Nicholas Urfe, MC; Maurice Conchis, Anthony Quinn; Lily, Candice
Bergen; Anne, Anna Karina; Meli, Paul Stassino; Anton, Julian Glover; Kapetan,
Takis Emmanuel.

TOO LATE THE HERO (UK: 27 August 1970)
1970
Robert Aldrich, 144 minutes; DVD.
Producer: Robert Aldrich; Associate Producer: Walter Blake; Screenplay: Robert
Aldrich, Lukas Heller; Story, Robert Aldrich, Robert Sherman; Photography:
Joseph Biroc; Editor: Michael Luciano.
Cast: Pte Tosh Hearne, MC; Lt Lawson, Cliff Robertson; Thornton, Ian Bannen;
Col Thompson, Harry Andrews; Capt Hornsby, Denholm Elliott; Campbell,
Ronald Fraser; Cpl McLean, Lance Percival; Johnstone, Percy Herbert; Capt
Nolan, Henry Fonda; Maj Yamaguchi, Ken Takakura.

SIMON SIMON
1970
Graham Stark, 30 minutes.
Producer: Peter Shillingford; Screenplay: Graham Stark; Photography: Derek
Van Lynt, Harvey Harrison Jnr; Editor: Bunny Warren.
Cast: 1st workman, Graham Stark; 2nd workman, John Junkin; Typist, Julia
Foster; Fireman, Norman Rossington; and Peter Sellers, MC, Ernie Wise, Eric
Morecambe, Bernie Winters and Bob Monkhouse.

GET CARTER (UK: 11 March 1971)
1971
Mike Hodges, 112 minutes; DVD.
Producer: Michael Klinger; Screenplay: Mike Hodges; Photography: Wolfgang
Suschitzky; Editor: John Trumper; Stunt Director: Johnny Morris.
Cast: Jack Carter, MC; Anna Fletcher, Britt Ekland; Cyril Kinnear, John
Osborne; Eric Paice, Ian Hendry; Cliff Brumby, Bryan Mosley; Glenda,
Geraldine Moffat; Margaret, Dorothy White; Keith, Alun Armstrong; Albert
Swift, Glynn Edwards.

THE LAST VALLEY (UK: 8 April 1971)
1971
James Clavell, 128 minutes; DVD.
Executive Producer: Martin Baum; Producer: James Clavell; Associate Producer:
Robert Porter; Screenplay: James Clavell; Photography: John Wilcox; Editor:
John Bloom; Music: John Barry.
Cast: Captain, MC; Vogel, Omar Sharif; Erica, Florinda Bolkan; Gruber, Nigel
Davenport.

KIDNAPPED (UK: 4 May 1971)
1971
Delbert Mann, 107 minutes; VHS.
Producer: Frederick H. Brogger; Screenplay: Jack Pulman; Photography: Paul Beeson; Editor: Peter Boita; Music: Roy Budd.
Cast: Alan Breck, MC; Lord Grant, Trevor Howard; Capt Hoseason, Jack Hawkins; Ebenezer Balfour, Donald Pleasence; Charles Stewart, Gordon Jackson; Catriona, Vivien Heilbron; David Balfour, Lawrence Douglas; Cluny, Freddie Jones.

ZEE AND CO (US: X, Y AND ZEE) (UK: 24 February 1972)
1972
Brian G. Hutton, 110 minutes.
Executive Producer: Elliott Kastner; Producers: Jay Kanter, Alan Ladd Jnr; Screenplay: Edna O'Brien; Photography: Billy Williams; Editor: James Clark; Music: Stanley Myers.
Cast: Zee Blakeley, Elizabeth Taylor; Robert Blakeley, MC; Stella, Susannah York; Gladys, Margaret Leighton; Gordon, John Standing; Rita, Mary Larkin; Gavin, Michael Cashman.

PULP (UK: 17 August 1972)
1972
Mike Hodges, 95 minutes; DVD.
Producers: Michael Klinger Mike Hodges; Screenplay: Mike Hodges; Photography: Ousama Rawi; Editor: John Glenn; Music: George Martin.
Cast: Mickey King, MC; Preston Gilbert, Mickey Rooney; Ben Dinuccio, Lionel Stander; Princess Betty Cippola, Lizabeth Scott; Liz Adams, Nadia Cassini.

SLEUTH (UK: 12 July 1973)
1972
Joseph L. Mankiewicz, 139 minutes; DVD.
Executive Producer: Edgar J. Schenck. Producer: Morton Gottlieb; Screenplay: Anthony Shaffer; Photography: Oswald Morris; Editor: Richard Marden; Music: John Addison.
Cast: Andrew Wyke, Laurence Olivier; Milo Tindle, MC.

THE BLACK WINDMILL (UK: 18 July 1974)
1974
Don Siegel, 106 minutes; VHS.
Executive Producers: Richard D. Zanuck, David Brown; Producer: Don Siegel; Screenplay: Leigh Vance; Photography: Ousama Rawi; Editor: Anthony Gibbs; Music: Roy Budd.
Cast: Maj John Tarrant, MC; Sir Edward Julyan, Joseph O'Connor; Cedric Harper, Donald Pleasence; McKee, John Vernon; Alex Tarrant, Janet Suzman; Ceil Burrows, Delphine Seyrig; Chief Supt Wray, Joss Ackland.

THE MARSEILLE CONTRACT (UK: 3 October 1974)
1974
Robert Parrish, 89 minutes.
Producer: Judd Bernard; Screenplay: Judd Bernard; Photography: Douglas
Slocombe; Editor: Willy Kemplen; Music: Roy Budd.
Cast: Johnny Deray, MC; Steve Ventura, Anthony Quinn; Jacques Brizard, James
Mason; Lucienne Brizard, Maureen Kerwin.

THE WILBY CONSPIRACY (10 July 1975)
1975
Ralph Nelson, 105 minutes; VHS.
Executive Producer: Helmut Dantine; Producer: Martin Baum; Screenplay:
Rod Amateau, Harold Nebenzal; Photography: John Coquillon; Editor: Ernest
Walter; Music: Stanley Myers; Stunt Arranger, Bob Simmons.
Cast: Shack Twala, Sidney Poitier; Jim Keogh, MC; Major Horn, Nicol
Williamson; Rina van Niekirk, Prunella Gee; Persis Ray, Persis Khambatta;
Muckerjee, Saeed Jaffrey.

PEEPER
1975
Peter Hyams, 87 minutes; VHS.
Producers: Irwin Winkler, Robert Chartoff; Screenplay: W. D. Richter;
Photography: Earl Rath; Editor: James Mitchell; Music: Richard Clement.
Cast: Leslie Tucker, MC; Ellen Prendergast, Natalie Wood; Mianne Prendergast,
Kitty Winn; Frank Prendergast, Thayer David.

THE ROMANTIC ENGLISHWOMAN (UK: 16 October 1975)
1975
Joseph Losey, 115 minutes; DVD.
Producer: Daniel M. Angel; Screenplay: Thomas Wiseman, Tom Stoppard;
Photography: Gerry Fisher; Editor: Reginald Beck; Music: Richard Hartley.
Cast: Elizabeth Fielding, Glenda Jackson; Lewis Fielding, MC; Thomas
Hursa, Helmut Berger; David Fielding, Marcus Richardson; Isabel,
Kate Nelligan.

THE MAN WHO WOULD BE KING (UK: 18 December 1975)
1975
John Huston, 129 minutes; DVD.
Producer: John Foreman; Screenplay: John Huston, Gladys Hill; Photography:
Oswald Morris; Editor: Russell Lloyd; Music: Maurice Jarre; Stunt
Co-ordinator: James Arnett.
Cast: Daniel Dravot Sean Connery; Peachy Carnehan, MC; Rudyard Kipling,
Christopher Plummer; Billy Fish, Saeed Jaffrey; Roxanne, Shakira Caine.

HARRY AND WALTER GO TO NEW YORK
August 19, 1976
Mark Rydell, 120 minutes; VHS.
Executive Producer: Tony Bill; Producers: Don Devlin, Harry Gittes; Screenplay:
John Byrum, Robert Kaufman; Photography: Laszlo Kovacs; Editor: Frederic

Steinkamp, David Bretherron, Don Guidance; Music: David Shire, Alan
Bergman, Marilyn Bergman.
Cast: Harry Dighby, James Caan; Walter Hill, Elliott Gould; Adam Worth, MC;
Lisa Chestnut, Diane Keaton.

THE EAGLE HAS LANDED (UK: 1 April 1977)
1976
John Sturges, 135 minutes; DVD.
Producers: Jack Wiener, David Niven Jnr; Screenplay: Tom Mankiewicz;
Photography: Anthony Richmond; Editor: Anne V. Coates; Stunt Co-ordinator:
Gerry Crampton.
Cast: Lt-Col Kurt Steiner, MC; Liam Devlin, Donald Sutherland; Lt-Col Max
Radl, Robert Duvall; Molly Prior, Jenny Agutter; Heinrich Himmler, Donald
Pleasence; Admiral Wilhelm Caneris, Anthony Quayle; Joanna Grey, Jean
Marsh; Father Philip Vereker, John Standing; Pamela Vereker, Judy Geeson.

A BRIDGE TOO FAR (UK: 24 June 1977)
1977
Richard Attenborough, 175 minutes; DVD.
Producers: Joseph E. Levine, Richard P. Levine; Screenplay: William Goldman;
Photography: Geoffrey Unsworth; Editor: Antony Gibbs; Music: John Addison.
Cast: Lt-Gen Frederick Browning, Dirk Bogarde; Staff Sgt Eddie Dohun, James
Caan; Lt-Col J. O. E. Vandeleur, MC; Maj Gen Robert Urquhart, Sean
Connery; Lt-Gen Brian Horrocks, Edward Fox; Col Bobby Stout, Elliott Gould;
Maj-Gen Stanislaw Sosahowski, Gene Hackman; Lt-Col John Frost, Anthony
Hopkins; Maj-Gen Ludwig, Hardy Kruger; Dr Spaander, Laurence Olivier;
Brig-Gen James M. Gavin, Ryan O'Neal; Maj Julian Cook, Robert Redford;
Lt-Col Wilhelm Bittrich, Maximilian Schell; Kate ter Horst, Liv Ullman.

SILVER BEARS (24 February 1978)
1978
Ivan Passer, 113 minutes; VHS.
Executive Producer: Martin C. Schute; Producers: Arlene Sellers, Alex Winitsky;
Screenplay: Peter Stone; Photography: Anthony Richmond; Editor: Bernard
Gribble; Music: Claude Bolling.
Cast: Doc Fletcher, MC; Debbie Luckman, Cybill Shepherd; Prince Gianfranco
Pietro Annunzio di Siracusa, Louis Jourdan; Shireen Firdausi, Stephane Audran;
Agba Firdausi, David Warner.

THE SWARM (28 July 1978)
1978
Irwin Allen, 116 minutes.
Producer: Irwin Allen; Screenplay: Stirling Silliphant; Photography: Fred J.
Koenekamp; Editor: Harold F. Kress; Music: Jerry Goldsmith.
Cast: Brad Crane, MC; Helena, Katharine Ross; Gen Slater, Richard Widmark;
Dr Hubbard, Richard Chamberlain; Maureen Schuster, Olivia de Havilland;
Felix, Ben Johnson; Dr Andrews, Jose Ferrer; Clarence, Fred MacMurray;
Dr Krim, Henry Fonda.

ASHANTI (UK: 26 January 1979)
1979
Richard Fleischer, 117 minutes; VHS.
Producer: Georges-Alain Vuille; Screenplay: Stephen Geller; Photography:
Aldo Tonto; Editor: Ernest Walter; Music: Michael Melvoin.
Cast: Dr David Linderby, MC; Prince Hassan, Omar Sharif; Suleiman, Peter
Ustinov; Brian Walker, Rex Harrison; Dr Anansa Linderby, Beverly Johnson.

CALIFORNIA SUITE (UK: 23 March 1979)
1978
Herbert Ross, 103 minutes; DVD.
Producer: Ray Stark; Screenplay: Neil Simon; Photography: David M. Walsh;
Editor: Michael A. Stevenson; Music: Claude Bolling.
Cast: Sidney Cochran, MC; Diana Barrie, Maggie Smith; Bill Warren, Alan Alda;
Hannah Warren, Jane Fonda; Dr Willis Panama, Bill Cosby; Dr Chauncey
Gump, Richard Pryor; Marvin Michaels, Walter Matthau; Millie Michaels,
Elaine May.

BEYOND THE POSEIDON ADVENTURE (UK: 3 August 1979)
1979
Irwin Allen, 114 minutes; VHS.
Producer: Irwin Allen; Screenplay: Nelson Gidding; Photography: Joseph Biroc;
Editor: Bill Brame; Music: Jerry Fielding.
Cast: Capt Mike Turner, MC; Celeste Whitman, Sally Field; Stefan Svevo, Telly
Savalas; Frank Mazzetti, Peter Boyle; Harold Meredith, Jack Warden; Hannah
Meredith, Shirley Knight; Gina Rowe, Shirley Jones; Wilbur Hubbard, Karl
Malden; Tex, Slim Pickens; Suzanne Constantine, Veronica Hamel.

DRESSED TO KILL (UK: 26 September 1980)
1980
Brian de Palma, 105 minutes; DVD.
Executive Producer: Samuel Z. Arkoff; Producer: George Litto; Screenplay:
Brian de Palma; Photography: Ralf Bode; Editor: Jerry Greenberg; Music: Pino
Donaggio; Stunt Co-ordinator: Vic Magnotta.
Cast: Dr Robert Elliott, MC; Kate Miller, Angie Dickinson; Liz Blake, Nancy
Allen; Peter Miller, Keith Gordon.

THE ISLAND (UK: 14 November 1980)
1980
Michael Ritchie, 114 minutes; VHS.
Producers: Richard D Zanuck, David Brown; Screenplay: Peter Benchley;
Photography: Henri Decae; Editor: Richard A. Harris; Music: Ennio Morricone.
Cast: Blair Maynard, MC; Nau, David Warner; Angela Punch McGregor, Beth;
Dr Windsor, Frank Middlemass; Rollo, Don Henderson.

THE HAND
1981
Oliver Stone, 104 minutes; VHS.
Executive Producer: Clark L. Paylow; Producer: Edward E. Pressman;
Screenplay: Oliver Stone; Photography: King Baggot; Editor: Richard Marks;
Music: James Homer; Special Effects, Carlo Rambaldi.
Cast: Jon Lansdale, MC; Anne Lansdale, Andrea Marcoviac; Stella Roche, Anne
McEnroe; Brian Fergusson, Bruce McGill.

ESCAPE TO VICTORY (UK: 4 September 1981)
1981
John Huston, 117 minutes; VHS.
Executive Producer: Gordon McLendon; Producer: Freddie Fields; Screenplay:
Evan Jones, Yabo Yablonsky; Photography: Gerry Fisher; Editor: Roberto Silvi;
Music: Bill Conti.
Cast: Robert Hatch, Sylvester Stallone; Capt John Colby, MC; Luis Fernandez,
Pelé; Terry Brady, Bobby Moore; Carlos Rey, Osvaldo Ardiles; Sid Harmor,
Mike Summerbee; Arthur Hayes, John Wark; Maj Karl von Steiner, Max von
Sydow.

DEATHTRAP (UK: 15 October 1982)
1982
Sidney Lumet, 116 minutes; DVD.
Executive Producer: Jay Presson Allen; Producer: Burtt Harris; Screenplay: Jay
Presson Allen; Photography: Andrzej Bartkowiak; Editor: John J. Fitzstephens;
Music: Johnny Mandel.
Cast: Sidney Bruhl, MC; Clifford Anderson, Christopher Reeve; Myra, Dyan
Cannon; Helga ten Dorp, Irene Worth.

EDUCATING RITA (UK: 7 May 1983)
1983
Lewis Gilbert, 110 minutes; DVD.
Executive Producer: Herbert L. Oakes; Producer: Lewis Gilbert; Screenplay:
Willy Russell; Photography: Frank Watts; Editor: Garth Craven; Music: David
Hentschel.
Cast: Dr Frank Bryant, MC; Rita, Julie Walters; Brian, Michael Williams; Trish,
Maureen Lipman; Julia, Jeanne Crowley.

THE HONORARY CONSUL (US: BEYOND THE LIMIT)
(UK: 6 January 1984)
1983
John MacKenzie, 104 minutes; DVD.
Producer: Norma Heyman; Screenplay: Christopher Hampton; Photography:
Phil Meheux; Editor: Stuart Baird; Music: Stanley Myers.
Cast: Charley Fortnum, MC; Dr Plarr, Richard Gere; Col Perez, Bob Hoskins;
Clara, Elpidia Carrillo; Leon, Joaquim de Almeida.

BLAME IT ON RIO (UK: 17 August 1984)
1984
Stanley Donen, 100 minutes; DVD.
Executive Producer: Larry Gelbart; Producer: Stanley Donen; Screenplay:
Charlie Peters, Larry Gelbart; Photography: Reynaldo Villalobos; Editors,
George Hively, Richard Maiden.
Cast: Matthew Hollis, MC; Victor Lyons, Joseph Bologna; Karen Hollis, Valerie
Harper; Jennifer Lyons, Michelle Johnson; Nicole Hollis, Demi Moore.

WATER
1985
Dick Clement, 95 minutes; VHS.
Executive Producers: George Harrison, Dennis O'Brien; Producer: Ian La
Frenais; Co-Producer: David Wimbury; Screenplay: Dick Clement, Ian la
Frenais, Bill Persky; Photography: Douglas Slocombe; Editor: John Victor Smith;
Music: Mike Moran.
Cast: Baxter Thwaites, MC; Pamela, Valerie Perrine; Dolores, Brenda Vaccaro;
Sir Malcolm Leveridge, Leonard Rossiter; Delgado, Billy Connolly.

THE JIGSAW MAN (unreleased)
1985
Terence Young, 98 minutes; DVD.
Executive Producer: Mahmud Sipra; Producer: Benjamin Fisz; Screenplay:
Jo Eisinger; Photography: Freddie Francis; Music: John Cameron.
Cast: Sir Philip Kimberley/Sergei Kuzminsky, MC; Admiral Scaith, Laurence
Olivier; Penny Kimberley, Susan George; Jamie Fraser, Robert Powell; Sir James
Chorley, Charles Gray.

THE HOLCROFT COVENANT (UK: 20 September 1985)
1985
John Frankenheimer, 112 minutes; VHS.
Executive Producer: Mort Abrahams; Producers: Edie Landau, Ely Landau;
Co-Producer: Otto Plaschkes; Screenplay: George Axelrod, Edward Anhalt, John
Hopkins; Photography: Gerry Fisher; Editor: Ralph Sheldon; Music: Stanislas.
Cast: Noel Holcroft, MC; Johann Tennyson, Anthony Andrews; Heldon
Tennyson, Victoria Tennant; Aithene Holcroft, Lilli Palmer; Jurgen Maas, Mario
Adorf; Manfredi, Michael Lonsdale; Leighton, Bernard Hepton.

HANNAH AND HER SISTERS (UK: 19 July 1986)
1986
Woody Allen, 106 minutes; DVD.
Executive Producers: Jack Rollins, Charles H. Joffe; Producer: Robert Greenhut;
Screenplay: Woody Allen; Photography: Carlo Di Palma; Editor: Susan E.
Morse.
Cast: Mickey Sachs, Woody Allen; Elliot, MC; Hannah, Mia Farrow; April,
Carrie Fisher; Lee, Barbara Hershey; Evan, Lloyd Nolan; Norma, Maureen
O'Sullivan; Dusty, Daniel Stern; Frederick, Max von Sydow; Holly, Dianne
Wiest.

MONA LISA (UK: 5 September 1986)
1986
Neil Jordan, 104 minutes; DVD.
Executive Producers: George Harrison, Dennis O'Brien; Producers: Stephen Woolley, Patrick Cassavetti; Co-Producers: Chris Brown, Ray Cooper, Nik Powell; Screenplay: Neil Jordan, David Leland; Photography: Roger Pratt; Editor: Lesley Walker; Music: Michael Kamen.
Cast: George, Bob Hoskins; Simone, Cathy Tyson; Mortwell, MC; Thomas, Robbie Coltrane; Anderson, Clarke Peters; Cathy, Kate Hardie; Jeannie, Zoe Nathenson; May, Sammi Davis.

SWEET LIBERTY (UK: 12 September 1986)
1986
Alan Alda, 107 minutes; VHS.
Executive Producer: Louis A. Stroller; Producer: Martin Bergman; Screenplay: Alan Alda; Photography: Frank Tidy; Editor: Michael Economou; Music: Bruce Broughton; Stunt Co-ordinator: Victor Paul.
Cast: Michael Burgess, Alan Alda; Elliott James, MC; Faith Healy, Michelle Pfeiffer; Stanley Gould, Bob Hoskins; Gretchen Carlsen, Lise Hilboldt; Cecelia Burgess, Lillian Gish.

THE FOURTH PROTOCOL (UK: 20 March 1987)
1987
John MacKenzie, 119 minutes; DVD.
Executive Producers: Frederick Forsyth, Wafic Said, MC; Producer: Timothy Burrill; Screenplay: Frederick Forsyth; Photography: Phil Meheux; Editor: Graham Walker; Music: Lalo Schifrin.
Cast: John Preston, MC; Maj Petrofsky, Pierce Brosnan; Borisov, Ned Beatty; Irina Vassileevna, Joanna Cassidy; Brian Harcourt Smith, Julian Glover; Sir Bernard Hemmings, Michael Gough; Gen Karpov, Ray McAnally; Sir Nigel Irvine, Ian Richardson; George Berenson, Anton Rodgers; Angela Berenson, Caroline Blakiston.

HALF MOON STREET (UK: 24 April 1987)
1986
Bob Swaim, 90 minutes; VHS.
Executive Producers: Edward R. Pressman, David Korda. Producer: Geoffrey Reeve; Screenplay: Bob Swaim, Edward Behr; Photography: Peter Hannan; Editor: Richard Marden; Music: Richard Harvey.
Cast: Lauren Slaughter, Sigourney Weaver; Lord Bulbeck, MC; Gen Sir George Newhouse, Patrick Kavanagh; Lady Newhouse, Faith Kent; Lindsay Walker, Ram John Holder.

THE WHISTLE BLOWER (UK: 29 May 1987)
1986
Simon Langton, 100 minutes; DVD.
Executive Producers: Phillip Nugus, John Kelleher, James Reeve; Producer: Geoffrey Reeve; Screenplay: Julian Bond; Photography: Fred Tammes; Editor: Robert Morgan; Music: John Scott.

Cast: Frank Jones, MC; Lord, James Fox; Bob Jones, Nigel Havers; Sir Adrian
Chapple, John Gielgud; Cynthia Goodburn, Felicity Dean; Charles Greig,
Barry Foster; Bruce, Gordon Jackson; Bill Pickett, Kenneth Colley; Government
Minister, David Langton.

JAWS: THE REVENGE
1987
Joseph Sargent, 99 minutes; VHS.
Producer: Joseph Sargent; Screenplay: Michael de Guzman; Photography: John
McPherson; Editor: Michael Brown; Music: Michael Small.
Cast: Ellen Brody, Lorraine Gary; Michael Brody, Lance Guest; Jake, Mario Van
Peebles; Carla Brody, Karen Young; Hoagie, MC.

SURRENDER (UK: 20 November 1987)
1987
Jerry Belson, 95 minutes; VHS.
Executive Producers: Menahem Golan, Yorum Globus; Producers: Aaron
Spelling, Alan Greisma; Screenplay: Jerry Belson; Photography: Juan Ruiz
Anchia; Editor: Wendy Greene Bricmont; Music: Michel Colombier.
Cast: Daisy Morgan, Sally Field; Sean Stein, MC; Marty Caesar, Steve
Guttenberg; Jay Bass, Peter Boyle; Ace Morgan, Jackie Cooper; Hedy, Iman;
Ronnie, Julia Kavner.

WITHOUT A CLUE (UK: 28 April 1989)
1988
Thom Eberhardt, 107 minutes; DVD.
Producer: Mark Stirdivant; Writers, Larry Strawther, Gary Murphy;
Photography: Alan Hume; Editor: Peter Tanner.
Cast: Sherlock Holmes, MC; Dr Watson, Ben Kingsley; Lestrade, Jeffrey Jones;
Lesley, Lysette Anthony; Greenhough, Peter Cook; Moriarty, Paul Freeman;
Smithwick, Nigel Davenport.

DIRTY ROTTEN SCOUNDRELS (UK: 30 June 1989)
1988
Frank Oz, 110 minutes; DVD.
Executive Producers: Dale Launer, Charles Hirschhorn; Producer: Bernard
Williams; Screenplay: Dale Launer, Stanley Shapiro, Paul Henning; Photography:
Michael Ballhaus; Editors, Stephen A. Rotter, William Scharf; Music: Miles
Goodman.
Cast: Freddy Benson, Steve Martin; Lawrence Jamieson, MC; Janet Colgate,
Glenne Headley; Inspector Andre, Anton Rodgers; Fanny Eubank, Barbara
Harris.

A SHOCK TO THE SYSTEM (UK: 26 October 1990)
1990
Jan Egleson, 87 minutes; DVD.
Executive Producer: Leslie Morgan; Producer: Patrick McCormick; Screenplay:
Andrew Klavan, Alice Arlen; Director of Photography: Paul Goldsmith; Editors,
Peter C. Frank, William A. Anderson; Music: Gary Chang.

Cast: Graham Marshall, MC; Stella Anderson, Elizabeth McGovern; Robert
Benham, Peter Riegert; Leslie Marshall, Swoozie Kurtz; Melanie O'Connor,
Jenny Wright; Detective Laker, Will Paton; Tara Liston, Haviland Morris;
Lillian, Barbara Baxley; Henry Parker, Philip Moon; George Brewer, John
McMartin.

MR DESTINY (unreleased)
1990
James Orr, 105 minutes; DVD.
Producers: James Orr, Jim Cruickshank; Screenplay: James Orr, Jim
Cruickshank; Director of Photography: Alex Thomson; Editor: Michael R
Miller; Music: David Newman.
Cast: Larry Burrow, James Belushi; Ellen Burrows, Linda Hamilton; Mike,
MC; Clip Metzler, Jon Lovitz; Niles Pender, Hart Bockner; Leon Hansen, Bill
McCutcheon; Cindy Jo, Rene Russo; Jackie Earle, Jay O Sanders; Guzelman,
Maury Chaykin; Harry Burrows, Pat Corley; Roswell, Douglas Seale; Jewel
Jagger, Courteney Cox.

BULLSEYE! (UK: 12 November 1990)
1990
Michael Winner, 102 minutes; VHS.
Producer: Michael Winner; Screenplay: Leslie Bricusse, Lawrence Marks and
Maurice Gran; Director of Photography: Alan Jones; Editor: Michael Winner;
Music: John Du Prez.
Cast: Sidney Lipton/Doctor Daniel Hicklar, MC; Gerald Bradley-Smith/Sir
John Bevistock, Roger Moore; Willie, Sally Kirkland; Flo Fleming, Deborah
Barrymore; Darrell Hyde, Lee Patterson; Nigel Holden, Mark Burns; Inspector
Grosse, Derren Nesbitt; Francesca, Deborah Leng; Death's Head, Christopher
Adamson; Donna Dutch, Steffanie Pitt.

NOISES OFF (UK: 24 July 1992)
1992
Peter Bogdanovich, 104 minutes; VHS.
Producer: Frank Marshall; Screenplay: Marty Kaplan; Director of Photography:
Tim Suhrstedt; Editor: Lisa Day.
Cast: Lloyd Fellowes, MC; Dotty Otley/Mrs Clackett, Carol Burnett; Selsdon
Mowbray/The Burglar, Denholm Elliott; Poppy Taylor, Julie Hagerty; Belinda
Blair/Flavia Brent, Marilu Henner; Timm Allgood, Mark Linn-Baker; Frederick
Dallas/Philip Brent, Christopher Reeve; Garry Lejeune/Roger Tramplemain, John
Ritter; Brooke Ashton/Vicki, Nicollette Sheridan.

BLUE ICE (UK: 9 October 1992)
1992
Russell Mulcahy, 105 minutes; VHS.
Producers: Martin Bregman, MC; Screenplay: Ron Hutchinson; Director of
Photography: Denis Crossan; Editor: Seth Flaum; Music: Michael Kamen.
Cast: Harry Anders, MC; Stacy Mansdorf, Sean Young; Sir Hector, Ian Holm;
Buddy, Bobby Short; Osgood, Alan Armstrong; George, Sam Kelly; Stevens, Jack
Shepherd; Westy, Philip Davis; Sam Garcia, Bob Hoskins.

THE MUPPET CHRISTMAS CAROL (UK: 18 December 1992)
1992
Brian Henson, 86 minutes; VHS.
Producers: Brian Henson, Martin G. Baker; Screenplay: Jerry Jahl; Director of
Photography: John Fenner; Editor: Michael Jablow; Music: Miles Goodman.
Cast: Ebenezer Scrooge, MC; the Muppets.

ON DEADLY GROUND (UK: 11 March 1994)
1994
Steven Seagal, 100 minutes; VHS.
Producers: Steven Seagal, Julius R. Nasso, A. Kitman; Screenplay: Ed Horowitz,
Robin U. Russin; Director of Photography: Ric Waite; Editors, Robert A.
Ferretti, Don Brochu; Music: Basil Poledouris.
Cast: Forrest Taft, Steven Seagal; Michael Jennings, MC; Masu, Joan Chen;
MacGruder, John C. McGinley; Stone, R. Lee Ermey; Liles, Shari Shattuck;
Homer Carlton, Billy Bob Thornton; Hugh Palmer, Richard Hamilton; Silook,
Chief Irvin Brink; Tunrak, Apangulak Charlie Kairaiuak.

BULLET TO BEIJING (unreleased)
1996
George Mihalka, 104 minutes; VHS.
Producers: Alexander Goloutva, John Dunning, Andre Link; Screenplay: Peter
Welbeck; Directors of Photography: Peter Benison, Terence Cole; Editor:
Francois Gill; Music: Rick Wakeman.
Cast: Harry Palmer, MC; Nick, Jason Connery; Natasha, Mia Sara; Alex,
Michael Gambon; Craig, Michael Sarrazin; Colonel Gradsky, Lev Prygunov;
Yuri Stephanovich, Anatoly Davidov; Jean, Sue Lloyd; Kim Soo, Burt Kwouk.

MIDNIGHT IN ST PETERSBURG (unreleased)
1997
Doug Jackson, 105 minutes; VHS.
Producers: Edward Simons, Kent Walwin, Alexander Goloutva, John Dunning,
Andre Link; Screenplay: Peter Welbeck; Director of Photography: Peter Benison;
Editor: Vidal Beique; Music: Rick Wakeman.
Cast: Harry Palmer, MC; Nick, Jason Connery; Natasha, Mia Sara; Alex,
Michael Gambon; Craig, Michael Sarrazin; Brandy, Michelle Rene Thomas;
Tatiana, Tanya Jackson; Dr Vestry, Serge Houde; Yuri, Anatoly Davidov; Hans
Schreiber, Vlasta Vrane; Louis, John Dunn-Hill; Colonel Gradsky, Lev Prygunov.

BLOOD AND WINE (UK: 7 March 1997)
1996
Bob Rafelson, 100 minutes; DVD.
Producer: Jeremy Thomas; Screenplay: Nick Villiers, Alison Cross; Director of
Photography: Newton Thomas Sigel; Editor: Steven Cohen; Music: Michael
Lorenc.
Cast: Alex Gates, Jack Nicholson; Jason, Stephen Dorff; Gabriela, Jennifer
Lopez; Suzanne, Judy Davis; Victor Spansky, MC; Henry, Harold Perrineau
Jr; Dina Reese, Robyn Peterson; Mike, Mike Starr; Frank Reeze, John Seitz.

LITTLE VOICE (UK: 5 November 1998)
1998
Mark Herman, 97 minutes; DVD.
Producer: Elizabeth Karlson; Screenplay: Mark Herman; Director of
Photography: Andy Collins; Editor: Michael Ellis; Music: John Altman.
Cast: Mari, Brenda Blethyn; LV, Jane Horrocks; Billy, Ewan McGregor; George,
Philip Jackson; Sadie, Annette Budland; Ray Say, MC; Mr Boo, Jim Broadbent.

CURTAIN CALL (unreleased)
1998
Peter Yates, 94 minutes.
Producer: Andrew Korsch; Screenplay: Todd Alcott; Director of Photography:
Sven Nykvist; Editor: Hughes Winborne; Music: Richard Hartley.
Cast: Stevenson Lowe, James Spader; Julia, Polly Walker; Max Gale, MC; Lily
Marlowe, Maggie Smith; Charles Van Allsburg, Buck Henry; Will Dodge, Sam
Shepard; Brett Conway, Frank Whaley; Michelle Tippet, Marcia Gay Harden;
Amy, Frances Sternhagen.

SHADOW RUN (unreleased)
1998
Geoffrey Reeve, 98 minutes; DVD.
Producer: Geoffrey Reeve; Screenplay: Desmond Lowden; Director of
Photography: Eddy van der Enden; Editor: Terry Warwick; Music: Adrian
Burch, David Whitaker.
Cast: Haskett, MC; London-Higgins, James Fox; Joffrey, Matthew Pochin;
Julie, Rae Baker; Larcombe, Kenneth Colley; Melchior, Christopher Cazenove;
Maunder, Rupert Frazer; Liney, Leslie Grantham; Daltrey, Tim Healy.

THE DEBTORS (unreleased)
1999
Evi Quaid.
Producers: Kara Meyers, Evi Quaid; Screenplay: Jordan Roberts, Jeremy Pikser,
Evi Quaid; Director of Photography: Eric Edwards; Editors, Jon Gregory,
William S. Scharf; Music: Simon Boswell.
Cast: MC, Randy Quaid, Catherine McCormack, Jamie Kennedy, Udo Kier.

THE CIDER HOUSE RULES (UK: 17 March 2000)
1999
Lasse Hallstrom, 126 minutes; DVD.
Producer: Richard N. Gladstein; Screenplay: John Irving; Director of
Photography: Oliver Stapleton; Editor: Lisa Zeno Churgin; Music: Rachel
Portman.
Cast: Homer Wells, Tobey Maguire; Candy Kendall, Charlize Theron; Mr Rose,
Delroy Lindo; Wally Worthington, Paul Rudd; Dr Wilbur Larch, MC.

GET CARTER(UK: 24 June 2000)
2000
Stephen Kay, 108 minutes; DVD.
Producers: Mark Canton, Elie Samaha, Neil Canton; Screenplay: David
McKenna; Director of Photography: Mauro Fiore; Editor: Jerry Greenberg;
Music: Tyler Bates.
Cast: Jack Carter, Sylvester Stallone; Gloria, Miranda Richardson;
Doreen, Rachael Leigh Cook; Geraldine, Rhona Mitra; Jeremy Kinnear,
Alan Cumming; Cliff Brumby, MC; Thorpey, John Cassini; Cyrus Paice,
Mickey Rourke.

QUILLS (UK: 19 January 2001)
2000
Philip Kaufman, 124 minutes; DVD.
Producers: Nick Wechsler, Julia Chasman, Peter Kaufman; Screenplay: Doug
Wright; Director of Photography: Rogier Stoffers; Editor: Peter Boyle; Music:
Stephen Warbeck.
Cast: the Marquis De Sade, Geoffrey Rush; Madeleine, Kate Winslet; Coulmier,
Joaquin Phoenix; Royer-Collard, MC; Madame LeClerc, Billie Whitelaw;
Delbene, Patrick Malahide; Simone, Amelia Warner.

MISS CONGENIALITY (UK: 23 March 2001)
2000
Donald Petrie, 110 minutes; DVD.
Producer: Sandra Bullock; Screenplay: Mark Lawrence, Katie Ford, Caryn
Lucas; Director of Photography: Laszlo Kovacs; Editor: Billy Weber; Music: Ed
Shearmur.
Cast: Gracie Hart, Sandra Bullock; Victor Melling, MC; Eric Matthews,
Benjamin Bratt; Kathy Morningside, Candice Bergen; Stan Fields, William
Shatner.

SHINER (UK: 14 September 2001)
2000
John Irvin, 99 minutes; DVD.
Producers: Geoffrey Reeve, Jim Reeve; Screenplay: Scott Cherry; Director of
Photography: Mike Molloy; Editor: Ian Crafford; Music: Paul Grabowsky.
Cast: Billy 'Shiner' Simpson, MC; Frank Spedding, Martin Landau; Georgie,
Frances Barber; Stoney, Frank Harper; Mel, Andy Serkis; Karl, Danny Webb;
Ruth, Claire Rushbrook; Golden Boy, Matthew Marsden; Gibson, Kenneth
Cranham; Chris, David Kennedy; DI Grant, Peter Wright; DS Garland, Nicola
Walker.

LAST ORDERS (UK: 18 January 2002)
2001
Fred Schepisi, 110 minutes; DVD.
Producer: Elisabeth Robinson; Screenplay: Fred Schepisi; Director of
Photography: Brian Tufano; Editor: Kate Williams; Music: Paul Grabowsky.
Cast: Jack, MC; Vic, Tom Courtenay; Lenny, David Hemmings; Ray, Bob
Hoskins; Amy, Helen Mirren; Vince, Ray Winstone; young Jack, J. J. Feild;

young Vic, Cameron Fitch; young Lenny, Nolan Hemmings; young Ray, Anatol
Yusef; young Amy, Kelly Reilly; young Vince, Stephen McCole; Bernie, George
Innes.

QUICKSAND (unreleased)
2002
John Mackenzie, DVD.
Producer: Geoffrey Reeve; Screenplay, Timothy Prager; Director of Photography:
Walter McGill; Editor: Graham Walker; Music: Anthony Marinelli.
Cast: Martin Raikes, Michael Keaton; Jack Mallows, MC; Lela Forin, Judith
Godreche; Oleg Burraskaya, Rade Serbedzija; Michael Cote, Matthew Marsh.

AUSTIN POWERS IN GOLDMEMBER (UK: 26 July 2002)
2002
Jay Roach, 94 minutes; DVD.
Producers: Joan S. Lyons, Mike Myers, Eric McLeod, Demi Moore, Jennifer
Todd, Suzanne Todd; Screenplay: Mike Myers, Michael McCullers; Director of
Photography: Peter Deming; Editors, Jon Poll and Greg Hayden; Music: George
S. Clinton.
Cast: Austin Powers/Dr Evil/Fat Bastard/Goldmember, Mike Myers; Foxxy
Cleopatra, Beyoncé Knowles; Scott Evil, Seth Green; Basil Exposition, Michael
York; Number Two, Robert Wagner; Nigel Powers, MC.

THE QUIET AMERICAN (UK: 29 November 2002)
2002
Philip Noyce, 101 minutes; DVD.
Producers: Staffan Ahrenberg, William Horberg; Screenplay: Christopher
Hampton, Robert Schenkkan; Directors of Photography: Christopher Doyle,
Huu Tuan Nguyen, Dat Quang; Editor: John Scott; Music: Craig Armstrong.
Cast: Thomas Fowler, MC; Alden Pyle, Brendan Fraser; Phuong, Do Thi Hai
Yen; Hinh, Tzi Ma.

THE ACTORS (UK: 16 May 2003)
2003
Conor McPherson, 92 minutes; DVD.
Producers: Stephen Woolley, Neil Jordan, Redmond Morris; Screenplay: Conor
McPherson; Director of Photography: Seamus McGarvey; Editor: Emer
Reynolds; Music: Michael Nyman.
Cast: Anthony O'Malley, MC; Tom, Dylan Moran; Barreller, Michael Gambon;
Dolores Barreller, Lena Headey; Mrs Magnani, Miranda Richardson.

SECONDHAND LIONS (UK: 24 October 2003)
2003
Tim McCanlies, 105 minutes; DVD.
Screenplay: Tim McCanlies; Producers: David M. Kirschner, Corey Sienega,
Scott Ross; Director of Photography: Jack Green; Editor: David Movitz; Music:
Patrick Doyle.
Cast: Garth, MC; Hub, Robert Duvall; Walter, Haley Joel Osment.

THE STATEMENT (UK: 27 February 2004)
2003
Norman Jewison, 115 minutes; DVD.
Producer: Robert Lantos; Screenplay: Ronald Harwood; Director of
Photography: Kevin Jewison; Editor: Stephen Rivkin; Music: Normand Corbel.
Cast: Pierre Brossard, MC; Annemarie Livi, Tilda Swinton; Colonel Roux,
Jeremy Northam; Armand Bertier, Alan Bates; Nicole, Charlotte Rampling;
Commissaire Vionnet, Frank Finlay.

Bibliography

Michael Caine

Anon, 'Bond and contrabond', *Sunday Telegraph*, 29 November 1964.

Anon, 'Mrs Bloom in £70,000 club deal', *Sunday Telegraph*, 8 August 1965.

Anon, 'Mr Caine finds Hollywood so bracing', *Sunday Express*, 13 February 1966.

Anon, 'The guttural poor', *Daily Telegraph*, 1 September 1966.

Anon, 'Caine's new outlook', *Evening Standard*, 26 September 1966.

Anon, 'The young man shows his medals', *Time*, 17 February 1967.

Anon, 'Richard Harris to sue film company', *Daily Telegraph*, 27 February 1968.

Anon, 'Cockney Caine fails in his first bid to play the country squire', *Daily Express*, 22 July 1969.

Anon, 'Minda's new life', *Sunday Express*, 11 June 1972.

Anon, 'Quit Britain? No way, says Michael Caine', *Sunday Express*, 8 September 1974.

Anon, 'Home sick Caine tired of the endless sunshine', *Sunday Express*, 9 November 1975.

Anon, 'I spy Caine as the film Philby', *Daily Mirror*, 10 February 1976.

Anon, 'Is Caine the right cover?', *Sunday Telegraph Magazine*, 19 December 1976.

Anon, 'A fillip for Philby', *Daily Express*, 11 July 1977.

Anon, 'Caine's mutiny', *Evening Standard*, 3 October 1977.

Anon, 'Caine mutiny: no tax exile for Michael', *Evening Standard*, 21 February 1978.

Anon, 'Star Michael aims to become US citizen', *Daily Mirror*, 7 August 1980.

Anon, 'Michael Caine: a method in his mutiny', *Films*, October 1982.

Anon, 'Beware the betelwok, my son', *Guardian*, 14 July 1984.

Anon, 'John Frankenheimer', *Films and Filming*, February 1985.

Anon, 'Michael Caine hopes for Tory victory', *Daily Telegraph*, 26 May 1987.

Anon, 'Home to a touch of quality', *Daily Mail*, 19 January 1988.

Anon, 'St Michael', *Sunday Telegraph*, 23 October 1994.

Anon, interview with Caine, *Film Review*, February 1999.

Anon, interview with Caine, *Independent on Sunday*, 24 November 2002.

Anotonowicz, Anton, 'I'll take care of you now, David', *Daily Mirror*, 13 May 1991.

Austen, David, 'Playing Dirty', *Films and Filming*, April 1969.

Austen, David, 'Making it or breaking it', *Films and Filming*, May 1969.

Barber, Lynn, 'The Caine scrutiny', *Vanity Fair*, December 1992.

Barrett, Sara, 'Loudmouth Langan and the saga of Caine and table', *Daily Mail*, 14 April 1986.

Benson, Ross, 'California sweet life', *Daily Express*, 23 March 1979.

Billson, Anne, *My Name Is Michael Caine*, Muller, 1991.

Bishop, David, *Starring Michael Caine*, Reynolds and Hearne, 2003.

Blair, Gordon, 'My daughter and Prince Andrew? Blimey, she only cares about horses', *Sunday Mirror*, 23 August 1981.

Bracewell, Michael, 'Man in the Mirror', *Guardian*, 8 February 1997.

Brandreth, Gyles, 'I owe it all to everyone', *Weekly Telegraph*, no 545.

Brodie, Ian, ' "Ruinous taxes" force Michael Caine to quit Britain', *Daily Telegraph*, 21 September 1977.

Brompton, Sally, 'Luxury? Not for me, says Michael Caine's mother', *Sunday Express*, 4 December 1966.

Brompton, Sally, 'Caine joins the tax mutiny . . .', *Daily Mail*, July 18, 1974.

Burke, Michael, 'Caine bans blood from Ripper film', *Daily Star*, October 8, 1988.

Caine, Michael, 'Roots', *Sunday Express*, December 14, 1986.

Caine, Michael, *What's It All About?*, Century, 1992.

Caine, Michael, *Acting in Film: An Actor's Take on Movie Making*, Applause, 1997.

Caine, Michael, 'My London', *Evening Standard*, 14 September 2001.

Callan, Paul, 'Our man in Hollywood', *Daily Mirror*, 14 April 1984.

Case, Brian, 'Return of the Native', *Time Out*, 1992; reprinted in *The Time Out Book of Interviews*, Penguin, 1998.

Castell, David, 'The Michael Caine marathon', *Films Illustrated*, August 1975.

Coleman, Terry, 'All squired on the home front', *Guardian*, 23 November 1985.

Crystal, Anna, 'A private audience with Woody Allen, Mia Farrow and Michael Caine', *Films and Filming*, June 1986.

d'Arcy, Susan, 'The funny side of Michael Caine', *Films Illustrated*, February 1977.

Dougary, Ginny, 'A Knight's Tale', *Times Magazine*, 15 September 2001.

Dunford, Simon, 'A very English movie legend', *Eastern Daily Press*, 23 November 2002.

Dunford, Simon, 'The Norfolk job', *Eastern Daily Press*, 14 March 2003.

Dunford, Simon, 'My name is . . . Baron Fitznoodle', *Eastern Daily Press*, 31 October 2003.

Durgnat, Raymond, 'Michael Caine', in *International Dictionary of Films and Filmmakers, vol 3: Actors and Actresses*, Nicholas Thomas (Ed.), St James Press, 1992.

Eastaugh, Ken, 'The Caine scrutiny', *Sun*, 12 August 1972.

Eimer, David, 'Caine finds his voice', *Culture, Sunday Times*, 13 December 1998.

Ethan, Olivia, 'Raising Caine', *Daily Express Magazine*, 20 September 2003.

Evans, Peter, 'Michael Caine . . . backed by his mother while he mutinied', *Daily Express*, 30 January 1964.

Evans, Peter, 'I had to leave, or die a pauper in the workhouse', *News of the World*, 24 April 1983.

Evison, Sue, 'The good feud guide', *Sun*, 18 March 1986.

Finn, Philip, 'Caine: I'll join exiles', *Daily Mail*, 19 September 1977.

Flett, Scarth, 'The happy star with just one ambition left', *Sunday Express*, 20 November 1988.

Freedland, Michael, *Michael Caine*, Orion, 1999.

van Gelder, Lawrence, untitled interview, *New York Times*, 14 August 1987.

Gibbons, Fiachra, 'Caine gives Bafta tributes a cutting edge', *Guardian*, 10 April
    2000.
Gibbons, Fiachra, 'Caine mutiny opens acting class divide', *Guardian*, 14 April
    2000.
Gilbert, Lewis, 'All About Alfie', *Guardian*, 4 May 2001.
Goodridge, Mike, 'Quiet Confidence', *Screen International*, 17 January 2003.
Gris, Henri, 'Michael Caine talking' *Sunday Citizen*, 12 March 1967.
Haden-Guest, Anthony, 'Slang it to me in rhyme', *Daily Telegraph Magazine*,
    7 December 1971.
Hall, William, *Raising Caine*, Sidgwick and Jackson, 1981.
Harlow, John, 'Caine mutiny puts him back on track for Oscar', *Sunday Times*,
    22 September 2002.
Harvey, Alex, 'How Caine won and lost the battle of the bulge', *Sun*, 22 Decem-
    ber 1983.
Hickey, William, 'The beautiful reason Caine's bachelor days will end this year',
    Daily Express, 4 March 1970.
Hirschhorn, Clive, 'My flash days are over, says Michael Caine', *Sunday Express*,
    27 August 1972.
Hirschhorn, Clive, untitled piece, *Sunday Express*, 11 July 1975.
Honan, Corinna, 'The Class War of Michael Caine', *Mail on Sunday*, 20 Septem-
    ber 1992.
Horner, Rosalie, 'Why British TV can't afford me', *Daily Express*, 5 October
    1988.
Iley, Chrissy, 'Doctor Love', *Sunday Times Magazine*, 12 March 2000.
Jack, Ian, 'Citizen Caine', *Observer Magazine*, 7 September 1986.
Johnston, Sheila and Roddick, Nick, 'The boys are back in town', *Stills*, October
    1984.
Johnston, Sheila, 'No rest for the wicked', *Independent*, 28 November 2003.
Kobal, John, 'Michael Caine', *Films and Filming*, January 1985.
Lee, Emma, 'Lots of folk will now know of Caine's Norfolk link', *Eastern Daily
    Press*, 4 November 2003.
Lewin, David, 'Why there's a man with a gun under Michael Caine's bedroom
    window', *Daily Mail*, 8 August 1966.
Lewin, David, 'Why my daughter must be a lady', *Daily Mail*, 25 February 1967.
Lewin, David, 'Billion Dollar Caine', *Daily Mail*, 15 November 1967.
Lewin, David, 'Why I bar sex and violence: Len Deighton talking', *Daily Mail*,
    6 December 1967.
Lewin, David, 'The rich revenge of Michael Caine', *Daily Mail*, 14 March 1983.
Lewin, David, 'Why Caine's coming home', *Daily Mail*, 17 September 1985.
Lewin, David, 'Mr Caine's one-night stand', *Mail on Sunday*, 2 October 1988.
'Mandrake', 'The rising star of citizen Caine' *Sunday Telegraph*, 8 July 1973.
'Mandrake', 'Cockney Caine joins Julie, the urchin charmer', *Sunday Telegraph*,
    22 August 1982.
'Mandrake', 'The able Caine has more than a touch of class', *Sunday Telegraph*,
    23 August 1984.
'Mandrake', 'What not many people know about Deighton', *Sunday Telegraph*,
    13 October 1985.
Mann, Roderick, 'Big money has altered my life, says Mr Caine', *Sunday Express*,
    25 July 1965.

Mann, Roderick, 'Why Mr Baker may lose his biggest gamble', *Sunday Express*, 27 February 1966.

Mann, Roderick, 'I enjoy success says Mr Caine', *Sunday Express*, 8 January 1967.

Mann, Roderick, 'The gift that made Mr Caine cry . . .', *Sunday Express*, 31 March 1968.

Mann, Roderick, 'The change in Mr Caine', *Sunday Express*, 10 November 1968.

Mann, Roderick, 'How Mike and Omar are beating boredom', *Sunday Express*, 12 October 1969.

Mann, Roderick, 'I don't deserve my "off-screen" image, says Michael Caine', *Sunday Express*, 16 May 1971.

Mann, Roderick, 'Call me Larry, Lord Olivier tells Mr Caine', *Sunday Express*, 21 May 1972.

Mann, Roderick, untitled piece, *Sunday Express*, 19 November 1973.

Mann, Roderick, 'It was the bees' fault', *Sunday Express*, 3 September 1978.

Mann, Roderick, 'I'd only earn half as much in Britain', *Sunday Express*, 21 March 1982.

Marlborough, Douglas, 'No spies in specs for Mike', *Daily Mail*, 3 December 1968.

Marshall, William, 'I don't need one more friend', *Daily Mirror*, 4 September 1981.

Marshall, William, 'Healthy, wealthy and not guilty', *Daily Mirror*, 16 August 1982.

Marshall, William, 'I'm too old and rich to do things I don't enjoy', *Daily Mirror*, 1 February 1986.

Matloff, Jason, 'Idol Chatter: Michael Caine', *Premiere*, January 1999, p42.

McKee, Victoria, 'A childhood: Michael Caine', *The Times*, 19 December 1992.

Mohan, Dominic, 'I'm the original Austin Powers', *Sun*, 9 July 2002.

Monetti, Sandro, 'Mutinous Caine: I want younger leading ladies', *Sunday Express*, 2 January 2000.

Moore, Jane, 'To have the chance to play this role . . . it was wonderful', *Sun*, 22 December 1998.

Mortimer, John, 'My lunch with Maurice', *Sunday Telegraph*, 14 October 1990.

Munn, Mike, 'We may not see much more of Michael Caine', *Film Review*, May 1976.

Naughton, John, 'The man who is king', *Empire*, April 1997.

O'Sullivan, Kevin, 'I'm no pie and eels yob who got lucky . . . I'm a good actor', *Daily Mirror*, 8 April 2000.

Palmer, Martyn, 'Why the young stars all look up to Caine', *Sunday Express*, 26 March 2000.

Parsons, Tony, 'The man who would be Caine', *Arena*, autumn 1988.

Paskin, Barbara, 'A better class of actor', *Sunday Express*, 6 February 1994.

Pearce, Garth, 'Caine the quiet man cometh', *Daily Express*, 17 October 1986.

Pearce, Garth, 'My weird recipe for a successful marriage', *Now*, 9 February 2000.

Pearce, Garth, 'Caine takes the Michael (but only out of himself)', *Sunday Express*, 28 July 2002.

Perry, George, 'Why I'm just wild about Jollywood', *Sun*, 12 June 1984.

Perry, George, 'Raising Caine', *Sunday Times Magazine*, 24 November 2002.

Pulver, Andrew, 'Now don't mess abaht', *Guardian*, 23 February 1998.

Rayment, Tim, 'Outraged Harris fires broadside at Caine mutiny', *Sunday Times*, 6 August 1995.

Riddell, Mary, 'Caine scrutiny', *Daily Mail*, 5 January 2002.

Rosen, Marjorie, 'The man who would be Caine', *Film Comment*, July–August 1980.

Ross, Ally, 'What's it all about', *Sun*, 8 January 1999.

Sutcliffe, Thomas, 'Hollywood Greats: Michael Caine', *Independent*, 12 March 2003.

Thompson, Douglas, 'Why I've been driven away', *Daily Mail*, 21 September 1977.

Thomson, David, 'Truly a class act. Not a lot of people know that', *Independent*, 30 November 2002.

Tresidder, Megan, 'The "cockney sparrow" who says he's a vulture', *Sunday Telegraph*, 11 October 1992.

Wansell, Geoffrey, 'Michael Caine', *Sunday Telegraph Magazine*, 6 July 1986.

Ward, Christopher, 'Caine and Marco's gourmet deal', *Sunday Express*, 4 January 1996.

Weatherby, W. J., 'Caine plays it for crazy', *Guardian*, 11 August 1981.

White, Lesley, 'What's it all about?', *Sunday Times Magazine*, 23 July 1995.

Wigmore, Barry, 'The exile', *Daily Mirror*, 3 October 1980.

Film; history

Ackroyd, Peter, *London: The Biography*, Vintage, 2001.

Adams, Mark, *Mike Hodges*, Pocket Essentials, 2001.

Aitken, Jonathan, *The Young Meteors*, Secker & Warburg, 1967.

Amis, Kingsley, *The James Bond Dossier*, Jonathan Cape, 1966.

Anon, 'US backs Stanley Baker', *Daily Telegraph*, 2 January 1966.

Appleyard, Bryan, *The Pleasures of Peace: Art and Imagination in Post-War Britain*, Faber, 1989.

Armes, Roy, *A Critical History of the British Cinema*, Secker and Warburg, 1978.

Baxter, John, *Ken Russell: An Appalling Talent*, Michael Joseph, 1973.

Bernstein, George L., *The Myth of Decline: The Rise of Britain Since 1945*, Pimlico, 2004.

Billen, Andrew, 'Swinging in the Sixties', *New Statesman*, 5 January 2004.

Bogdanor, Vernon and Skidelsky, Robert (Eds), *The Age of Affluence: 1951–1964*, Macmillan, 1970.

Booker, Christopher, *The Neophiliacs: A Study of the Revolution in English life in the Fifties and Sixties*, Collins, 1969.

Booker, Christopher, *The Seventies: Portrait of a Decade*, Allen Lane, 1980.

Bracewell, Michael, 'Time on their side', *The Times*, 5 June 2004.

Bragg, Melvyn, *Rich: The Life of Richard Burton*, Hodder and Stoughton, 1988.

Braine, John, *Room at the Top*, Eyre and Spottiswoode, 1957.

Brett, Simon, *A Shock to the System*, Macmillan, 1984.

Brien, Alan, 'America's "Method" actors come to the Aldwych', *Sunday Telegraph*, 24 January 1965.

Broccoli, Cubby with Zec, Donald, *When the Snow Melts: The Autobiography*, Boxtree, 1998.

Callow, Simon, *Being an Actor* (revised edn), Penguin, 1995.

Campbell, John, *Margaret Thatcher* (two volumes), Jonathan Cape, 2000, 2003.

Cannadine, David, *Class in Britain*, Penguin, 2000.

Cannadine, David, *History in our Time*, Penguin, 2000.

Cannadine, David, *In Churchill's Shadow: Confronting the Past in Modern Britain*, Allen Lane, 2002.

Carpenter, Humphrey, *That Was Satire That Was: the Satire Boom of the 1960s*, Gollancz, 2000.

Carpenter, Humphrey, *The Angry Young Men*, Penguin/Allen Lane, 2002.

Catterall, Ali and Wells, Simon, *Your Face Here: British Cult Movies since the Sixties*, Fourth Estate, 2001.

Caughie, John (Ed.), *Theories of Authorship*, Routledge & Kegan Paul, 1981.

Caute, David, *Joseph Losey: A Revenge on Life*, Faber and Faber, 1994.

Chibnall, Steve, *British Film Guide 6: Get Carter*, IB Tauris, 2003.

Clarke, Nick, *The Shadow of a Nation: The Changing Face of Britain*, Weidenfeld and Nicolson, 2003.

Clarke, Peter, *Hope and Glory: Britain 1900–1990*, Allen Lane, 1996.

Connolly, Ray (Ed.), *In the Sixties*, Pavilion, 1995.

Cory, Desmond, *Deadfall*, Corgi, 1967.

Coveney, Michael, *Maggie Smith: A Bright Particular Star*, Gollancz, 1992.

Craig, Patricia, *Brian Moore: A Biography*, Bloomsbury, 2002.

Davies, Steven Paul, *Get Carter and Beyond: The Cinema of Mike Hodges*, Batsford, 2002.

Deighton, Len, *The Ipcress File*, Hodder and Stoughton, 1962.

Deighton, Len, *Funeral in Berlin*, Jonathan Cape, 1964.

Deighton, Len, *Billion Dollar Brain*, Jonathan Cape, 1965.

Dyer, Richard, *Stars* (new edn), BFI, 1998.

Edwards, Sydney, 'Osborne at 40: beating Caine at his own game', *Evening Standard*, 28 August 1970.

Falk, Quentin, *Travels in Greeneland: The Cinema of Graham Greene*, Quartet, 1984.

Feeney Callan, Michael, *Richard Harris: Sex, Death and the Movies: An Intimate Biography*, Robson, 2003.

Finstad, Suzanne, *Natasha: The Biography of Natalie Wood*, Century, 2001.

Fisher, Clive, *Noel Coward*, Weidenfeld and Nicolson, 1992.

Foot, Paul, *The Politics of Harold Wilson*, Penguin, 1968.

Fowles, John, *The Magus*, Jonathan Cape, 1966.

Fowles, John, *The Journals: Volume 1*, Jonathan Cape, 2003.

French, Philip, 'Alan Bates: 1934–2003', *Observer*, 4 January 2004.

Geist, Kenneth L., *Pictures Will Talk: The Life and Films of Joseph L. Mankiewicz*, Scribners, 1978.

Gillett, Philip, *The British Working Class in Postwar Film*, Manchester University Press, 2003.

Goodwin, Cliff, *Behaving Badly: The Life of Richard Harris 1930–2002*, Virgin, 2003.

Green, Jonathon, *All Dressed Up: The Sixties and the Counterculture*, Jonathan Cape, 1998.

Greene, Graham, *The Quiet American*, Heinemann, 1955.

Greene, Graham, *The Honorary Consul*, Bodley Head, 1973.

Grobel, Lawrence, *The Hustons*, Bloomsbury, 1990.

Harris, Richard, 'A sharp kick from a man called Horse', letter to the *Sunday Times*, 6 August 1995.

Hattersley, Roy, *Who Goes Home: Scenes from a Political Life*, Little, Brown, 1995.

Hewison, Robert, *In Anger: Culture in the Cold War 1945–60*, Weidenfeld & Nicolson, 1981.

Hewison, Robert, *Too Much: Art and Culture in the Sixties 1960–75*, Methuen, 1986.

Hirsch, Foster, *Joseph Losey*, Twayne, 1980.

Hoberman, J., *The Dream Life: Movies, Media, and the Mythology of the Sixties*, The New Press, 2003.

Hobsbawm, Eric, *Interesting Times: A Twentieth Century Life*, Allen Lane, 2002.

Hoggart, Richard, *The Uses of Literacy*, Chatto and Windus, 1957.

Honey, John, *Does Accent Matter?: The Pygmalion Factor*, Faber, 1989.

Jefferys, Kevin, *Finest and Darkest Hours: The Decisive Events in British Politics from Churchill to Blair*, Atlantic, 2002.

Jenkins, Peter, *Mrs Thatcher's Revolution: The Ending of the Socialist Era*, Jonathan Cape, 1987.

Kael, Pauline, *Reeling*, Marion Boyars, 1977.

Kael, Pauline, *When the Lights Go Down*, Holt Rinehart Winston, 1980.

Kael, Pauline, *Taking It All In*, Marion Boyars, 1986.

Kael, Pauline, *State of the Art*, Arena, 1987.

Kael, Pauline, *Hooked*, Marion Boyars, 1990.

Kidel, Mark, 'Let Us Play', *Times Literary Supplement*, 10 January 2003.

Kurlansky, Mark, *1968: The Year that Rocked the World*, Jonathan Cape, 2004.

Lee, Christopher, *This Sceptred Isle: Twentieth Century*, Penguin, 2000.

Leitch, David, 'Superstar Shaw gets Philby role', *Sunday Times*, 18 September 1977.

Levin, Bernard, *The Pendulum Years: Britain and the Sixties*, Jonathan Cape, 1970.

Levy, Shawn, *Ready, Steady, Go!: Swinging London and the Invention of Cool*, Fourth Estate, 2002.

Lewis, Roger, *The Life and Death of Peter Sellers*, Century, 1994.

Lewis, Roger, *The Real Life of Laurence Olivier*, Century, 1996.

Lewis, Ted, *Get Carter* (originally published as *Jack's Return Home*), Allison and Busby, 1998.

Lodge, David, *Ginger, You're Barmy* (revised edn), Penguin, 1982.

Longmate, Norman, *How We Lived Then: A History of Everyday Life During the Second World War*, Hutchinson, 1971.

MacDonald, Callum, *Britain in the Korean War*, Blackwell, 1990.

MacDonald, Ian, *Revolution in the Head: The Beatles Records and the Sixties* (revised edn), Fourth Estate, 1997.

McFarlane, Brian, *An Autobiography of British Cinema*, Methuen, 1997.

McFarlane, Brian, *The Encyclopedia of British Film*, Methuen, 2003.

Magee, Bryan, *Clouds of Glory: A Hoxton Childhood*, Jonathan Cape, 2003.

Marwick, Arthur, *Class: Image and Reality in Britain, France and the USA since 1930*, Collins, 1980.

Marwick, Arthur, *The Sixties*, Oxford University Press, 1998.

Masters, Brian, *The Swinging Sixties*, Constable, 1985.

Masters, Brian, *Getting Personal: A Biographer's Memoir*, Constable, 2002.

Melly, George, *Revolt into Style: The Pop Arts in the 50s and 60s* (revised edn), Oxford University Press, 1989.

Milne, Tom, *Losey on Losey*, Secker and Warburg, 1967.

Moline, Karen, *Bob Hoskins: An Unlikely Hero*, Sphere, 1988.

Morgan, Kenneth O., *Britain Since 1945: The People's Peace* (third edn), Oxford University Press, 2001.

Murphy, Robert, *Sixties British Cinema*, BFI, 1992.

Naughton, Bill, *Alfie*, Panther (film tie-in edn), 1966.

O'Brien, Edna, *Zee & Co*, Weidenfeld and Nicolson, 1971.

Orwell, George, *Down and Out in Paris and London* (revised edn), Penguin, 1975.

Orwell, George, *The Complete Works: Vol. X, 'A Kind of Compulsion'* (Ed. Peter Davison), Secker and Warburg, 1998.

Osborne, John, *A Better Class of Person: An Autobiography 1929–1956*, Faber, 1981.

Osborne, John, *Almost a Gentleman: An Autobiography 1955–1966*, Faber, 1991.

Osborne, John, *Damn You, England: Collected Prose*, Faber, 1994.

O'Toole, Peter, *Loitering with Intent: The Apprentice*, Macmillan, 1996.

Palmer, James and Reilly, Michael, *The Films of Joseph Losey*, Cambridge University Press, 1993.

Porter, Roy, *London: A Social History*, Hamish Hamilton, 1994.

Priestley, J. B., *English Journey* (new edn), Penguin, 1977.

Rainer, Peter (Ed.), *Love and Hisses: The National Society of Film Critics Sound Off on the Hottest Movie Controversies*, Mercury House, 1992.

Rampton, James, 'Don't make me laugh', *Independent*, 7 May 2003.

Rham, Edith de, *Joseph Losey*, Andre Deutsch, 1991.

Rissik, Andrew, *The James Bond Man: The Films of Sean Connery*, Elm Tree, 1983.

Robbins, Keith, *The British Isles: 1901–1951*, Oxford University Press, 2002.

Rosenstone, Robert A. (Ed.), *Revisioning History: Film and the Construction of a New Past*, Princeton University Press, 1995.

Roud, Richard (Ed.), *Cinema: A Critical Dictionary*, Secker and Warburg, 1980.

Russell, John, *Braque*, Phaidon, 1959.

Shaffer, Anthony, *Sleuth*, Calder and Boyars, 1971.

Shaffer, Anthony, *So What Did You Expect: A Memoir*, Picador, 2001.

Shipman, David, *The Great Movie Stars: the International Years*, Angus and Robertson, 1980.

Siegel, Don, *A Siegel Film*, Faber, 1993.

Sikov, Ed, *Mr Strangelove: A Biography of Peter Sellers*, Sidgwick and Jackson, 2002.

Sillitoe, Alan, *Saturday Night and Sunday Morning*, W. H. Allen, 1958.

Sklar, Robert, *City Boys*, Princeton University Press, 1992.

Stamp, Terence, *Coming Attraction*, Bloomsbury, 1988.

Stamp, Terence, *Double Feature*, Bloomsbury, 1989.

Stead, Peter, *Film and the Working Class*, Routledge, 1989.

Storey, Anthony, *Stanley Baker: Portrait of an Actor*, W. H. Allen, 1977.

Strachan, Alan, obituary of Anthony Shaffer, *Independent*, 8 November 2001.

Sylvester, David, *London Recordings*, Chatto & Windus, 2003.

Taylor, John Russell, *Anger and After: A Guide to the New British Drama*, Methuen, 1962.

Theroux, Paul, *Doctor Slaughter*, Hamish Hamilton, 1984.

Thomson, David, *The New Biographical Dictionary of Film*, Little Brown, 2002.

de Toth, Andre with Slide, Anthony, *de Toth on de Toth: Putting the Drama in Front of the Camera*, Faber, 1996.

Updike, John, *Self-Consciousness*, Knopf, 1989.

Vansittart, Peter, *In the Fifties*, John Murray, 1995.

Walker, Alexander, *Hollywood UK: The British Film Industry in the Sixties*, Stein and Day, 1974.

Walker, Alexander, *Peter Sellers*, Weidenfeld and Nicolson, 1981.

Walker, Alexander, *National Heroes: British Cinema in the Seventies and Eighties*, Harrap, 1985.

Warburton, Eileen, *John Fowles: A Life in Two Worlds*, Jonathan Cape, 2004.

Whitehead, Phillip, *The Writing on the Wall: Britain in the Seventies*, Michael Joseph with Channel 4, 1985.

Wollen, Peter, *Signs and Meaning in the Cinema*, Secker and Warburg/BFI, 1969.

Wood, Robin, *Personal Views: Explorations in Film*, Gordon Fraser, 1976.

Wood, Robin, *Hitchcock's Films Revisited* (revised edn), Columbia University Press, 2002.

Wood, Robin, *Hollywood from Vietnam to Reagan . . . and Beyond*, Columbia University Press, 2003.

Woodward, Ian, *Glenda Jackson: A Study in Fire and Ice*, Weidenfeld and Nicolson, 1985.

Young, Hugo, *One of Us*, Pan, 1990.

Acknowledgements

Books are no more solitary efforts than are movies, and like the Oscar-winner of cliché I should like to make my thanks to this production's many backroom boys and girls.

Paul Fisher, who helped me come up with the original idea for the book on one of our many Somerset walks, has been such an engaging friend these past few years that I sometimes find it difficult to separate what I think from what he does.

The novelist, biographer and critic David Taylor, who has written for me for many years at the *Daily Telegraph*, helped me make a rough idea a saleable proposition. David's wife Rachel came to my rescue when I had sapped his own inspiration.

John Saddler, the agent with whom the Taylors put me in touch, has been a constant spur and splint. My editor, Walter Donohue, has borne my unproductive stretches and furtive silences with the patient faith that is born of wisdom. Also at Faber, Lesley Felce and Ian Bahrami edited my copy with firm but fair hands.

Mark Sweeting of the Wilson's School Alumni helped me contact fellow pupils of the adolescent Maurice Micklewhite. Norman and Vernon Tucker, Old Wilsonians both, were most kind in helping me with my enquiries. Bryan Forbes, Glenda Jackson and Jim Broadbent shared recollections of working with Caine. Caine himself would not speak to me, for which he can hardly be blamed. To have authorized one biography and authored one's own memoir is enough self-admission for any man.

Lisa Allardice, Mark Amory, Jason Cowley, Jan Dalley, Philip Dodd, Mark Ellen, Suzi Feay, Caroline Gascoigne, Susanna Gross, David Hepworth, Blake Morrison, Ferdinand Mount, Paul Du Noyer, Jude Rogers, Nancy Sladek, Kate Summerscale, Boyd Tonkin, Jeremy Treglown, John Walsh and numerous other of the London literary and arts editors have kept me working on material that related however tangentially to the bigger project in hand. George Perry, long-time film writer on the *Sunday Times* and the author of many a movie book had some sage advice for a struggling first-timer.

Rachel Simhon, my editor at the *Telegraph*, was kind enough to grant me a three-month sabbatical to finally cuff the book into shape.

I owe her more thanks than she knows. I cannot promise to be any more faithful to her in the future, but I can promise her more mentions like this.

Also at the *Telegraph*, picture editor Mike Spillard was kind enough to take on some extracurricular research for me. Matt Pritchett and his father Oliver came to my rescue in tracking down a half-remembered quote from V. S. Pritchett (respectively, their grandfather and father).

Simon Dunford, feature writer on the *Eastern Daily Press*, helped me with young Maurice Micklewhite's Norfolk years.

The staffs of the London Library, the British Film Institute and the *Daily Telegraph* have all aided me well beyond the call of duty.

Tim Roberts was always on hand to remind me quite how many clunkers Michael Caine has appeared in. Sinclair McKay, a colleague and friend at the *Telegraph*, was always around to reassure me I am not the only one who finds solace and sustenance in bad movies.

Tracking down all those movies was a task in itself. My brother Alistair Bray taped rather too many for me than seemed fair; my cousin Daniel Bray forgot to tape almost as many.

To my brother Kingsley – another biographer, though of a rather more rarefied kind – I owe too much to begin even skating across. Nobody has talked with me about so much with such perspicacity. His enjoyment of one sentence of this book will be reason enough to have written it.

More than thirty years have passed since the television première of *Deadfall*, during which broadcast my father commented that 'Michael Caine never could bloody act!' To this moment of incisive criticism I have always dated my interest in the aesthetics of performance. I have no reason to believe a reading of this book will lead my father to modify his opinion; nonetheless, to him and to my mother – and not only for their eventual mastery of the mysteries of satellite television recording – all the thanks in the world.

And to Sharon Kemp, a woman of such abiding strength she conceded to letting me watch *Billion Dollar Brain* a third time in the space of a week, even more.

Index

This index is compiled on a word-by-word basis so that, for example, New York Times precedes Newman, Paul.

All films in which Michael Caine appeared are listed together under, Caine, Michael, films.